Shadow States

Since the mid-twentieth century, China and India have entertained a difficult relationship, erupting into open war in 1962. *Shadow States* is the first book to unpack Sino-Indian tensions from the angle of competitive state-making – through a study of their simultaneous attempts to win the approval and support of Himalayan people. When China and India tried to expand into the Himalayas in the twentieth century, their lack of strong ties to the region and the absence of an easily enforceable border made their proximity threatening: observing China's and India's state-making efforts, local inhabitants were in a position to compare and potentially choose between them. Using rich and original archival research, Bérénice Guyot-Réchard shows how India and China became each other's 'shadow states'. Understanding these recent, competing processes of state formation in the Himalayas is fundamental to understanding the roots of tensions in Sino-Indian relations.

Bérénice Guyot-Réchard teaches international and South Asian history at King's College London. She was previously Research Fellow at Emmanuel College, Cambridge. Her research explores the effects of social, political, and environmental processes on South Asia's contemporary international relations. She has recently published in *Contemporary South Asia* and *Modern Asian Studies*.

Shadow States

India, China and the Himalayas, 1910–1962

Bérénice Guyot-Réchard

King's College London

CAMBRIDGE
UNIVERSITY PRESS

CAMBRIDGE
UNIVERSITY PRESS

University Printing House, Cambridge CB2 8BS, United Kingdom

One Liberty Plaza, 20th Floor, New York, NY 10006, USA

477 Williamstown Road, Port Melbourne, VIC 3207, Australia

4843/24, 2nd Floor, Ansari Road, Daryaganj, Delhi – 110002, India

79 Anson Road, #06–04/06, Singapore 079906

Cambridge University Press is part of the University of Cambridge.

It furthers the University's mission by disseminating knowledge in the pursuit of education, learning, and research at the highest international levels of excellence.

www.cambridge.org
Information on this title: www.cambridge.org/9781107176799

First published 2017

Printed in the United Kingdom by Clays, St Ives plc

A catalogue record for this publication is available from the British Library.

ISBN 978-1-107-17679-9 Hardback

To Max

Contents

Figures

Maps

Acknowledgements

This book began as a dissertation charting late colonial and early independent India's incorporation of the region once considered South Asia's 'largest *terra incognita*': the eastern Himalayas. I soon realised that I could not separate this story from what was happening across the border. Indian state-making in what we now call Arunachal Pradesh was always conditioned by the shadow of China, especially after the People's Republic of China (PRC) annexed nearby Tibet. And the conditioning went both ways, it appeared. This book is an effort to explore this interaction and its consequences, albeit from a primarily Indian angle.

I first wish to thank the Gates Cambridge Trust and Trinity College, Cambridge, for their financial support during my PhD. I acknowledge the support of the Mary Euphrasia Mosley Travel Fund, the Cambridge History Faculty's Prince Consort Fund and Members' History Fund, the Smuts Memorial Fund, the Cambridge Humanities Research Scheme, the Frederick Williamson Fund, and Emmanuel College, Cambridge.

Research for this book has taken me to many places: London, Delhi, Assam, Meghalaya, and Arunachal. I am truly grateful to Barmati Dai, Oshong Ering, K.C. and Sudha Johorey, Egul Padung, Yeshe Dorjee Thongchi, Mamang Dai, and B.J. Verghese for sharing their stories with me. I thank the staff of the Asian & African Studies Reading Room at the British Library; Jaya Ravindran and her staff at the Indian National Archives; the staff of the Nehru Memorial Library; Darmeshwar Sonowal, Nupur Barpatra Gohain, Nripen Sarma, Arun Kashyap, Hareswar Baishya, and everyone at the Assam State Archives; and the North-Eastern Regional Centre of the Indian Council of Social Science Research in Shillong. In Itanagar, my gratitude goes to Tage Tada and the Research Department – particularly Batum Pertin, R.N. Koley, Kime Ampi, and Noni Sali, thanks to whom I trawled the Arunachal Pradesh State Archives, discovered Arunachali food, and learnt a few words of Apatani (sadly mostly forgotten). In Naharlagun, I thank the Arunachal Pradesh Information and Public Relations

Department for permission to reproduce pictures from their photographic collection. I am also grateful for the warm welcome Prafulla Govinda Baruah, P.K. Baruah, and Wilson Matthews always gave me at the *Assam Tribune* in Guwahati. Finally, I wish to thank the people who made the Centre of South Asian Studies at Cambridge a wonderful research home for all these years, and whose assistance I benefited from innumerable times: Kevin Greenbank, Barbara Roe, and Rachel Rowe.

Many more people helped along the way. Sarit Chaudhuri, Udayon Misra, Bhupen Sarma, Arupjyoti Saikia, and Tanka Subba gave me precious advice on conducting research in north-eastern India. In Delhi, the Khullar family, Aparajita Mazumdar and Siddarth Chowdhury, and Mr and Mrs Bhardwaj gave me homes away from home at different stages of my research. So too did the Talukdar family in Guwahati and Christine Wanglat in Itanagar. Jarpum Gamlin, Satbir Bedi, and Sukrit Silas helped me discover Arunachal in ideal conditions. Jishnu Borua's generosity facilitated my research at the Assam State Archives. Bonita Baruah and Kawaldeep Kaur translated two Assamese books into English, and Babita Rajkhowa kindly put me in touch with Bonita.

I have tremendously benefited from the advice of scholars at Cambridge and beyond. My thanks must first and foremost go to Joya Chatterji, an extraordinary supervisor, mentor, and friend. Vivek Bhandari, Katia Buttefrille, Peter Caterall, Graham Chapman, Leigh Denault, Laurence Gautier, Rebecca Gnüchtel, Anton Harder, Ben Hopkins, Emma Hunter, Beatrice Jauregui, Harshan Kumarasingham, Rachel Leow, Fiona McConnell, Sanghamitra Misra, Rana Mitter, Zilpha Modi, Ishan Mukherjee, Partha Pratim Shil, Kaushik Roy, Tsering Shakya, Jayita Sharma, Benno Weiner, Arne Westad, and Benjamin Zachariah – all helped at various stages of this project. I particularly wish to thank Willem van Schendel, David Washbrook, and David Ludden for their constant support. Equally, I thank Gunnel Cederlöf, Jason Cons, Tanja Hüber, Stella Krepp, Li Wenjie, Andrès Rodriguez, and Willem van Schendel for reading certain book chapters, and Rebecca Gnüchtel and Toni Huber for commenting on the whole manuscript and sharing some of their work with me.

I benefited enormously from my time as a research fellow at Emmanuel College, Cambridge. The friendship and support of my colleagues – particularly Julie Barrau, Tom Johnson, Larry Klein, Jon Lawrence, David Maxwell, Geraint Thomas, and Elisabeth van Houts – was invaluable in writing this book. A one-year visiting fellowship at the Graduate Institute in Geneva enabled me to finish it, and I thank Gareth Austin, Gopalan Balachandran, and Davide Rodogno for welcoming me there.

I further wish to thank the colleagues at my new academic home, King's College London, for their warm welcome. Thank you also to Tina Bone for the beautiful maps and to my editor Lucy Rhymer, the anonymous reviewers, and the whole team at Cambridge University Press.

Last but not least, this book would not have been possible without my family. This book is a very small reward for their love, support, and patience, but it is to them – and above all to Max – that it is dedicated.

Transcription and Terminology

This book refers to the inhabitants of the eastern Himalayas as 'tribes' or 'tribals'. While these terms belong to a contested 'vocabulary of power',[1] they are in common use in Arunachal Pradesh, where they can be used with pride.[2] *Adivasi*, today the more consensual term elsewhere in India, refers to indigenous communities originally from the rest of the subcontinent who arrived in colonial Assam to work in tea gardens. Moreover, the Indian constitution recognises the indigenous populations of NEFA/Arunachal as Scheduled Tribes, with attendant rights and privileges.

A related issue is how to designate Arunachal and Assam's various Scheduled Tribes. The most important ones are listed below: the terms most widely recognised today first, and older or alternative ones second. The newer names tend to be endonyms, whereas the earlier ones had often been given by outsiders and can be considered derogatory – 'Abor', for instance, means 'ungoverned, untamed' in Assamese. For this reason and because they were replacing older terms by the end of the 1950s, this book uses the most familiar names today.

In the PRC, the state-sanctioned term is *minzu* (nationality). Like 'tribe', the concept of *minzu* – and the classification of the PRC's inhabitants in this light – has a fraught history. Chinese authorities currently recognise fifty-five minority *minzu* alongside the Hans. Among them, the Tibetans, the Monbas (Monpas and Membas), and the Lhobas inhabit the eastern Himalayas. The last term, derived from Tibetan, subsumes a variety of non-Buddhist people, such as the Adis or the Mishmis (the latter also known as Deng).[3]

---

[1] Willem van Schendel, 'The dangers of belonging: Tribes, indigenous peoples and home-lands in South Asia', in *The politics of belonging in India: Becoming Adivasi*, ed. by Daniel Rycroft and Sangeeta Dasgupta (London: Routledge, 2011), pp. 19–43.

[2] Stuart Blackburn, *Himalayan tribal tales: Oral tradition and culture in the Apatani Valley* (Boston; Leiden: Brill, 2008), p. 9.

[3] Colin Mackerras, 'Introduction', in *Ethnic minorities in modern China*, ed. by Colin Mackerras, 4 vols (London; New York: Routledge, 2011), I, pp. 1–25.

Adi – Abor
Hrusso – Aka
Bugun – Khowa
Galo – Gallong
Khamti – Khampti
Lisu – Yobin
Meyor – Zakhring
Monpa – Mönba, Lama
Memba – Drukpa, Tshangla, Pemaköpa
Mishing – Miri
Digaru Mishmi – Taraon Mishmi
Idu Mishmi – Chulikata Mishmi
Miju Mishmi – Kaman Mishmi
Nyishi (Bangni in Kameng) – Dafla
Puroik – Sulung
Singpho – Kachin

The transcriptions I have chosen are meant to be intelligible to a wide audience. For Mandarin, I follow the pinyin system, except for names like Chiang Kai-shek and Sun Yat-sen, more widely recognised than Jiang Jeshi and Sun Yixian. For Hindi, Tibetan, and local languages, I chose what seemed the most pronounceable renderings for non-specialist, English-speaking readers.

Chronology

1873	British India creates an Inner Line between Assam and the eastern Himalayas.
1910	Zhao Erfeng conquers Dzayül and Pomé. Chinese troops invade Lhasa.
1911	March: Murder of Noel Williamson. October: The first of a series of uprisings against the Qing Empire erupts in Wuhan. British India launches the Abor Expedition and the Miri and Mishmi missions.
1912	January–February: The Republic of China is declared; the last Qing Emperor abdicates. Chinese officials are expelled from Tibet, Kham, and the eastern Himalayas over the course of the year.
1913	Start of a period of *de facto* independence for Dalai Lama-ruled Tibet.
1914	British Indian and Tibetan representatives sign a secret boundary agreement in the eastern Himalayas.
1933	The thirteenth Dalai Lama dies.
1942	March: Japan occupies Burma. Lhasa tries to strengthen control over Monyül.
1943	April: London, Delhi, and Assam agree to bring the eastern Himalayas under 'effective control'.
1946	Civil war resumes between the Guomindang and the Chinese Communist Party (CCP).
1947	August: India attains independence.
1949	October: The CCP wins the Chinese Civil War and proclaims the People's Republic of China (PRC).
1950	August: A major earthquake hits the eastern Himalayas. October: The People's Liberation Army (PLA) marches on Chamdo to force Tibet to negotiate its peaceful negotiation. India commits to incorporating the eastern Himalayas.
1951	February: Indian authorities take over Tawang. May: The PRC annexes Tibet under the Seventeen Point Agreement.

1953   October: Achingmori Massacre. December: Verrier Elwin appointed Adviser for Tribal Areas.

1954   North-East Frontier Agency (NEFA) formally created. April: India and the PRC sign a trade agreement and proclaim their 'peaceful coexistence'.

1956   The Khampas in Sichuan, Yunnan, and Qinghai revolt against China. April: Inauguration of the Preparatory Committee for the Autonomous Region of Tibet.

1959   January: Zhou Enlai formally informs Nehru that the PRC rejects the McMahon Line. March: Uprising in Lhasa. The fourteenth Dalai Lama flees to India. August: Longju Incident. September: India decides to militarise NEFA.

1962   October 20: China invades NEFA. November 20: China declares a unilateral ceasefire. Parts of NEFA occupied until early 1963.

Acronyms and Abbreviations

AG	Adviser to the Governor of Assam (Nari Rustomji 1948–1954, K.L. Mehta 1954–1959, Nari Rustomji 1959–1963)
AICC	All India Congress Committee
APCC	Assam Pradesh Congress Committee
APO	Assistant Political Officer
APSA	Arunachal Pradesh State Archives
ASA	Assam State Archives
ATA	Adviser for Tribal Areas (i.e. Verrier Elwin)
BL	British Library
BRO	Border Roads Organisation
CSAS	Centre of South Asian Studies, Cambridge
DIPR	Directorate of Information and Public Relations, Government of Arunachal Pradesh
IFAS	Indian Frontier Administrative Service
IOR	India Office Records
MP	Member of Parliament
NAI	National Archives of India
NEFA	North-East Frontier Agency
NHTA	Naga Hills Tribal Area
NMML	Nehru Memorial Museum & Library
PB	Parliamentary Board
PLA	People's Liberation Army
PO	Political Officer
PRC	People's Republic of China
SECGA	Secretary to the Assam Governor
SOAS	School of Oriental and African Studies
SRC	States Reorganisation Commission
UKNA	United Kingdom National Archives, Kew

Glossary

T: *Tibetan, H: Hindi, A: Assamese, Ad: Adi*

Amban (Manchu)	commissioner representing the Qing Empire in Tibet
Beyül (T)	a Buddhist 'hidden land', where believers can attain enlightenment
Bharat darshan (H)	a tour to discover India, with a view to nation-building (literally, 'pilgrimage to India')
Chaprasi (H)	junior office worker
Depön (T)	general in the Tibetan army
Dim Dam (Ad)	a particularly aggressive species of flies, endemic in the eastern Himalayas
Dobashi (H)	interpreter
Duar (A, H)	foothill passes connecting the eastern Himalayas and the floodplains of Assam
Dzong (T)	Tibetan or Bhutanese fort, often hosting a local government official
Dzongpön (T)	governor of a *dzong* (district) in the traditional Tibetan government
Gam (Ad), gaonbura (A)	village headman
Gelugpa	the dominant school of Tibetan Buddhism. The Dalai Lama is its foremost member
Gompa (T)	Tibetan Buddhist monastery or hermitage
Jamadar (H)	low-ranking official
Jawan (H)	Indian soldier
Kaiya (H)	Marwari merchant/shopkeeper
Kebang (Ad)	village council in the Adi areas
Khenpo (T)	abbot of a Tibetan Buddhist monastery
Lama (T)	spiritual leader in Tibetan Buddhism

Lhopa (T)	Tibetan name for the inhabitants of NEFA (literally, 'southern barbarian')
Mahout	an elephant driver
Mekhela Chador (A)	the traditional dress of Assamese women, historically worn by some NEFA communities
Mibong (Ad)	'colonial official' in some Adi languages
Momo (T)	Tibetan dumplings
Monlam (T)	the greatest Tibetan Buddhist festival
Nyertsang (T)	Tibetan Buddhist monastic official, in charge of maintaining the accounts and perceiving tribute
Posa (A)	tribute or rent
Sarkar (H)	government
Stupa (T)	mound-like Buddhist monument hosting sacred relics
Tsampa (T)	roasted barley flour, a staple diet of Tibet
Tangka (T)	Tibetan coins
Tusker	(Indian) Border Roads Organisation staff
Ulag (T)	corvée labour, a form of taxation in the Tibetan political system

Characters

Fourteenth Dalai Lama, Tenzin Gyatso (1935–present) – The reincarnation of the thirteenth Dalai Lama, discovered in Amdo in the late 1930s. Enthroned in 1950 after the PLA crossed into Tibet. Fled to India in 1959.

Tungno – Headman of the Miju Mishmi village of Pangum, in the upper Lohit Valley, around 1910. Informed British Indian authorities of the conquest of Dzayül by Zhao Erfeng.

Lu Chuanlin (1836–1910) – Han official during the late Qing Empire. Governor-General of Sichuan at the start of the twentieth century. Advocated direct rule over Kham.

Feng Quan (?–1905) – Han official serving the Qing Empire as assistant *amban*. Tasked with increasing Qing control over eastern Tibet. His actions around Batang led to his murder, insurrections across Kham, and Zhao Erfeng's conquests.

Zhao Erfeng (1845–1911) – Han official who led military campaigns across Kham in the last decade of the Qing. Launched radical attempts to firmly incorporate it under Qing sovereignty, but was killed at the start of the revolution that ended the empire.

Francis Younghusband (1863–1942) – British army officer and explorer. Led a 1903–1904 armed expedition to Lhasa, which resulted in the British invasion of Tibet and the signature of a treaty with the Dalai Lama.

Thirteenth Dalai Lama, Thupten Gyatso (1876–1933) – Spiritual and temporal leader of Tibet. Presided over a period of *de facto* independence for Tibet after the fall of the Qing Empire.

Noel Williamson (?–1911) – British colonial official. Assistant Political Officer at Sadiya between 1906 and 1911. Advocated British Indian expansion into the Himalayas. Murdered during an armed expedition into the Adi country in March 1911.

Frederick Bailey (1882–1967) – British intelligence officer and explorer. Veteran of the Younghusband Expedition. Travelled extensively in

Tibet and the Himalayas. Led an unauthorised expedition to south-eastern Tibet, Monyül, and the Lohit Valley in 1911–1912.

Mazanon – Digaru Mishmi headman. Witnessed the attempts of Qing and British officials to expand into the Lohit Basin in the early twentieth century.

W.C.M. Dundas – British colonial official. Succeeded Noel Williamson as Assistant Political Officer, Sadiya. Appointed Political Officer, Central and Eastern Sectors (Sadiya Frontier Tract), at the head of an expanded frontier administration in 1912. Worked to assert British Indian claims in the Lohit Valley against the Qing and expand administration in the Adi foothills.

Liu Wenhui (1895–1976) – One of the main warlords in Sichuan and eastern Kham during Republican and Nationalist China.

Sun Yat-sen (1866–1925) – Chinese revolutionary and statesman. Played a crucial role in the fall of the Qing Empire and the establishment of the Republic of China.

Henry McMahon (1862–1949) – British diplomat and colonial official. As Indian Foreign Secretary, led territorial negotiations with China and Tibet in 1913–1914. Gave his name to the Indo-Tibetan boundary in the eastern Himalayas.

Chiang Kai-shek (1887–1975) – Chinese political and military leader. Head of the Guomindang Party from 1925 and, from 1928, of the Nationalist Chinese government. Fled to Taiwan upon his defeat by the CCP.

Olaf Caroe (1892–1981) – British Indian administrator, specialist of frontier issues. Indian Foreign Secretary between 1939 and 1946. Played a leading role in shaping Indian expansion in the eastern Himalayas and policies towards China. Wrote extensively about Central Asia and the Pakistan–Afghanistan borderlands after 1947. Continued to entertain an active interest in South Asian and Tibetan affairs, for example as President of the Tibet Society.

Frank Kingdon-Ward (1885–1958) – British explorer and botanist. Undertook dozens of expeditions through Tibet, Assam, western China, and Burma between the 1910s and the 1960s. His unauthorised attempts to enter Tibet via the North-East Frontier Tracts caused Indian authorities to rediscover the existence of the McMahon Line.

James Philip Mills (1890–1960) – Colonial administrator and anthropologist, specialist of the Naga Hills. Appointed to the new position of Adviser to the Assam Governor in 1943 to spearhead expansion into the eastern Himalayas. Had to resign shortly before independence. Taught Cultural Anthropology at the School of Oriental and African Studies (SOAS) in London until 1954.

Paul Mainprice – Colonial frontier official. Joined the Indian Civil Service in 1937 and served in various parts of India before being appointed British Trade Agent at Gyantse, Tibet in 1942. Appointed Political Official for the Lohit Valley in 1943.

Peter James – Colonial frontier official. Appointed to the North-East Frontier Tracts in 1944. Specialist of the Adi areas. Stayed on as an Assam tea planter after 1947.

Christoph von Fürer-Haimendorf (1909–1995) – Austrian anthropologist. Born in an aristocratic family. Received his PhD for a study of the Nagas. Befriended Philip Mills in the Naga Hills in 1936. Interned by British Indian authorities as an enemy citizen when the Second World War broke out. On special appointment by the Assam Governor, explored the Apatani and Nyishi country in 1944–1945. Appointed at SOAS, where he became one of the major anthropologists of South Asia. Made further visits to NEFA/Arunachal and Nagaland between 1962 and 1980.

Jawaharlal Nehru (1889–1964) – Indian politician and statesman. One of the main leaders of the Indian National Congress' fight for independence in the last decades of colonial rule. First Prime Minister of independent India.

Nari Rustomji – Adviser to the Governor of Assam (1947–1953, 1959–1962). Parsi from Bombay. Colonial administrator in Assam prior to 1947. Became the first Indian appointed to the post of Adviser, tasked with leading the incorporation of NEFA into India.

Mao Zedong (1893–1976) – Chinese Communist revolutionary and statesman, founder and leader of the PRC from 1949 to 1976.

Vallabhbhai Patel (1875–1950) – Indian National Congress Leader and major figure in India's freedom struggle. Deputy Prime Minister from 1947 till his death.

Kathing, Ralengnao (Bob) (1912–1990) – Frontier official who took over Tawang for India in 1951. Born in Manipur to a Tangkhul Naga family. Served in the V Force during the Second World War before a brief spell in the Manipur government and the Assam Rifles. Appointed Assistant Political Officer to the Sela Sub-Agency in 1950. Had a distinguished career in the NEFA, Nagaland, and Sikkim administrations before being appointed ambassador to Burma.

K.L. Mehta (1913–1991) – Adviser to the Governor of Assam (1954–1959). Born in Rajasthan in an aristocratic family, studied at the London School of Economics before joining the Indian Civil Service in the late 1930s. Succeeded Rustomji as Adviser after the Achingmori Massacre. Left for the External Affairs Ministry in June 1959, where his expertise on border issues and the PRC was in high demand. Replaced by his predecessor, Rustomji.

S.M. Krishnatry – Former major in the Indian army recruited by the NEFA administration for the first batch of the Indian Frontier Administrative Service (IFAS) in 1954. Chosen because of his long experience of various Indian frontiers: had served on the North-West Frontier during the Second World War, commanded Indian army escorts in Tibet and Sikkim in the late 1940s, and served as Trade Agent at Gyantse (1950–1954).

Verrier Elwin (1902–1964) – Autodidact anthropologist, tribal activist, and government official. Born in Britain and naturalised by India after 1947. Went to India in 1927 as a missionary; converted to Hinduism in 1937. Having become an authority on the tribes of central and eastern India, was appointed adviser to Nehru on tribal areas and put at the head of NEFA's research administration.

Ram Manohar Lohia (1910–1967) – Indian political leader. Fought for India's independence as a member of the Congress Socialist Party. Broke with Nehru and the Congress in 1948. Founder and chairman of the Socialist Party in 1955, often in opposition to the Nehru government. Early critic of the policies followed in NEFA, particularly Inner Line restrictions. Attempted to publicise the issue by entering NEFA without permission several times in 1958 and 1959, courting arrest. Finally permitted to enter NEFA after the 1962 war, under escort.

Oshong Ering (1932/1933–) – Padam Adi who was among NEFA's very first batches of students. Finished high school in 1955 and graduated three years later from St Edmund's College in Shillong. One of the first indigenous inhabitants to join the NEFA administration, in 1960. In post at Pasighat during the 1962 war, where he helped with evacuation and intelligence gathering. Went on to a distinguished career in the NEFA/Arunachal government.

Zhou Enlai (1898–1976) – Prime Minister of the PRC from 1949 to 1976. Led the unsuccessful boundary discussions with India prior to the 1962 war.

Kunga Samten Dewatshang (1914–1985) – Khampa trader and key founder and leader of the Chushi Gangdruk resistance movement against the PRC. Escaped to NEFA with his family in 1959 and resettled there.

Sawthang La (1917–?) – Native Bhutanese who was Assistant Tibetan Agent for the NEFA authorities. Joined service in 1941. Assigned to the Lohit Valley in the mid-1950s. Tasked with monitoring Chinese movements and persuading the Mishmis, Dzayülis, and Meyors of the greater benefits of Indian sovereignty.

Kamasha (?–?) – Tibetan carpenter from Rima, active in Dzayül and the Lohit. Favourably impressed by the Indian administration due to its more generous policies towards the inhabitants (compared to China's).

Tarun Bhattacharjee (1931–?) – Young NEFA frontier official, born in Shillong. Base Superintendent at the Shimong Adi village of Yingkiong during the 1962 war. Published extensively about NEFA and his life there.

Katon Borang (c. 1937–) – An Adi student who experienced the 1962 war. Later an administrator and politician in NEFA and Arunachal Pradesh.

Introduction

In early October 2013, two young Indian archers missed their flight to China. Immigration authorities at Delhi's Indira Gandhi International Airport had refused to let them pass: the Chinese visa they had been granted to attend an archery competition in Guangzhou was not stamped, as for other Indian citizens, but stapled. This was no coincidence. The two women were from Arunachal Pradesh, a Himalayan state on India's north-eastern extremity that is roughly the size of Austria. Chinese authorities thereby indicated that they considered Delhi's rule over the region, and the archers' Indian citizenship, to be dubious at best (Map 1).

This was not the first time Arunachalis had been issued stapled visas. Athletes or sports representatives from the state had many times been denied visits to the People's Republic of China (PRC) on that basis. Before, Beijing had altogether refused issuing visas for Arunachalis: China held Arunachal to be part of Tibet – and the Arunachalis, ergo, to be Chinese citizens. The row over stapled visas led Delhi to cancel plans to ease restrictions on PRC visitors to India.

The spat was but the latest in a series of incidents. Just before the new Chinese Prime Minister's visit to Delhi in May 2013, a three-week standoff between Indian troops and the People's Liberation Army (PLA) had taken place in Ladakh, high in the western Himalayas. Meanwhile, Indian naval authorities worried about Chinese activism in the Indian Ocean.[1] But the year 2013 was not an extraordinary one for Sino-Indian relations. Tensions have plagued the relationship between China and India for decades, and they have gone well beyond diplomatic spats and armed stand-offs. Back in 1962, war erupted between the two countries high up in the Himalayas. In 1987, another military escalation was averted. Delhi and Beijing have officially agreed to maintain

---

[1] Fayaz Bukhari, 'China, India troops set up rival camps in Himalayan desert', *Reuters*, 20 April 2013; 'After Ladakh incursions, China flexes its muscles in Indian Ocean' (IBN Live, 14 May 2013).

1

'peace and tranquillity' on their vast Himalayan border since then, but incidents occur on a regular basis.

A voluminous scholarship has tried to explain these tensions between the world's two biggest countries. The disputed Sino-Indian boundary looms large in many of these accounts. From afar, the Himalayas look like a wall between the Tibetan plateau and the Indian subcontinent, but on the ground, India and China have antagonistic views of where their territories end and meet. Delhi stands by boundary lines inherited from British times, deeming them identical to India's historical and natural borders: the Ardagh–Johnson Line in the north-west of the Himalayas, near Ladakh, and the McMahon Line, on the massif's eastern extremity. Beijing's boundary claims lie far to the south of Indian assertions. The result is a dispute over the ownership of more than a hundred thousand square kilometres of territory, mainly near Ladakh (the Aksai Chin) and in the eastern Himalayas (Arunachal). An intense debate surrounds the validity of both claims.[2]

For many analysts, however, the boundary dispute hides a broader rivalry. China and India consider themselves great powers and expect to be treated as such, but their ambitions overlap across Tibet, South Asia, and even South-East Asia and the Indian Ocean.[3] Their conceptions of national security also seem at odds. For India, a non-threatening South Asia is one devoid of Chinese influence and under Indian leadership; for China, South Asia can only be a safe hinterland if Indian hegemony is kept at bay.[4] The Tibet question adds to the antagonism. India had strong cultural and economic ties with the plateau historically and had inherited special rights in the region from British rule. Since 1959, it has hosted the Dalai Lama's government-in-exile and the biggest Tibetan refugee community in the world.[5]

---

[2] For instance: Alastair Lamb, *The China–India border: The origins of the disputed boundaries* (London: Oxford University Press, 1964); Neville Maxwell, *India's China war* (London: J. Cape, 1970); Elliot Sperling, 'The politics of history and the Indo-Tibetan border (1987–88)', *India Review*, 7:3 (2008), 223–239; Parshotam Mehra, 'India–China border: A review and critique', *Economic and Political Weekly*, 17:20 (1982), 834–838; Karunakar Gupta, 'Distortions in the history of Sino-Indian frontiers', *Economic and Political Weekly*, 30 (1980), 1265–1270.

[3] *The India–China relationship: Rivalry and engagement*, ed. by Francine R. Frankel and Harry Harding (New Delhi: Oxford University Press, 2004); Mohan Malik, *China and India: Great power rivals* (Boulder, CO: First Forum, 2011); Harsh V. Pant, 'Rising China in India's vicinity: A rivalry takes shape in Asia', *Cambridge Review of International Affairs*, 25:3 (2013), 1–18; David Brewster, *India's ocean: The story of India's bid for regional leadership* (London: Routledge, 2014).

[4] John W. Garver, *Protracted contest: Sino-Indian rivalry in the twentieth century* (New Delhi: Oxford University Press, 2001).

[5] Dawa Norbu, 'Tibet in Sino-Indian relations: The centrality of marginality', *Asian Survey*, 37:11 (1997), 1078–1095; Steven A. Hoffmann, 'Rethinking the linkage between Tibet

This book argues that these existing analyses miss a fundamental element of the Sino-Indian rivalry: the difficulty of coexisting in the Himalayas, a region whose distinct human landscape exposes India and China's imperial nature. It is not just the boundary dispute or power games that create tension, but the fact that India and the PRC both seek to consolidate their presence in the regions east of Bhutan by achieving exclusive authority and legitimacy over local people.

The Indian Union and the PRC alike derive their geographical claims to the Himalayas from the conquests of a foreign empire (Manchu for China, British for India), but these empires' territorial inheritance in the Himalayan regions east of Bhutan was fragile, if not flimsy. Chinese and Indian authorities' presence there is in fact very recent. Indeed, it truly dates back to the 1950s. Effective, lasting state expansion largely happened *after* formal decolonisation.

The story of China and India is that of two post-colonial *and* imperial polities seeking to deepen their rule over Himalayan regions where they encounter people starkly different from their 'core' citizenry. China and India's brutal experience of Western colonialism long obscured their own imperial tendencies, but there is growing recognition that Qing China was an expansionist empire comparable to European powers. Moreover, its successor states employed colonial policies on China's geographic peripheries – Tibet included.[6] As for independent India, its long freedom struggle and professed unity-in-diversity ideal coexist with imperial strategies towards Kashmir or Nagaland. Decolonisation is nowhere as clear cut or emancipatory a process as official history would have it.[7]

This intimate entanglement between the imperial and the national has shaped China's and India's expansion in particular ways. The 'process

---

and the China–India border conflict: A Realist approach', *Journal of Cold War Studies*, 8:3 (2006), 165–194.

[6] Laura Hostetler, *Qing colonial enterprise: Ethnography and cartography in early modern China* (Chicago: University of Chicago Press, 2001); Peter C. Perdue, 'China and other colonial empires', *Journal of American–East Asian Relations*, 16:12 (2009), 85–103; Kirk W. Larsen, 'The Qing Empire (China), imperialism, and the modern world', *History Compass*, 9:6 (2011), 498–508; Justin M. Jacobs, 'Empire besieged: The preservation of Chinese rule in Xinjiang, 1884–1971' (unpublished doctoral thesis, University of California, San Diego, 2011); Benno Weiner, 'The Chinese Revolution on the Tibetan frontier: State building, national integration and socialist transformation, Zeku (Tsékhok) County, 1953–1958' (unpublished PhD dissertation, Columbia University, 2012).

[7] Dipesh Chakrabarty, 'Introduction', in *From the colonial to the postcolonial: India and Pakistan in transition*, ed. by Dipesh Chakrabarty (New Delhi; Oxford: Oxford University Press, 2007).

of empire' has been put to the service of nationalism.[8] Colonial trauma renders Chinese and Indian authorities particularly sensitive to their perceived status (whether past glory or current prestige), driving them to assertiveness on questions of sovereignty.[9] On the one hand, India and China see themselves as victims of imperialism; on the other, they resort to claims and governance methods inherited from it. The tension between the two imbues them with a lasting sense of anxiety and vulnerability, particularly strong in the eastern Himalayas. There, Chinese and Indian authorities have encountered people not only culturally distinct, but also ready to move – whether in search of better opportunities or to escape a polity seen as oppressive. People's mobility has been a source of deep anxieties for states, and China and India are no exception. From the perspective of officials on either side, border populations cannot be easily pinned down by coercive measures; worse, their location gives them the option to 'defect' to the other side.[10]

In the absence of an easily enforceable border and of strong legal, cultural, emotional, or historical claims to the eastern Himalayas' inhabitants, China and India's proximity became inherently threatening. Local men and women did not identify with (or care for) either polity, but the possibility to look on the other side meant that they could at least compare the two states, from the threat they might pose to the trade, welfare, and development opportunities they might bring. Indian and Chinese state-making and nation-building turned into processes of mutual observation, replication, and competition to prove themselves the better state – becoming in short, anxiety-fuelled attempts at self-definition against one another.

In Westminster political systems, the opposition's leaders collectively and individually 'shadow' each and every member of the Cabinet, closely following their government department's policies and questioning them in parliament. This Shadow Cabinet offers people an alternate choice of

---

[8] David Ludden, 'The process of empire: Frontiers and borderlands', in *Tributary empires in global history*, ed. by Christopher Bayly and Peter Fibiger Bang (New Delhi: Palgrave Macmillan, 2011), pp. 132–150; Uradyn Bulag, *Collaborative nationalism: The politics of friendship on China's Mongolian frontier* (Lanham, MD; Plymouth: Rowman & Littlefield, 2010); Dibyesh Anand, 'China and India: Postcolonial informal empires in the emerging global order', *Rethinking Marxism*, 24:1 (2012), 68–86.

[9] Manjari Chatterjee Miller, *Wronged by empire: Post-imperial ideology and foreign policy in India and China* (Stanford, CA: Stanford University Press, 2013).

[10] Arjun Appadurai and Carol Breckenridge, 'On moving targets', *Public Culture*, 2 (1989), i–iv; James C. Scott, *The moral economy of the peasant: Rebellion and subsistence in Southeast Asia* (New Haven: Yale University Press, 1976); Benjamin D. Hopkins, 'The frontier crimes regulation and frontier governmentality', *Journal of Asian Studies*, 74:2 (2015), 369–389.

programme and leadership, forcing the incumbent government to always try to keep one step ahead.[11] This idea of an always discernible, readily available, and equally viable *alternative* political project is a key element of bilateral tensions. China and India see themselves as each other's 'shadow state' in the Himalayas.

This book is an attempt to study China–India relations not through their high politics, but from the ground up, and to show how this yields novel possibilities to understand tensions between the two countries. To do so, it explores India's attempts to entrench itself in the eastern Himalayas from 1910 onwards, and how they collided with China's own plans to deepen its hold over Tibet. It suggests that this led to the emergence of competitive 'state shadowing' between Chinese and Indian authorities and eventually participated in the outbreak of war between the two countries in 1962.

Anatomy of a Borderland

The region described here as the 'eastern Himalayas' lies to the east of Bhutan, at the juncture of the Himalayan range and two lower massifs, the Hengduan and the Patkai. There, monsoon winds come crashing against the mountains, sometimes eight months out of twelve. Heat and humidity foster the growth of dense jungles and high biodiversity. At higher altitudes, subtropical environments give way to temperate or alpine ones. Higher still are the snowline and the glaciers. The dry, windy landscape of the Tibetan plateau only starts under the 'rain shadow', beyond the highest peaks. But even there, zones of warmer temperatures, higher rainfall, and tangled forests subsist. Powerful rivers tumble down the Himalayas. Some have broken through the upper range, and where they do, their valleys act as funnels that propel the rain-carrying winds further, all the way to the plateau (Figure I.1).[12]

The most powerful of these rivers, the Tsangpo, has its source 1,700 kilometres away in far western Tibet. For most of these, it follows a leisurely course across the plateau, its braids-like channels turning surrounding areas into Tibet's agricultural heartland. As it approaches the Himalayas' easternmost peak, Namcha Barwa, the Tsangpo picks up

---

[11] Joel Bateman, *In the shadows: The Shadow Cabinet in Australia* (Australian Government – Department of Parliamentary Services, 2008).

[12] Mark Aldenderfer and Yinong Zhang, 'The prehistory of the Tibetan plateau to the seventh century AD', in *The Tibetan history reader*, ed. by Gray Tuttle and Kurtis R. Schaeffer (New York: Columbia University Press, 2013), pp. 3–48; Francis Kingdon-Ward, *Riddle of the Tsangpo Gorges: Retracing the epic journey of 1924–25 in South-East Tibet*, ed. by Kenneth Cox (additional material by Kenneth Cox, Kenneth Storm, Jr. and Ian Baker) (Woodbridge: Garden Art Press, 2008).

Figure I.1 The Lohit Valley, c. 1945
© Centre of South Asian Studies (CSAS), Cambridge. Mainprice
Collections, Box 19

the pace. Its waters now follow but one narrow channel, fighting their way
through jungle-clad gorges overlooked by glaciers. Instead of
pushing further east, the river circles Namcha Barwa, carving out the
world's deepest canyon, and, its U-turn completed, plunges down the
Himalayas to emerge in the Assam plain as the Brahmaputra River – 240
kilometres further and 3,000 metres below (Map 2).

Though sparsely populated, the eastern Himalayas' human landscape
is a complex one. Its northern edge straddles two Tibetan regions: central
Tibet, culturally and politically the heartland of the Dalai Lama's government, and Kham, which has a distinct identity and history. Besides
Tibetan populations, the eastern Himalayas host a variety of groups
who practise Tibetan Buddhism and Bon (the pre-Buddhic religion of
Tibet) and use classical Tibetan as a written language. The Monpas who
inhabit alpine regions near Bhutan have their own idiom. So do their
southern neighbours, the Sherdukpens, and the Membas of Pemakö.
People from various parts of Kham have also moved near the Tsangpo's
Great Bend.

But not all the eastern Himalayas belong to a greater Tibetan sphere. A great variety of groups inhabit the valleys – Hrussos, Puroiks, Apatanis, to cite but a few – and some, like the Adis, the Nyishis, or the Mishmis, have their own subgroups. Beneath these differences, these populations share a similar material culture, such as the widespread use of bamboo, speak Tibeto-Burman languages, and have oral rather than written traditions. Historically, most of them also practised shifting cultivation and held 'animist' beliefs.

The eastern foothills, near the plains of Assam, are inhabited by yet different people. The Khamtis and the Singphos follow Theravada Buddhism and have close links to the populations of the South-East Asia highlands. So do the non-Buddhist Tangsas, Noctes, and Wanchos who inhabit the lower mountains of the Patkai and are related to Naga populations living in the central part of the range. It is there that population densities are at their highest. Shared socio-economic ties and cultural practices often blurred the boundaries between supposedly different groups. The Nyishis of the upper Subansiri traditionally dressed their hair in Tibetan fashion, when those further south tied it into a bun on their forehead.[13] To the east, the Bokar Adis' indigenous beliefs were interspersed with Buddhist practices, whereas the Padam Adis, nearer to the plains, sometimes wore Assamese dress and peppered their language with Assamese words.[14] Identities and belonging could form complex assemblages, for instance among Tibetan Buddhist groups, whose shared religious identity and sense of difference vis-à-vis non-Buddhists were tempered by strong regional identifications (Map 3).

This linguistic, cultural, and religious diversity and ambiguity betrayed the historical fluidity of human settlement in the region, assumed to have ultimately originated from either Tibet or the Yunnan–Burma borderlands. Migration was not a single, en masse movement but a constant, protracted, small-scale process. People moved at different times, for different reasons, and to different places. Individuals, families, at times entire villages could migrate, and sometimes move on, yet again. Some moved in search of better land, others because of a famine, a feud, a disaster, or an epidemic; some moved to marry or join relatives; some moved to benefit from trade opportunities; some migrated for religious reasons, or because of war and political strife; some moved due to the

---

[13] New Delhi, NAI, External Affairs Proceedings (1945), Tour diaries of Capt Davy in the Dafla hills, 241-CA/45 (26 January entry).

[14] See respectively Tarun Kumar Bhattacharjee, *The frontier trail* (Calcutta: Manick Bandyopadhyay, 1993), p. 80; Gindu Borang, 'Trade practices of the Adis with special reference to Padams', *Yaaro moobang: A land of peace, prosperity and happiness*, 1 (2001), 14–18 (pp. 16–17).

migratory pressures of other groups; some wanted to escape punishment; and some moved, not of their own accord, but because they had been captured and enslaved.[15] Seasonal migrations added to this fluidity. Every winter, the Sherdukpens descended from their altitude villages to camp in the Assam plains, profiting from their warmer clime and the trade opportunities.[16] Many Tsona Monpas similarly relocated to Tawang over the cold season.[17] Northern Adis travelled to Tibetan-speaking areas as seasonal labourers.[18]

Contact and interaction accompanied migration. People travelled to visit relatives, to build alliances, to search for prey – men among the non-Buddhist groups were skilled hunters – and above all, to trade. Himalayan people depended on the plateau and the plains for essential commodities such as salt, agricultural implements, or weapons, which they exchanged against available surpluses. Barter, often through a series of intermediaries, was the most widespread form of exchange. The Buddhist Membas acted as middlemen between the Tibetan plateau and their southern Ramo, Pailibo, and Galo neighbours, giving them wool, weapons, or beads and ornaments in exchange for hides, cane, chillies, and Assamese silk.[19] The Mishmis' chief source of wealth was their export of poisonous and medicinal plants.[20]

---

[15] Stories of origins and migration play an unusually important role in constructing the continuity and distinctiveness of local identities. The Nas and the Mras of the Subansiri Basin tell how their ancestors descended from the sky to settle on the Tibetan plateau before migrating south. Neighbouring groups, such as the Nyishis, also believe they came from the north, but their legendary ancestor is a trickster called Abotani. *Origins and migrations in the extended eastern Himalayas*, ed. by Stuart Blackburn and Toni Huber (Leiden; Boston: Brill, 2012). Buddhist migration into Pemakö thus began in the seventeenth century, when war, political turmoil, and religious oppression sent many people searching for sacred 'hidden lands' (*beyül*). It continued over the next centuries, under different guises and with different degrees of importance. Kerstin Grothmann, 'Population, history and identity in the hidden land of Pemakö', *Journal of Bhutan Studies*, 26 (2012), 21–52.

[16] Yeshe Dorjee Thongchi. Interview with the author, 8 February 2014, Itanagar (Arunachal Pradesh).

[17] Interview with Karma Wangdu (Interview #46M). Interviewed by Rebecca Novick on 13 April 2010 (held at the Tibet Oral History Project), www.tibetoralhistory.org/interviews.html (accessed 27 January 2015). Monyül also hosted small semi-migratory herder communities, the Pangchenpas and Thingbupas. Bibhas Dhar, *Transhumants of Arunachal Himalayas: The Pangchenpas and the Thingbupas of Tawang District* (Guwahati: Geophil, 2009).

[18] Stuart Blackburn, 'Memories of migration: Notes on legends and beads in Arunachal Pradesh', *European Bulletin of Himalayan Research*, 25/26 (2003–2004), 15–60 (p. 25).

[19] R.K. Billorey, 'Oral history in north-east India', in *Proceedings of the North-East India History Association, Second Session* (Shillong: Singhania Press, 1981), pp. 14–22 (pp. 19–20).

[20] Sudatta Sikdar, 'Tribalism vs. colonialism: British capitalistic intervention and transformation of primitive economy of Arunachal Pradesh in the nineteenth century', *Social Scientist*, 10:12 (1982), 15–31 (p. 17).

Local and regional trading networks coexisted with long-distance caravan routes, particularly for rice and salt. These generally involved currency and followed three main corridors: in the far west, the route from Charduar in Assam to Tawang, Tsona, and Lhasa; in the far east, the Sadiya–Rima route through the Lohit Valley, which connected Assam to Kham and western China; and the Hukawng Valley route to Burma.[21] Lhasa stationed an official at Tsona specifically to control the purchase of rice from the plains, either sold to locals or used for New Year celebrations in Lhasa; in return, he gave Monpa intermediaries equally precious salt.[22]

Pilgrimages acted as another nexus of trade. Tibetan Buddhists could go as far as Lhasa; pilgrims conversely flowed in, attracted by the great monastery at Tawang or the eastern Himalayas' 'hidden lands', earthly paradises where believers could find refuge, a place to settle, and Buddhist liberation. Pemakö was considered the purest of them. Tsari, north of the Subansiri, was the holiest mountain of Tibet. Every twelve years, 20,000 people from around Tibet circumambulated it. Of all the Tibetan Buddhist pilgrimages, this was the greatest and the most dangerous. Some pilgrims, finally, passed through en route to the Buddhist sites of Assam.[23]

The reach of the Dalai Lama's government over the eastern Himalayas' Tibetanised regions was highly uneven on the eve of the twentieth century. Scholars generally agree that the Tibetan state did not exercise direct, unlimited, or exclusive control over land and people. Lhasa ruled both through temporal mechanisms – government officials such as the *dzongpön*s, in charge of districts where they had much day-to-day autonomy – and spiritual ones, through the influence of Gelugpa monasteries. Its authority diminished the farther one got from the capital.[24]

Configurations of 'Tibetan' power were particularly complex in the eastern Himalayas, which Lhasa considered a geographic and

---

[21] J.B. Bhattacharjee, 'The eastern Himalayan trade of Assam in the colonial period', in *Proceedings of the North-East India History Association, First Session* (Shillong: Singhania Press, 1980), pp. 174–192 (p. 176); R.B. Pemberton, *Report on the Eastern Frontier of British India* (Guwahati: Department of Historical and Antiquarian Studies, 1991 [1835]).

[22] Short Interview with Karma Wangdu (Interview #46M). For an overview of these trans-Himalayan trade networks, see Blackburn, 'Memories of migration' (pp. 33–34).

[23] Toni Huber, *The cult of Pure Crystal Mountain: Popular pilgrimage and visionary landscape in southeast Tibet* (New York; Oxford: Oxford University Press, 1999); Toni Huber, *The Holy Land reborn: Pilgrimage and the Tibetan reinvention of Buddhist India* (Chicago, IL: University of Chicago Press, 2008).

[24] William M. Coleman IV, 'Making the state on the Sino-Tibetan frontier: Chinese expansion and local power in Batang, 1842–1939' (unpublished doctoral thesis, Columbia University, 2014), pp. 6–10.

civilisational periphery. Monyül – the land of the Monpas – and nearby Chayül were administered by Lhasa-appointed *dzongpön*s, who collected taxes, requisitioned labour, and administered justice.[25] So was Dzayül, on the other end of the eastern Himalayas. But other regions remained outside of secular authorities' influence. Pomé, north of Pemakö, was a semi-independent kingdom.[26] Finally, since the eastern Himalayas historically served both as a space of refuge from the Tibetan state or a place of exile, some Tibetanised communities were fully outside of Lhasa's reach.[27]

Non-Tibetan Buddhist societies had seen fewer processes of local state formation. While the Khamtis had forged a small kingdom, most people lived in relatively egalitarian socio-political structures. Sources of authority were varied – clan, village council, chieftain, or head of the household. The highest of them was seldom at the level of the entire tribe.

A complex political economy had linked the lower Himalayan slopes and Assam prior to the colonial period. The foot of the hills was an area of overlapping authority and resource use between highland-centred groups and polities such as the Ahoms, a kingdom that ruled most of Assam for six centuries. Local forests played a crucial role in nearby hill dwellers' subsistence, while Ahom subjects formed villages in their vicinity. Relations were managed through *posa*, a practice whereby Ahom officials relinquished part of these settlements' revenues to the Nyishis or the Adis to guarantee peaceful relations. For the latter, *posa* was a form of rent, due to them as the first users of land others now wished to occupy.[28]

The transitional regions at the foot of the trade corridor between Assam, Monyül, and Tibet were a particularly complex area, where a variety of Bhutanese, Mughal, Hrusso, or Monpa power holders enjoyed seasonal or time-limited control. This fluid system was maintained through the exchange of 'tribute' in multiple directions, and trade

---

[25] Monyül had been permanently annexed by Lhasa at the end of the 5th Dalai Lama's reign, in 1680. His successor, the 6th Dalai Lama, was born there. Michael Aris, *Hidden treasures and secret lives: A study of Pemalingpa (1450–1521) and the sixth Dalai Lama (1683–1706)* (London: Kegan Paul, 1989).

[26] Santiago Lazcano, 'Ethno-historic notes on the ancient Tibetan kingdom of sPo Bo and its influence on the eastern Himalayas', *Revue d'Etudes Tibétaines*, 7 (2005), 41–63.

[27] Toni Huber, 'Pushing south: Tibetan economic and political activities in the far eastern Himalaya, ca. 1900–1950', in *Sikkim Studies: Proceedings of the Namgyal Institute Jubilee Conference, 2008*, ed. by Alex McKay and Anna Balikci (Gangtok: Namgyal Institute, 2011) (p. 261).

[28] On indigenous notions of space and authority, see Gunnel Cederlöf, *Founding an empire on India's north-eastern frontiers, 1790–1840: Climate, commerce, polity* (Delhi: Oxford University Press, 2013), chapter 2.

fairs played a crucial role in the adjustment of these dynamic politico-economic arrangements.[29]

In short, the eastern Himalayas were historically a world of active (if not always large-scale) movement and interaction between many ethnic, linguistic, and cultural groups. The formidable landscape did not preclude these exchanges but shaped them in specific ways. Political interaction and conceptions of space and authority followed complex logics. This was a world where different actors could share, at different times or for different aspects, ownership and use of a place, its produce, and its people. Authority tended to be located in socio-economic relations, in control over people, rather than over territory.[30] This interaction should not be romanticised. Conflict, tensions, competition, prejudice, and civilising missions were present.[31] But this was a world articulated in ways starkly different from Western frameworks of sovereignty and 'international' relations.

The Eastern Himalayas around 1900

Under today's dominant geographic representations, the eastern Himalayas straddle three world regions: South, East, and South-East Asia.[32] Yet these notions are recent and, indeed, rooted in historical and political struggles and scholarly biases. Following Willem van Schendel, many scholars in fact consider the area and the neighbouring highlands to form a distinct region, Zomia. Beyond shared cultural, linguistic, or socio-economic ties, Zomia is above all characterised by its historical location on the periphery, and often on the outside, of valley-dominated states and their formation – a marginality that renders it invisible on current world maps.[33] This book dissects the contested and

---

[29] Sanghamitra Misra, *Becoming a borderland: The politics of space and identity in colonial northeastern India* (New Delhi: Routledge, 2011).

[30] Ibid. Greater emphasis on control over people was historically widespread across Tibet and the Himalayas. Geoffrey Samuel, *Civilized shamans: Buddhism in Tibetan societies* (Washington; London: Smithsonian Institution Press, 1993); Catherine Warner, 'Flighty subjects: Sovereignty, shifting cultivators, and the state in Darjeeling, 1830–1856', *Himalaya, the Journal of the Association for Nepal and Himalayan Studies*, 34:1 (2014), 23–35.

[31] Huber, 'Pushing south'; Sara Shneiderman, 'Barbarians at the border and civilizing projects: Analyzing ethnic and national identities in the Tibetan context', in *Tibetan borderlands*, ed. by Christiaan Klieger (Leiden: Brill, 2006), pp. 9–34.

[32] David Ludden, 'Where is Assam?', *Himal South Asian*, November (2005) http://himal mag.com/component/content/article/1676-Where-is-Assam?.html (accessed 17 March 2010).

[33] Willem van Schendel, 'Geographies of knowing, geographies of ignorance: Jumping scale in Southeast Asia', *Environment and Planning D: Society and Space*, 20 (2002), 647–668.

unfinished processes through which a part of Zomia was reconfigured as part of South and East Asia.

Neither the Qing nor the British empires, predecessors to today's China and India, could boast of a concrete state presence in the eastern Himalayas in the early twentieth century. Like the Ahoms' dealings with the Adis or the Nyishis, relations between Tibetan areas and China-based empires did not resemble modern structures of political hierarchy and authority. The Dalai Lama stood under Beijing's protection but he was also the Emperor's religious tutor, and as such superior to him in certain spheres.[34]

The relationship dated back to the middle of the twelfth century when Tibet had pledged submission to the Mongols. But the Yuan dynasty had not actively intervened in Tibet, and their successors, the Ming, lost authority over the country. It was only when Qing troops ousted the Zhunghar Mongols from Lhasa in 1720 that the priest–patron relationship between China and Tibet resumed – this time with the Dalai Lama, whose government had brought the plateau under control in the mid-seventeenth century. The Qing Empire had stationed troops and implemented reforms to ensure Tibet's stability and allegiance, most notably by installing a representative in Lhasa, the *amban*. Yet its presence on the plateau had waxed and waned, and it did not seek directly to administer the country. The Dalai Lama continued to manage affairs in central Tibet quite autonomously.[35]

The situation was different in eastern Kham, where the Qing claimed suzerainty over the myriad local principalities, installing military garrisons and investing local strongmen with titles. There too the aim was to achieve military and political control rather than direct administration. In practice, the presence of the Chinese state across eastern Kham was thin and its influence far from paramount – especially since Lhasa enjoyed much spiritual authority. There were few Qing officials, and, bar some exceptions, their tasks were limited. Imperial troops were present only in strategic points, unevenly distributed, and often of poor calibre.[36] Qing title investitures were used by local power holders as one among many instruments to assert their own power.[37] Traders played a crucial role as conduits for imperial power given this shallow formal

[34] Xiuyu Wang, *China's last imperial frontier: Late Qing expansion in Sichuan's Tibetan borderlands* (Lanham, MD: Lexington Books, 2011), p. 20.

[35] Melvyn C. Goldstein, *The snow lion and the dragon: China, Tibet, and the Dalai Lama* (Berkeley: University of California Press, 1997); Gray Tuttle, *Tibetan Buddhists in the making of modern China* (New York; Chichester: Columbia University Press, 2005).

[36] Elliot Sperling, 'The Chinese venture in Kham 1904–11, and the role of Chao Er-feng', *Tibet Journal*, 1:2 (1976) (p. 11).

[37] Wang, *China's last imperial frontier*, chapters 1–2.

presence.[38] Kham's extremely complex and fluid political patchwork defied concrete subordination to any external power.

By 1900, the Qing Empire's position in Tibetan areas was significantly weaker. The autonomy of the Dalai Lama's government had grown, and Beijing had failed to intervene in wars between Tibet and other powers.[39] In Kham, imperial troops had 'dwindle[d] to insignificance', leaving only 'a light sprinkling of state power' over the region.[40] As for the eastern Himalayas, located at the junction of western Kham and central Tibet, they had never seen Chinese troops or officials.[41]

Meanwhile, European colonialism had reached Assam. Over the nineteenth century, the British gradually conquered the Brahmaputra Valley and much of its mountainous hinterland. By 1900, the eastern Himalayas were among the last surrounding regions not to have been annexed. Indeed, they were not considered part of the British Empire. Colonial authorities held the 'Outer Line' of their territory to stop at the foot of the Himalayas. Regular administration itself did not go that far, but was confined within an 'Inner Line' drawn at a distance from the hills.

The Inner Line aimed to control interaction between Assam and the Himalayas. British subjects were forbidden from crossing it without a permit, assorted to specific activity restrictions. As for people living across the Inner Line, violating it carried the threat of retaliatory expeditions by Assam district officials. British Indian sovereignty had many internal frontiers. The foot of the hills was a transitional zone of rule, where colonial authorities proposed not to interfere 'politically', save to exert order and punishment. But the Himalayas themselves lay outside the bounds of this layered sovereignty.

The policy followed a familiar rationale for the British Empire. In the nineteenth century, attempts had been made to find trade routes to China through the region. But, unlike the Assam plains – which became targets for agricultural expansion and tea, timber, or rubber production – these trade routes and the eastern Himalayas were seen as offering too few economic benefits to justify the cost of

---

[38] C. Patterson Giersch, 'Commerce and empire in the borderlands: How do merchants and trade fit into Qing Frontier History?', *Frontiers of History in China*, 9:3 (2014), 361–383.

[39] Goldstein, *The snow lion and the dragon*, pp. 21–22.

[40] Wang, *China's last imperial frontier*, p. 43.

[41] Hsiao-Ting Lin, 'Boundary, sovereignty, and imagination: Reconsidering the frontier disputes between British India and Republican China, 1914–47', *Journal of Imperial and Commonwealth History*, 32:3 (2004), 25–47 (p. 26).

administration. The formidable terrain factored in these calculations.[42]

This 'non-interference' policy also derived from colonial characterisations of the eastern Himalayas' inhabitants as tribes. In the classification and identification schemes that played so central a role in colonial rule, the term embodied not so much certain cultural traits as an assemblage of negative markers – primitiveness, isolation, savagery, anarchy, paganism – that stood in opposition to ideas of civilisation, modernity, but also caste and Hinduism. Tribes were those whom civilisation and history had forgotten. What's more, tribalness belonged to a specific geography: the hills. Hills and plains were constructed as separate and antagonistic worlds, the latter – the realm of civilisation, of British subjects, and, above all, the seat of capitalist interests – being in need of protection from the former.[43]

British India's presence on their doorstep had important consequences for the inhabitants of the Himalayan foothills, and sometimes farther up. To claim the resources of the Brahmaputra's north bank, Europeans strove to impose unambiguous, bounded spheres of authority and property on the area.[44] Boxed up into the category of hill savages, the tribes' rights to plains territory went unrecognised, despite the lowlands' importance in their resource base and their notions of space. Hunting, fishing, or cultivation grounds were claimed or threatened by state and private actors, who treated them as wasteland.[45] Assam officials regulated trade with the Himalayas through Inner Line agencies and trade fairs in the foothills, where they held assemblies and popularised manufactured goods to assert their might. They reframed *posa* as illegitimate blackmail, paid only to protect the plains' from the highlands' savagery. The practice became a monetised and tightly regulated transaction meant to keep the

---

[42] T.T. Cooper, *The Mishmee hills: An account of a journey made in an attempt to penetrate Thibet from Assam to open new routes for commerce* (London: HS King, 1873); Sikdar, 'Tribalism vs. colonialism', (pp. 19–21, 26); Cederlöf, *Founding an empire*, chapter 3.

[43] Willem van Schendel, 'The dangers of belonging: Tribes, indigenous peoples and homelands in South Asia', in *The Politics of belonging in India: Becoming Adivasi*, ed. by Daniel Rycroft and Sangeeta Dasgupta (London: Routledge, 2011), pp. 19–43; Sanghamitra Misra, 'The nature of colonial intervention in the Naga Hills, 1840–80', *Economic and Political Weekly*, 33:51 (1998), 3273–3279.

[44] Misra, *Becoming a borderland*, pp. 55–66.

[45] The armed columns sent to the Hrusso country in 1883–1884, to Padam villages in 1893–1894, to the Apatani Valley in 1897, and to Idu settlements at the mouth of the Dibang Valley in 1899–1900 were among the most notable instances of promenades. For more details, see Robert Reid, *History of the frontier areas bordering on Assam, 1883–1941* (Delhi: Eastern Publishing, 1983), p. 270; Sanghamitra Misra, 'Law, migration and new subjectivities: Reconstructing the colonial project in an eastern borderland', *Indian Economic and Social History Review*, 44:5 (2007), 425–461.

foothills' inhabitants at bay and was generalised to groups who had not engaged in it.[46]

The Inner Line was instituted partly to regulate the activities of capitalist entrepreneurs beyond Assam's settled areas. In the second half of the nineteenth century, a worldwide rubber boom had driven European speculators to tap forest resources closer and closer to the foothills. Marwari traders from western India (*kaiyas*) followed. Many foothills' inhabitants became involved in the extraction of rubber, spending their earnings in *kaiya* shops on salt or manufactured goods from across the world, as well as on opium, whose sale and consumption accompanied colonial entrenchment in the plains. Assam's transformation into a frontier of global capitalism was 'restructur[ing] the conditions of human action and volition' among people living closer to the plains.[47]

These transformations created new avenues of conflict. Some Singphos and Khamtis competed against another for rubber tapping, while Mishings fell trees in forests claimed by Adis. Conflict between tribals and capitalist actors was rife, whether due to unfair wages, the over-exploitation of forest resources, deforestation, or restrictions on elephant hunting.[48] In the early nineteenth century, pitched battles had taken place between tribes such as the Khamtis and British troops. Later, tribals raided sawmills, officials, tea gardens, opium shops, or merchants. British officials retaliated by sending in brutal military 'promenades' beyond the Inner Line, which also helped to provide information about the eastern Himalayas.

Colonial officials saw the Inner Line as a protective barrier around British India's territorial and economic base. The eastern Himalayas' inhabitants were to remain in a 'temporal outside of the historical pace of development and progress ... where the time of the law did not apply;

---

[46] Boddhisattva Kar, 'When was the postcolonial? A history of policing impossible lines', in *Beyond counter-insurgency: Breaking the impasse in northeast India*, ed. by Sanjib Baruah (New Delhi: Oxford University Press, 2009), pp. 49–77.

[47] Boddhisattva Kar, 'Historia elastica: A note on the rubber hunt in the north-east frontier of British India', *Indian Historical Review*, 36:1 (2009), 131–150. British officials had initially paid *posa* with opium and took it on journeys to the hills to manage encounters with the inhabitants. Cultivation spread to the Adi foothills, whose inhabitants used it for smoking and as a medicine. Opium trade routes opened up between eastern India, China, and Burma through the Hukawng Valley. Shops selling the drug cropped up near the Inner Line. Guwahati, ASA, Assam Secretariat, General Department Files (1878), Trade route to China, 167J; A. Hamilton, *In Abor jungles of North-East India* (New Delhi: Mittal Publications, 1983 [reprint]), p. 36; F.M. Bailey, *China–Tibet–Assam: A journey, 1911* (London: Jonathan Cape, 1945), p. 141; A.W. Porter, 'Report on the expedition to the Hukawng Valley and Naga Hills (Burma), Season 1928–29' (Maymyo: Government Branch Press, 1929) (p. 1).

[48] Kar, 'Historia elastica'; Kar, 'When was the postcolonial?'.

where slavery, headhunting, and nomadism could be allowed to exist'.[49] This intended divide could never be effective, and not merely because of the Himalayas' and the Assam plains' connected histories. Colonial capitalism was itself creating new connections between them, affecting many tribals in the process. But it did mean that British India's material presence in the eastern Himalayas was still 'most shadowy' at the start of the twentieth century – like China's.[50]

Sources at the Border

It is important to stress that the aim in this book is not to provide a full picture of the Sino-Indian relationship, or of the eastern Himalayas in the twentieth century. Conducting research on these topics is not straightforward, and so the goal is rather to make the most of the sources available at present to understand the nature of low politics between China and India. On the Indian side, research on Arunachal Pradesh has long been constrained by difficulties in accessing the region. Once barred from entering it, foreign scholars can now visit it for limited amounts of time. Many Indian government sources have yet to be traced or accessed. Another constraint is that, in a region characterised mainly by oral cultures, and where most people remained illiterate in 1963, written sources by local people are extremely few. Insofar as they exist, they consist of reminiscences written or transcribed decades after the experiences they mention. The conduct and publication of oral history is, however, hampered by the region's sensitive context; it is only recently, through the work of a few ethnographers, that material has begun to be gathered. Third-party sources for the 1940s and 1950s are lacking, since access to NEFA was strictly regulated. Visitors and press parties were periodically allowed in under administrative supervision, but most of the time the region was cordoned off. In any case the press was not very interested: the majority of newspapers contented themselves with government communiqués and reports.

Researching the Indian side of the border is comparatively easier than for the Chinese side, however.[51] This is so at the level of high politics, which has led much of the scholarship on Sino-Indian relations to focus on the Indian side, but even more if one attempts to analyse the

---

[49] Kar, 'When was the postcolonial?' (pp. 51–52).
[50] London, BL, Reid Collection (7 November 1941), 'A note on the future of the present excluded, partially excluded and tribal areas of Assam' by Robert Reid, Mss Eur E278/4, p. 1.
[51] Starting with Foreign Ministry collections, access to Chinese archives has generally tightened up under the Xi Jinping government, at the time of writing and researching this book.

relationship from the ground up. Travel north of the international border is restricted, and sources about them are hardly accessible at the moment. This problem of access is reflected in the paucity of work done by Tibetologists and China specialists on this specific part of Tibet.

What we do have nonetheless is a wealth of Indian government archives and private papers that, by and large, have never been mined. Sometimes this is because they come from recently released files, but more often because they do not pertain to high-level diplomatic or military decision-making and are located, not in Delhi or London, but in Assam and Arunachal. They include the collections of the NEFA Secretariat held in Itanagar, the Arunachal state capital; the private papers and memoirs of state and non-state actors (retired officers, political parties, cultural organisations, local inhabitants); the mostly untapped archives of the NEFA Branch of India's External Affairs Ministry; the same ministry's documents on Tibet and Himalayan affairs, including recently released files; colonial archives in London; press reports; and, finally, interviews with retired frontier officials – including some of the earliest indigenous officers and teachers – and journalists who visited NEFA in the 1950s.

It is therefore on the Indian side of the border, on the regions today administered as Arunachal Pradesh, that this book focuses to get a glimpse of the mechanics of state shadowing. The incorporation of the eastern Himalayas into India has never been studied in depth. Read against the grain, local government records such as the NEFA adminis-trative tour diaries can reveal the agency of frontier populations in the process – if not their own perspectives on it.

Touring the length and breadth of the eastern Himalayas was crucial to the engagement between state representatives and the inhabitants. From the 1940s onwards, diary keeping became a core duty of touring officials. It was through these diaries that senior Indian administrators learnt about the region, devising policies from their observations. In and of them-selves, they hint that state-making was not a simple top–down process.[52] Moreover, all officials alike were asked to record their observa-tions and experiences. Many wrote long, textured anecdotes about their encounters with the inhabitants and reported popular complaints and demands. This does not mean they comprehended them, or the motivations that lay behind. But often, the result was that tour diaries surreptitiously informed the discourse contained in higher-level archives. It is by supplementing and confronting these sources with oral interviews, popular petitions recorded in government files, and local

---

[52] I am grateful to Toni Huber for first alerting me to the abundance and potential of tour diaries.

memoirs that the complex, changing, and above all fragile nature of state–society relations can be provisionally reconstructed.

What local-level Indian sources reveal is the constant preoccupation of frontier officials with Himalayan people's awareness of Chinese initiatives across the border, and how they might appraise them against their own. For Indian state agents, entrenching themselves in the eastern Himalayas was always done under the shadow of China. To assess whether Chinese state agents might have conversely considered India as a shadow state, a more indirect approach is necessary. This book therefore cross-examines Indian material regarding the Chinese side of the border with what we know of Chinese policies in Tibet.

Fortunately, there is a rapidly growing scholarship concerning the engagement of successive Chinese states with Tibet and China's 'minorities', from the Qing Empire (1644–1911) to Republican and Nationalist China (1912–1949) and the PRC (from 1949 onwards). We also have a significant corpus of oral history collections on Tibet, some containing interviews of inhabitants of the eastern Himalayas, as well as memoirs by Tibetans who lived or passed through the region.[53]

Recent work highlights the late Qing Empire's formal imperialism in Tibetan areas, which elaborated on modern ideas of sovereignty. Warlords, intellectuals, and the Guomindang government recuperated the project between the 1910s and 1940s.[54] This state-making process was a contingent one, where official discourse of strength and ideological commitment to a united, internally sovereign China was not matched on the ground. Chinese authorities had to negotiate with Tibetan power holders who manipulated both their and Lhasa's policies and ideas for their own purposes.[55] Works on the PRC continue this critique of a teleology of overpowering, coercive incorporation, emphasising the hearts-and-minds policies followed by Communist authorities and the

---

[53] 'Tibet Oral History Project', www.tibetoralhistory.org/interviews.html (accessed 27 January 2015); 'Minnesota Tibetan Oral History Project', http://collections.mnhs .org/ioh/index.php/10000814 (accessed 27 January 2015); Case Western Reserve University Melvyn C. Goldstein, 'Tibet Oral History and Archive Project (TOHAP)', http://tibetoralhistoryarchive.org (accessed 27 January 2015).

[54] Mark Elliott, 'Frontier stories: Periphery as center in Qing History', *Frontiers of History in China*, 9:3 (2014), 336–360.

[55] For instance: Joseph D. Lawson, 'Warlord colonialism: State fragmentation and Chinese rule in Kham, 1911–1949', *Journal of Asian Studies*, 72:2 (2013), 299–318; Wang, *China's last imperial frontier*; Hsiao-ting Lin, *Modern China's ethnic frontiers: A journey to the west* (London: Routledge, 2011); Coleman IV, 'Making the state on the Sino-Tibetan frontier'; Scott Relyea, 'Gazing at the Tibetan plateau: Sovereignty and Chinese state expansion in the early twentieth century' (unpublished doctoral thesis, University of Chicago, 2012); Yudru Tsomu, 'Taming the Khampas: The Republican construction of eastern Tibet', *Modern China*, 39:3 (2013), 319–344.

PLA and the importance of the actions, attitudes, and ambitions of non-state actors in shaping Chinese state-making in Tibet.[56] Viewed in a comparative light, China's efforts to impose itself in the region in the twentieth century seemed marked by vulnerabilities not too dissimilar to those of India.

To discern how these Chinese vulnerabilities may have played out in the eastern Himalayas, this book triangulates the observations of Indian frontier officials about their neighbour (which are abundant, given the aforementioned obsession) and Tibetan testimonies with this varied secondary literature on Chinese policies in Tibetan and minority areas. We know, for instance, of many instances where PRC cadres used medical treatment as part of their hearts-and-minds policies; on that basis, Indian reports that CCP cadres used health care for propaganda purposes may be taken as having a reasonable degree of likelihood. From the sketch that can then be attempted, it appears that from the perspective of PRC officials, it was India that was casting a long shadow.

Recent scholarship on the Qing Empire has emphasised the need to explore China's protracted, unfinished 'empire to nation' transition in a comparative perspective.[57] This book suggests that such a comparative perspective is all the more crucial with respect to India. Not only did the two countries veer towards 'state-nations' in parallel, but an instinct for comparison animated state agents on either side – instinct-driven, in either case, by the anxieties arising out of borderland spatialities.[58]

State Expansion: A Not-So-Perfect Story

If the origins of China and India's difficult interaction lie somewhere, they are to be found in the challenges and contradictions of state-making and nation-building processes at play since the start of the twentieth century. Save for the regions that went to Pakistan, India inherited the territory of the British Indian Empire upon independence in August 1947. Officially, this included the mountains north of Assam. But this inheritance existed

---

[56] Tsering W. Shakya, *The dragon in the land of snows: A history of modern Tibet since 1947* (London: Pimlico, 1999); Melvyn C. Goldstein, *A history of modern Tibet* (Berkeley: University of California Press, 1989–), 3 vols; Sulmaan Wasif Khan, *Muslim, trader, nomad, spy: China's Cold War and the Tibetan borderlands* (Duke, NC: UNC Press, 2015).

[57] William C. Kirby, 'When did China become China? Thoughts on the twentieth century', in *The teleology of the modern nation-state: Japan and China*, ed. by Joshua A. Fogel (Philadelphia: University of Pennsylvania Press, 2005), pp. 105–114; Perdue, 'China and other colonial empires'; Larsen, 'The Qing Empire, imperialism, and the modern world'.

[58] *Crafting state-nations: India and other multinational democracies*, ed. by Alfred C. Stepan, Juan J. Linz, and Yogendra Yadav (Baltimore: Johns Hopkins University Press, 2011).

primarily on maps, and even such maps were hard to come by. On the ground, the presence of colonial authorities was scarce, to say the least. Most of the region remained un-administered, if not unexplored. In places, Tibet's influence extended far south of the cartographic border. Even the notion of areas 'under effective control' was slightly fanciful. For departing British officials, the eastern Himalayas remained the 'largest *terra incognita*' in South Asia.[59]

This state of affairs betrayed the fact that – as in the Chinese case – Indian state expansion was not, and would not be, a linear process. Twice, in the early 1910s and during the Second World War, Assam colonial authorities tried to extend their administration to the eastern Himalayas. Twice, this activism was followed by stagnation, if not by retrenchment. It was only in the 1950s, and rather due to external events than to the advent of independence, that the Indian state consolidated its presence.

In moments of euphoria in the 1950s, the Indian press talked of the inexorable, methodical progress of the independent Indian state through the 'North-East Frontier Agency', or NEFA. (Arunachal had yet to be invented.) Local inhabitants were being liberated from backwardness and colonial neglect. They were joining their rightful home: India.[60] Frontier authorities projected a vision of tribal people learning to be Indian through the nurture of a benevolent state, descended among them to lift them up while respecting their 'own genius'. Indeed, state expansion was presented as a philosophy: a 'NEFA Philosophy'.[61]

Beneath this perfect story lay a different reality. Under the veneer of strength, state expansion and consolidation were protracted processes over which frontier authorities had precarious control. In late colonial times as under Jawaharlal Nehru (1947–1964), the frontier revealed the Indian state to be a fragmented, vulnerable, contingent entity, more often than not possessed of contradictory impulses and priorities – and even when purposeful, not necessarily adept at realising its plans.[62]

Some of the constraints were external. From a state perspective, the eastern Himalayas' rugged, jungle-clad terrain and humid climate present considerable difficulties. The narrow, dangerous trails criss-crossing the

---

[59] London, BL, IOR (1936–1947), Excluded and partially excluded areas of Assam: Constitutional position, IOR/L/PS/12/3115A (Committee of the Constituent Assembly on Tribal and Excluded Areas, c. May 1947).

[60] B.N. Mullik, *My years with Nehru: The Chinese betrayal* (Bombay: Allied Publishers, 1971), pp. 136–140.

[61] Verrier Elwin, *A philosophy for NEFA*, 1st edn (Shillong: North-East Frontier Agency, 1957).

[62] See also Joel S. Migdal, *State in society: Studying how states and societies transform and constitute one another* (Cambridge: Cambridge University Press, 2001), p. 22.

region were of little help to project state power, and building the transport infrastructure necessary to permit it raised enormous logistical and engineering problems. Too isolated to be supplied during the rains, many outposts long had to be withdrawn at the end of winter. For years, Indian authorities struggled to be more than a fair-weather state – an entity able to enforce its pretensions to sovereignty only when the skies were clear.

But climate and terrain tell only part of the story. Fault lines within the state apparatus played as big a role in the contingency of late colonial and early independent India's expansion. The British Empire was composed of different parts, each with their specific priorities or interests. In a border province like Assam, this meant not only the India Office in London and the Viceroy's government in Delhi, who presided over a 'sub-empire', but also provincial officials animated by their own 'sub-imperialism'.[63] The farther removed from daily frontier management, the more likely were colonial authorities to weigh expansion there against other priorities, often negatively.

India's independence removed one level in this hierarchy, London, but did not lead to more unity of purpose. Various central authorities had divergent views of the urgency of state expansion. While the External Affairs officials entrusted with the administration of the region pushed for it, Nehru himself had other pressing matters, particularly in the aftermath of India and Pakistan's Partition. The Finance and Defence ministries showed little interest for much of the 1950s. The former focused on financial retrenchment; the latter doubted that the eastern Himalayas presented a geo-strategic risk, believing it impassable for military forces. What's more, channels of command and communication between frontier administration and New Delhi were defective.

These conflicting motives and priorities had serious consequences. Central authorities were seldom in the driving seat in the 1950s. Instead, the state-making impetus largely came from the actions of frontier administrators. But these 'men on the spot' waged a constant battle against material, financial, and manpower shortages, and so, while they subscribed to the idea that international boundaries mark the pinnacle of territorial sovereignty, for long it made more sense to use their small resources on population centres than to exhaust themselves in a futile attempt to materialise their boundary claims.[64] The result was that, even in the early 1960s, India's north-eastern

---

[63] John Darwin, *The empire project: The rise and fall of the British world-system, 1830–1970* (Cambridge: Cambridge University Press, 2009); John S. Galbraith, 'The "turbulent frontier" as a factor in British expansion', *Comparative Studies in Society and History*, 2:2 (1960), 150–168; Cederlöf, *Founding an empire*; Sameetah Agha, 'Sub-imperialism and the loss of the Khyber: The politics of imperial defence on British India's North-West Frontier', *Indian Historical Review*, 40:2 (2013), 307–330.

[64] Itanagar, APSA, NEFA Secretariat (1955), Expansion programme for Subansiri for 1955–56 P189/55, pp. 11–12. The influence of 'men on the spot' was also evident in

frontier remained poorly manned, with a minimal transport and communication infrastructure, and chunks of territory under fragile control. Indian sovereignty was far from a fait accompli.

But state-making is not a one-way process that is a function of a state's strength or weakness. It rather results from the encounter between the state and a variety of other actors, starting with local societies – interactions that take on multiple forms, from negotiation and cooperation to confrontation, and that shift through time and space, playing out differently in different locales.

Terrain, climate, and state brittleness made the state–society relationship especially crucial in NEFA. The possibility for state expansion, and even more so for its permanence, hinged in the last resort on the eastern Himalayas' inhabitants. Their internal diversity notwithstanding, the Tagins, the Monpas, or the Mishmis were starkly different from the bulk of India's population. Moreover, Indian authorities' capacity to coax them into submission was limited: the use of force was costly and prone to backfire. Without the locals' willingness to negotiate with frontier officials – to supply them, work for them, inform them – India's state presence hung by a thread.

Until the last few years of colonial rule, the eastern Himalayas' inhabitants were in their majority reluctant to countenance this presence. Gradually, some individuals, some villages accepted to let the state in, and even began to support it. That they chose to do so partly stemmed from state weakness and contingency, which offered the possibility to subvert and manipulate Indian officials' presence to obtain leverage in local, micro-level politics between clans, families, or villages. Letting the state in could also be beneficial, provided its activities could be directed for one's own purposes: having a school, a dispensary, or an airstrip built near the village; obtaining goods unavailable from existing trade networks; experimenting with new agricultural methods.

From the late 1940s onwards, development schemes played a key role in India's protracted consolidation in the eastern Himalayas. Indian authorities painted this as an ideological choice, but theirs was mainly a pragmatic solution to a situation where tribal support for state presence stemmed from the demands people could make upon it. As such, development schemes rested on a constant negotiation between frontier authorities and local inhabitants. Bargaining capacity shifted through time and space, and between different sections of local communities.

the 'Tibet Cadre'. Alex McKay, *Tibet and the British Raj: The frontier cadre 1904–47* (London: Curzon, 1997).

At first, this favoured people who had had earliest access to the state: they were inevitable stepping stones for the administration's expansion and consolidation. Once most people had come in contact with outposts and development schemes, in the late 1950s, inter-tribal competition for limited state resources and capabilities gave the NEFA administration more leverage. External factors however prevented it from getting an unambiguous upper hand. As such, the Indian state sketched out in this book is starkly different from its portrayal as a controlling, coherent entity possessed with an innate will and a consistent strategy that it imposes on a population and a territory.[65] Indeed, at times, Indian authorities rather appeared as a 'standoffish state', particularly before 1950 – contesting the idea that states are always obsessed with legibility, control, and extraction.[66]

What's more, the governmentality expressed by development schemes was a contested one. Post-colonial scholarship tends to see the Nehruvian state as a coercive, top–down machine imposing itself on 'target' populations through development schemes, particularly through planning.[67] In NEFA at least, things were not so simple. Indian authorities did pretend to the consistent, pervasive, and spatially homogeneous exercise of power over passive populations, yet, on the ground, it was anything but that. The energy state representatives spent on proclaiming a 'philosophy' of incorporation was an attempt to gain composure in unstable circumstances.

The eastern Himalayas' incorporation into India cannot, therefore, be reduced to what James Scott calls a 'conscious strategy of engulfment and eventual absorption', pitting the State against People refusing to be governed.[68] Scott's insight that statelessness can be a conscious strategy is an invaluable analytical tool, but the demarcation between 'state space' and 'non-state space' was anything but clear. The trade or pilgrimage networks that crossed the eastern Himalayas acted as conduits of power, including state influence, and opposing or evading the state was not the

[65] Judith M. Brown, *Modern India: The origins of Asian democracy*, 2nd edn (Oxford: Oxford University Press, 1994); Donald A. Low, *Eclipse of empire* (Cambridge: Cambridge University Press, 1991); Rasheeduddin Khan, 'The total state: The concept and its manifestation in the Indian political system', in *The state, political processes, and identity: Reflections on modern India*, ed. by Zoya Hasan, Rasheeduddin Khan, and S.N. Jha (New Delhi: Sage, 1989), pp. 33–72.

[66] Dan Slater and Diana Kim, 'Standoffish states: Nonliterate leviathans in Southeast Asia', *TRaNS: Trans-Regional and -National Studies of Southeast Asia*, 3:01 (2015), 25–44.

[67] Partha Chatterjee, 'Development planning and the Indian state', in *The state and development planning in India*, ed. by Terence J. Byres (New Delhi: Oxford University Press, 1994), pp. 51–72.

[68] James C. Scott, *The art of not being governed: An anarchist history of upland Southeast Asia* (New Haven, CO; London: Yale University Press, 2009), p. 325.

only attitude evinced by local inhabitants.[69] Accommodation, acceptance, and even invitation and engagement were also in evidence. What is at stake, then, is to discern what led to these variations.

This book shows that, under given circumstances, a *certain kind* of state presence could be acceptable or even welcomed. Essential to the phenomenon were the dynamics internal to the highlands, from relations between different groups, individuals, or villages, to prior interaction, in some regions, with another polity – Tibet. Identities or beliefs could play a significant role in shaping the encounter between state actors and local populations, but not a predetermined one. In a region treated by Lhasa as an inferior and barbarian land, even Tibetan Buddhists could envision Indian rule, provided it supported local religious practices and beliefs. Power relations in the eastern Himalayas were like shifting sands, where the state, or rather its representatives, were often in an uneasy posture.

Shadow States in the Himalayas

If relations between Himalayan inhabitants and Indian officials were crucial and yet unstable, it was also because India's expansion attempts rubbed against those of another polity: China. From the beginning, Indian state-making was strongly conditioned by its neighbour's initiatives in their shared borderland. Eventually, China would become India's shadow state in the Himalayas.

It was concerns over late Qing expansionism that prompted British India's first forays in the eastern Himalayas in the early 1910s, followed by the negotiation of an Indo-Tibetan boundary agreement that gave birth to the McMahon Line. Three more times between the 1940s and 1960s, fears over Chinese expansionism revived Indian activism in the eastern Himalayas: during the Second World War, when Assam and its hinterland became a bulwark against Japan and the last land link between Nationalist China and British India; in 1950, when the newly founded PRC 'peacefully liberated' Tibet; and in 1959, when revolt erupted in Lhasa and China explicitly rejected the McMahon Line.

Chinese state-making not only generated decisive momentum for India's expansion; it also gave paramount importance to state–society relations. Given the absence or seasonality of Indian state presence in the first half of the twentieth century, it was mainly through local inhabitants that Assam frontier authorities learnt of Chinese activities.

---

[69] Charles Patterson Giersch, 'Across Zomia with merchants, monks, and musk: Process geographies, trade networks, and the Inner-East–Southeast Asian borderlands', *Journal of Global History*, 5:2 (2010), 215–239.

People's initiatives helped India maintained its claim to the region, as when some portrayed themselves as British Indian subjects to enquiring Qing parties. Cultivating ties with them was therefore essential. The PRC's annexation of Tibet in 1951 caused Delhi to commit to the incorporation of NEFA into India. It also made the establishment of constructive relations with local people a core priority. Indian authorities viewed Communist China's presence on the Tibetan plateau as an inherent threat, but not primarily a military one. Their main fear was that the PRC would win the loyalty of NEFA's inhabitants. Frontier officials were painfully aware that, lack of a clearly delimited boundary notwithstanding, there was no real topographical, economic, or cultural watershed between the plateau and the Himalayas. India's choice of a development-centric expansion strategy in the 1950s answered the perceived need to convince NEFA's tribal inhabitants not to look towards China.

Shadow state conditioning went both ways. PRC authorities had their own reasons to worry about Indian state expansion – and not merely because they viewed at least some of NEFA as part of Tibet. If 'India' was a fragmented entity, criss-crossed by tensions between civilian and military authorities, different ministries, and various levels of power, so too was 'China'. Communist China could ill afford to maintain itself in Tibet through the ostensible use of force. In an attempt to win the people over, PRC authorities delayed socialist reforms and left the Dalai Lama's government in place in the early 1950s.

In south-eastern Tibet, however, this strategy encountered a destabilising factor: India's nearby presence. Confronted with two parallel state expansion processes, borderlanders were comparing what each one brought them, in both negative and positive terms, and some made direct overtures to the Indian administration. In a mirror effect, Chinese authorities came to fear that the eastern Himalayas' inhabitants might prefer the neighbouring state: India.

Throughout the 1950s, Indian and PRC frontier authorities consistently monitored what happened on the other side, formulating, adapting, and re-articulating their welfare and development schemes in response to each other's initiatives. In the early part of the decade, Delhi and Beijing were proclaiming their 'peaceful coexistence' to the world. Yet beneath this ostensible diplomatic honeymoon, the very fact of their coexistence on the ground precluded genuine peace. Proving the Chinese or the Indian state's greater capacity to deliver so as to steer the population in one's favour was at the heart of their competition.

By emphasising the importance of ever-changing state–society relations on either side of the eastern Himalayas, this book proposes a radically different approach to conventional understandings of the Sino-Indian rivalry. At best, the rich literature on the relationship treats the people of the Himalayas as a footnote; at worst, it ignores them entirely, presenting the China–India borderlands as an uninhabited space. This is partly because of an overwhelming preoccupation with high politics, namely top-level military and political decision-making and diplomatic relations. In these accounts, the Himalayas are but the object of China and India's antagonistic ambitions, a piece of unchanging physical territory to be seized rather than a space to be studied in its own right. That the other main terrain of dispute is the Aksai Chin, a barren desert in the Himalayas' far north-west, adds to the silence.

For it is the Aksai Chin, ostensibly, that has been the main block in the way of a territorial solution. In 1960, Delhi rejected an unofficial offer by Beijing to renounce its claim to NEFA, in exchange for India recognising PRC sovereignty over the Aksai Chin. This was the last time China and India tried to discuss their dispute before the outbreak of war between them, and it would take decades for border talks to resume. Many scholars think the PRC's offer was genuine, betraying its need to compromise at a time of domestic and international uncertainty.[70] This would make the territorial dispute over NEFA a secondary one, a bargaining ploy, even.

But China and India's friction in the eastern Himalayas did not depend on one or the other side's irredentism, although competing territorial claims heightened it. Rooted in unstable biopolitics and China and India's spatial proximity, the dynamics of shadowing sufficed to sustain it. Himalayan inhabitants had no intrinsic stake or interest in China or India; but parallel, uneven state-making processes gave them a measure of choice, of agency vis-à-vis these giants. And as China and India came to see themselves as each other's alternative, they became each other's threat.

The result was that, by 1962, a *multidimensional* security dilemma had coalesced in the eastern Himalayas. Worsening bilateral relations and Chinese efforts to crush Tibetan rebellion in the region had led both India and China to rush their troops towards the McMahon Line. Delhi had gone back on its 1950 decision not to militarise NEFA and was pushing its forces perilously near the border. What is not recognised,

---

[70] Garver, *Protracted contest*, p. 100; M. Taylor Fravel, *Strong borders, secure nation: Cooperation and conflict in China's territorial disputes* (Princeton, NJ; Oxford: Princeton University Press, 2008), chapters 2, 4.

however, is that the security dilemma had an eminently biopolitical dimension. Shadowing had escalated in tandem with military canvassing. Chinese and Indian authorities in the NEFA–Tibet borderlands were now determined to outdo each other's development and welfare initiatives at the border, hoping to convince people on their side of the border not to look across – but thereby only increasing the benefit of doing so.

In October 1962, the PLA invaded NEFA and Ladakh, magisterially defeating Indian forces over the course of a month-long war. Interpretations of the conflict variously focus on the Cold War, the boundary dispute, or China and India's rival power ambitions. Yet, the war should also be seen in the light of the fraught – and, at that time, increasingly impossible – coexistence between the two neighbours. If the immediate cause for Beijing's decision was to secure the Aksai Chin by teaching Delhi a lesson, war also presented a chance to end the other, older security dilemma in China's favour. Invading and *occupying* NEFA was an attempt to control the terms of the PRC's hearts-and-minds competition with India through a definitive demonstration of state superiority, in a display not just of military prowess but also of the ability to deliver the goods and opportunities local inhabitants demanded. War was a state-making performance, and its audience was as much Himalayan people as Indian authorities or Chinese domestic audiences.

On the face of it, it seems impossible to see the 1962 war as anything but an unmitigated debacle for India and a triumph for the PRC. The long-term impact of the defeat on India's foreign and defence policy, particularly vis-à-vis China, contributes to this received wisdom.[71] And yet, if the conflict is viewed through the lens of shadowing, a different picture takes shape.

That the Indian government suffered a major military defeat is incontestable. So is the fact that the PRC increased its hold over the Aksai Chin. But controlling strategic territory was not the war's only purpose. PRC authorities also meant to prevent India from ever seeming a viable alternative for Tibet's populations, and conversely to convince NEFA's inhabitants not to accept India's presence among them. In short, they intended to create a popular resistance that would have made it very difficult for beleaguered Indian authorities, ousted from NEFA, to return to the eastern Himalayas – solving, or at least easing, the friction of coexistence.

---

[71] *The India–China relationship*, ed. by Frankel and Harding, chapter 2; Sarbari Bhaumik, 'Unsettled border', *Himal South Asian*, January 2011; Dibyesh Anand, 'Remembering 1962 Sino-Indian border war: Politics of memory', *Journal of Defence Studies*, 6:4 (2012), 177–196.

The PRC's attempt to get the upper hand did not work. By portraying themselves as invincible – something India had never been capable of – Chinese authorities wrested frontier communities of their own agency, of their capacity to accept the state on their own terms. Instead of rejecting the Indian administration, the inhabitants of NEFA accepted its return. Their *relative* preference went to an Indian state that was less efficient, but also more malleable. As for the Tibetan side of the border, it would continue to experience far more popular resistance to PRC rule than NEFA vis-à-vis India. On that count, China's success in 1962 might well have proved a pyrrhic victory.

Part I

1910–1950

1   False Starts
The First Rush towards the Eastern Himalayas

Around May 1910, two Tibetans arrived in Pangum, a small Mishmi village high up in the Lohit Valley. They brought word that Chinese troops had occupied the Tibetan town of Rima, a few days' march away. The astonished villagers were informed that Dzayül's new rulers expected them to carve them a track all the way from Tibet to the plains of Assam – one 'broad enough for two horsemen to ride abreast', at that.

Pangum's people had no desire to follow such orders. Tungno, their chief, decided to inform British Indian authorities of this turn of events. After a long, long trek, he presented himself to their station at Sadiya, on the edge of Assam. The local official soon got confirmation of Tungno's report. Other Mishmis said the Chinese had planted flags well south of Dzayül, near an area called Walong, and were trying to encourage Han immigration into the region. They had also banned trade between the Miju Mishmis and areas under their control.

Dzayül's conquest was not an isolated event. All along the Himalayan range, signs of Qing activism were being reported. In the east, Chinese troops were marching through Kham, and Yunnan authorities were probing their borderlands with British Burma. Further west, Qing soldiers were being sent to Monyül, Lokha, and Kongpo on the south-eastern edge of the Tibetan plateau. They had ensconced themselves across the borders of the principality of Sikkim, and the imperial court had sent envoys to Kathmandu. Unconfirmed reports spoke of Chinese tents pitched in far western Tibet, where the survey done by an imperial party had fuelled suspicion that China planned to build a fortress in the region. The king of Bhutan had been informed that his small Himalayan kingdom was China's protectorate, following which he was duly ordered to let Chinese currency circulate freely in the country and to confine his diplomatic relations to Beijing only.

Only one conclusion could be drawn, it seemed: Qing China had embarked on a forward policy all along India's Himalayan frontier.[1] These developments caught India's colonial authorities on the back foot in the eastern Himalayas. They had neither troops nor officials in the mountains, and their twenty outposts or so were at a distance from the foothills. Some were 'positively microscopic': there were only a few hundred men from the military police to guard the Inner Line, which ran for some 400 miles on the north bank of the Brahmaputra. This 'Lakhimpur Battalion' had little training, morale, or discipline.[2] As for the administrative side, it consisted of two frontier officers.

London had always refused to entertain any thought of expanding into the eastern Himalayas. The India Office's stance was that the region was not worth the cost of expansion, and that conquering chunks of the foothills only led to further annexation. Such was London's disinterest that no 'Outer Line' of British influence had ever been defined for the Mishmi areas. Where it existed, it only came up to the foot of the hills.[3]

The realisation that the Qing coveted territory British India had never ostensibly claimed would, for the first time, spur colonial authorities to expand in the eastern Himalayas. This first episode of competitive state expansion would not survive the fall of the Chinese Empire in 1912 and the outbreak of the First World War, but it would leave behind a problematic legacy – an Indo-Tibetan boundary born in murky circumstances and with largely partial knowledge of the areas it was supposed to divide. When independent India would try to concretise it decades later, this officially neat line would turn out to make sense neither to local government officials nor to the people of the eastern Himalayas (Map 5).

A New Turn in Qing Frontier Policy

British–Qing competition in the eastern Himalayas broke out at an important juncture in modern Chinese history. Since the late nineteenth century, a protracted, non-linear transition from empire to nation-state had begun throughout the Qing dynasty's territories, from the Burma

---

[1] London, BL, IOR (1912), Chinese activity on the Mishmi border (JE Shuckburgh, India Office, 9 September 1912), IOR/L/PS/20/MEMO30/8. Beijing was also insisting on a Chinese inspector for Burma's Chinese schools and had reiterated its demand, first made in 1905, to establish a consulate at Calcutta. A local council had also been formed within the Chinese chamber of commerce in Rangoon, tasked with reporting about Burma's Han community to China's provincial assembly.

[2] George Dunbar, *Frontiers* (Delhi: Omsons Publications, 1984 [c.1932]), p. 77.

[3] BL, IOR/L/PS/20/MEMO30/8 ('The North East Frontier: Tribal territory north of Assam', 3 December 1910), p. 20.

border to Xinjiang and the Han-majority regions.[4] Atomised and locally managed 'frontier policies' had metamorphosed into a more integrated, top–down strategy to tackle external challenges, starting with the discontiguous, multifaceted threat of competing empires such as British India. The birth of this 'foreign policy' was co-constitutive with the evolution of Chinese thought about sovereignty and attempts to centralise and homogenise the empire.[5]

Qing China's novel expansionism was likely driven by the alleged Great Game between Russia and British India. In 1900, Lu Chuanlin, China's Governor-General in Sichuan, published a collection of writings that forcefully advocated establishing absolute, exclusive control over Kham. Doing so, he argued, was the only way to restrict Russian and British access to Tibet and have Lhasa's subordination to Beijing recognised. This would in turn fend off European expansionism, for 'under the law of states, countries do not invade each other'.[6] If Qing China wanted to compete with European powers and be treated as their equal, it would have to adopt their model of international relations and internal governance.

Some scholars see the spectre of the Great Game as a mere pretext for late Qing expansionism; the Russo-British rivalry in Inner Asia did not present a direct threat to Imperial China's own claims and influence. Indeed, Lu Chuanlin's arguments could be interpreted differently.[7] The very idea of sovereignty was deeply connected with imperialism.[8] By establishing itself as a full participant in the 'law of states', China would justify its expansionism in Tibetan areas and elsewhere.

What is certain is that by the start of the twentieth century, officials on the marches of Kham were using the Great Game to push China to adopt

---

[4] William C. Kirby, 'When did China become China? Thoughts on the twentieth century', in *The teleology of the modern nation-state: Japan and China*, ed. by Joshua A. Fogel (Philadelphia, PA: University of Pennsylvania Press, 2005), pp. 105–114; Justin M. Jacobs, 'Empire besieged: The preservation of Chinese rule in Xinjiang, 1884–1971' (unpublished doctoral thesis, University of California, San Diego, 2011), p. 27.

[5] Matthew M. Mosca, *From frontier policy to foreign policy: The question of India and the transformation of geopolitics in Qing China* (Stanford, CA: Stanford University Press, 2013).

[6] Scott Relyea, 'Yokes of gold and threads of silk: Sino-Tibetan competition for authority in early twentieth century Kham', *Modern Asian Studies*, 49:4 (2015), 963–1009 (p. 22).

[7] Xiuyu Wang, *China's last imperial frontier: Late Qing expansion in Sichuan's Tibetan borderlands* (Lanham, MD: Lexington Books, 2011); William M. Coleman IV, 'Making the state on the Sino-Tibetan frontier: Chinese expansion and local power in Batang, 1842–1939' (unpublished doctoral thesis, Columbia University, 2014), pp. 215–216.

[8] Dibyesh Anand, 'The Tibet question and the West: Issues of sovereignty, identity and representation', in *Contemporary Tibet: Politics, development and society in a disputed region*, ed. by June T. Dreyer and Barry Sautman (London: M.E. Sharpe, 2006), pp. 285–304 (pp. 288–289).

Western concepts of sovereignty, territoriality, and statehood. Doing away with indirect frontier rule was the first step in that direction. Sichuan soon set out to enhance their reach over Kham. Rapid modernisation was taking place there after the Boxer Rebellion, and increased involvement in Kham enabled provincial authorities to obtain agricultural and mineral resources for it.[9] Beijing too felt the need for a more active policy in the Tibetan area. In 1904, it shifted the post of assistant *amban* from Lhasa to western Kham, with instructions to raise troops and reclaim land in the region.

The incumbent, a Han official called Feng Quan, proved far more activist than his imperial brief demanded. Keen to enhance his career prospects, he defied orders to install himself in western Kham and instead moved further east, to Batang. The area offered greater agricultural potential and hence far more promise for administrative and military presence. There, Feng Quan launched a comprehensive land reclamation programme that soon generated strong resistance among local inhabitants. Khampas clashed with Chinese farm colonies around Batang until, in March 1905, the violence escalated into a general uprising.[10]

Chinese repression was brutal. On Beijing's orders, Sichuan sent troops to subdue Batang, where secular and monastic authorities had joined forces against China. It took five days of harsh fighting for Qing troops to take the town and its fortified monastery, after which Khampa chieftains, high-ranking monastic officials, and hundreds of monks were murdered. Batang's fate only spurred other parts of eastern Kham to rise against China. It would take until 1906 and an enormous logistical, financial, and human investment to break the resistance.[11] The Qing had never waged such an extensive military operation in Tibetan lands.

In stark contrast to previous military expeditions, Chinese state presence was not scaled back after the end of the uprising. Zhao Erfeng, the principal leader of the campaign, instead began a systematic attempt to conquer, annex, and incorporate Kham into the Qing Empire. In the biggest centres of Khampa resistance, he destroyed or downsized monasteries, abolished the system whereby indigenous leaders ruled on behalf of the emperor, and issued regulations to curtail religious authority, alter

---

[9] Samuel Adshead, *Province and politics in late Imperial China: Viceregal government in Szechwan, 1898–1911* (London: Curzon, 1984).

[10] Elliot Sperling, 'The Chinese venture in Kham 1904–11, and the role of Chao Er-feng', *Tibet Journal*, 1:2 (1976), 10–35 (pp. 13–15). Feng Quan himself was murdered by local inhabitants as he tried to leave town in the wake of the uprising.

[11] Wang, *China's last imperial frontier*, chapter 5; Wim van Spengen, 'Frontier history of southern Kham: Banditry and war in the multi-ethnic fringe lands of Chatri, Mili, and Gyethang 1890–1940', in *Khams Pa histories: Visions of people, place and authority*, ed. by Lawrence Epstein (Leiden: Brill, 2002), pp. 7–29.

Tibetan cultural practices, and assert the Khampas' subjecthood.[12] He then set out to establish direct rule over Kham as a whole. Whereas it had rejected similar ideas back in 1900, Beijing granted full support to Zhao Erfeng's plans: militarising Kham, harnessing its mineral and agricultural resources, intensifying trade with China, and, finally, promoting Chinese education among the population. Appointed head of a Sichuan–Yunnan Frontier Affairs Commission specially created for the purpose, Zhao received further sign of imperial support when his brother became Governor of Sichuan. He could now use the province's revenues to further Chinese state expansion in Kham.

Between 1906 and 1911, Zhao Erfeng launched intensive political, economic, and acculturative reforms in Kham. His was a modern colonial enterprise, consciously inspired by Japanese and European models of imperialism while retaining its distinctiveness. Thirty counties and administrative divisions were created and systematic attempts were made to curb the monasteries' authority and to sinicise Kham. Mines were opened, a Chinese public–private monopoly over the lucrative tea trade was established, and Hans were encouraged to start farming colonies in the region.[13]

While Sichuan officials were mainly preoccupied with Kham, Beijing was even more concerned with central Tibet. In 1904, a British military expedition led by Francis Younghusband had invaded Tibet, laying bare the extent of Qing weakness in Lhasa. Other than pleading meekly and unsuccessfully with the Dalai Lama to start negotiations, its *ambans* had failed to do anything.[14] Eventually, Tibetan authorities had been forced to concede Sikkim's protectorate to British India and to sign a trade convention enabling the latter to maintain trade marts, supervised by colonial representatives, in three Tibetan towns. India had also wrested the right to maintain military escorts and a physical infrastructure (land, buildings, rest houses, hospitals, telegraph, and eventually missions) in Lhasa-held territory and to conduct diplomatic relations with the Dalai Lama's government. It would soon create an administration to manage them.[15] In effect, British India had extended its influence to Tibet.

---

[12] Wang, *China's last imperial frontier*, chapter 6; Relyea, 'Yokes of gold'; Coleman IV, 'Making the state on the Sino-Tibetan frontier', chapter 5.

[13] Wang, *China's last imperial frontier*, Chapter 8; Relyea, 'Yokes of gold'; Joseph D. Lawson, 'Warlord colonialism: State fragmentation and Chinese rule in Kham, 1911–1949', *Journal of Asian Studies*, 72:2 (2013), 299–318 (p. 300).

[14] Wang, *China's last imperial frontier*, pp. 90–91.

[15] Alex McKay, *Tibet and the British Raj: The frontier cadre 1904–47* (London: Curzon, 1997).

Excluded from these agreements, Qing China was determined to recover its power over Lhasa. A window of opportunity soon opened up. In exile since the Younghusband Expedition, the Dalai Lama struggled to control his government from afar. As for the British, they soon decided that undermining Qing China's claim to Tibet risked playing into Russia's hands; in 1906, they signed an Anglo-Chinese Convention recognising Beijing's suzerainty over Lhasa.

In late 1906, the imperial court decided to 'rectify Tibetan affairs'. A diplomat seasoned in European politics was despatched to Lhasa, where he blocked direct correspondence with British India and drafted an ambitious programme to reform Tibet's political and socio-cultural structures. When ill health and internecine feuds within Lhasa's Chinese circles caused his transfer, Beijing replaced him with Zhao Erfeng himself. Zhao was reluctant to take up his new post. He was more interested in consolidating Chinese rule in Kham and felt that advancing into Tibet without secure supply lines could do no good. When Beijing refused to retract the appointment, he responded by a time-honoured *amban* tactic: he did not proceed to Lhasa.[16]

Whatever Zhao Erfeng's own intentions, the announcement of his appointment as *amban* fuelled anti-Chinese sentiment in Lhasa. Zhao had earned himself such a reputation for cruelty for his actions in Kham that some people, both in government and among the masses, threatened revolt and a mass exodus if 'Butcher Zhao' crossed the Upper Yangtze. Furious, Beijing ordered its troops to march on Lhasa in February 1910. Barely returned from exile, the Dalai Lama had to flee again, but from a different invader. It was the first time the Qing had marched on Tibet against the overwhelming opposition of its population.[17]

Between the occupation of Lhasa and its imperialism in Kham, Qing China's expansionism had acquired such momentum that, by the middle of 1910, its troops were now trespassing into the forests of Kongpo, north of the Siang Basin. It was at that point that news of Dzayül's takeover reached the ears of British administration in Assam.

Assam Officials Have Their Way

Local frontier authorities reacted to the news of Chinese advance in Dzayül with the same intensity as their Sichuan counterparts in the face of European advances. In November 1910, they petitioned the Government

---

[16] David Dahpon Ho, 'The men who would not be *amban* and the one who would: Four frontline officials and Qing Tibet policy, 1905–1911', *Modern China*, 34:2 (2008), 210–246.

[17] Hugh Richardson, *Tibet and its history*, 2nd edn (Boulder: Shambhala, 1984), pp. 98–99.

of India for a firm reaction: 'Should the Chinese establish themselves in strength or obtain complete control up to our outer line, they could attack us whenever they pleased, and the defence would be extremely difficult.'[18]

In raising the alarm about China's expansionism, Assam hoped to obtain what it had unsuccessfully campaigned for since 1908: an end to the official non-interference policy beyond the Inner Line.[19] Its repeated suggestions for expansion had all been vetoed. Noel Williamson, the official posted at Sadiya, had proposed building a road between Assam and Dzayül and imposing poll tax on Adi villages in the foothills to make them 'realise they were within British territory'. But Assam's argument that the 'policy of aloofness' was unproductive – since 'proximity to civilization has failed in any way to redeem the tribes from their native savagery' – had left the Government of India and the India Office unconvinced. The only thing they were ready to countenance were a few non-punitive forays beyond the Inner Line in the Adi foothills, under strict conditions.[20]

The Qing's occupation of Dzayül had provided Assam officials with ammunition to sway their superiors towards expansion. They were not the only ones to advise a strong reaction. In Sichuan, the British Consul thought that letting Zhao Erfeng have his way would result in 'a Chinese agricultural colony that will gradually spread' into Burma and Assam.[21] Considering that Han military-agricultural colonies had played a key role in China's assimilation of frontier regions in the past, the fear was not irrational.[22]

Military authorities agreed that the lack of colonial state presence in the eastern Himalayas was 'strategically unsound'. In late 1910, the Government of India decided to reinforce its influence over Bhutan and began to contemplate the necessity of creating a buffer in the eastern Himalayas, 'so far as might be necessary by arranging that the tribes ... should have no relations or intercourse with any Foreign Power other than the British Government'.[23]

---

[18] Robert Reid, *History of the frontier areas bordering on Assam, 1883–1941* (Delhi: Eastern Publishing, 1983) (Eastern Bengal & Assam Secretariat, March 1911, Nos. 45–46), quoted p. 221.
[19] Between 1905 and 1911, Assam was administered together with eastern Bengal. For the sake of clarity, I retain the shorthand 'Assam' when talking about frontier administration.
[20] Reid, *History of the frontier areas.* Quote pp. 212–215. As proof of the Pasis' and Minyongs' savage and unredeemable nature, the authorities stressed that they were threatening to stop sawmills contractors from entering their country to cut timber.
[21] BL, IOR/L/PS/20/MEMO30/8 ('Chinese "forward" policy on the Indian frontier'), p. 1.
[22] Peter C. Perdue, *China marches west: The Qing conquest of Central Eurasia* (London: Belknap Press, 2005), pp. 232–233.
[23] BL, IOR/L/PS/20/MEMO30/8 ('Chinese advances – GOI's position'), pp. 22–23. In 1910, the Government of India passed a new treaty with Bhutan, under which the latter agreed to surrender the conduct of its foreign relations to its southern neighbour.

Within a few months, however, central authorities in Delhi reverted to their earlier position: non-interference. Zhao Erfeng notwithstanding, they saw 'no necessity at present for incurring the risks and responsibilities entailed by a forward movement'. London, which had rejected earlier plans for expansion, probably lay behind this change of mind. The Assam frontier administration had but one consolation. Their superiors had allowed them to venture beyond the Outer Line to gather information – though if, and only if, this could be done 'without risk of complications [or] any general increase of activity'.[24]

Williamson, the Sadiya official who had so pushed for expansion, decided to make the most of the narrow latitude given to him. In January–February 1911, he departed for the Lohit Valley and pushed as far as Walong. The trip revealed that China had now expanded its claim on Mishmi areas. Its flags were found flying over a place called Menilkrai, an area south of Walong at the end of a flat, arable expanse of land extending all the way to Dzayül.[25]

On his return to Sadiya, Williamson immediately left for another tour, this time up the Adi-inhabited Siang Valley. Two years earlier, he had ventured thirty-two miles upriver, something no European had ever done. This time he planned to go even farther. His previous visit had gone without incident, and he thought that the tour would enable him to detect potential Tibetan influence in the higher reaches of the valley. On 8 March, Williamson set out for the Siang Basin with three servants, two orderlies, and forty-four Mishing and Gurkha porters. Accompanying him was J.D. Gregorson, a tea garden doctor.[26]

Three weeks later, Williamson, Gregorson, and most of their party were dead. On 30 and 31 March 1911, they were murdered within a few miles of each other near the villages of Komsing and Pangin. Never before had such a large-scale massacre of a government party occurred since the British arrival at the foot of the eastern Himalayas. Apparently, Williamson had never informed his superiors of his initiative, and had explicitly been forbidden to venture beyond the Outer Line. This was a disaster.

Assam authorities argued for the strongest retaliation possible: the massacre was a direct show of defiance against the British Empire, 'as much a deliberate attack upon us as if the [Adis] had come into our country'. Armed columns should visit every single Pasi and Minyong settlement to extract reparation. Those who would submit should pay a fine or work for free for the government; those who would not should be

---

[24] Reid, *History of the frontier areas*. Quoted p. 222.   [25] Ibid. (p. 217).
[26] Dunbar, *Frontiers*, pp. 105–106.

burnt. To make the most of the occasion, these systematic visits of the lower Adi country should be used 'to survey and map it as far as possible ... [in order] to consider whether ... to enter into any treaty with these people ... [as done] with Sikkim and Bhutan'. Under the guise of a comprehensive punitive expedition, Williamson's murder had given Assam another occasion to rally its superiors to their views.[27]

This time, the British and Indian governments were ready to listen. By spring 1911, Qing forces were planning to invade Pomé and Pemakö, on the northern edge of the Siang Basin.[28] Assam officials themselves had raised the spectre of China in their retaliation proposal: exploring the Siang Basin in the wake of the military promenade would provide 'an excellent opportunity of ascertaining [Chinese] movements' and prevent them 'from establishing their influence over the [Adis] as over the Mishmis'.[29]

For the Government of India, it was now imperative to explore different parts of the eastern Himalayas. The goal was not yet to expand administration but to survey the area. Geographical knowledge – embodied in supposedly scientific and hence perfect maps – was a key instrument in asserting colonial rule. From the late eighteenth century onwards, surveys and maps had legitimised and historicised British possession of India, shaping a certain idea of it. By surveying the eastern Himalayas, British Indian authorities wished to fix the region onto India's geo-body.[30] The surveys would help devise a future boundary, and expeditions for the purpose would ensure that the tribes would be 'in no manner of doubt as to their being under us'. This time, London did not object. On 24 July 1911, it wired full permission to India's proposal.[31]

Like Zhao Erfeng's campaigns, the British Empire's decision to move away from non-interference was therefore driven by competitive

---

[27] Reid, *History of the frontier areas* (Eastern Bengal and Assam to Government of India, 16 May 1911), quoted pp. 223–224. Since Williamson had paid for his adventurousness with his life, the Government of India refrained from issuing a formal reprimand against the defunct officer.

[28] Santiago Lazcano, 'Ethno-historic notes on the ancient Tibetan kingdom of sPo Bo and its influence on the eastern Himalayas', *Revue d'Etudes Tibétaines*, 7 (2005), 41–63 (pp. 56–57).

[29] Reid, *History of the frontier areas* (Eastern Bengal and Assam to GOI, 16 May 1911), quoted p. 224.

[30] Matthew H. Edney, *Mapping an empire: The geographical construction of British India, 1765–1843* (Chicago; London: University of Chicago Press, 1997); Ian J. Barrow, *Making history, drawing territory: British mapping in India, c.1756–1905* (New Delhi; Oxford: Oxford University Press, 2003); David Vumlallian Zou and M. Satish Kumar, 'Mapping a colonial borderland: Objectifying the geo-body of India's Northeast', *Journal of Asian Studies*, 70:1 (2011), 141–170.

[31] Reid, *History of the frontier areas* (GOI to Indian Secretary of State, 29 June 1911, and Indian Secretary of State to GOI, 24 July 1911), p. 225.

concerns. The parallels went deeper. In both cases, the drive for expansion was coming from below, from the province – Sichuan for China, Assam for India – or even from an individual, a 'man on the spot'. It was not that imperial capitals were uninterested in the frontier, but they were too far from it to take the measure of potential opportunities and threats there, and often too engrossed in other issues. In India's case, the fact that the colonial Government of India answered to the India Office in London added yet another layer of complexities and divergent priorities.[32]

This disjuncture also spoke to the fact that Qing and British central authorities sought to palliate imperial weakness on the frontier by empowering the province to carry out frontier policy. The Tibetan plateau's extreme environment and remoteness from Beijing had led the Qing to make Sichuan their key intermediary in south-western China.[33] British India similarly delegated frontier matters to Assam, though that province's fortunes were not tied to imperial frontier policies to the same extent as Sichuan's.

As a result, 'Chinese' and 'British Indian' expansionism meant more Sichuan and Assam expansionism than that of Beijing or Delhi, though the latter's financial backup was essential. Frontier officials had their own conception of the state's goals and interests and regularly acted on their own initiative. Zhao Erfeng's prioritisation of Kham over central Tibet was a case in point. In 1911, he had even refused the governorship of Sichuan in order to stay in Kham. There was also a strange parallel between the murder of Feng Quan and of Noel Williamson. Both officials had ignored their superiors' orders to limit their geographical reach, both had much greater plans for the frontier than their orders planned for, and both ended up ushering, through their violent death, a momentum of state expansion that might otherwise have been more subdued.

Punitive Columns and Exploratory Missions

At the end of October 1911, a colonial force gathered at the entrance of the narrow, wall-like gorges of the Siang River. The enterprise was officially called the Abor Expedition (after the colonial name for the Adi tribes), but there could be no doubt about its punitive nature. Though two civilian officers were present, the force was headed by a Major-

---

[32] On the divergent worlds inhabited by local and central officials and their contrasting priorities, see also Gunnel Cederlöf, *Founding an empire on India's north-eastern frontiers, 1790–1840: Climate, commerce, polity* (Delhi: Oxford University Press, 2013).

[33] Yingcong Dai, *The Sichuan frontier and Tibet: Imperial strategy in the early Qing* (Seattle: University of Washington Press, 2009).

General. Four army battalions had been summoned to reinforce 725 military police members. The men were Gurkha, Sikh, Naga, Mizo, or Bengali. They had alongside them a small contingent of Europeans, local tea planters or troops from the Assam Valley Light Horse. And then there were the Naga porters, no less than 4,000 of them. Twenty elephants had also been brought in. The scale of the operation was unprecedented.

While the bulk of the force went up the Siang Gorges, another column turned west, entering the Galo country. Wherever villages offered resistance – guerrilla attacks, booby traps, stone shoots, poisoned defences – they were burnt along with their crops. The expedition culminated in the fall of the Adi village of Kebang on 9 December. Where culprits of Williamson and his men's murder could be identified and caught, they were tried and sentenced to imprisonment or transportation. For the British, this violence was merely a special 'operation'; among the inhabitants, it became known as 'Poju Mimak', the Anglo-Abor War of 1911. By New Year's Eve 1912, Adi resistance was broken. The leaders of the Abor Expedition could now launch the second part of their expedition: the reconnaissance of the vast Siang Basin.[34]

Colonial concerns over Chinese expansionism had increased during preparations for the expedition. Zhao Erfeng had created a Chinese province – Xikang – in Khampa territory, and the Qing had made further strides in the eastern Himalayas. With the visit of an imperial party to the Hrusso country, their presence had been felt near the Assam plains and south-eastern Bhutan. In the Lohit Valley, Mishmi headmen had been pressured to go to Dzayül and pledge submission to the Chinese. The very Siang Basin that the Abor Expedition proposed to explore could shortly come under Qing influence: the kingdom of Pomé, just north of the area, was under Chinese occupation, and the Qing seemed ready to send a force down the Siang.

It was the turn of the Government of India to get truly anxious. Should Pemakö be occupied, this could 'lead to [Chinese] claims to tribal territory which do not at present exist, if not to more serious complications'. From now on, it became imperative to arrive at a 'sound strategical boundary between China cum Tibet and the tribal territory'. The Viceroy thought that the border should follow the divide between Tibetan and tribal territory. But in the absence of concrete knowledge about the higher Himalayan reaches, it was impossible to ascertain where that lay. The explorations that would follow the retaliatory mission therefore acquired an unprecedented importance.[35]

---

[34] Reid, *History of the frontier areas*, pp. 229–231; Dunbar, *Frontiers*, pp. 144–170.
[35] Reid, *History of the frontier areas* (GOI to Secretary of State, 21 September 1911), p. 227.

Over the winter, three major reconnaissance and flag-carrying expeditions toured the Lohit, Subansiri, and Siang basins to establish or strengthen relations with tribals, assess the Chinese threat, and survey the country – all in preparation for a future boundary. By the time they wound up in early 1912, India's colonial authorities were in a lighter mood. Their forces had penetrated deeper into the eastern Himalayas than ever before and had faced neither humiliating defeats nor big losses of life. The Abor Expedition had managed to visit most of the Minyong Adi villages. The column had summoned certain strongmen to inform them that they should now be loyal subjects of the King, this time assorting coercion with trade inducements: Adis would now be 'entitled to trade where they liked'. Closer to the plains, subsidiary parties visited the important Padam village of Damro and the southern Galo area. Several Assam Rifles outposts had been established very close to the foothills, most notably at Pasighat near the mouth of the Siang, a settlement that would one day become the most important Indian government centre in the eastern Himalayas. Assam thereafter successfully lobbied Delhi to remove one hierarchical layer in frontier policy: freed from the supervision of neighbouring District Commissioners, their Political Officers (POs) now directly answered to the provincial Governor. To give territorial reality to this administrative reorganisation, the eastern Himalayas were divided into two sectors, a Central & Eastern one and a Western one. Intensive information gathering had taken place. Expedition reports contained a wealth of new details about the landscape and its inhabitants: lists of villages; inter-tribal relations and feuds; socio-cultural practices; systems of government; fighting strength of the tribes; or major communication corridors. A geographical mystery that had gripped European imaginations had been solved in the bargain. It was now almost beyond doubt that the Tsangpo, the lifeline of Tibet, was one and the same as the Siang River, and thus as India's Brahmaputra.

As far as identifying the best 'military line' between India and Tibet was concerned, the results were less clear cut.[36] The Abor Expedition had gone far but not so far as to reach the end of Adi territory. To the west, the Miri Mission tasked with exploring as much of the Subansiri Basin as possible had failed to fulfil even its more conservative ambitions. Although it contacted many villages never before visited, it had not succeeded in going far inland. Two months of the precious dry season had been wasted due to immense difficulties with finding and retaining 300 porters. Bad weather also prevented advance parties from reaching the projected base camp in the hills. By the time the tour had started,

[36] Ibid. (pp. 181, 233–234).

in January 1912, its itinerary had been drastically curtailed. Even that could not be fully realised. By February, the rains had started again, slowing down the expedition's progress; local guides often proved unavailable due to latent hostility or poor inter-village relations; and the party finally had to retrace its steps when, still in the lower reaches of the Subansiri, it was attacked by a Nyishi village. As a result, the Miri Mission never came close to the Tibetan plateau and left a huge part of the Subansiri Basin unexplored. Its guess that there was no interaction between Tibet and the basin's upper reaches would later be disproved.[37]

The challenges encountered by this expedition exemplified the chasm between colonial beliefs in the possibility of perfect cartographic knowledge and the messy reality of mapping.[38] They also revealed long-term constraints on Indian and Chinese state expansion in the Tibet-Himalayan borderlands, starting with the extreme nature of their climate and terrain. In the eastern Himalayas, the monsoon is so long and so powerful that the government's working season was limited to the dry winter months. All administrative actions and expeditions took place between November and March. As the Miri Mission found out, even during those months dry weather was no guarantee. When expansion was secured through the establishment of outposts, the latter were seldom permanent, for it was hardly possible to supply them, or indeed to reach them, during the flood and landslide season. Just like roads in the region would for long be just 'fair-weather' tracks, state presence too would remain seasonal.

Projecting state power in such conditions was hard; maintaining and consolidating it was harder. The Abor Expedition had to cross very difficult terrain – starting with the impressive Siang Gorges – to reach the Adi villages it proposed to punish, with little hope of obtaining supplies from the sparsely populated surroundings. Zhao Erfeng's troops had faced similar problems. To attack Batang, they had marched huge distances and crossed five parallel mountain ranges, some averaging 6,000 metres in altitude, and hauling supplies and weaponry in their wake. The journey had taken them three months. Having subdued the town, they battled to maintain their troops, officials, and runners there, in the absence of stable supplies of grain.

Hence it was not a coincidence that in much of the Himalayas and on the Tibetan plateau, one of the core prerogatives of rulers was the *ulag*

---

[37] Guwahati, ASA (1912), Report on the Miri country and the operations of the Miri Mission, 1911–12; Guwahati, ASA (c.1912), Miri Mission 1911–12: Report on the survey operations.

[38] Thomas Simpson, 'Bordering and frontier-making in nineteenth-century British India', *The Historical Journal*, 58:2 (2015), 513–542.

system of corvée labour, often supplied as free transport to officials. The lack of roads, and the difficulty of using mules in many places, meant that expeditions required disproportionate amounts of manpower – as the thousands of porters roped in for the Abor Expedition showed. To reach Batang in 1905, Qing troops had found themselves at the mercy of local chieftains and monasteries to obtain transport. Notwithstanding the fact that neither bribes, gifts, nor ultimatums made local cooperation forthcoming, porters tended to flee. So desperate was the logistical situation that they began recruiting porters directly, even paying them – against *ulag* customs.[39] Transport would remain at the heart of the challenge to ensure the projection and continuity of state power in the eastern Himalayas well into the second half of the twentieth century.

A Cat-and-Mouse Game in the Mishmi Hills

British expansion had first targeted the Adi-inhabited Siang Basin, but it was in the Lohit Valley that the competition became obvious. News of China's push in the area kept reaching Sadiya in the second half of 1911. A veteran of the Younghusband Expedition, Frederick Bailey, had travelled from Dzayül to Assam that summer. North of the boundary flags put up by the Qing, he had met two Mishmi headmen on their way to a Chinese outpost in Dzayül. They had been threatened with retaliatory military actions if they persisted in refusing its summons. Bailey tried to convince them not to go, and instead to seek British advice at Sadiya. The two men turned back but did not go further than their own villages.

Further evidence of Chinese attempts to assert authority over Mishmis was surfacing. Tungno, the chief of Pangum, had ignored yet another summons to Rima. He had heard about Zhao Erfeng's expedition to Pomé and feared being enlisted. A Digaru Mishmi headman, Mazanon, reported that a large Qing party had entered his land. Its leader had told the villagers that though the Chinese Empire was not coming to tax them, it expected them to follow its orders. The first was to raise imperial flags closer to Assam, the second to build a road down the valley for the passage of imperial troops. Finally, the Qing official had distributed nine bags of salt, enjoining them to eat Chinese salt as well as British. Mazanon had deflected their first demand, suggesting they use the Lohit Valley route taken by the British; as for the flags, the Digaru headmen had replied that the Chinese could plant them themselves. They did accept the nine loads of salt, but only ate half of it for fear of a British reaction. The next day, the

[39] Wang, *China's last imperial frontier*, p. 195.

party departed, threatening to send in 300 soldiers if the Mishmis defied China's authority.

Given these incidents, British Indian authorities considered it imperative to send a third expedition to the Lohit Basin to ascertain the extent of Chinese advance and take countermeasures. In December 1911, the new frontier official at Sadiya, W.C.M. Dundas, left at the head of a Mishmi Mission. Tungno's and Mazanon's tales proved to be largely true. Headmen in the Delei Valley were found in possession of fifteen sealed and signed 'warrants of protection', issued in Zhao Erfeng's name. The documents declared that their holders had made submission to the Qing Empire and were now under the protection of Sichuan authorities. The Chinese party that had distributed them had told the Digarus 'to show [them] to any Chinese official they might meet while trading in Tibet, or to any British official who might enter the tribal country'.

Qing China had also increased its territorial claim in the Lohit Valley. At Menilkrai, Dundas discovered flags bearing the symbol of a four-clawed dragon. A wooden board stood nearby, with the inscription: 'The southern frontier of Zayul on the borders of the Szechuan Province of the Chinese Empire.'[40] Of the Chinese themselves, there was no sign. This likely proved fortunate, for the Government of India had given contradictory orders: the expedition was not to confront any Qing troops present there, but would still have to make them withdraw 'into recognised Tibetan–Chinese limits' – by force if needed.[41]

Before returning to Sadiya, the British party persuaded the Digarus to surrender their Chinese documents.[42] Dundas had his men place a cairn of stones and a bilingual notification affirming that Menilkrai was, in fact, British territory. Yet, when the government party returned to the same spot a few months later, a second Chinese pillar stood, reiterating Qing sovereignty. Three Chinese officials had apparently come down from Dzayül shortly after Dundas' departure, looked at the British boundary notification at Menilkrai, and ordered their Mishmi porters to put up another Qing pillar alongside it.[43]

In China, uprisings had erupted against the Qing. But Assam frontier authorities could not know its outcome yet; for now, they considered Chinese intentions over the Lohit corridor to be more threatening than ever. They petitioned Delhi to fund more decisive expansion. Should British India not capitalise on the Mishmi Mission, any future boundary negotiation with China would be hampered 'by an apparent renunciation

---

[40] BL, IOR/L/PS/20/MEMO30/8 (Chinese activity), pp. 149–152.
[41] Reid, *History of the frontier areas*, p. 237.   [42] Ibid. (p. 243).
[43] BL, IOR/L/PS/20/MEMO30/8 (Chinese activity), p. 151.

of territory', they argued. Moreover, Dundas had succeeded in establishing peaceful relations with many inhabitants. Should this expansion opportunity be squandered, the Mishmis might interpret it as a sign of weakness, which the Chinese might exploit to expand their influence among them, for instance by giving them firearms – many tribals had asked the colonial party for firearms, but their requests had been turned down.[44]

In October 1912, Delhi wired sanction to expand administration beyond Assam's Inner Line – not without some reluctance from London. Expansion in the Lohit Basin was the priority. Promoted PO, Dundas got four officials to assist him. The plan was to establish a military police position at Menilkrai, with intermediate outposts on the main river confluences to Sadiya. A cart-and-bridle road would be built all the way to Walong, and connected by porter tracks to the main passes leading to Tibet. Another track would go through the Dibang Valley, to the west, and a telegraph line would link Sadiya to the outposts. Engineering companies would be raised specifically for the constructions of these posts and roads. The whole of the Mishmi hills would be subject to extensive surveying.

Expansion plans for the rest of the Himalayas were less ambitious, but momentous compared to earlier colonial policies. In the Western Sector, where Chinese influence had not seemed a concern, a PO would be charged with getting to know the area in more detail before formulating proposals for it. In the Adi country, the positions established at Balek, Pasighat, and Kobo during the expeditions of 1911–1912 would be transformed into seasonal outposts, and a trade mart established at the vanquished village of Kebang to foster relations with the tribes of the upper Siang Basin. Further survey missions would be dispatched to evaluate Tibetan influence around Pemakö.[45]

For the next two years, Assam officials worked to realise these expansion plans. In the Lohit Valley, the cat-and-mouse game with Chinese officials seemingly continued. In early 1914, a British Indian party spotted another Chinese boundary marker at Menilkrai. The wooden pillar stood on a hill slope between two pine trees, a thatch roof for cover. It was a small protection against the elements, but it had succeeded in its task: the Qing inscription could still be read. At first, local Mishmi villages denied knowing anything about it. Eventually, some let it slip that in early 1912, a few months after Dundas' departure, two rifle-carrying Chinese officials had come down from Rima on a lightning visit. They had

[44] Reid, *History of the frontier areas* (Assam to GOI, 7 July 1912), pp. 240–243.
[45] Ibid. (pp. 246–248).

stayed around just for the time it took their Tibetan coolies to erect the boundary post. Upon leaving, they told the headmen: 'Show the post to the English, if they come again.'

This time, the Chinese pillar was not left in its state. The British official removed it and left it to rot in the jungle. But the situation could not be allowed to continue, he argued. If India let Chinese officials have their way at Menilkrai, they would control one of the rare zones of flat, arable land in this part of the Himalayas. The small colonial garrison stationed in the Lohit Valley would not be able to support itself other than by getting supplies from Sadiya, 172 miles downstream. British control of the entire Mishmi hills would be at risk.[46]

The Fall of the Qing

In reality, the Chinese expansion momentum had collapsed. By the time British officials put up their third boundary pillar at Menilkrai, the Qing Empire was no more: it had crumbled almost in simultaneous time with India's Himalayan expeditions. By 1 January 1912, China had become a Republic. Sichuan had been among the first provinces in China to rise against the empire; the unprecedented taxation imposed to finance modernisation and the Kham campaigns had made it ripe for rebellion.[47]

Tibet was almost immediately affected. In Lhasa, Chinese troops mutinied and started looting the city. Tibetans retaliated, boosted by the Dalai Lama who coordinated the uprising from his Sikkimese exile. Not all the monasteries sided with the revolt, and the bitter fighting that ensued saw a third of Lhasa turned to ruins. By early 1912, Chinese forces had been defeated, paving the way for the Dalai Lama's return. By January 1913, the Tibetan leader had negotiated the full surrender of the remaining Qing soldiers, officials, and their retinue, and forced them to leave Lhasa – not via Kham, but through India.[48] China had been thrown out of Tibet.

Kham too was in upheaval. Anti-Chinese uprisings rocked the region, and Zhao Erfeng was not there to quell them. Having gone to Sichuan, he had been murdered by revolutionaries in late 1911. A long period of unrest and violence followed, reducing Chinese state control back to its pre-Zhao Erfeng days. Han farmers fled or were killed, military officials

---

[46] London, BL, IOR (1914), Walong promenade (tour) 1914, IOR/L/MIL/7/16894 (O'Callaghan's diary for February 1914).
[47] Adshead, *Province and politics in late Imperial China*.
[48] Ho, 'The men who would not be *amban*' (pp. 28–29).

were put under siege, and 90 per cent of the 300 Chinese government schools were destroyed within a few years.[49]

Competition between various warlords and Han forces loyal to the new Republic – not to mention attacks by a virtually autonomous Yunnan – hampered Chinese attempts to retake control of the region. In 1917–1918, Lhasa's armies wrested control of western Kham. They were poised to go further when the British consul intervened. Ten years later, a powerful warlord, Liu Wenhui, conquered Sichuan and parts of eastern Kham. But he was largely independent for most of the 1930s, and of the surviving administrative units Zhao Erfeng had established, most were in the east and back under indigenous leaders.[50] The de facto boundary between Lhasa-ruled areas and Chinese-influenced areas would stay east of Dzayül until 1950.

Chinese expansionism ended quickly in the eastern Himalayas. Dzayül and Pomé had been among the last regions conquered by Zhao Erfeng, and they were just south of Kham's first centres of anti-Chinese rebellion after the fall of the Qing. Erected in June 1912, the third Chinese boundary post erected at Menilkrai was in fact one of Qing China's last actions in the eastern Himalayas. Imperial forces were expelled from their base in Dzayül shortly afterwards, apparently by a Lhasa official. Pomé's inhabitants had risen against Zhao's expeditionary force even earlier, using their knowledge of the landscape to thwart its advance. By the end of 1911, two-thirds of the Chinese troops had retreated, and Pomé soon came back under the fragile control of its local dynasty.[51]

Chinese state presence disappeared from the eastern Himalayas for the next thirty years. This did not mean the new Republic had given up its claims on Kham and central Tibet. Sun Yat-sen, the revolutionary leader who had briefly held the presidency, proclaimed China as a 'Republic of Five Nationalities' – a Han-centric polity where Tibetans, Hans, Mongols, Manchus, and Huis would eventually fuse into one nation and one state. His successor, Yuan Shikai, still hoped to revive China's supremacy over Tibet. In early 1913, he telegraphed the Dalai Lama, apologising for the violence in Lhasa and 'restoring' him in his Manchu titles.[52]

[49] Relyea, 'Yokes of gold' (pp. 35–36).
[50] Hsiao-ting Lin, *Tibet and Nationalist China's frontier: Intrigues and ethnopolitics, 1928–49* (Vancouver: University of British Columbia Press, 2006), part I.
[51] Lazcano, 'Ethno-historic notes' (p. 57).
[52] Melvyn C. Goldstein and Gelek Rimpoche, *A history of modern Tibet, Volume 1: The demise of the Lamaist state, 1913–1951* (Berkeley: University of California Press, 1989), pp. 58–59.

The Dalai Lama rejected them and instead announced his assumption of total rule over Tibet, both spiritual and temporal, and without Chinese interference. The proclamation was not couched in the Western terms of a declaration of independence, but it amounted to one. Faced with what had become a de facto independent Tibet and unable to do much about it so long as China remained divided between different warlords, Han leaders would nevertheless continue to assert their sovereign right to Tibet in verbal discussions with British officials as well as in political propaganda. And, once Chiang Kai-shek would have nominally reunified China in 1928, his Guomindang government would vocally proclaim its commitment to recovering 'lost' territories. Though Zhao Erfeng's advances into the eastern Himalayas had collapsed with him, China would never cease to assert its 'cartographic' sovereignty over the region.[53]

The Simla Convention

Under the circumstances, British Indian authorities remained wary. The eastern Himalayas was not experiencing the unrest engulfing much of Kham, but frontier officials feared Assam was not completely safe from China. The political status of Tibetan areas was uncertain, and the un-administered Mishmi hills were 'like a screen behind which the progress of the policy and movement of the Chinese near our vulnerable north-east salient cannot be observed from within our administrative border'.[54]

London and Delhi therefore sanctioned Assam's enhanced expansion proposals and shifted their policy on Tibet. Whereas they had hitherto accepted or even protected Chinese claims to suzerainty in order to thwart Russia's influence, they now favoured a self-governing Tibet: not only was China incapable of stabilising it, it threatened India's Himalayan frontier.[55] By the same token, working towards a 'strategically sound' Indo-Tibetan boundary north of Assam remained crucial.

The goal seemed within grasp. Relations between British India and Lhasa had greatly improved since the Younghusband Expedition. The Dalai Lama had begun to see China as the primary threat to Tibet's autonomy and had returned to Lhasa through the mediation of British officials. Two invasions in ten years had convinced him that Tibet needed to obtain full mastery over its own affairs.[56]

[53] Hsiao-ting Lin, *Modern China's ethnic frontiers: A journey to the west* (London: Routledge, 2011).

[54] Reid, *History of the frontier areas* (Assam, 7 July 1912), quoted p. 243.

[55] Clive J. Christie, 'Great Britain, China and the status of Tibet, 1914–21', *Modern Asian Studies*, 10:4 (1976), 481–508 (pp. 482–486).

[56] Goldstein and Rimpoche, *A history of modern Tibet, Volume 1*.

Such mastery would be hard to come by unless the border with China was stabilised; Lhasa could not hope to resist a Chinese military offensive. External support was essential to start negotiation and guarantee an agreement. British India was ready to offer it. Like Tibet, Delhi shared a strong interest in stabilising the volatile Kham borderlands. Together with redefined Sino-Tibetan relations, a boundary agreement would protect Assam's hinterland from Chinese encroachment and provide British India with a buffer state on its northern boundary. To bring Beijing to the negotiating table, Britain threatened to withdraw financial assistance to the flagging Chinese Republican regime – adding, for good measure, the threat of denying it diplomatic recognition. Beijing reluctantly accepted to participate in a tripartite conference. In October 1913, a Chinese representative arrived in the Indian hill station of Shimla (Simla).

The negotiations were to produce an agreement on Tibet's political status and its boundary with China. Tibetan areas were to be divided into two zones. One, Inner Tibet, would be a shared zone of influence between Lhasa and Beijing; the other, Outer Tibet, would be under Lhasa's sole control, though China would retain titular suzerainty. This definition fell short of declaring Tibet's independence, but Lhasa's representative was ready to accept it to ensure a boundary agreement.

Disagreements quickly surfaced. Delhi and Lhasa insisted on an Inner–Outer Tibet boundary replicating the general watershed between Qing and Tibetan influence at the start of the twentieth century. The Chinese, however, defended the boundary set by Zhao Erfeng at the height of his campaigns. This amounted to englobing the whole of Kham under Chinese influence, including Dzayül and Pomé. Delhi and Lhasa would not countenance this.

News from Assam steeled British resolve against China's expansive proposals. Frontier officials were reporting the presence of Chinese troops at Menkong, on the Salween River. It was ten long days from there to Rima by mule track, but, still, an army could mobilise there and march on Dzayül, without colonial authorities ever knowing about it. Letting Chinese authority come even closer would be even worse.

But the Chinese would not back down either. Though China's plenipotentiary had initialled the Simla Convention, Beijing refused to ratify it and withdrew from the negotiations.[57] Now reduced to Delhi and Lhasa, the conference continued along different lines. Henry McMahon, the British Indian representative, favoured ratifying it bilaterally, without

[57] Attempts to reopen negotiations at the end of the First World War would similarly flounder. Christie, 'Great Britain, China and the status of Tibet' (pp. 493–496).

China's involvement. London refused, fearing this would be tantamount to a formal recognition of Tibet's independence.

Delhi therefore reduced its ambitions at the Simla Conference to its second goal: establishing a boundary between India and Tibet in the eastern Himalayas. Between Assam's constant reminders of the frailty of colonial influence and China's expansive definition of Inner Tibet, British Indian authorities were convinced that the issue was more pressing than ever. In July 1914, they succeeded: the British Indian and Tibetan representatives concluded their bilateral discussions by an exchange of notes, fixing an international boundary north of Assam. It would soon come to be known as the McMahon Line, after the man who had negotiated it on British India's behalf.

The 850-mile-long line, which ran from Bhutan's northern edge to upper Burma, reflected colonial concerns for a militarily defensible boundary alignment. Several areas recognised as part of the Tibetan realm were englobed into Indian territory. In the Lohit, the agreement placed the boundary just above Walong and well in advance of Menilkrai, the spot disputed between Qing and Assam frontier officials. The latter had convinced their superiors that only Walong, with its arable, flat land, offered the potential to become a self-sufficient government position.[58]

In the extreme west, much of Monyül, an area under 'active and continuous control' by Tibetan government officials and the Drepung Monastery, had also been made Indian territory. Military authorities and the official responsible for British India's Tibet policy, the Sikkim PO, had insisted that this 'Tibetan wedge' between Bhutan and tribal regions had to be removed, especially as there were signs that China coveted the area. Controlling the town of Tawang and its vicinity also offered several advantages: tours to the area had revealed its strong agricultural potential; the shortest route between Assam and Lhasa passed through it; the monsoon was clement; and, finally, its inclusion would provide India with 'a good clean line on the map'.[59]

In practice, the McMahon Line had been drawn based only on partial, or superficial, understanding of the eastern Himalayas' human and physical geography. The Indo-Tibetan boundary was officially meant to follow the watershed or the highest range of the eastern Himalayas, yet

---

[58] Reid, *History of the frontier areas*, p. 251.
[59] Itanagar, APSA, NEFA Secretariat (1943), Towang, 48/43-AD (PO Sikkim to External Affairs Secretary, 2 July 1943), p. 19. The Simla agreement recognised the rights of certain Tibetan families who held estates south of the McMahon Line, near Tawang and Mechuka, to continue their activities there. H.K. Barpujari, *Problem of the hill tribes: North-East Frontier, Volume 3: 1873–1962, Inner Line to McMahon Line* (Guwahati: Spectrum, 1981), pp. 282–283.

no real principles underlined its alignment. In 1914, knowledge of the upper regions' topography was still too scant to permit an accurate assessment of where that watershed or highest crest lay. Visited by two surveys and by several officers' parties, the Lohit Valley was one of the exceptions; but there, the watershed principle was not applied. When officials would be sent to claim the McMahon Line, they would soon find that they lacked guidelines, both cartographic and on the ground, to ascertain the boundary's precise location. At the time, however, the problem was not apparent, and London and Delhi had in any case no clear administrative intentions towards the upper reaches of Assam's north-east frontier.

McMahon recommended that steps be taken to assume concrete control over the new boundary, especially Tawang. Assam officials agreed. They had not remained idle during the Simla Conference. For the first time, a British officer had visited Dzayül – at the insistent invitation of the region's reinstated Tibetan authorities. While the extent of Lhasa's control over Dzayül prior to 1910 is unclear, the Dalai Lama's government was now intensifying its rule over the area. Cultivating good relations with British frontier officials on the ground was important in the context of the Simla Conference, and Dzayül's *dzongpön*s strove to develop cordial relations with the Sadiya PO.

But the latter was convinced that even with Lhasa's increased control over Dzayül, the territory claimed by British India was not safe: 'Who [could] say but that with internal stability, China will endeavour to realise … her ambition to reduce Tibet to the position of a regularly administered province.' It was essential that India continue to push its administration forward from Sadiya.[60] In 1919, another territorial reorganisation created three 'Frontier Tracts': Balipara in the west, Sadiya for the Adi and Mishmi hills, and Lakhimpur in the south-east. Sections of the tracts were then brought under 'loose control'. Termed 'Backward Tracts', the region was excluded from the Montagu–Chelmsford Reforms that took place that year and devolved some power to Indian actors at the provincial level.

This did not translate into much advance on the ground. For when, in May 1914, Assam submitted a third proposal – this time to increase state penetration in the Adi areas by building a bridle path through the Siang Gorges and pushing outposts farther inland – they were disappointed. Delhi would not sanction the scheme. Just like China two years earlier, British India's state expansion momentum was about to die out.

[60] BL, IOR/L/MIL/7/16894 (O'Callaghan Tour Diary for February 1914).

A Line Drawn in the Dark and Kept in the Dark

Just as McMahon gave the final touch to the Indo-Tibetan boundary that would bear his name, the First World War reared its head. Between the situation in Europe and the latency of the Chinese threat, expanding the empire on a remote Himalayan frontier dropped from London's agenda. In fact, even the cartographic sovereignty established in the wake of the Simla negotiations was not asserted.

Having signed the agreement creating the McMahon Line, British authorities decided not to publicise it. Their initial fear was that doing so might antagonise Russia, but even after the collapse of the Czarist Empire, they kept the agreement secret. Should the McMahon Line's existence be revealed, the likely consequence would be renewed Chinese interest in Tibet and accusations of British imperialism. Accordingly, the 1914 Simla agreement was not included in the 1929 edition of Aitchinson's *Treaties*.[61]

Assam frontier officials found themselves back in the pre-1911 situation – having to make do with whatever funds and permissions they could obtain from their superiors. In an attempt to concretise the cautious programme sanctioned back in 1912, Dundas extended his authority over the Adi inhabitants of the foothills, working to control all the villages that had cultivation in the plains east of the Siang River. He also expanded administration west of the river to incorporate villages on the south of the first Himalayan ridge, arguing they were friendly, and brought their disputes to Pasighat. By early 1918, he was satisfied that all the Singphos and Khamtis were now under the Sadiya headquarters, as well as many important Padam, Pasi, and Minyong Adi villages and small Mishmi settlements of the foothills.[62]

In practice, 'bringing under administration' meant little more than yearly tours to collect poll tax and settling disputes. Moreover, the expansion momentum in the Lohit Valley had died out. In 1916, Delhi refused sanction to further expenditure on the Lohit Valley road beyond Tidding, in the foothills. The bridges that had been built further up began to crumble, and the road had begun to erode.

The end of the war did not return India's north-east frontier to the attention of Delhi and London. In 1920, Assam obtained permission to send a punitive column against some Idu Mishmis in retaliation for the murder of a Gurkha soldier, but after great difficulty. The provincial

---

[61] Hsiao-Ting Lin, 'Boundary, sovereignty, and imagination: Reconsidering the frontier disputes between British India and Republican China, 1914–47', *Journal of Imperial and Commonwealth History*, 32:3 (2004), 25–47 (p. 31).
[62] Reid, *History of the frontier areas*, pp. 252–253.

Chief Commissioner had forcibly argued that 'well-disposed tribesmen are already amazed and bewildered at ... the inexplicable delay of the British government in seeking reparation from the open murder of its servant and the open capture of its subjects'.[63] When, two years later, Assam again requested approval for 'a definite programme of operations' in the Mishmi and Adi areas, Delhi took a year to reply and opposed a flat refusal. Notwithstanding the dire state of government finances, expenditure would not be justified since the main justification for expansion – Chinese pressure – had disappeared. In fact, the time had come to reduce the cost of frontier administration, and drastically so. The Government of India favoured restricting expenditure on the Lohit Valley Road further, abolishing the recently created post of PO Balipara, and withdrawing outposts.

Several times over the next few years, Assam tried to reverse this retrenchment, stressing its adverse consequences for colonial presence and relations with tribal people. If expeditions were cancelled and bridges left to rot, officers would not be able to exert 'even the loosest control' over the eastern Himalayas.[64] In fact, the damage would be double because the bridges had enabled many Mishmis to cross unfordable rivers to come trade with Sadiya, argued frontier officials: this had been an important factor in the welcome shown by many of them to British presence. Had the Government of India not admitted that abandoning big projects, such as the Lohit Valley Road, would be 'a retreat and regarded as evidence of weakness'? Powerful Adi villages would take retrenchment as a signal to reassert themselves. As for the Balipara Frontier Tract, so little had been achieved there, and withdrawing its sole officer would leave the tea gardens open to predatory tribal raids.[65]

Delhi only consented to a few changes. The Lohit Valley Road would be maintained until Tidding, but to a very reduced standard. Outposts at the entrance of the Dibang Valley would be withdrawn. The position of PO Balipara would remain, but his tours would be limited 'to the bare minimum compatible with the measure of control necessary in the interests of the security of the plains'. By 1923–1924, retrenchment had been fully effected. In the file sanctioning it, a manuscript note read: 'a humiliating decision which will probably in the long run prove very expensive'.[66]

[63] London, BL, IOR (4 February 1920–22 March 1926), Future control of North East Frontier: Sadiya and Balipara tracts; Lohit Valley Road IOR/L/PS/12/3113 (Assam Chief Secretary to Foreign & Political Department, 7 December 1919).
[64] Ibid. (Government of India to Wakely, 4 October 1922).
[65] Guwahati, ASA, Assam Secretariat, Political Branch (1923), Closure of the Sadiya and Balipara Frontier Tracts p. 7.
[66] BL, IOR L/PS/12/3113 (Botham, 20 December 1923, and Draft telegram, September 1923).

Imaginary Sovereignties

The first episode of competitive Sino-Indian expansion in the eastern Himalayas had died out almost as quickly as it began. Ironically, the polity that would make concrete strides in the region in the two decades after the Simla Convention – for there was one – was Tibet. The thirteenth Dalai Lama was convinced that to protect the de facto independence acquired in 1913, Tibet had to modernise. This meant reforming the bureaucracy and building the embryonic Tibetan army, but also asserting more centralised control over outlying regions.[67] Eyed on by both the Chinese and the British, the eastern Himalayas were a prime target for Lhasa.

This expansionism had older antecedents. Tibetan Buddhist world views saw the region as the 'periphery of civilisation'; its inhabitants were no more than barbarians. Since the start of the century, this had turned the northern Himalayan slopes into a political and economic playground not just for the Tibetan government but for various adventurers or entrepreneurs more or less connected to it. In 1906, the Dalai Lama's troops had decimated the Nas of the upper Subansiri Basin, forcing them to scatter into two groups who would end up divided by the McMahon Line.[68]

The 1920s and 1930s would see increased expansionism by Lhasa and regional powerholders. A powerful Lhasa official tried to start tea gardens in Na territory, sparking resistance and yet more killings. South of Mechuka, a Tibetan aristocrat tried, through violence, to open up new areas for taxation and corvée labour among the Ramos and Pailibos.[69] Meanwhile, Lhasa strove to bring Pomé under control. When its king consequently stopped paying tribute and prevented the Dalai Lama's officials from entering his territory, Tibetan troops occupied the kingdom. A brutal war ensued, and the monarch fled to Sadiya. Secured through the presence of two garrisons, Pomé became an administrative district under the rule of Lhasa-appointed officials. The latter increased their demands on local Buddhist populations, causing many to take refuge in Sadiya. By the 1930s, Lhasa's intermediaries and the powerful Sera monastery would be working to expand their tax and corvée area yet further, into Adi-inhabited areas.[70] Chinese and Indian state presence, meanwhile, had effectively withdrawn.

---

[67] Goldstein and Rimpoche, *A history of modern Tibet, Volume 1*, pp. 65–138.
[68] Toni Huber, 'Pushing south: Tibetan economic and political activities in the far eastern Himalaya, c.1900–1950', in *Sikkim Studies: Proceedings of the Namgyal Institute Jubilee Conference, 2008*, ed. by Alex McKay and Anna Balikci (Gangtok: Namgyal Institute, 2011) (pp. 259–263).
[69] Ibid. (pp. 262–266).
[70] Dundul Namgyal Tsarong, *In the service of his country: The biography of Dasang Damdul Tsarong, Commander General of Tibet*, ed. by Khenmo Trinlay Chödron (Ithaca, NY:

And yet, in the late 1950s, China and India would hark back to the events of the 1910s to justify their claim to the eastern Himalayas against one another. Neither Nationalist China – as the Chinese Republic would become known after its superficial reunification by Chiang Kai-shek, in 1928 – nor the PRC would admit that Zhao Erfeng had not pushed beyond Pomé or southern Dzayül, and that his conquests were swept away after a mere two years. India, meanwhile, would present the boundary settled at Simla as the paramount proof of the legality of its presence in Walong, Tawang, or Pemakö. That the handful of outposts built after 1910 disappeared within a few years, or that many areas supposedly englobed in Indian territory would not see a British official till the 1940s and 1950s, would not be mentioned. Just as people in western Kham probably knew little about the Chinese Republic, few Monpas knew they supposedly fell under the Indian government.

In the case of China, warlords and Republican leaders would at least consistently promote a 'cartographically existing' authority over Tibet and the eastern Himalayas.[71] But the British Empire would long keep the Simla agreement secret. Even after its publication, London and Delhi did not act to ensure that the McMahon Line became well known. The result was that certain British or American maps and atlases ignored its existence – when they did not place the Indo-Tibetan boundary at the foot of the hills.[72] The contrast between Republican China's sensitivity towards its imaginary sovereignty and the British Empire's apparent forgetfulness in this regard are connected with the fact that British and Qing expansion attempts had very different 'sovereignty goals' in the eastern Himalayas.

Delhi and London's vision followed an imperial logic: the eastern Himalayas should be a buffer between India and its neighbourhood. Confronted by Chinese expansionism, their aim was limited to achieving *external* sovereignty over the region – that is, to ensure that no foreign power would intrude into the eastern Himalayas, and that local people

Snow Lion, 2000), p. 58; Lazcano, 'Ethno-historic notes' (pp. 58–61); Hugh Richardson, *High peaks, pure earth: Collected writings on Tibetan history and culture*, ed. by Michael Aris (London: Serindia, 1998), p. 564.

[71] Lin, 'Boundary, sovereignty, and imagination' (p. 26).

[72] Itanagar, APSA, NEFA Secretariat (1958), Tour diary of RR Pal Sharma, Assistant Research Officer Kameng R-172/56 (Foreign Secretary to Secretary of State, 17 August 1936); New Delhi, NAI, External Affairs Proceedings (1943), Claim by the Tibetan government that Tibetan subjects settled in Bhutan should be repatriated to Tibet. Measures taken to stabilize the MacMahon Line, 63/X/43 (Caroe, 12 January 1944); New Delhi, NAI, External Affairs Proceedings (1944), Tibetan intelligence reports received from CIO. Assam comments of the British mission, Lhasa, and the PO Sikkim on reports about the Chinese ultimatum, 576/CA/44 (Lambert's Tibet Intelligence Report, 29 July 1944).

would have 'no relations or intercourse with any Foreign Power other than the British Government'.[73] It was to formalise this buffer that they worked towards an Indo-Tibetan boundary agreement. Since this could not be done without some active presence on the ground, colonial authorities accepted to create outposts and build roads, but only the minimum required to fulfil their purpose. When the possibility of foreign influence recessed, they all but disappeared along with it.

In this context, it was the late Qing Empire, long seen as a victim of foreign imperialism and its own incapacity to change, that went the farthest in its attempts to apply and enhance Western notions of sovereignty – with its external *and* internal dimensions – and statehood over the Tibeto-Himalayan borderlands, by colonising them. Zhao Erfeng's expansionism was a thoroughly modern endeavour, one in which an empire was gradually evolving into a multi-nation-state.[74] And even if Zhao's Republican successors had limited capacity to implement it, they would recuperate this state-making project.

---

[73] BL, IOR/L/PS/20/MEMO30/8.

[74] William M. Coleman IV, 'The uprising at Batang: Khams and its significance in Chinese and Tibetan history', in *Khams Pa histories: Visions of people, place and authority*, ed. by Lawrence Epstein (Leiden: Brill, 2002), pp. 31–56; Adshead, *Province and politics in late Imperial China*; Kirk W. Larsen, 'The Qing Empire (China), imperialism, and the modern world', *History Compass*, 9:6 (2011), 498–508.

Figure 1.1 Dirang Dzong, c. 1938
© The Royal Geographical Society. Francis Kingdon-Ward Collection

2　The Return of the Fair-Weather State
The Second World War and the Himalayas

In late 1935, an angry letter from Lhasa reached Delhi. A certain 'King-da', a British subject apparently, had entered Tibet without authorisation. Olaf Caroe, India's Foreign Secretary, was perplexed: he did not know of any King-da and British subjects were not supposed to trespass beyond Assam's Inner Line, let alone venture into Tibet. Upon enquiry, the man turned out to be Frank Kingdon-Ward, an explorer and botanist well known to colonial authorities who had gone plant-hunting through the eastern Himalayas and had reached Tawang, where Tibetan *dzongpöns* permitted him to go further into Tibet – or so he claimed.[1] Indian authorities were furious. Kingdon-Ward's wanderlust had not only caused tensions with Lhasa, his travels had also unveiled a disturbing situation in Assam's Frontier Tracts. Far from respecting the McMahon Line, Tibet controlled Tawang. Indeed, its influence spread south of the Sela Pass. Kingdon-Ward thought that, 'while the main [Himalayan] range might be the *de jure* frontier, . . . the *de facto* frontier lay much further south'.[2]

There was more. Prompted to confirm where the McMahon Line lay so that Delhi raise the matter with Lhasa, Assam replied that they did not know anything about a boundary, and had anyhow no influence beyond the foothills.[3] Twenty years after Shimla, colonial authorities realised their mistake in not concretising their Himalayan border. With no maps to announce its existence and no state presence to materialise it on the ground, the McMahon Line's insubstantial nature had been laid bare.

The discovery came just as Nationalist China was making headway in Tibet. After resuming relations with Lhasa in 1930, Chiang Kai-shek's

---

[1] Alastair Lamb, *Tibet, China & India, 1914–1950: A history of imperial diplomacy* (Hertingfordbury: Roxford Books, 1989), p. 422.
[2] Francis Kingdon Ward, 'The Assam Himalaya: Travels in Balipara I', *Journal of The Royal Central Asian Society*, 25:4 (1938), 610–619 (p. 613).
[3] Itanagar, APSA, NEFA Secretariat (1958), Tour diary of RR Pal Sharma, Assistant Research Officer Kameng R-172/56 (Foreign secretary to HMG Under-Secretary, 17 August 1936).

Guomindang government had capitalised on the death of the thirteenth Dalai Lama in December 1933 to recover a presence in the country, for the first time since 1912: the Guomindang had obtained Tibet's permission to maintain two officials and a wireless station in Lhasa.[4] Using the Communist Long March as a pretext, the regime had also improved its influence in Sichuan and eastern Kham and was countering Lhasa and the warlord Liu Wenhui by tacitly supporting Khampa autonomy movements.[5] It had officially relaunched Xikang, the province Zhao Erfeng had created. Chinese maps showing the Assam Frontier Tracts under it had freshly been printed, dividing the region into three districts: Loyül, Lower Dzayül, and Monyül.[6]

Whether this signified a more substantive return of China's influence and ambitions in Tibet is debatable. Xikang had no reality west of the Upper Yangtze, and hence in the eastern Himalayas. Moreover, there are signs that Chiang Kai-shek's frontier policy was mainly instrumentalist and pragmatic. Strident claims for the recovery of 'lost' territories such as Tibet served to buttress the regime's brittle domestic political legitimacy and authority.[7]

From an Indian standpoint, however, it seemed self-evident that Nationalist China would eventually seek to control Tibet. Should this happen, the risk was that it would use Lhasa's hold over Tawang to justify its annexation and even that of Sikkim and Bhutan. The circumstances forced London to include the McMahon Line in Survey of India maps in 1936. Taken but reluctantly, the decision would hopefully prevent China from claiming ignorance about the boundary.

Assam maintained this was insufficient. Asserting the McMahon Line cartographically would mean very little if, as in 1914, nothing was done to ensure a measure of control over Tawang and its vicinity. Seeing their expansion proposals repeatedly quashed from above, frontier officials had used visits like that of Kingdon-Ward to keep an eye on the eastern

---

[4] Hsiao-ting Lin, *Tibet and Nationalist China's frontier: Intrigues and ethnopolitics, 1928–49* (Vancouver: University of British Columbia Press, 2006), Chapter 4.

[5] Peng Wenbin, 'Frontier processes, provincial politics and movements for Khampa autonomy during the Republican Period', in *Khams Pa histories: Visions of people, place and authority*, ed. by Lawrence Epstein (Leiden: Brill, 2002), pp. 57–84.

[6] The re-creation of Xikang was part of a general readjustment of Nationalist China's outlying territories in 1928, but the Guomindang remained absent from most of these regions. Hsiao-Ting Lin, 'Boundary, sovereignty, and imagination: Reconsidering the frontier disputes between British India and Republican China, 1914–47', *Journal of Imperial and Commonwealth History*, 32:3 (2004), 25–47 (pp. 29–30).

[7] Lin, *Tibet and Nationalist China's frontier*, Part 2. For Lin, an actual extension of 'Chinese' control over Kham or Tibet was not in Chiang Kai-shek's interest: it would likely have reinforced local warlords' power.

Himalayas. The Balipara PO had given his blessing to the plant hunter's trip and assisted him extensively.[8]

Constitutional changes might have given further fillip to Assam colonial authorities' push for expansion. Under the 1935 Government of India Act, an elected indigenous ministry would soon govern lowland Assam. Excluded from the reforms, the Frontier Tracts and other parts of the Assam highlands would continue to be ruled by the British Governor in his full discretion – one of the last preserves of total colonial rule.

Eventually, London agreed to despatch someone to Tawang to assess the situation and reassert British India's claims. The Balipara PO returned from a tour of Monyül in spring 1938. Assam frontier authorities now wanted to conduct more comprehensive tours. But London and Delhi had second thoughts about expansion. War with Germany was on the horizon. In the circumstances, financing a costly activist policy in the eastern Himalayas did not seem a priority. Soon, concerns about the McMahon Line receded into the background.[9]

For the second time since the start of the twentieth century, war preparations had cancelled British Indian plans to expand in the eastern Himalayas. This time, however, it would not take decades for senior colonial authorities to take an interest in the region again. On the contrary, the extension of the Second World War to Southeast Asia would soon generate India's first significant expansion momentum in the eastern Himalayas – and, once again, the fear of China's own plans would stand at its core (Map 5).

Uneasy Allies

On 7 December 1941, Japan declared war on the United States and on British Malaya. Within two months, Kuala Lumpur and Singapore had fallen, the Dutch East Indies were invaded, and Rangoon was under siege. By late March 1942, most of South-East Asia was under Japanese control – including Burma. The Guomindang government found itself in a dire situation. At war with Tokyo since 1937, it had retreated further and further into China, eventually losing access to the sea; retrenched in Sichuan, it desperately needed overland supplies from the British and the Americans. With the loss of Burma, the last such land route had been cut off.

[8] Lamb, *Tibet, China & India, 1914–1950*, p. 421. Chinese Nationalist officials similarly leveraged foreign expeditions for information and strategic advantage in warlord-held areas. Justin M. Jacobs, 'Nationalist China's "Great Game": Leveraging foreign explorers in Xinjiang, 1927–1935', *Journal of Asian Studies*, 73:1 (2014), 43–64.
[9] Melvyn C. Goldstein and Gelek Rimpoche, *A history of modern Tibet, Volume 1: The demise of the Lamaist state, 1913–1951* (Berkeley: University of California Press, 1989), Chapter 8.

British India's position was not easy either. The Japanese advance had stopped at the foot of the Patkai Range, on the Indo-Burmese border. All that lay between India and Japanese-held Burma were Assam and the surrounding highlands. Lest eastern India's weak defences be shored up and a link with south-western China re-established, the collapse of the Guomindang and the invasion of India were distinct possibilities.[10]

In a few months, the internal situation and bilateral relationship of British India and Nationalist China radically changed. The two countries found themselves wartime partners, under direct threat from a common enemy. For both of them, the eastern Himalayas were now of unprecedented significance. Of all Allied-controlled areas, Assam lay closest to Chiang Kai-shek's besieged forces. But the Sadiya Frontier Tract and the Patkai were also precariously close to Japanese positions and completely unprotected – their formidable climate and landscape at once a shelter and an obstacle.

The Guomindang was the first to gauge the region's new importance. Pursuing an active frontier policy had been a mere expedient for the regime before 1937; with the Japanese invasion, however, Nationalist China's centre of gravity shifted west, to regions where its writ had been minimal and whose ethnic minorities were actively courted by Tokyo. Increasing its hold over these regions, eastern Tibet included, became a key condition of the regime's survival.[11]

When Japan severed China's railway to French Indochina in late 1940, Guomindang authorities decided to carve a new road to the sea via the shortest route possible: Dzayül and the Lohit Valley. The project participated in an intense infrastructure programme in China's western borderlands, betraying the regime's wartime unification strategy. Like Han youth's 'frontier service', geological surveys, or land reclamation, road building was meant to further Guomindang state-making among warlords and minorities.[12]

In February 1941, Chiang Kaishek and senior Guomindang officials ordered the construction of a highway via the Sadiya Frontier Tract. Two

---

[10] Christopher Bayly and Tim Harper, *Forgotten armies: The fall of British Asia, 1941–1945* (London: Allen Lane, 2004).

[11] Hsiao-ting Lin, *Modern China's ethnic frontiers: A journey to the west* (London: Routledge, 2011).

[12] See respectively: Andres Rodriguez, 'Building the nation, serving the frontier: Mobilizing and reconstructing China's borderlands during the War of Resistance (1937–1945)', *Modern Asian Studies*, 45:2 (2011), 345–376; Judd Kinzley, 'Crisis and the development of China's southwestern periphery: The transformation of Panzhihua, 1936–1969', *Modern China*, 38:5 (2012), 559–584; Joseph D. Lawson, 'Unsettled lands: Labour and land cultivation in western China during the War of Resistance (1937–1945)', *Modern Asian Studies*, 49:5 (2015), 1442–1484.

survey parties journeyed to Dzayül for reconnaissance. The Regent of Tibet – acting on behalf of the young fourteenth Dalai Lama – had no intention of letting the road happen. Fearing a Chinese machination to expand in Tibet, Lhasa despatched officials to prevent the surveyors from reaching Dzayül. Local *dzongpöns* expelled the party and destroyed bridges on the Yangtze to prevent further trespassing. Confronted with Lhasa's clout over western Kham and unable to afford an armed confrontation with it in the midst of Japanese attacks, Guomindang authorities bode their time.[13]

When Japan's invasion of Malaya and Singapore turned the Government of India into a wartime ally, Guomindang authorities revived their plans of an India-China highway. In February 1942, Chiang Kai-shek visited Delhi to strengthen the new alliance and proposed his project to India – this time via an alternative route from Assam to Yunnan via northern Burma. Within a couple of months, however, the Allies had lost control of Burma. Nationalist China revived its idea of a route through the eastern Himalayas.[14]

British Indian authorities were in a quandary over Chinese road-building proposals. China, their rival in Tibet and the eastern Himalayas, was now their ally as well – an ally that needed urgent and massive help if Japan was to be contained. Boosting trade between Sichuan and India by building a road gave added weight to the scheme. Assam itself had recently proposed to build one through that same Lohit Valley.[15] On the other hand, a trade route was a long-term project that would do little for the immediate war effort. It was more likely that it would prove a conduit for Chinese influence, undermining both the Tibet and Frontier Tract buffers. Many British officials were convinced that China would never abandon its ambition to retake Tibet.

Torn between wartime imperatives and persisting apprehensions about China's inner motives, London and Delhi took the initiative in order to control the situation. They informed the Guomindang that they would not build roads without Tibetan consent – which was not forthcoming – but simultaneously pressured Lhasa to authorise the transhipment of goods from India to China. This was to be done not through an Assam–Sichuan motorway but through pack transport on other routes.

The Guomindang agreed to a tripartite administration of trade but immediately proposed that the pack route follow the southern Kham road through Chamdo and Lhasa. This southern route was still far too

[13] Lin, 'Boundary, sovereignty, and imagination' (p. 34).
[14] Goldstein and Rimpoche, *A history of modern Tibet, Volume 1*, pp. 378–390.
[15] Robert Reid, *History of the frontier areas bordering on Assam, 1883–1941* (Delhi: Eastern Publishing, 1983), pp. 264–265.

close to Tibet's centres of power and to the eastern Himalayas for Lhasa's or Delhi's liking. India instead proposed the longer north road and, to placate China, worked to open up further pack routes through Xinjiang.[16] The Allies also embarked on a long-term infrastructure project to restore a motorable route to China: the Ledo Road. Starting from upper Assam and crossing the Patkai to reach Bhamo in northern Burma, and then connect with Yunnan, its 500-mile trajectory carefully avoided the eastern Himalayas.

In parallel, an innovative way was found to save the Guomindang from military and economic asphyxiation. Since crossing the eastern Himalayan 'Hump' was difficult and not to the liking of colonial authorities, the Allies would go over it. In April 1942, a gigantic military airlift operation began. For the next forty-two months, American planes flew across the Frontier Tracts and the nearby Naga Hills on an almost daily basis to deliver 650,000 tons of goods and weapons to China.[17] By December 1943, 10,000 tons of goods a month were being delivered to Yunnan.[18]

If British India and Nationalist China found themselves united around the common imperative of defeating Japan, their antagonistic goal to protect and strengthen their claim to the eastern Himalayas had therefore not disappeared. Wartime tensions and competition between the Allies and the Guomindang are well known, especially concerning Burma, but the question of the eastern Himalayas was equally destabilising.[19] In fact, discussions on using the region as a wartime link between China and India fuelled fears that the conflict would benefit the other side. London's sense of strategic vulnerability even led it to contemplate creating a Crown Colony in Assam's highlands, separate from both India and Burma.[20] The result was an uneasy alliance, made all the more

[16] Lin, *Tibet and Nationalist China's frontier*, pp. 125–132.

[17] Yikun Ge and Wei Li, 'Links between Yunnan and India during the Second World War', in *India and China in the colonial world*, ed. by Madhavi Thampi (New Delhi: Social Science Press, 2005), pp. 193–198.

[18] John D. Plating, *The Hump: America's strategy for keeping China in World War II* (College Station: Texas A&M University Press, 2011).

[19] Hans van de Ven, 'Stilwell in the stocks: The Chinese Nationalists and the Allied powers in the Second World War', *Asian Affairs*, 34:3 (2003), 243–259; Chan Lau Kit-ching, 'Symbolism as diplomacy: The United States and Britain's China policy during the first year of the Pacific War', *Diplomacy & Statecraft*, 16:1 (2005), 73–92; E. Bruce Reynolds, 'Failed endeavours: Chinese efforts to gain political influence in Thailand during World War II', *Intelligence and National Security*, 16:4 (2001), 175–204; J.E. Williams, 'Chiang Kai-shek's intervention in Indian politics: An episode in Sino-British relations, February–September 1942', *International Relations*, 5:5 (1977), 49–70.

[20] Frontier officials serving on the Assam–Burma border in 1930 had mooted the idea back in 1930. Robert Reid, the Governor of Assam in 1942, staunchly advocated reviving it. While London's main concern was strategic, Reid's support for the Crown Colony

uncomfortable by the fact that wartime circumstances emphasised just how little presence either China or India had on the ground.[21] Within a year, this unvoiced antagonism would result in British India's first real expansion momentum. In the event, it was not China's action that triggered it, but Tibet.

Towards Consensus

In winter 1942, two Tibetan generals (*depöns*) arrived in Tawang on an 'enquiry commission' to put a stop to migration between Tawang, Tsona, and Bhutan. This was unusual: senior Lhasa officials were not in the habit of visiting Monyül. While the *depöns* and their large retinue inspected the area and listed all its inhabitants and their property, Lhasa informed Bhutan that it expected its cooperation in the matter, invoking a 1799 mutual repatriation agreement.

Olaf Caroe was dismayed. Tibet's actions not only breached India's protectorate over Bhutan, they also indicated its continued disregard for the McMahon Line. Indeed, Lhasa claimed to have lost all records regarding their boundary with India. The Foreign Secretary's wariness grew when a telegram arrived from Assam soon after. A 'little trouble' had occurred in Balipara: headmen south of the Sela Pass had received 'peremptory and threatening' orders from the *depöns* to attend a gathering of Tibetan subjects. The PO had succeeded in convincing the Sherdukpens not to go, but Monpas further north had apparently obeyed the summons. For intelligence authorities, the implication of the *depöns*' actions was clear: 'either he's got his maps wrong, or this is a definite move forward by Tibet.'[22]

Indian officials were not far from the truth. Tibet was not a passive actor in the Himalayas. Under the new Regent, Lhasa authorities had resumed the thirteenth Dalai Lama's attempts to reform the state and increase control over Tibet's geographic periphery. These efforts were accompanied by initiatives to highlight Tibet's sovereign persona and

Scheme derived more from his self-proclaimed love for highland tribes, seen as in need of protection from the rest of India. Conveniently, this also meant wresting important chunks of colonial territory from elected Indian ministries. London, British Library, Reid Collection (1937–42), Letters and papers as Governor of Assam, Mss Eur E278/4 (5 January 1942).

[21] Jui-te Chang, 'An imperial envoy: Shen Zonglian in Tibet, 1943–1946', in *Negotiating China's destiny in World War II*, ed. by Hans J. van de Ven, Diana Lary and Stephen R. MacKinnon (Standford, CA: Stanford University Press, 2015), pp. 52–69.

[22] New Delhi, NAI, External Affairs Proceedings (1943), Claim by the Tibetan government that Tibetan subjects settled in Bhutan should be repatriated to Tibet. Measures taken to stabilize the MacMahon Line, 63/X/43 (Central Intelligence Officer Shillong to DIB, 30 January).

bolster foreign support for its recognition. A Foreign Affairs Bureau had been formed in 1942, and Lhasa had received two American envoys, hoping to be invited at the peace conference after the war.[23] The *depöns'* arrival in Monyül was thus part of a broader scheme of state-making, meant to reinforce Tibet not just vis-à-vis China *but also vis-à-vis India.*

None of this was to Caroe's or Assam's liking: Tibet's encroachment was worrying enough, but what if China used it for its own purposes? Had the Guomindang not 'publicly stated as one of their post-war desiderata' the settlement of Tibet's status? Lest 'some reality [be] given to the McMahon Line before the war ends', a peace conference between the Allies could well turn to India's disadvantage, territorially. The Governor-General agreed:

much would be gained by putting frontier disputes with Tibet behind us at the earliest possible moment. [The] main consideration ... is the possibility of Chinese establishing effective sovereignty over Tibet at the end of this war, or failing this using Tibet as stooges to encroach on Indian territory.[24]

Long discussions followed over the policy to adopt. As in 1910, Assam officials were the most forceful. '[M]aking the McMahon Line effective as soon as possible' was the only option, argued the Governor's Secretary, Phillip Mills.[25] Lhasa's behaviour was even more expansionist than initially thought. Supported by a substantial armed retinue, the *depöns* were levying as much tax as possible around Tawang. Their agents had descended to the foothills to conduct their census and assert Tibet's authority, presenting British India as a mere 'subordinate revenue collecting agency'.[26] 'Whereas we were formerly dealing with the misdemeanours of the local Monastery officials', concluded Mills, 'we are now dealing with the actions of an official of the Tibetan Government and there is now a Tibetan Post on Indian soil'.[27]

Assam authorities had other reasons to push for expansion. Since 1935, they had undertaken or sponsored several tours in the Himalayas. Expeditions to the Siang Basin had revealed another instance of Tibetan expansionism. After conquering the Pomé Kingdom north of Pemakö, Lhasa had expanded tax collection and corvée obligations as far

[23] Goldstein and Rimpoche, *A history of modern Tibet, Volume 1*, Chapter 11.
[24] NAI, External 63/X/43(Caroe, 13 February 1943, Secretary to the Assam Governor to Foreign Secretary, 27 January 1943, and Governor-General to Secretary of State for India, 11 March 1943).
[25] Itanagar, APSA, NEFA Secretariat (1943), Towang, 48/43-AD (Mills to Caroe, 23 February 1943).
[26] NAI, External 63/X/43 (PO Balipara to Secga, 8 March 1943).
[27] APSA, 48/43-AD (Mills to Clow, 15 March 1943).

as Karko, seventy miles south of the McMahon Line. In response, Assam officials had used whatever means were available to recover the initiative in the Adi areas: they had turned the foothills north of Pasighat into a 'control area' – ostensibly to fulfil the pan-Indian goal of abolishing slavery – and established temporary Assam Rifles outposts in the Upper Siang Basin.[28]

Without Delhi's sanction for extending 'control areas', frontier officials' ability to impose themselves vis-à-vis either the inhabitants or Lhasa's representatives was severely curtailed. Buddhist tax collectors merely waited for the monsoon and the closure of the outpost to descend on Adi areas; powerful villages such as Karko and Riga reinstated trade blocks and slave raids, affirming their political autonomy as soon as the last rifleman had left. Nothing less than London and Delhi's full financial, logistical, and political support would do.

In the External Affairs Department, Caroe agreed that India needed to take definite steps 'to occupy such points permanently as may be necessary' to fend off Tibet's 'encroachments' – in Tawang and along the McMahon Line. A formal protest had been lodged with Lhasa on their boundary violation and correspondence with Bhutan. Yet, while Lhasa had subsequently accepted dealing with the latter via Sikkim and recognised British jurisdiction over the Sherdukpens, it had carefully eschewed mentioning the McMahon Line.

The views of British India's Tibet cadre also had to be ascertained, and they were far more circumspect than those of Assam. The Sikkim Political Officer agreed that China presented a strategic threat. Some expansion was therefore warranted. But he also warned that, if India acted in Tawang as in the past, namely by contenting itself with a flag-waiving expedition, it would only succeed in antagonising Tibet without securing control over the region. His colleague in Lhasa was even more lukewarm: an Indian takeover of Tawang would only succeed in provoking Nationalist China to expand in Kham. It was better to limit India's reaction to a written protest mentioning the McMahon Line.

Advocates of a forward policy in the eastern Himalayas won the day. On 16 April 1943, the Secretary of State for India sanctioned the policy – and accepted to shoulder its costs. For the first time, authorities at every echelon of the colonial hierarchy had agreed to assert 'effective control' over the eastern Himalayas.[29]

---

[28] Reid, *History of the frontier areas*, pp. 257–262.
[29] NAI, External 63/X/43 (PO Sadiya to Mills, 31 March, Caroe, 13 February, Foreign Secretary to PO Sikkim, 20 March, Gould to Mills, 14 February, Ludlow to Gould, 10 March, 13 February, and Secretary of State to Governor-General, 16 April 1943).

Temporising on Tawang, Advancing Elsewhere

Major issues remained to be settled. Given the war and the lay of the land, deciding how to best administer the eastern Himalayas was not easy. Under Foreign Office pressure, London had put several caveats to its support of expansion. First, defeating Japan took priority. Advances in the Frontier Tracts could not be allowed to hamper the war effort. Second, frontier authorities should strictly avoid military clashes with Tibet. Relations with Lhasa had to be preserved, and the Guomindang should not be given any chance of 'stirring up propaganda in China and the US'.[30]

Respecting these two conditions was no small hurdle for frontier authorities. Control over the Assam Rifles, the semi-military force responsible for the Frontier Tracts, had been handed over to the army. Most of them were now engaged in the fight against Japan, over on the Burma border. In the circumstances, the Assam Governor was tentatively open to transferring responsibility for Balipara to the Sikkim Political Officer. Not only did the latter have his own troops, but Tawang was more easily reached from Bhutan than from Assam. Compared to the Tashigang route, which offered a motorable gradient, good potential railway connections, and a supply of local labour, the Sela route was longer and more difficult.[31]

Another question had to be answered: should India vindicate the whole of the McMahon Line or should it relinquish Tawang? London had made it clear that expansion in the Himalayas should not derail its alliance with China and the United States. Insisting on controlling Monyül, which had clearly been Tibetan territory for centuries and did not seem strategically essential, might do just that. London therefore instructed to go 'slow and carefully' on Tawang. The India Office even pondered whether, in order to achieve 'a good frontier ... for us', free of Tibetan encroachments, India might perhaps do better by making territorial concessions to Lhasa.[32]

This time, Sikkim and Assam spoke in unison: they rejected the idea of a transfer. Insisting on an Indian presence in Tawang was not a good idea vis-à-vis Lhasa, but the region was too important – whether in its own right or as a potential headquarters for other parts of the Himalayas – for India to relinquish it, argued the Sikkim PO. Moreover, 'any large abatement of claim ... [could] impair the 1914 Convention as a whole'. Assam

[30] Ibid. (Peel to Caroe, 22 April 1943).
[31] Ibid. (Preliminary report on routes to Towang, Gould, May 1943).
[32] Ibid. (Secretary of State to Governor-General, 17 April 1943).

was even more adamant: unless they occupied Tawang, there was nothing to keep the areas south of the Sela Pass free from Tibetan interference.[33]

Delhi, Assam, and Sikkim eventually compromised: expansion in Tawang would be divorced from the vindication of the McMahon Line elsewhere in the Frontier Tracts, and be dealt with at a more opportune time. Bar Tawang then, expansion would reconnoitre the different river basins and establishing a presence at strategic points in each of them. Indian authorities settled that the administration of the eastern Himalayas would remain with the Assam Governor, as Agent to India's Governor-General. Finally, a new administrative position was created specifically to spearhead state expansion: Adviser to the Governor. The incumbent was none other than Mills, the Assam official who had so strongly campaigned for a change of policy. On 20 July 1943, an express letter arrived in London: the Government of India was ready to move into the eastern Himalayas.[34]

By late 1943, the urgency of spreading Indian presence in the region had increased. In a book called *China's Destiny*, Chiang Kai-shek proclaimed the upcoming restoration of 'lost territories' to China.[35] Delhi and Assam's concerns were heightened by reports that Lhasa feared an imminent Guomindang invasion.[36] Meanwhile, the Second World War was taking a new turn on the Assam-Burma frontier. The Allies had registered several military successes in Burma, the construction of the Ledo Road was proceeding apace, and Assam's railway system was finally increasing its capacity. The press was starting to dream of an upcoming Allied victory.[37]

Mills, who had come into his new functions in early September, had but a few months before him to make the most of the 1943–1944 dry season. The Adviser to the Governor immediately set out to reorganise the Frontier Tracts' administrative set-up, shore up frontier staff, and assign them priority missions. Two sub-agencies were created in Balipara, one for the Subansiri Basin and one for the regions south of the Sela Pass.

---

[33] The *depön* in person had visited the region in April 1943. Ibid. (Sikkim to Foreign Secretary, 18 June).

[34] Ibid.   [35] Lin, *Tibet and Nationalist China's frontier*, pp. 140–141.

[36] New Delhi, NAI, External Affairs Proceedings (1943), Lhasa weekly letters, 62/X/43. In fact, the military crisis along the Sino-Tibetan border betrayed not so much a plan for the re-conquest of Tibet as a stratagem, engineered by Chiang Kai-shek, to impose direct control over the warlords of southwest China. Hsiao-ting Lin, 'War or stratagem? Reassessing China's military advance towards Tibet, 1942–1943', *China Quarterly*, 186 (2006), 446–462.

[37] 'Reconstruction after war: Development schemes for Assam', *Assam Tribune*, 24 December 1943.

Finding staff to explore them was easier said than done. The army had agreed to spare two Assam Rifles battalions for civilian use, but the Governor, worried about 'internal security' in the Assam plains, was reticent to assign them all to the eastern Himalayas. Even more difficult was the recruitment of civilian personnel, starting with frontier officers. The ideal candidate was a man who could face hiking hill after hill to meet largely unknown – and perhaps hostile – populations, that is, a 'young, stout, intelligent officer ... interested in tribal and jungle exploration', with a good deal of energy and a strategic mind. Few colonial officials fit these requirements even at the best of times, and the war had sent most of them to the Burma front.

In Sadiya, Mills had to appoint a PO considered much too junior for his responsibilities, but who at least spoke an Adi language and was in good physical shape. His assistant was a police officer of even greater youth, called Peter James. The search for the Lohit Valley PO took even longer: the head of the British Mission in Lhasa was needed there, his predecessor refused the Subansiri job on health grounds, and Kingdon-Ward was still persona non grata.[38] Eventually, Assam settled on an inexperienced officer from the Tibet cadre with no familiarity with Assam. Paul Mainprice had only been British Trade Agent in Tibet for eleven days when an External Affairs telegram ordered him to proceed immediately to Assam to 'do the Lohit Valley'.[39] The Subansiri would have to wait.

Expansion, Finally

It was in the Sela Sub-Agency, where thwarting Tibet's influence was the most urgent, that frontier authorities took their first step forward. Sherdukpens, Mijis, Hrussos, and Monpas were informed that any attempt at tax collection by Lhasa or Tawang envoys was henceforth illegal, and payments to Buddhist monasteries entirely voluntary (and preferably in kind). To prevent Tibetan officials from crossing the Sela Pass, the seasonal Assam Rifles station that had survived among the Sherdukpens since 1942 was transformed into a year-round administrative outpost.

In the Monpa country, the administration adopted a more circuitous strategy. A small dispensary opened at Dirang Dzong in February 1944. It was only once it proved popular enough among locals that a second permanent administrative outpost was sited there, nine months later. To create further support, the Rupa and Dirang outposts defended the Monpas and

---

[38] NAI, External 63/X/43 (Weightman, 4 October).
[39] Cambridge, CSAS (1936–1949), F.P. Mainprice Papers (20–25 October).

Sherdukpens against their neighbours' raids, and the PO told them that they need not feel forced to graze the *dzongpöns*' cattle free of charge. This did not quite succeed in stopping the latter from entering the sub-agency or demanding tribute, however.[40]

In the Lohit Valley, similar attempts to displace Tibetan influence generated tension. The new PO, Mainprice, had reached Walong after a long, arduous journey in early 1944. Mainprice had built a semi-permanent camp near Menilkrai and made a start on a permanent outpost at Walong itself when he was forced to go back to Gyantse – the Tibet cadre too faced personnel shortages. On his return in late 1944, he found that Dzayül's *dzongpöns* had pulled down the Walong outpost's stone foundations and retaliated against the Mishmis who had helped his party. Mainprice rebuilt the outpost and established staging houses to help communications but abandoned the idea of manning the McMahon Line itself: the Assam Rifles stationed at Walong were too dependent on the goodwill of Dzayül's *dzongpöns* (Figures 2.1 and 2.2).[41]

In the Siang Basin, the Sadiya PO and his assistant conducted extended tours to explore Adi areas and identify cooperative communities and individuals. Taking advantage of long-term warfare between many villages, they focused on interfering in, and eventually solving, inter-tribal disputes. The success of the enterprise was not a given, for several villages in the Upper Siang Basin had openly defied government parties. In the end, these tours ended without much incident. Even villages that had been particularly hostile in the past, or that were ready to resist the party according to settlements further downstream, in fact accepted its arrival. By summer 1944, the outposts of Riga and Karko had been revived, this time on a year-round basis.[42]

Expansion went far more slowly in Balipara's Subansiri Sub-Agency. Unable to find a Briton to explore it, Delhi accepted Mills' recommendation to hire an Austrian anthropologist, Christoph von Fürer-Haimendorf.[43] He departed for the Subansiri on a purely exploratory mission in early 1944. When he came back several months later, it was with positive news for Indian authorities. Fürer-Haimendorf had toured well beyond the areas visited by the Miri Mission of 1911–1912, and while he had not been able to go up to the snow line, he did not think economic ties with the Tibetan plateau translated into Lhasa's political control.[44]

[40] NAI, External 63/X/43.
[41] F.P. Mainprice Papers; Itanagar, APSA, NEFA Secretariat (1950), Tour Diary of Assistant Political Officer Lohit, B.C. Bhuyan, GA-12/50.
[42] Itanagar, APSA, NEFA Secretariat (1940), Tour diaries of the APO Pasighat for November 1940–April 1944.
[43] NAI, External 63/X/43.
[44] London, SOAS, Fürer-Haimendorf Papers (1945), Diary of Fürer-Haimendorf's first tour to the Apa Tani Valley, 1944–45, PP MS 19, Box 3; London, SOAS,

Figure 2.1 Paul Mainprice's expedition, c. 1945
© CSAS, Cambridge. Mainprice Collections, Box 19

Mills concluded that there was no need to rush to the McMahon Line in the region and that Assam's frontier administration should rather increase contact with the Apatanis and southern Nyishis. By early 1945, a Political Officer was appointed to establish the region's first outpost.

By the end of their second season of expansion, Indian authorities had recovered the foothold into the eastern Himalayas lost after 1914; indeed, they had for the first time succeeded in implanting outposts inland, several of them permanent, and acquired more knowledge of the region. Moreover,

Fürer-Haimendorf Papers (1945), Diary, Camp Duta, May 1944–February 1945, PP MS 19, Box 4.

Figure 2.2 Wartime expansion in the Lohit Valley: The Changwinti
outpost
© CSAS, Cambridge. Mainprice Collections, Box 19

these forays had not, as in the past, caused violent incidents with the inhabitants of the Frontier Tracts. In Charduar, Pasighat, and Tirap, officers had
begun experimenting with agriculture, planting seeds or teaching terrace
cultivation to foothill inhabitants.[45]

But this was only the beginning. Much of the region remained unexplored, especially the Subansiri and Dibang basins, and, even in the few
areas where it had established a year-round presence, India's 'effective

---

[45] Itanagar, APSA, NEFA Secretariat (1945), Annual administration report of the Balipara
Frontier Tract for 1944–1945, Ex/BFT/8/45; Itanagar, APSA, NEFA Secretariat (1943),
Tour diaries of the PO Tirap, EX/225/43.

control' was still in its infancy. Across the Himalayan range, however, these developments were of growing concern for Nationalist China.

The Dangers of Trade

In mid-1944, British authorities noticed that newly published Guomindang maps included the Frontier Tracts in Chinese territory. Pressed for an explanation by the British ambassador, the Guomindang government replied that it did not see the problem and played down the issue: the map was but an unprecise draft, to be corrected later on.[46]

Some time later, two men came to see the Sadiya PO. They wanted permission for a large-scale trade scheme through the Lohit Valley. The men, who introduced themselves as Mr. Chen from the Tai Kyi Company and Mr. Thomas from the Peking Syndicate, said that their interest in the Lohit Valley was eminently pragmatic. The route was much shorter than the Kalimpong-Lhasa route used to tranship goods between China and India and not so plagued by banditry. The PO pointed out this would mean carrying 30,000 coolie and 10,000 mule loads per season, notwithstanding arranging for ferries, trucks, and godowns. Chen and Thomas replied that they would themselves organise ferries, strengthen the bridges, and maintain the road. As for coolies and mules, their agents were already recruiting in south-eastern Tibet.

Assam frontier officials balked at the idea. The Tai Kyi scheme would entail 6,000 porters constantly plying the Lohit Valley and the posting of many customs and security staff in the area, clashing with colonial road building and burdening Sadiya's already overstretched administrative corps. It was also likely to harm colonial authorities' relations with the Lohit's inhabitants: the latter's fragile human and material resources – the valley was sparsely populated and, at that time at least, food and fuel deprived – were already under pressure due to Indian outposts and road construction.

A far more strategic reason lay behind these justifications. Like the Central Intelligence Bureau and the Tibet cadre, Assam officials feared the Guomindang's hand behind the project. Chen and Thomas claimed they had Lhasa's approval to launch a route through Dzayül, and indeed that it was participating in its construction. Indian intelligence services thought otherwise. Why would Tibetan authorities support a Sadiya–Rima trade route when they had doggedly rejected the prospect two years before? And why did the Tai Kyi Company and Peking

---

[46] Itanagar, APSA, NEFA Secretariat (1945), Inaccuracies in the delineation of Sino-Burma and Indo-Tibetan boundaries, Misc/16/45AD.

Syndicate want to trade for three years, when the Ledo Road was about to be completed?[47]

British officials in Tibet rather suspected another attempt to extend Guomindang influence: the trade route 'would give China a dominant position in South-Eastern Tibet' and hamper Assam's influence among the Mishmis. If the proposal became reality, the majority of traders on the route would be Han or pro-Chinese Khampas. India would prove unable to furnish the security staff required to prevent banditry around Dzayül or retaliation by the Mishmis, and 'the next step would be Chinese armed escorts for the convoys on the Tibetan section'. And, if that was not enough, Delhi would not have the capacity to introduce registration for subjects crossing the McMahon Line, making trans-border smuggling – already flourishing – and a Chinese population influx very likely.[48]

Just as in 1942, Indian authorities avoided a clash with China by going via Tibet. While Assam officials were instructed to be 'blandly non-cooperative' towards Chinese traders, Delhi tactically informed Lhasa of the Tai Kyi proposal. As expected, Tibetan authorities' opposition to a Sichuan–Assam trade route had not abated, leaving India free to shelve the project out of respect for Tibet. To smoothen the diplomatic situation, the Indian government instructed its Supply Department to undertake the delivery of private Chinese goods – *through the Kalimpong route*.

Was the Guomindang truly behind the Tai Kyi Company's proposal to open a major trade route through Sadiya and Rima? The possibility should not be discounted. Nationalist China had successfully used the transhipment of goods through Lhasa and Kalimpong to increase its influence and sent agents disguised as merchants.[49] Given that China was then at a disadvantage in the eastern Himalayas (unlike Zhao Erfeng, the Guomindang could not reach Dzayül or Pomé), the trade route proposal might well have been a creative strategy to mitigate it without seeming overtly expansionist.[50]

---

[47] New Delhi, NAI, External Affairs Proceedings (1944), Sadiya–Rima route – export to China – attempts to dispatch supplied by Tai Kyi Trading company, and Peking syndicate and Tung Hsing Co Sadiya. Customs due on Tibetan traders using the Lohit Valley route, 263/CA/44. Suspicions might also have been heightened by rumours, in late 1943, of a proposed postal service between Assam and Sichuan. New Delhi, NAI, External Affairs Proceedings (1944), Lhasa weekly letters, Gyantse and Yatung news reports, and other misc. reports on affairs in Tibet, Bhutan, and Sikkim, 182/CA/44 (Tibetan intelligence report, 22 December 1943).

[48] NAI, External 263/CA/44 (Richardson, 4 January 1945, and Central Intelligence Officer Assam, 24 December 1944).

[49] NAI, External 62/X/43 (Yatung report, 15 January).

[50] British Indian intelligence officials viewed with concern the increased presence of Chinese merchants in Tibet and its main outlet, the north Indian town of Kalimpong. They were convinced that trade was a means for China to assert its suzerainty over Tibet.

As in 1910, the fear of China was key in persuading Delhi and London to undertake a forward policy. And just as in 1910 – in a pattern that would recur time and again between China and India – internally driven developments, and their interpretation across the border, ended up affecting their relations.

There had been no repeat of the cat-and-mouse game with the Qing around Menilkrai, however. If competition there was, the war made it both more diffuse and indirect than at the start of the twentieth century: diffuse, because China and British India's concurrent designs over the eastern Himalayas had to be balanced with their common interest – protecting the region from Japan, preserving connections between China and the Indian subcontinent, and maintaining wartime alliances; indirect, because these imperatives interacted with the Tibetan state's own expansionism.

Indian officials were convinced that Tibet was taking advantage of the war to further its position south of the McMahon Line. Lhasa's preoccupations were more likely defensive in nature. Confronted with Chiang Kai-shek's attempts to penetrate Kham through road building, Tibetan authorities could reasonably fear a Sino-British strategic realignment at their expanse. In 1942, the British had ostensibly sided with the Guomindang by forcing Lhasa to agree to the transhipment of goods through Tibet. Securing Tibetan territory, in those conditions, might have appeared essential.

Domestic considerations likely played a part in Tibet's eastern Himalayan policy. In the uncertain wartime climate, the Tibetan Regent once again sought to modernise the state apparatus, starting with its army. The power struggle with aristocratic and monastic estates over the raising of funds and manpower for the purpose began anew.[51] In this context, the eastern Himalayas might have presented an alternative way to expand state resources and capabilities without increasing pressures on the Tibetan plateau. The result was a triangular competition between China, India, and Tibet, each side seeking to increase its authority vis-à-vis the other two.

Another Guomindang survey party apparently explored the Sadiya–Rima route in 1944, carefully noting the boundary signs placed around Menilkrai. New Delhi, NAI, External Affairs Proceedings (1944), Tibetan intelligence reports received from CIO. Assam comments of the British mission, Lhasa, and the PO Sikkim on reports about the Chinese ultimatum, 576/CA/44 (CIO Shillong to Intelligence Bureau, 5 June 1944 and Tibet Intelligence Report, 18 January 1944).

[51] Goldstein and Rimpoche, *A history of modern Tibet, Volume 1*, chapters 11–12.

The Consensus Disintegrates

For Mills and his colleagues in the Assam frontier cadre, India would win the contest by expanding further; they were confident that this momentum would last. The Second World War was slowly coming to an end in the 'China–Burma–India Theatre'. In July 1944, an attempted Japanese invasion of India had been thwarted at Kohima and Imphal, near the Burma border. Soon, Allied armies would leave, and Mills hoped that many expansion constraints would disappear. As the army would release doctors and engineers, the stranglehold that had prevented India from manning Frontier Tracts dispensaries or getting started on their big infrastructural project – a road through the Lohit Valley – would ease. The Adviser to the Governor had already received a most positive piece of news: military authorities had accepted to supply frontier posts by plane.[52]

In this optimistic atmosphere, the PO for the Tirap Frontier Tract – a previously scantly administered region south of the Lohit Valley, associated with Balipara and Sadiya upon its creation in 1943 – drew up a 'blueprint for post-war reconstruction'. Proposals were made to start educational facilities.[53] Meanwhile, Mainprice returned from another tour to the Lohit Valley, convinced that the McMahon Line should be redrawn to India's advantage. If Delhi wanted to spread its influence and intelligence powers over Kham (and it should), Walong would not do. India should rather shift the boundary further north and incorporate Dzayül, with its rich rice-growing lands, sizeable population, and abundance of flat land.

The PO dreamed of a time when the Lohit Valley Road would go right up to Walong, redirecting 'all the trade and animal traffic of Eastern Tibet ... right down to India'; the revised McMahon Line would then enable India to control both the 'easy summer route' between Assam and Kham and the route into northern Burma.[54] Mainprice's superiors accordingly obtained sanction to continue the Lohit Valley Road, and his successor was instructed to invite the Rima *dzongpöns* to Walong to smooth out relations and obtain their acceptance of Indian expansion.[55]

---

[52] New Delhi, NAI, External Affairs Proceedings (1945), Recruitment of 150 porters and 5 sardars for transporting ration to posts in Siang Valley, Assam, 259-CA/45.

[53] London, BL, Miscellaneous papers relating to the North-East Frontier of India (1945), 'Blueprint for Sadiya: A post-war reconstruction plan for Sadiya Frontier Tract', by GED Walker, MSS Eur D1191/11.

[54] New Delhi, NAI, External Affairs Proceedings (1946), Ratification of the McMahon Line below Rima, 307-CA/46 (Mainprice to Mills, 12 September 1945).

[55] New Delhi, NAI, External Affairs Proceedings (1946), Meeting between the Assistant Political Officer, Lohit Valley, and Rima Dzongpön, 49-NEF/46.

In fact, the unstable alignment of goals among India's metropolitan, central, and regional authorities that had coalesced after 1942 was about to disintegrate. Instead of freeing up material resources and manpower, the end of the Second World War would cause Indian state expansion to stall, yet again. External Affairs officials excepted, central authorities quickly reverted to the position that administering the eastern Himalayas was not essential to India's security.

Defence and military authorities were among the first to lose their faith in the region's geopolitical importance. In August 1945, Caroe organised a meeting to convince key ministries that expansion in the Frontier Tracts was 'a matter of vital importance'. But the Defence Department was categorical: the army had no interest in maintaining road communications in the Frontier Tracts. Instead of pursuing the Lohit Valley Road project, Assam frontier officials would do better to limit themselves to the maintenance of the existing track. The maximum the military would commit to was to create 'forward observation posts in time of need'.[56]

By September 1945, twelve of Assam's eighteen airfields had been designated as being surplus to defence requirements. The army decided that even the Sadiya airfield was not essential to their purposes and that, should it be maintained, 'it should be only for its political value'.[57] The Defence Ministry, which had initially promised to continue airdrops to outposts after the war, suddenly decided in April 1946 that the border did not warrant the air force's investment in time, efforts, personnel, money, or infrastructure.[58]

Several factors explained the novel disinterest of many central authorities for the eastern Himalayas. Not everyone agreed that China continued to present a severe challenge to India's claim to the region. Many officials believed that the 'grain of the country' was 'a barrier but not a route', and that north-eastern India was hence naturally protected from Chinese invasion.[59] Chiang Kai-shek's troops, meanwhile, had begun leaving Assam, and the provincial government was taking steps to deport Chinese civilians present there.[60] Most importantly, civil war had just

---

[56] New Delhi, NAI, External Affairs Proceedings (1945), Programme of political work in the North East Frontier Agency for 1945–46, 257-CA/45 (Minutes of a meeting to consider the policy for the Tribal Areas on the NEF).

[57] New Delhi, NAI, External Affairs Proceedings (1946), Post-war maintenance of airfields on the NEF, 61-NEF/46.

[58] New Delhi, NAI, External Affairs Proceedings (1947), Maintenance of airfields in the North East Frontier, 117-NEF.

[59] London, BL, Reid Papers (1946), Assam and the North East Frontier of India, Mss Eur E278/19, Chapter 9.

[60] Guwahati, ASA, Home – Miscellaneous Files (1945), Deportation of certain Chinese subjects from India HMI/23/45.

resumed in China. With the Communists and the Guomindang at each other's throat, the Indian General Staff felt confident that China would not try expanding in the eastern Himalayas any time soon. Jawaharlal Nehru, independent India's first Prime Minister, would accordingly command the Assam Governor to keep commitments to a minimum.[61]

External Affairs authorities disagreed. In August 1946, the Guomindang formally complained about India's activities in the region. 'Anxious, in consonance with the traditional friendly relations between China and Great Britain, to maintain the present [boundary] position', Nationalist China was ready to 'assume that [these] acts of aggression on Chinese territorial sovereignty [were] not the intention of the British Indian frontier officials' but demanded India's immediate withdrawal from the Lohit.[62] Delhi did not comply, but External Affairs officials rejected Mainprice's proposal and abandoned the idea of organising bilateral meetings with the Dzayül *dzongpöns*.[63] A brutal internal conflict did not mean Chinese leaders had lost sight of Tibet and the eastern Himalayas.

This was not sufficient to convince the rest of the Indian government to maintain full support for state expansion. With the end of the Second World War, the issue of India's independence had come back to the centre of subcontinental politics. Countenanced by London when India's north-eastern frontier had seemed directly vulnerable, the Crown Colony scheme was quickly abandoned by British authorities: the scheme was deemed too costly, and its benefits not worth causing huge nationalist opposition in India.[64] As for the Indian National Congress, whose leaders were about to take over the Interim Government, they had little time to consider expansion on a frontier they hardly knew anything about.

For the second time in the twentieth century, Indian state expansion in the eastern Himalayas fizzled out after a short effervescence. Assam's frontier administration found itself more starved for cash and materials than ever. When a young official was sent to explore the Subansiri in March 1945, the only way he succeeded was by

[61] New Delhi, NAI, Home Affairs Proceedings (1947), Expansion of special police forces. Question of the utilisation of the Assam Rifles in the settled area of Assam, 18/8/47-Police.
[62] Itanagar, APSA, NEFA Secretariat Files (1947), Protest by the Chinese government regarding the Indian government's policy on the MacMahon Line, 24/C/47.
[63] New Delhi, NAI, External Affairs Proceedings (1947), Meeting in December 1945–January 1946 between F.P. Mainprice, APO Lohit, and Rima Dzongpön to establish personal contacts, 61-NEF/47.
[64] *The transfer of power, 1942–47*, ed. by N. Mansergh and E.W.R. Lumby, 12 vols (London: H.M.S.O., 1980), Volume V (Amery to Wavell, 28 September 1944).

relying on US troops and on the black market for his stores: no British military depots were left in Assam.[65] Meanwhile, after several years of supporting their outposts by air, local authorities were forced to requisition tribal porters once again.[66]

The staff situation was hardly better. In early 1947, the Sadiya Officer acted as assistant for the headquarters, oversaw the Lohit Valley Road project in the absence of a District Engineer, and somehow still managed to spare 188 days a year for touring. The overstretch worsened after August 1947, when the Indian Civil Service disappeared. To make matters worse, the Assam government failed to request additional posts for frontier staff. As a result, the newly appointed Subansiri PO now doubled as PO for Balipara, and his colleague for Sadiya for both the Abor and Mishmi hills.[67]

So difficult was the replacement of European officers that a young Parsi from Bombay with only six years of service was chosen as the new Adviser to the Governor: Nari Rustomji. By his own admission, Rustomji did not have 'a single day's experience of administration in the hill areas'. Two weeks of briefings was all he got before stepping into a role that involved 'the laying down and implementation of policy on issues as divergent as devolution of power to indigenous tribal institutions and defence of a frontier several thousand miles long'. In the event, Rustomji would quickly come into his own as Adviser. For now, he could only count on the advice of a few British officers, temporarily retained for the sake of continuity and to remediate manpower shortages.[68]

So far as it could, the frontier administration tried to maintain administrative and infrastructural projects. A permanent outpost in the Subansiri was established at Kure, near the Apatani Valley.[69] The Interim Government adopted a five-year development plan for the Frontier Tracts after difficult negotiations with the central Finance Department. At the core of the Rs 12,800,000 scheme was the build-up

---

[65] New Delhi, NAI, External Affairs Proceedings (1945), Tour diaries of Capt Davy in the Dafla hills, 241-CA/45.

[66] NAI, 61-NEF/46; New Delhi, NAI, External Affairs Proceedings (1947), Supply-dropping operations on the NEF. Division of responsibility between the civil and military authorities, 31-NEF/47.

[67] New Delhi, NAI, External Affairs Proceedings (1947), Appointment of Captain Campbell, Major Kathing and Captain Sailo for work in the Assam Tribal Areas, 80-NEF/47.

[68] Nari Rustomji, *Imperilled frontiers: India's north-eastern borderlands* (Delhi: Oxford University Press, 1983), pp. 39–40.

[69] Ursula Graham Bower, *The hidden land* (London: John Murray, 1953).

of infrastructure. With the exception of the Lohit Valley Road, most of it would remain unrealised.[70]

The Limbo of Independence

India became independent on 15 August 1947, but the expansion lull continued. The clearest sign of it was the Ledo Road in Tirap. Seen as too expensive and 'serving no useful purpose', its maintenance beyond Hell's Gate was abandoned in 1947. Built at extraordinary human and material cost, the road quickly fell into disrepair. From a military corridor, it became an informal trade route. Indian traders who requested its reopening saw their demands ignored. 'It will be unfortunate if the firm suffers loss ... through being unable to move the surplus stores which it has purchased', deplored the Indian Home Ministry, 'but this is not sufficient justification for bringing on ourselves the difficulties in the way of frontier and excise control which the opening of the road would entail'.[71]

Far from harnessing opportunities to enhance its reach, the newly independent Indian state was reluctant to exercise certain functions in the eastern Himalayas. India's north-east frontier had been at best a passing preoccupation for Indian nationalist circles. If Nehru repeatedly mentioned the Himalayas in *A Discovery of India*, written during the war, it was the north-west of the range, and particularly Kashmir, that he mainly had in mind. The contrast was all the greater with Han intellectuals, actively engaged in re-imagining a Chinese national space encompassing minorities such as Tibetans.[72] Moreover, Pan-Asianism and the fight against colonialism had brought the Congress leadership and the Guomindang together in the 1930s. Although the cooperation faltered after the end of the Second World War, the break had more to do with conflicting views of internationalism and communism than with Indian fears of Chinese Nationalist expansion.[73]

In any case, the immediate priorities of the new Indian authorities lay elsewhere. For Nehru, the most pressing matter was to manage the consequences of the creation of Pakistan: drawing up a border;

---

[70] London, BL (1946), North-East Frontier Agency and Tribal Areas Five-Year Plan, Mss Eur D1191/17; New Delhi, NAI, External Affairs Proceedings (1946), Political work in the tribal areas of Assam for 1946–47, 65-NEF/46.

[71] New Delhi, NAI, Home Affairs Proceedings (1948), Opening of the Ledo Road upto Pangsa Pass, 51/67/48-Public.

[72] Jawaharlal Nehru, *The discovery of India* ([S.l.]: Meridian Books, 1945); Yudru Tsomu, 'Taming the Khampas: The Republican construction of eastern Tibet', *Modern China*, 39:3 (2013), 319–344.

[73] Brian Tsui, 'The plea for Asia – Tan Yunshan, Pan-Asianism and Sino-Indian relations', *China Report*, 46:4 (2010), 353–370.

controlling communal riots; organising the relief and rehabilitation of Partition refugees; reorganising the administration. Moreover, a deep antagonism was emerging between India and Pakistan. The immediate attentions of Indian defence authorities went to the border with their new neighbour. As for India's economic and financial structures, Partition had dealt them an important blow. The Finance Ministry had to advocate staunch financial retrenchment.[74]

To divert India's attention further, there was growing unrest on the Assam–Burma border. A self-determination movement had taken root among Naga groups during transfer of power negotiations. A Naga National Council was demanding autonomy within India and the right to determine their status (with or without it) after some time. Partly for this, partly for fear of China, Indian frontier authorities intensified their activities in the Naga Hills Tribal Area, thinly administered before the Second World War. Placed under the authority of the Adviser to the Governor like the nearby Himalayas, it was now prioritised over them. Vast discrepancies in Assam's requirements for red cloth – given to cooperative chiefs and notables – hint that Delhi considered it far more important to build support in the Naga Hills than in the Frontier Tracts.[75]

The last reason for retrenchment was that, in 1947, administrative powers over the Frontier Tracts had been transferred from the Assam Governor to the elected government of the province. This other transfer of power petered out. The local government had few funds or personnel at its disposal to implement a real frontier policy; it also considered it far more pressing to mitigate the Partition's economic consequences and convince the Assamese that having a non-colonial government did make a difference.[76] The administration and development of the Frontier Tracts could wait.

---

[74] For example, New Delhi, NAI, External Affairs Proceedings (1947), Budget estimates for the year 1948–49 for five year development plan of Assam Tribal Areas, 132-NEF/47; New Delhi, NAI, External Affairs Proceedings (1947), Implementation of the education scheme of the five year development plan of the Assam Tribal Areas, 103-NEF/47.

[75] Itanagar, APSA, NEFA Secretariat (1947), Supply of red cloth for NEFA A/204/47.

[76] Assam's plantation economy and lack of political significance meant that it was 'in private hands'. Stabilising its public finances had been a constant problem. David Ludden, 'Spatial inequity and national territory: Remapping 1905 in Bengal and Assam', *Modern Asian Studies*, 46:3 (2012), 1–43 (p. 19). The Partition only worsened the situation. Assam's richest district was transferred to East Pakistan. Relief and rehabilitation challenges abounded: refugees from communal riots poured in, and Sylheti Hindus preferred to move to nearby parts of Assam. And the creation of East Pakistan had virtually cut Assam off from the rest of India and from its natural trade outlets. Anindita Dasgupta, 'Remembering Sylhet: A forgotten story of India's 1947 partition', *Economic and Political Weekly*, 43:31 (2008), 18–22.

This did not mean there was a 'blackout' in the Indian presence in the eastern Himalayas as in 1914.[77] Between 1947 and 1950, the skeleton-like frontier administration somehow tried to build on wartime initiatives. But in the end, the most significant action taken by the Indian state with regard to the Frontier Tracts immediately after independence was their formal incorporation into the new Union of India.

Since they had been partially or totally excluded from political reforms linked to the Government of India Act, 1935, the fate of Assam's highlands was not a foregone conclusion. The Constituent Assembly created a North-East Frontier (Assam) Tribal and Excluded Areas Sub-Committee to formulate constitutional proposals relative to these regions. The underlying principle was that their ethnic and cultural distinctiveness and their political isolation would necessitate specific provisions.

In November 1948, constitution makers adopted a 'Sixth Schedule', giving Assam's hill tribes a series a series of political and socio-economic safeguards, including the formation of Autonomous Districts and Regions headed by councils with a wide range of powers. This stood in sharp contrast with the containment of group rights in the constitution as a whole.[78] The Frontier Tracts and the Naga Hills Tribal Area's position within the Schedule was an awkward one. Their legal status in colonial times had been blurry in the extreme. Though the plains areas of the Frontier Tracts counted as 'Excluded Areas', and thus part of British India, the bulk of the region was classified as a 'Tribal Area'. As such, it belonged to a territorial limbo – being 'not part of British India or of Burma or of any Indian State' and certainly not, since this was about imperial views, part of a foreign power.[79] Signalling independent India's claim to the succession of British Indian territory was therefore particularly crucial in the eastern Himalayas and the northern Patkai.

---

[77] BL, MSS Eur D1191/111.

[78] Rochana Bajpai, *Debating difference: Minority rights and liberal democracy in India* (New Delhi: Oxford University Press, 2010).

[79] London, BL, IOR (c.1937), Burma–Assam border: Extension of the control area in the Naga Hills, IOR/L/PS/12/3116 – Coll 22/4 (Unsigned letter, c. 1942). In 1936, a Government of India (Excluded and Partially Excluded Areas) Order had earmarked the whole of the Frontier Tracts as 'excluded areas' and thus as constitutionally part of Assam. A year later, however, the Centre decided to reserve that status only to the 'administered' parts of the eastern Himalayas, turning the rest into 'Tribal Areas', defined under the Government of India Act 1935. Further discussions on whether the decision had been legally proclaimed show the confusion that reigned about the so-called 'administration' of the eastern Himalayas in the late colonial period. London, BL, IOR (1936–1947), Excluded and partially excluded areas of Assam: Constitutional position, IOR/L/PS/12/3115A (External Affairs Secretary to Under-Secretary, 10 December 1945).

Accordingly, the Assam Frontier Tracts and the Naga Hills Tribal Areas were listed under the Sixth Schedule – with the provision that its key aspects, like political representation and administrative autonomy, would not yet be implemented there. The Constituent Assembly's Sub-Committee on Assam had come back from a series of tours of the province – about to become a state – with the conviction that giving Balipara, Sadiya, or Tirap's inhabitants political citizenship was for now unadvisable, 'until ... an area is or can be brought under regular administration'. Made on the basis of a most cursory visit to the Frontier Tracts, the justification was that the Nagas, the Mishmis, or the Nyishis were not ready to participate in India's political life.[80]

The decision had in fact as much to do with India's still extremely limited presence in the eastern Himalayas. Granting the region's inhabitants the right to take part in the country's democratic process would have exposed the fact that the Indian state knew not the size of the population of the region, nor indeed where it lived, and could not possibly organise elections given the fact it had not yet completed a single road through it.

The Far Shores of War

For many of the Frontier Tracts' inhabitants, the creation of a government outpost was but part of the more general upheaval caused by the Second World War. After Japan conquered Burma in 1942, Assam saw Allied troops pouring in by the thousands. Barracks, arsenals, depots, military hospitals began to dot the countryside in much of Upper Assam and the Patkai, while rail and road networks were drastically expanded.

If Balipara was comparatively less affected, the Sadiya Frontier Tract saw troops and supply organisations settle at the foot of the hills, especially east of the Siang River. Soldiers from Britain, China, Australia, Africa, or the United States implanted themselves around places like Sadiya, with their rest camps, their airfields, their equipment stores.[81] In the Tracts' plains areas, forests were cut 'to make room for enormous military camps' and hills 'slashed out for the construction of roads'.[82] Tirap, through which the Ledo Road was being built, was particularly affected. In the process, the Inner Line's capacity to limit interaction between Assam's administered districts and 'loose control' areas eroded.

---

[80] *The framing of India's constitution: A study*, ed. by B. Shiva Rao, 5 vols (New Delhi: Indian Institute of Public Administration, 1968), Volume III, pp. 703–705.

[81] Oshong Ering. Interview with the author, 11 February 2014, Pasighat (Arunachal Pradesh).

[82] Eleanor Bor, *Adventures of a botanist's wife* (London: Hurst & Blackett, 1952), p. 161.

Chinese and American troops were there in support of the massive operations over the Hump. Supply planes initially flew over the Patkai, but in 1944, their itinerary was diverted directly on the eastern Himalayas.[83] For the remote villages that saw them fly over their heads, these planes appeared as huge, menacing birds making an atrocious tumult. Sometimes the birds would fall to the ground: between the mountains, the rain, and the limits of aerial technology, it was not rare for planes to come crashing down. Confronted by strange-looking men and stranded cargo, villagers might both take some unknown artefacts and help an injured crew member. The encounter was often followed by another one, this time with a dedicated American rescue team often expecting the inhabitants' assistance.[84]

This was but one of the ways in which the population of the Frontier Tracts participated in the war effort. In early 1942, the speed of Japan's advance across Burma generated a gigantic exodus of European and Indian refugees along with Allied troops. Mishmis, Khamtis, or Padam Adis lived along some of these escape routes. Many saved exhausted refugees from certain death.[85]

Far more widespread was the recruitment of tribals from the foothills as porters or road workers. Anterior to the war, the practice by which a frontier official summoned a community to supply a given number of men and women to carry loads increased dramatically, even farther than the Himalayan foothills. Villages who refused to comply could be fined and their notables arrested.[86] Government parties were confronted with women pleading for their men not to be requisitioned, or with old men hoping to persuade them that they could not work anymore.[87] Sometimes participation was such that it endangered cultivation.[88] While porterage or roadworks were not favoured activities, the Allies' insatiable need for manpower made them lucrative, unlike in peacetime. Many tribals from the foothills already engaged in casual work in the plains, for example as cane cutters; others tapped rubber to sell it in the settled areas. The Assam frontier administration began to use US Air Force or Royal Air Force planes as an alternative means of supplying outposts in the later

---

[83] London, BL, IOR (1944), Tour notes of the Adviser to the Governor of Assam for Tribal Areas and States, 1944–1946 – 1944 Tour notes, IOR/L/PS/12/3120, p. 3.

[84] Itanagar, APSA, NEFA Secretariat (1945), Reports on air crashes, Misc-32/45-AD.

[85] Geoffrey Tyson, *Forgotten frontier* (Calcutta: W.H. Targett & Co, 1945); Egul Padung. Interview with the author, 11 February 2014, Pasighat (Arunachal Pradesh); Cambridge, CSAS, Mackrell Collection (1942), Rescue operations (film), Film 1.

[86] APSA, Tour diaries of the APO Pasighat 1940–1944, pp. 19–20, 25, 45.

[87] SOAS, PP MS 19, Box 3, p. 18.

[88] London, BL, IOR (1943), Report on the Frontier tribes of Assam for the year 1942–1943, IOR/V/10/121.

stages of the war.[89] This decreased the obligation to porter for the administration itself (generally for little pay), so some Galos or Minyong Adis who had engaged in other forms of wage labour in the plains chose roadworks or bridge building, provided it was short term and ideally in the cold season.

Increased contact with external actors went together with the ever-greater penetration of capital, sometimes quite far inland. The transformation of much of the eastern Himalayas into a satellite economy accelerated. In parts of the Siang Basin, villagers began to descend en masse to the Assam plains in winter to work for local sawmills or to cultivate the fields of influential Pasighat tribals. By the end of the war, even isolated Adis from the Siang–Subansiri borderlands had begun to do the same.

Changes in the political economy often led to a novel relationship with frontier officials. On tour, the more welcoming villages were often those who sent many of their members to the plains. Some men from the Adi foothills joined the Assam Rifles. Even people not involved in wage labour were more likely to come down to Pasighat than before the war, hoping to benefit from expanding commercial networks.[90]

The number of shops on the edge of the Inner Line increased alongside the number of troops. Their mostly Marwari owners were there to fulfil the military's immense requirements, but they also took advantage of growing monetisation among certain Himalayan communities. In their stores, tribals freshly released from roadworks or porterage found a host of articles on which to spend newly acquired cash – from yarn and the indispensable bag of salt to tea, cloth, or cigarettes.[91] Equally, a Mishmi or a Padam might come down from his village to sell his produce at the store. Most were agricultural produce, like rice, which Galos living as far north as the edge of the Bori country would exchange for cash in the plains, before buying their own needs,[92] but experience showed that some manufactured articles, like the beautiful Adi rugs, were popular among American troops. Tribal dress styles were evolving, touring officers noticing an increasing number of men and women clad in garments bought in the bazar, like the Yambo shawl of *markin* cloth.[93]

The dynamic betrayed intensifying human and economic flows across the borderlands of the China–Burma–India Theatre. Notwithstanding the

---

[89] For example, NAI, External 259-CA/45.
[90] Itanagar, APSA, NEFA Secretariat (1946), Tour diaries of PLS James for August 1945–December 1946, pp. 9, 21, 29, 33.
[91] Cambridge, CSAS, FP Mainprice Papers (1936–49), 'Paul, 1943 Diaries', Box I, Part I.
[92] APSA, James tour diaries August 1945–December 1946, p. 34.
[93] 'Paul, 1943 Diaries' (14 November); APSA, James tour diaries August 1945–December 1946, p. 21.

failure of the Sadiya–Rima road scheme, the Lohit Valley's importance as a trade route had increased. Tibetan silver currency was being siphoned off through Sadiya, and Chinese notes in quantity were on sale in Shillong, Assam's capital.[94] Traders were trying to open the Siang Valley as a long-distance trade route, hoping 'now that [the British administration] had gone forward to Karko, [Adis might not] persist in refusing through passage to them'.[95] Opium, guns, and ammunition circulated in abundance across the borderlands between Sichuan, Burma, Tibet, and the Himalayas.[96] Lower Adis visited the Pasighat ammunition shop. Mishmis had such an ample supply that they could afford to shoot even the smallest birds.[97]

Booming trade routes and the growing participation of certain tribal groups and individuals in the cash-based economy fuelled significant changes in networks of economic and political power. Opening new commercial opportunities and fulfilling the tribes' trade requirements enabled colonial administrators to connect them to the Indian state, even as it remained mostly at a distance from the hills. From the nineteenth century onwards, frontier marts or *kaiya* shops had begun to cause a 'general southern drift of trans-Himalayan trade'.[98] Assam authorities had purposely assorted their punitive and exploratory ventures in the eastern Himalayas with the creation of trading posts, pro-trade proclamations, and attacks on villages that acted as trade barriers; they had bitterly complained about Delhi post-1914 letting bridges built to favour trade go to rot.

By providing increased opportunities to interact with Himalayan inhabitants and introducing the latter to an ever-greater variety of goods – included when a plane and its plentiful cargo crashed inland – the war served the Assam administration's attempts to impose themselves as the 'government'. More than ever, trade was put to the use of state-making. Sadiya officials began to organise auctions of tribal produce. Ostensibly this was meant to ensure tribals would get a fair deal instead of dealing with 'shopkeepers [who] knew that a man who has walked down for

---

[94] London, BL, IOR (1946), Tibetan intelligence reports from the Central Intelligence Officer, Assam, 162-CA/46; BL, IOR/L/PS/12/3120 (Tour notes for the Lohit Valley, 1946), pp. 5–6.

[95] London, 162-CA/46 (TIR 8.46).

[96] Itanagar, APSA (1945), Tibet intelligence reports, Misc-35/45; London, 162-CA/46.

[97] APSA, James tour diaries August 1945–December 1946, p. 21; BL, IOR/L/PS/12/3120 (Tour notes for the Lohit Valley, 1946), p. 6.

[98] Stuart Blackburn, 'Memories of migration: Notes on legends and beads in Arunachal Pradesh', *European Bulletin of Himalayan Research*, 25/26 (2003–2004), 15–60 (pp. 33–34). This long-term tilt did not prevent the general redirection of Bhutan trade to Bengal, at the expense of the Brahmaputra Valley. Ratna Sarkar and Indrajit Ray, 'Trend of Bhutan's trade during 1907–26: Export', *Journal of Bhutan Studies*, 26 (2012), 100–122.

perhaps a fortnight to sell his stuff and buy his years' requirements of salt and thread cannot wait till he gets his price or take his stuff back unsold'. But it was no coincidence that this would also make them 'see the PO and APO when they come in'.[99]

The war also had contradictory effects, for it increased the leverage of some tribals vis-à-vis colonial officials in some respects. Minyongs or Nyishis once forced to carry loads almost free of charge for touring parties now received significant wages. Discussions of coolie rates or the salary to pay for a bridge to be built became fierce. In March 1944, a group of Galos insisted that they would only porter if given wages similar to those they had received on the Ledo Road – nothing paid better than military projects.[100] An increasing number of tribals were finding some benefit in negotiating with frontier officials.

These changes were not always to the advantage of the Indian state. Several officers feared that if some tribals were 'becoming *sirkari* [*sic*]' (government-minded), they might not conceive of the entity called 'government' as having a British Indian identity (or care whether it had one). During the war, the Hrussos or the Nyishis had as much contact with American military officers and troops as with British Indian officials. Hump planes regularly crashed in areas still largely terra incognita for the latter, yet 'American rescue parties, laden with tinned peaches and without maps, [were] always ready to plunge in' – with or without British permission. The risk was that India's sovereignty over the Himalayas would be undermined before even having been asserted.[101] To preserve Anglo-American relations and control encounters between inhabitants and Americans, POs tried to assist search crews after plane crashes, but tensions were never far away.[102] The fragility of the link between state-making and national awareness would remain in evidence even after India's independence.

A New Vocabulary of State Expansion

A new expansion mindset was simultaneously taking shape in the Assam frontier administration. When two powerful Adi villages had refused to send porters to the Abor Labour Corps in the early years of the war, the PO, unable to carry out a retaliatory promenade given Assam Rifles' shortages, had petitioned Shillong (unsuccessfully) to burn down their granaries by plane.[103] Different considerations began to temper this

---

[99] 'Paul, 1943 Diaries' (13 November) A similar phenomenon can be discerned in officials' attempts to regulate the sale of opium through a system of shops and licenses.
[100] SOAS, PP MS 19, Box 388, also pp. 30–30b.   [101] BL, IOR/L/PS/12/3120.
[102] APSA, Ex/BFT/8/45.
[103] NAI, External 63/X/43 (PO Sadiya to Mills, 31 March 1943).

punitive bent. In discussions surrounding a new forward policy in 1943, frontier officials articulated their positions not just in regard of a perceived Sino-Tibetan strategic threat, but of the need of colonial authorities to respect their 'obligations . . . towards the Monbas and others'. The Sikkim PO was adamant that, if India was to control Tawang, it needed to 'demonstrate, definitely and without delay, that our occupation is beneficial'. He accordingly insisted that 'liberal funds . . . [be given] for roads and other beneficent activities'.[104] The Adviser to the Assam Governor also professed pastoral concerns towards Buddhist communities as a reason to expand in Monyül. In early 1944, Mills demanded the abolition of the Assam Rifles' three *duar* outposts, arguing they were oppressive to tribesmen. 'They belong to an era when all hillmen were regarded as potential enemies and criminals', he argued; 'their continuance gives the tribes the impression that we are indifferent to what goes on in the hills provided no harm comes to plainsmen.'[105]

When, a year later, Mills began envisioning the possibilities for expansion that the end of the war could open up, he asked a frontier official to draw up a '[p]ost-war reconstruction plan for Sadiya Frontier Tract'. The officer, G.E.D. Walker, recommended the division of the tract into more manageable entities, but also insisted on the need to provide the inhabitants with medical and educational facilities and improve their agricultural methods. What Walker advocated was a form of state expansion at odds with earlier calls for 'pacification' through military subjugation yet distinct from older arguments about the civilising mission of the colonial endeavour:[106]

any form of development is a political and strategic necessity. . . . A contented loyal population is a strategic necessity of the highest importance . . . measures to achieve this, even if they are part of a long-term policy, are as essential as any plans bearing apparent immediate fruit.[107]

The old vocabulary of violence employed by the colonial state in the eastern Himalayas had by no means disappeared, but this new development mindset increasingly took root in the aftermath of the Second World War. Assam frontier officials spent much of the lead-up to decolonisation designing and negotiating sanction for a five-year development plan that, while prioritising road building, also articulated the need for welfare and

---

[104] Ibid. (PO Sikkim to Foreign Secretary, 'Vindication of the McMahon Line in the Towang area').
[105] BL, IOR/L/PS/12/3120 (Tour notes for 1944), p. 1.
[106] Sanghamitra Misra, 'The nature of colonial intervention in the Naga Hills, 1840–80', *Economic and Political Weekly*, 33:51 (1998), 3273–3279.
[107] BL, MSS Eur D1191/11, p. 2.

development schemes.[108] In 1947, a young Assamese woman married to a Mishing, a plains tribe closely linked to the Adis, was hired to build a frontier educational system.[109] Though its concrete effects would not clearly appear in the 1940s, a sort of development turn was taking shape in frontier governance. Its roots were complex and varied. The Second World War had completed a transformation of official perceptions of Assam's tribals, begun when some of them joined labour corps in the First World War. The suffering and help of Patkai people during the conflict had made a lasting impression on colonial officials; once seen as headhunting savages or predatory raiders, tribals were recast as authentic and heroic beings.[110] Their 'primitive' character ceased to be a cause for contempt to become a marker of cultural purity, a source of praise and admiration. Asked for his views on the transfer of power and its effect on tribes, Mills argued that it was 'more accurate to describe the culture of the hills as different from that of the plains than as inferior to it'.

This reappraisal had two corollaries. The first was that tribal culture had to be preserved against external influences, starting with the 'plains' Indians. The Inner Line logic evolved from guarding the plains from raids to protecting primitive, loyal cultures from the encroachment of Indian civilisation. The second was that Assam frontier officials assumed a guardian-cum-gatekeeper attitude towards the tribes, particularly in the Frontier Tracts. 'The danger of unwise, if well-intentioned, legislation is obvious', wrote Mills, 'but it is frequently said that the tribesmen of India do not need protection against deliberate exploitation by Indians. I unhesitatingly say they do.' The Sixth Schedule of the Constitution bore the stamp of the protectionist idea. This guardianship mindset was to mark frontier policy well beyond India's independence.[111]

These changes echoed pan-Indian, and indeed global, reflections on the link between development, authority, and legitimacy in a post-war world. In the 1930s and 1940s, Indian nationalists came to see planned, socialist development as a crucial component of the realisation of freedom.[112] During the war, colonial authorities had consequently

---

[108] SOAS, PP MS 19, Box 3 (21 May entry); APSA, Ex/BFT/8/45 (May report); BL, Mss Eur D1191/17; NAI, External 65-NEF/46.

[109] Indira Miri, *Moi aru NEFA [NEFA and I]* (Guwahati: Spectrum Publications, 2003).

[110] BL, Mss Eur E278/19.

[111] London, British Library, Archer Papers (1945), 'A note on the future of the Hill tribes of Assam and the adjoining hills in a self-governing India' by J.P. Mills, Mss Eur F236/357, p. 10, 1.

[112] Benjamin Zachariah, *Developing India: An intellectual and social history, c. 1930–50* (New Delhi; Oxford: Oxford University Press, 2005).

sought to contain Indian public opinion by pushing their own development rhetoric.[113]

Faced with the ineluctable perspective of decolonisation after 1945, colonial frontier authorities too were adjusting their strategy to fall in line with the new focus of development – a preoccupation their colleagues in Burma and Chinese nationalists shared. Given their ambivalence towards a soon-to-be Indian national project, however, their development strategy had a different flavour to that of Chinese officials, for whom development and 'reconstruction' were to educate minority elites about a China-centred national order.[114]

Proposing a development-based expansion strategy was also eminently pragmatic. It seemingly produced far better results among local populations than the punitive logic. No matter how undermanned or under-supplied, the tiny, ramshackle 'hospitals' built in the eastern Himalayas attracted a steady supply of patients. Epidemics helped to build legitimacy at little cost – provided enough medicine tablets could be found.[115] In areas where Tibetan influence was strong, dispensaries had the further advantage of undermining it without confronting Lhasa head on. When Mainprice made his way through the Lohit Valley in late 1943, his mandate was to launch 'very light administration *and medical and other services*' in the region.[116] Schools and educational facilities came under these 'other services'. While parents could be coerced to enrol their progeny, children themselves often saw this as a chance to satisfy their worldly and intellectual curiosity. Some Adi villages had begun to pay an Assamese teacher out of their own pockets.[117] Other parents had enrolled their children in missionary schools just across the Inner Line.[118]

Health care or schools offered the way to mitigate the enduring difficulties of frontier administration in securing a permanent presence in the eastern Himalayas. Officials approached each winter like a race against time, or rather against climate, trying to progress as much as possible before the start of the rains made touring impossible; inland outposts

[113] Sanjoy Bhattacharya and Benjamin Zachariah, '"A great destiny": The British colonial state and the advertisement of post-war reconstruction in India, 1942–45', *South Asia Research*, 19:1 (1999), 71–100.

[114] Rodriguez, 'Building the nation, serving the frontier'; Andres Rodriguez, '"Decolonizing" the borderlands: Yunnan–Burmese borderlands and the dilemmas of the early postwar period (1945–1948)' (paper presented at the 4th Asian Borderlands Research Network Conference, Hong Kong, December 2014).

[115] APSA, Ex/BFT/8/45; BL, IOR/L/PS/12/3120; Itanagar, APSA, NEFA Secretariat Files (1945), Epidemic in the NEFA, 13/29/45.

[116] 'Paul, 1943 Diaries'. Emphasis added.

[117] Oshong Ering. Interview with the author; Barmati Dai. Interview with the author, 12 February 2014, Pasighat (Arunachal Pradesh).

[118] Miri, *Moi aru NEFA [NEFA and I]*, p. 41.

either had to be removed during the rainy season or were in extremely poor shape by the end of it.[119] This seasonal state retrenchment rendered relations established with a given tribal group fragile. Mills deplored that the British visit to Tawang in 1938 had not been capitalised on, instating doubts among the Monpas about India's true claims to their territory and making them wary of welcoming a British officer again – those who had extended hospitality to the British PO were reportedly punished by the *dzongpöns*. As for the Sherdukpens, under pressure by Lhasa in 1943, they feared heeding the PO's advice not to obey, knowing that the *dzongpöns* might descend on their villages to punish them the minute the fair-weather Assam Rifles outpost had been withdrawn.[120] Faced with Indian expansion attempts, Tibetan officials' tactic was to wait till the start of the rains, when they could at leisure pull down the walls of an outpost or resume their tax collection south of the McMahon Line – just like some tribals bode their time until the riflemen's departure.[121]

By contrast, health-care, educational, or trade facilities often had a far more lasting impact than outpost creation – often because they enabled Indian authorities to 'act at a distance'.[122] But it would be several years before India would cease to be a fair-weather state in the eastern Himalayas.

[119] APSA, James tour diaries August 1945–December 1946.
[120] NAI, External 63/X/43.
[121] APSA, Tour diaries of the APO Pasighat 1940–1944, p. 17.
[122] Peter Dicken et al., 'Chains and networks, territories and scales: Towards a relational framework for analysing the global economy', *Global Networks: A Journal of Transnational Affairs*, 1:2 (2001), 89–112 (p. 96).

Part II

1950–1959

3   Exploration, Expansion, Consolidation?
State Power and its Limitations

While independent India put the final touch to its constitution in late 1949, the Chinese civil war had run its course. In October, Mao Zedong proclaimed the birth of a Communist People's Republic of China. The Guomindang's remnants soon fled to Taiwan. On 1 January 1950, Radio Peking announced that only a few territories remained to be liberated: Hainan, Taiwan – and Tibet. Nine months later, 40,000 PLA soldiers crossed into Lhasa-held territory.

Tibetan authorities had taken belated steps to build up their army in preparation for such an attack, but within days, Chamdo, their bulwark in western Kham, was encircled. Mao used his control of the town to force Lhasa to negotiate. Tibet's elites were ill prepared for this. Three years earlier, the country had teetered close to civil war. Animosity was rife between various factions, and disunion, confusion, and indecision reigned. Tibet had remained diplomatically isolated and its de facto independence unrecognised. In desperation, the Tibetan government enthroned the fifteen-year-old Dalai Lama and made a last-minute appeal for international intervention. To no avail: Tibet had little standing in the United Nations, which was in any case preoccupied by the Korean War, and Britain and the United States were not prepared to plead its case.[1]

Although it had inherited British rights in Tibet and had considered granting it military assistance and forging a new bilateral treaty, Delhi resisted helping its neighbour. Antagonising China and endangering India's non-alignment and leadership potential were too high a price for the preservation of Tibet's independence – an independence that no amount of international intervention could preserve, Nehru believed.[2]

---

[1] Tsering W. Shakya, *The dragon in the land of snows: A history of modern Tibet since 1947* (London: Pimlico, 1999), pp. 52–61; Melvyn C. Goldstein and Gelek Rimpoche, *A history of modern Tibet, Volume 1: The demise of the Lamaist state, 1913–1951* (Berkeley: University of California Press, 1989), pp. 707–736.
[2] *Selected works of Jawaharlal Nehru – Second series*, ed. by S. Gopal (New Delhi: Jawaharlal Nehru Memorial Fund, 1993), XV (Note, 18 November 1950), pp. 342–347; Shakya, *The dragon in the land of snows*, pp. 54, 61.

Lhasa capitulated. On 23 May 1951, its representative put his signature at the back of a seventeen-point agreement 'on measures for the peaceful liberation of Tibet'. The PRC had absorbed Tibet.

Despite their role in this turn of events, Nehru and his cabinet had strong misgivings about the future. No Chinese government had ever recognised the legality of the McMahon Line nor admitted knowing about its existence. India was now neighbours with a 'militaristic and aggressive nation' that might try to infiltrate and occupy pieces of India 'if there [was] no obstruction to this happening'.[3]

It was therefore worrying that, three years after independence, little had changed in the administration of the eastern Himalayas. The Sadiya Frontier Tract had been divided into two entities for greater manageability, the Abor Hills and Mishmi Hills Districts; a few outposts had been opened, notably on the Apatani plateau and at Along in the Adi heartland; and the administration had just completed the Lohit Valley Road. Yet these initiatives were limited. The order of the day had been consolidation, not expansion.[4]

All in all, the parts of India closest to Lhasa were under fragile control and separated from Tibet by the blurriest of borders. Vallabhbhai Patel, the Deputy Prime Minister, was especially worried. Inhabited by people with 'no established loyalty to India', the north-east frontier presented 'unlimited scope for infiltration'.[5] As Lhasa and Beijing parleyed in early 1951, Delhi set up a Border Defence Committee to examine the need for a new policy on India's Himalayan frontier. It returned from NEFA with a clear recommendation: establishing Indian sovereignty all the way to the border was a matter of the utmost urgency.[6]

---

[3] Quoted in Srinath Raghavan, 'Sino–Indian boundary dispute, 1948–60: A reappraisal', *Economic and Political Weekly*, 41:36 (2006), 3882–3892 (p. 3883). If the head of Indian intelligence services at the time is to be believed, infiltration fears extended to the Assam–Burma border. B.N. Mullik, *My years with Nehru: The Chinese betrayal* (Bombay: Allied Publishers, 1971), p. 111.

[4] P.N. Luthra, *Constitutional and administrative growth of the North-East Frontier Agency* (Shillong: NEFA, 1971), p. 11; London, BL, IOR (September 1944–March 1946), Programme of work for the North East Frontier Agency: McMahon Line; establishment of control, IOR/L/PS/12/3119.

[5] Vallabhbhai Patel, *Sardar Patel's correspondence, 1945–50*, ed. by Durga Das, 10 vols (Ahmedabad: Navajivan, 1971–1974), Volume X (Patel to Nehru, 7 November 1950), pp. 135–141.

[6] Delhi, NMML, Elwin Papers (1956), Report of the Ministry of External Affairs, 1955–56, S. No. 110 (Note on the political and administrative problems of the NEFA), pp. 66–67. It is difficult to say more about the so-called Himmatsinghji Committee (named after its chairman, the Deputy Defence Minister). Its report was never published, and the Indian Defence Ministry claims to have lost files pertaining to it. Claude Arpi, *1962 and the McMahon Line saga* (Delhi: Lancer, 2013), p. 412.

The winter of 1950–1951 marks a watershed in the history of the eastern Himalayas. In stark contrast to their intermittent efforts in the first half of the century, both China and India would now constantly seek to deepen their reach over the region. Delhi, which had financed only two new outposts in the Frontier Tracts in winter 1949–1950, sanctioned nine new centres a year later. Yet this shift was not accompanied by militarisation. It was not the Indian army that would spearhead state expansion but the civilian administration. In the light of the events of 1962, this decision may seem flawed and irrational. In fact, it was grounded in the specific conditions encountered by Indian authorities in the eastern Himalayas, particularly after the local outbreak – just a few months before Tibet's conquest – of a far more concrete crisis: the Assam earthquake of 1950 (Map 6).

Two Earthquakes

It was the evening of 15 August 1950. Exhausted from a long day of work in the fields, Monpa villagers had just gone home for some much-needed rest. Suddenly, a 'very deep and continued rumbling sound' rose out of the earth, and the walls began to shake, and to shake even more. People ran out of their crumbling homes: this was the *samberma* – the sign through which Loo, the Serpent-God, warned people to abandon their sinful activities by shaking the earth in anger. The first tremor was the longest and the worst, but many more followed over the next few days; mankind's faults must have been great indeed. By the time the deity's fury subsided, several dozen people had been killed, many more were injured, and Tawang's monastery had been damaged.[7]

At 8.6 degree of magnitude, the earthquake was one of the fiercest ever recorded.[8] Yet the Monpas had been spared the worst: the epicentre was near the other end of the Frontier Tracts, in Dzayül. In the Siang Basin, the Adis had just gone to sleep after celebrating Solung, their harvest festival, when *taromoton* struck.[9] When the main tremor died out, villagers around Pasighat could not believe their eyes: the mighty Siang had been reduced to a small stream, and hundreds of fish lay stranded on its dried-up bed. They did not know it yet, but massive landslides had blocked the

---

[7] Itanagar, APSA, NEFA Secretariat (1952), Extent of damage due to the earthquake of 1950, EG27/52.
[8] It ranks as the tenth strongest earthquake since 1900. 'Largest earthquakes in the world since 1900', *U.S. Geological Survey*, http://earthquake.usgs.gov/earthquakes/world/10_lar gest_world.php (accessed 14 December 2011).
[9] Tarun Kumar Bhattacharjee, *The frontier trail* (Calcutta: Manick Bandyopadhyay, 1993), p. 35.

narrow gorge upstream of the town. The worst was yet to come. A few days later, the natural dam burst. The monsoon-gorged river engulfed the countryside.[10]

From what the authorities could gather, 17,000 square miles lay ravaged across the Sadiya Frontier Tract.[11] Boulders and landslides had buried houses and inhabitants while the Lohit and Dibang rivers ran amok, flash floods washing away cattle and crops. In places, 'the mountains were silver as lepers with shining white scars, a country of death' with little sign left of human presence.[12] Attempts were later made to gauge the extent of the devastation: 952 deaths and 225,000 victims were reported, a large number for this sparsely populated region. In the Mishmi Hills, at least 15 per cent of houses and granaries, 80 per cent of standing crops, and 70 per cent of transport communications seemed badly damaged. The situation seemed even worse in Adi areas. Reports said that 30 per cent of tribal accommodation had collapsed, 35 per cent of cattle had been killed, 50 per cent of tracks and roads were destroyed, and 75 per cent of standing crops were lost.[13] However imprecise these estimates were, the eastern Himalayas had clearly experienced a human catastrophe of the first order.

Indian frontier authorities needed only to look at their own government infrastructure to guess the scale of the disaster. Entire portions of Pasighat had been submerged and its main access route partly washed away.[14] The town slowly recovered, but Sadiya was not so lucky. The Dibang River had radically changed its course, condemning it to a slow death by submersion.[15] In the hills, nothing was left of Theroliang, which the authorities planned to transform into a major outpost for the Mishmi country. The Lohit Valley Road had been badly damaged; in places, it had become the river bed. The forests at the foot of the hills – the administration's major source of revenue – were devastated.[16]

[10] Barmati Dai, Interview with the author, 12 February 2014, Pasighat (Arunachal Pradesh); *Boken Ete: An oddyssey*, ed. by Liju Ete (Naharlagun: The author, 2011), p. 21.

[11] 'Indo-Tibetan boundary: "no change to be permitted"', *Times of India*, 21 November 1950.

[12] Francis Kingdon-Ward, 'The Assam earthquake of 1950', *Geographical Journal*, 119:2 (1953), 169–182 (p. 181).

[13] New Delhi, NAI, Home Affairs Proceedings (1951), Question for the parliament of India by Shri Kamath regarding the loss of life and property wrought by the recent floods in Assam, 15/177-Public.

[14] *Boken Ete*, ed. by Ete, p. 22.

[15] Interview with G.T. Allen. Interviewed by 'Oral Archive: Plain Tales from the Raj' Series on 1972–74 (held at the SOAS Archives, London) (accessed 12 March 2015); New Delhi, NMML, APCC Papers (1954), Sadiya District Congress Committee, 1950–54, Packet 14 File 1.

[16] Kingdon-Ward, 'The Assam earthquake of 1950' (p. 181).

Indian authorities had seemingly suffered an enduring setback: the earthquake had caused a 'sudden, exogenous, and unexpected destruction of state capacity'.[17] But, in reality, what had been lost were but the few signs of the state's laborious expansion in the eastern Himalayas. Far from crippling Indian state-making, the 1950 earthquake was to give it momentum.[18]

The disaster was so spectacular that it temporarily highlighted the existence of Assam's Himalayan hinterland to the national press. Public and governmental sympathy swelled. Funds began pouring in. Nehru toured Assam to offer support and mobilise relief. Soon, the Prime Minister's Assam Relief Fund and the Governor's Earthquake Relief Fund were gathering help in cash and kind from all across India, stimulated by constant appeals by the media and political organisations. Delhi granted Rs 395,000 for relief expenditure on the people in the Abor and Mishmi Hills. The Assam government offered surplus clothing, the public donated Rs 270,000, and several countries and organisations contributed.[19]

On the ground, frontier officials sprang into action. A makeshift camp was built for 3,400 evacuees near Sadiya and an orphanage started for children who had lost their parents.[20] Airlift was organised for the stranded residents of Kobo's leper colony. An even more dramatic rescue took place at Nizamghat at the entrance of the Dibang Valley. Established a year before, the small settlement was now a rapidly sinking island in the middle of a furious river. The marooned inhabitants were saved from drowning at the last minute.[21] Meanwhile, frontier staff toured affected inland areas, calling the inhabitants to the outposts to receive medical help and collect food utensils or agricultural implements. People from the farthest reaches of the Siang Basin came down to Pasighat to obtain

[17] Tirthankar Roy, 'State, society and market in the aftermath of natural disasters in colonial India: A preliminary exploration', *Indian Economic Social History Review*, 45:2 (2009), 261–294 (p. 264).

[18] On the opportunity to reorder society and strengthen political legitimacy after natural disasters, see Janet Borland, 'Capitalising on catastrophe: Reinvigorating the Japanese state with moral values through education following the 1923 Great Kanto Earthquake', *Modern Asian Studies*, 40:4 (2006), 875–907; Gregory K. Clancey, 'The Meiji earthquake: Nature, nation, and the ambiguities of catastrophe', *Modern Asian Studies*, 40:4 (2006), 909–951.

[19] *Selected works of Jawaharlal Nehru – Second series*, ed. by Gopal, p. 166 (Broadcast to the Nation, 9 September 1950); New Delhi, NMML, APCC (1955), Proceeding Books of APCC Meetings, File 25; New Delhi, NAI, Home Affairs Proceedings (1950), Question in Parliament of India by Shri Kamath regarding Assam earthquake, 15/87-Public.

[20] Indira Miri, *Moi aru NEFA [NEFA and I]* (Guwahati: Spectrum Publications, 2003), p. 53.

[21] Delhi, NMML, Rustomji Papers (1963), Broadcasts, tour notes, articles, etc. (1959–1963), S. No. 8 ('Earthquake and flood: Operation rescue', June 1951).

essential items, returning home to distribute them.[22] Planes flew over the hills to drop bags of rice.[23] For many in the Frontier Tracts' hinterland, such relief was the first encounter with the *sarkar* (government). The earthquake was proving an unforeseen occasion for state-making. The young Republic of India had experience using relief and rehabilitation for such purposes. The influx of millions of partition refugees had made them a constitutive part of the assumption of freedom and a vital testing ground for the Nehruvian state's capabilities.[24] Moreover, Assam frontier officials might have remembered how their colonial predecessors had used humanitarian and paternalist actions to consolidate their rule over the Mizo Hills on the Burma border, in the wake of a rat plague.[25] British authorities had never undertaken relief in the eastern Himalayas. The opportunity to enhance independent India's legitimacy was all the greater.[26]

Operations were not an immediate or unequivocal success. They proved complex in areas where massive impediments had existed even before the disaster, such as the un-administered Dibang Valley.[27] There were also cases of mismanagement. In 1954, some Mishmis claimed that funds for their area had been misappropriated.[28]

Such failings notwithstanding, the disaster brought Indian authorities and frontier populations into unprecedented contact. It also coloured their relations in a different light. Colonial state presence had largely been defined in coercive terms; in contrast to punitive expeditions, relief cast the independent Indian state as a potential provider of tangible goods and benefits. The Adi evacuees were resettled in 'model villages' where

[22] 'Relief activity in Abor Hills District', *Assam Tribune*, 7 February 1951.
[23] Barmati Dai. Interview with the author.
[24] Joya Chatterji, *The spoils of partition: Bengal and India, 1947–1967* (Cambridge: Cambridge University Press, 2007), part II; Uditi Sen, 'Refugees and the politics of nation-building in India, 1947–1971' (unpublished doctoral thesis, Cambridge University, 2009).
[25] Sajal Nag, *Pied pipers in the hills: Bamboo flowers, rat famine and colonial philanthropy in North East India, 1881–1931* (Cambridge: University of Cambridge, Centre of South Asian Studies, 2008), pp. 276–279.
[26] Though many Assam planters helped after the earthquake, notably by providing their private planes for rescue efforts, the administration was cautious towards them: many of them were ex-frontier officers who had stayed in Assam after independence. Their past lives as state officials made them potential threats to the authority of their Indian successors. R.N. Koley, *East Siang in the last fifty years (1947–1997)* (Pasighat: District administration, East Siang, c. 1997), p. 35; Kew (London), UKNA, FOR (1950), Reports on Assam, Sikkim and Bhutan, FO 371/84250 (Calcutta special report no. 71), p. 78.
[27] New Delhi, NAI, External Affairs Proceedings (1950), Tribal Areas of Assam. Expenditure on projects, 146-NEF (Doulatram to Keskar, 15 August 1950).
[28] Delhi, NMML, APCC Papers, Correspondence with Chief Minister of Assam, 1953–54, Packet 33 File 1, p. 105.

development projects were soon started.[29] This new interaction pattern smoothened out state expansion. In Along, some people built their own landing ground, hoping to benefit again from the planes that had dropped relief goods on them.[30] Many Ramos and the Pailibos, who had contracted malaria during their stay in the plains, nevertheless accepted government expansion in the Upper Siang Valley a year later.[31]

In the eastern Himalayas, the geopolitical earthquake caused by China's march on Tibet thus came on the heels of a physical one. The PRC's conquest of the plateau turned the momentum created by the cataclysm into a comprehensive state-making attempt. Delhi became far more amenable to frontier administration's clamour for funds and personnel. But the earthquake also decisively shaped Indian authorities' perceptions of the Chinese threat and how to tackle it.

Viewed from Delhi, the Himalayas seemed an impassable natural frontier for invading armies.[32] Though in charge of the External Affairs portfolio, Nehru could not know better. The Prime Minister's acquaintance with Assam and its Frontier Tracts was minimal. His first visit in 1945 had been but a 'whirlwind electioneering tour' and had not taken him beyond the Inner Line.[33] His second, earthquake-related trip in late 1950 was limited to Pasighat or Sadiya.

By smashing the landscape of the Lohit Valley, the earthquake reinforced the idea that the Himalayas were a geographical fortress, susceptible to a takeover on the sly but not to a full invasion.[34] Nehru's ambassador in Beijing insisted that China's silence regarding the border dispute meant acceptance of the McMahon Line, reassuring the Prime Minister.[35] Indian authorities concluded that the main danger stemming from Tibet's 'peaceful liberation' was the possibility that NEFA populations might look towards China – and enable infiltration.

The result was that India's defence and military authorities remained aloof from frontier matters, preferring to let a branch of the External Affairs Ministry deal with them. Instead of militarisation, the Himmatsinghji Committee came back from its visit to the eastern

---

[29] Bhattacharjee, *The frontier trail*, pp. 64–66.   [30] *Boken Ete*, ed. by Ete, p. 23.
[31] Itanagar, APSA, NEFA Secretariat (1951), Malaria protection for the hill tribes coming down to the plains and plan for anti-malarial measures, M/94/51.
[32] 'The Himalayan Frontier: I – Background of quiet', *Times of India*, 22 November 1950.
[33] Mohammad Tayyebulla, *Between the symbol and the idol at last* (New Delhi; New York: Allied Publishers, 1964), p. 163.
[34] 'The Himalayan Frontier: I – Background of quiet'. Even in 1962, G.E.D. Walker, the last British Adviser to the Governor, expressed his doubts that the Chinese would ever be able to go down the Lohit Valley due to the earthquake. 'Assam Rifles post at Walong was set up in 1944', *Assam Tribune*, 15 November 1962.
[35] Raghavan, 'A reappraisal' (p. 3884).

Himalayas with recommendations directly taken from frontier officers' suggestions: expanding civilian administration and undertaking welfare and development activities among the tribes. For the earthquake had underscored a long-standing lesson: development could do far more than military expeditions to ensure acceptance, and so perhaps loyalty.[36]

The Birth of NEFA

The effect of these twin shocks soon became apparent. The most significant expansion step came in early 1951: India occupied Tawang. On 6 February that year, an Indian officer called Bob Kathing appeared on the outskirts of the town, along with sixty Assam Rifles. Not knowing what to make of their arrival, the *dzongpöns* received the party affably until they realised the nature of their mission. Swiftly appraised of the situation, Tibetan authorities protested: surely this ill-judged decision to annex their territory could only have been made by a lone frontier officer – could India not see that this would 'weaken their case vis-à-vis the Chinese'? The Indian representative replied that Tawang had been Indian since 1914. Delhi had only decided to 'vindicate what is rightly ours' lest the area become Chinese. As for India's readiness to relinquish Tawang, it had been 'naturally conditional' on Tibet accepting the rest of the boundary and had been rendered moot by its annexation.[37]

In Tawang itself, the earthquake helped present the Indian takeover in a palatable way. Because its habitations were made of stones, the population had suffered much more than neighbouring tribal groups. Frontier officials linked their arrival with earthquake relief, for instance helping to repair the monastery.[38] The administration further showcased its respect for Buddhism by organising a tour of India's major pilgrimage sites for Monpa notables in 1952.[39] They also canvassed support among the Monpa headmen, notably by shielding villages from *ulag* labour and the *dzongpön*'s taxes.[40]

[36] This echoes, from a different perspective, Srinath Raghavan's claim that Nehru's foreign policy – including towards China – was not irrational but predicated on specific conditions and tenable understandings. Srinath Raghavan, *War and peace in modern India* ([Basingstoke]: Palgrave Macmillan, 2010).

[37] New Delhi, NAI, External Affairs Proceedings (1951), Occupation of Tawang by the GOI, 18(C)51.

[38] Itanagar, APSA, NEFA Secretariat (1951), Occupation of Tawang, earthquake relief measures by Major Khathing's party, CGA/56/51; New Delhi, NMML, Elwin Papers (1954), Confidential reports on the NEFA 1952–4, S. No. 111.

[39] Itanagar, APSA, NEFA Secretariat (1952), Nari Rustomji – Confidential Reports on the North-East Frontier Agency for 1952, p. 19.

[40] Kazuharu Mizuno and Lobsang Tenpa, *Himalayan nature and Tibetan Buddhist culture in Arunachal Pradesh, India: A study of Monpa* (Berlin: Springer, 2015), p. 52.

Indian authorities were still anxious, however. The *dzongpöns* had retreated north of the border but the Tawang Monastery's parent institution, Drepung, could still make trouble: Buddhist monasteries were important seats of spiritual and secular power, and none more so than the big three monasteries of Lhasa, whose abbots were both key players in the Dalai Lama's administration and power holders in their own right. Two of them, Drepung and Sera, had a strong presence and influence in the eastern Himalayas – in Tawang and Pemakö, respectively.[41]

In December 1951, Drepung indeed sent a new *khenpo* (abbot) and *nyertsang* (monasterys accountant) to Tawang. While the abbot applied for an Indian sojourn permit only after significant pressure, the *nyertsang* completely ignored Indian summons to visit Assam for interrogation. His subordinates scrutinised Indian activities in Tawang, and he announced that Tawang would soon be returned to Tibet, for Chinese troops were on the way.[42]

Frontier authorities initially let these Tibetan officials stay and permitted monastic tribute to continue, but control of Tawang's monastery by 'foreigners' – ethnic Tibetans sent by Lhasa – was soon deemed too big a risk. The Tibetan government stood by its position that Tawang's cession had been contingent on Tibet remaining independent. Lhasa was not ready to confront Delhi over Monyül, but neither would it undermine its own claims to it. In mid-1952, Indian authorities replaced the Tibetan *nyertsang* by a local. The Monpas, who formed the bulk of the monastery's monks, had reportedly petitioned to have one of their own take over.[43]

Tawang's occupation was but the clearest sign that Indian authorities now planned to establish themselves everywhere south of the McMahon Line. In 1952–1953, they launched their first expeditions in the Ramo and Palibo country and to the upper Subansiri, partly to ascertain the extent of Tibetan taxation. An outpost was quickly opened in Mechuka, just south of the McMahon Line, where reports of Chinese tax collection had surfaced (false, as it were). Another was set up at Kibithoo in the Lohit Valley, while a series of Assam Rifles outposts and administrative centres were opened in the Siang

---

[41] NAI, External 18(C)51 (Indian Mission telegram, 20 April). On Sera's rule over the Membas, see Toni Huber, 'Pushing south: Tibetan economic and political activities in the far eastern Himalaya, ca. 1900–1950', in *Sikkim Studies: Proceedings of the Namgyal Institute Jubilee Conference, 2008*, ed. by Alex McKay and Anna Balikci (Gangtok: Namgyal Institute, 2011), pp. 259–276.

[42] New Delhi, NAI, External Affairs Proceedings (1952), Tibet policy: Top secret notes on India and China, 7(1)P/52.

[43] Itanagar, APSA, NEFA Secretariat (1952), Annual administrative report for the Sela Sub-Agency for 1952–53, Nil, p. 8; NMML, Elwin Papers, S. No. 111.

Basin.[44] Intelligence checkpoints were also set up.[45] The momentum of outpost creations continued unabated through the 1950s.

Territorial expansion came along with attempts to normalise the presence of the Indian state. The ad hoc nature of colonial interaction with the eastern Himalayas had left independent India's authorities in a tricky legal and administrative position. Few officials fully understood the legal status or geographical extent of the hodgepodge of territorial jurisdictions that supposedly formed the Frontier Tracts and the Naga Hills Tribal Area. This regularly made assigning administrative responsibilities a practical nightmare.[46] Worse, most of the frontier had been presumed to fall under the category of 'tribal area' in colonial times. In its purported quality as successor to the British, independent India was trying to establish its territorial jurisdiction over a region that had been defined as *legally outside* that colonial state! It was imperative to assert the Indian state's undivided, explicit jurisdiction over the eastern Himalayas.

In 1954, the Assam Governor promulgated a North East Frontier Areas (Administration) Regulation. Re-baptised as North-East Frontier Agency or NEFA – a name already in use unofficially – the eastern Himalayas were reorganised into six Frontier Divisions, each under a separate PO backed by several assistants: Kameng (formerly the Sela Sub-Agency); Subansiri; Siang (for the Abor Hills); Lohit (for the Mishmi Hills); and Tirap. The last one, Tuensang, was the reincarnation of the Naga Hills Tribal Area.

Administrative headquarters moved deep into the Himalayas. The region had hitherto been administered from the plains. The change had not been easy, for inland headquarters would hamper contact with Shillong and endanger supply lines. By 1951, however, post-earthquake floods and the transfer to the Assam state government of territory located in the plains had eased this long-standing dilemma.[47] With Sadiya about to disappear beneath the waters, the Lohit headquarters were hurriedly moved to Tezu. Other divisional headquarters also shifted inland (to Bomdila for Kameng, Ziro for the Subansiri, Along for the Siang, Khela for Tirap, and Tuensang for the eponymous division).[48]

---

[44] Itanagar, APSA, NEFA Secretariat (1958), List of administrative centres in NEFA, P66/58.

[45] Mullik, *My years with Nehru*, pp. 135–136. By 1958, there were twenty-two such IB checkpoints in NEFA.

[46] New Delhi, NAI, Home Affairs Proceedings (1953), Assam areas with which the Ministry of Home Affairs is concerned, 73/6/53-Pub.I.

[47] Guwahati, ASA, Assam Tribal Areas Department (1951), Correspondence between the Chief Minister and the Governor of Assam regarding the transfer of the plains portions of the Part B Tribal Areas to normal administration TAD/Con/55/51.

[48] NMML, Elwin Papers, S. No. 111, pp. 6–7, and Report for 1952.

Headquarters were created from scratch. Ziro was built near the Apatani plateau, a central location in the Subansiri that also hosted a community that was, from the administration's viewpoint, more advanced than surrounding Miris and Nyishis. Bomdila was built in the wild, on a spot deemed a convenient meeting place for the Sherdukpens, Buguns, Mijis, Hrussos, and Monpas.[49] The creation of an ever-greater number of administrative centres led to a small urban boom that became one of the major manifestations of Indian presence in NEFA.[50]

Administrative consolidation supposed that enough officials could be found. Hiring people to staff the frontier had been the Indian authorities' Achilles heel for years. Whether for administrative or technical positions, such as doctor or engineer, suitable candidates were few, willing ones even fewer.[51] In 1944, Delhi had so struggled to find an officer to explore the Subansiri that it hired Christoph von Fürer-Haimendorf, technically an enemy citizen. At least, Fürer-Haimendorf had something most of his colleagues did not possess: some knowledge of the area he was being sent to.[52] New recruits often did not have the slightest idea about where the eastern Himalayas lay, let alone a clue on how to reach their post. Thrown into the unknown, often alone with people whose language they could not speak, and forced to spend countless days hiking, many of them soon gave signs of wanting to leave. Retention, like recruitment, seemed a never-ending battle.[53]

From 1951 onwards, however, greater financial and policy support from the centre enabled frontier authorities to make sustained efforts to remedy its shortage of administrative staff. In 1954, a first batch of officers was chosen for frontier service after a special selection. Two years later, a distinct cadre of senior officers was created for NEFA: the Indian Frontier Administrative Service (IFAS).[54] Unlike earlier recruits, this

---

[49] New Delhi, NAI, External Affairs Proceedings (1962), Return of civil administration to NEFA, 49(4)/NI-62.

[50] Itanagar, APSA, NEFA Secretariat (1962), Extension of town development act in parts of NEFA 1/PC-157/62; Itanagar, APSA, NEFA Secretariat (1957), Tour diary of JN Ghose, Director of Health Services on his visit to Daporijo R-67/57.

[51] New Delhi, NAI, External Affairs Proceedings (1955), Reports on NEFA, 4(19)-P/55 (January report).

[52] P.C. Sen, *Two decades in NEFA and Arunachal, 1954–76* (Morekupur: Author, 2007), pp. 3–9.

[53] Ibid. (p. 24). Even Mainprice, the wartime official initially full of bravado and excitement about discovering the Mishmi Hills, soon became disillusioned. New Delhi, NAI, External Affairs Proceedings (1945), Tour notes and fortnightly reports on Assam Tribal Areas for 1945, 6/6-P/45 (Note by Mainprice, 13 July 1945).

[54] New Delhi, NAI, External Affairs Proceedings (1956), Election of NEFA officers and their appointment to the Indian Frontier Administrative Service, 18(5)-NEFA/56; New Delhi, NAI, Home Affairs Proceedings (1956), Election of NEFA officers to IFAS, 18(5)-NEFA/56 Vols I and II.

new generation of frontier officials – many of them from other tribal minorities in Assam, and with an army or police background – would receive intensive training, meant to endow them with a 'frontier mind'.[55]

A unique chain of command replaced the ad hoc administrative structure that had coalesced since the early twentieth century. This 'single line administration' was to smooth out decision-making and policy implementation. At its head stood the Adviser to the Governor, in Shillong. Under him, the administration was divided into an administrative branch and a development branch. While POs were responsible for overseeing and directing all administrative issues in their division, development schemes were entrusted to a newly appointed NEFA Development Commissioner, with various specialist departments under his responsibility.[56]

An essential prerequisite to the consolidation of state expansion, the normalisation of NEFA's territorial and bureaucratic structures also had symbolic importance. By instituting an 'Agency' under Delhi's direct control instead of liminal 'Tracts'; by imposing a single terminology of 'Frontier Divisions', endowed with defined boundaries and administrative headquarters; and by establishing POs as the counterparts of District Commissioners in the rest of Assam, the Indian state underscored that NEFA was now an integral part of India. It was not quite yet the 'settled' districts of the country, but it would be. State expansion was a performance, whose audience included local people and China alike.

State Presence with Feet of Clay

In early 1957, the External Affairs Ministry asked the Adviser to the Governor to take stock of six years of sustained expansion in NEFA. '[E]xpansion up to the border is already virtually complete in Kameng, Siang, Tirap and Tuensang', announced K.L. Mehta, Nari Rustomji's successor. This left the Subansiri and the Lohit, but the administration would remedy this shortly.[57] Lest Delhi get too complacent, Mehta added a note of caution:

remember that by an over-hasty expansion, in advance of our resources during this winter, we may leave other areas dangerously thin, and may well outrun our

---

[55] New Delhi, NAI, External Affairs Proceedings (1953), Notes by T.N. Kaul, N/53/1395/ 105 (Brief note on NEFA, 29 April).

[56] Luthra, *Constitutional and administrative growth*, pp. 21–22.

[57] New Delhi, NAI, External Affairs Proceedings (1956), Consolidation of NEFA administration up to the border, 7(31)-NEFA/56 (Points for Adviser's discussion regarding the expansion programme in New Delhi).

air supply . . . the whole administration of the NEFA will break down, if there is no efficient wireless [radio] communication.

Mehta did not exaggerate. If anything, the overstretch was greater than he could admit. At the turn of the 1960s, India's territorial expansion remained incomplete. The vast Dibang Basin was still un-administered, and a large area in the Subansiri, the Upper Kamla Valley, escaped government control. So did Vijaynagar, a strip of land in Tirap almost entirely surrounded by Burma.[58] As for Nehru's orders to push outposts 'forward to the farthest possible limit, so that our physical presence on the border signifies the boundary lines claimed by us', their concretisation was taking more time than planned.[59] Frontier officials had to choose between tackling border areas and prioritising the main population centres.[60] Expansion and consolidation stood in tension with one another.

This was tightly linked to the dismal state of transport and communication in NEFA, at least of the type favouring state expansion. Poor radio facilities made airdropping or the transmission of orders and information difficult. Where they existed, the haphazard manner in which radio stations had been purchased meant that different outposts held incompatible types of equipment.[61] Frontier administration experienced immense difficulties in building the roads necessary to establish a permanent link between administrative centres, headquarters, and the rest of India. On the eve of independence, NEFA had boasted of no motorable road other than the quickly deteriorating Ledo Road and only had a most limited network of bridle paths, often in very bad shape. The only way to communicate between Walong and Sadiya was by runner, a journey of nine to ten days. Even the most urgent messages took a week to reach the border. A tour to Rima took a minimum of three weeks.[62]

Indian authorities had prioritised road building ever since, but the rugged terrain and the absence of east–west corridors made for immense technical challenges. Blasting a road was costly, dangerous, time consuming. When a 'jeepable' road linking Tezpur to Bomdila was

---

[58] New Delhi, NAI, Home Affairs Proceedings (1963), Agricultural settlements in NEFA, 210(11)/63-NEFA; NAI, External 7(31)-NEFA/56.
[59] NAI, External 7(31)-NEFA/56 (PN Luthra, 16 February 1957).
[60] Itanagar, APSA, NEFA Secretariat (1955), Expansion programme for Subansiri for 1955–56 P189/55.
[61] NAI, External 7(31)-NEFA/56 (Mehta to Kaul, 5 September 1956).
[62] London, BL, Miscellaneous papers relating to the North-East Frontier of India (1944), JHF Williams, PO Sadiya Frontier Tract (with a note on the Lohit Valley), Mss Eur D1191/1, pp. 1–2 (Note on the Lohit Valley, November 1944).

inaugurated in 1959, the great pomp with which this was celebrated hid an uncomfortable fact: twelve years after independence, the road to Kameng's headquarters was the only major motorable artery in the whole of NEFA.[63] Bar a few short tarmac roads in the foothills, the rest of the agency could only be reached by the same tracks and bridle paths. Many trails remained, as in colonial times, 'only a few inches wide, high up on bare precipitous hillsides with no handholds, and at frequent intervals ... [one had to cross rock faces on] galleries of saplings, many of [them] ... in disrepair'.[64]

In the circumstances, frontier administration struggled to reduce 'the tyranny of distance'.[65] Frontier officers spent much of their time hiking at a snail's pace around the countryside. Most outposts could only be kept up by a tremendous airdropping schedule, costly and inefficient. Constrained by technology and the frequency of rain and fog, planes often cancelled their sorties or missed their target. Officials feared that, if such mishaps continued, some of their staff would starve.[66] Most large-scale initiatives were restricted to the four winter months, and much of the government's material infrastructure stood in need of a repair at the end of the rainy season. Without roads, Indian authorities could not reach NEFA's hinterland. And without access, their efforts to exercise control and authority could only be of limited effect.[67] Nor were the administration's efforts to solve financial, technical, and personnel shortages entirely successful. Shortages of engineering staff were particularly great, hampering the already sluggish growth of NEFA's road mileage.[68] Despite the greater support that frontier administration enjoyed in Delhi, not all central ministries were fully convinced of the

[63] 'Bomdila road opened', *Times of India*, 27 April 1959.

[64] London, BL, IOR (1947), Tour notes of the Adviser to the Governor of Assam, 1944–1946 IOR/L/PS/12/3120 (Tour notes for 1946 on the Lohit Valley Sub-Agency), p. 13.

[65] Penny Edwards, 'The tyranny of proximity: Power and mobility in colonial Cambodia, 1863–1954', *Journal of Southeast Asian studies*, 37:3 (2006), 421–443 (p. 427).

[66] Itanagar, APSA, NEFA Secretariat (1955), Commercial flights in Siang Frontier Division, SA194/55; Itanagar, APSA, NEFA Secretariat (1953), Nari Rustomji – Confidential Reports on the North-East Frontier Agency for 1953, p. 2; Itanagar, APSA, NEFA Secretariat (1955), Airdrop/airlift operation in NEFA – Requirements for 1955, SA/26/55.

[67] Mahnaz Z. Ispahani, *Roads and rivals: The political uses of access in the borderlands of Asia* (Ithaca, NY; London: Cornell University Press, 1989). The building of bridle tracks and roads had been essential to the entrenchment of colonial rule in the nearby Naga Hills District. Lipokmar Dzuvichu, 'Roads and the Raj: The politics of road building in colonial Naga Hills, 1860s–1910s', *Indian Economic and Social History Review*, 50:4 (2013), 473–494.

[68] New Delhi, NAI, External Affairs Proceedings (1957), Compendium of the Senior Officers Conference 1957, 3(13)-NEFA/57 (Recommendation of the engineering sub-committee meeting, 28 June 1957).

importance of India's north-eastern frontier. Army engineers, responsible for certain stretches of road, were often diverted elsewhere by their superiors.[69] Moreover, given the time it took to relay any decision or request in the absence of a good communications network, cumbersome bureaucratic procedures caused significant delays in the implementation of any decisions. POs and other NEFA officers consequently tended to undertake administrative or development schemes without official or financial sanction from above, counting on the latter being granted *ex post*.

Expansion and consolidation were further hampered by shortages of Assam Rifles, the semi-military force meant to accompany expeditions and man border checkpoints. Autonomy demands in the Naga-inhabited parts of Assam had morphed into an independence movement, fuelled by radical Naga leaders and Delhi and Assam's intransigence. In 1951, a plebiscite saw a majority of people in the Naga Hills District vote for independence. By early 1954, heavy-handed police actions radicalised Naga non-cooperation movements into armed militancy. As the Indian army moved in, the conflict escalated into a dirty war.

The Naga-inhabited Tuensang Division became a major frontline.[70] To stem the unrest, it was prioritised over other divisions for all government schemes, with little success. Following the demands of a convention of moderate Naga leaders, Tuensang was detached from NEFA in December 1957 and united with the Naga Hills District – a prelude to the constitution of a state of Nagaland in 1963. The agreement failed to stem what Indian authorities called the 'insurgency', however, and the conflict would continue for decades, ravaging Naga society.[71]

The Naga 'problem' had significant repercussions elsewhere in NEFA. Indian authorities created an ever-greater number of Assam Rifles battalions to tackle it. Yet, though they were supposed to be the backbone of border surveillance and law and order in NEFA, their resources were constantly being diverted to Tuensang and the Naga Hills District. External Affairs officials were reluctant to grant more troops to NEFA, counting on a rapid end of the Naga conflict.[72] NEFA's Himalayan divisions thus had but a skeleton police force.

---

[69] Itanagar, APSA, NEFA Secretariat (1955), Roads under construction by army engineers, 25/74/55-FA.

[70] Aosenba, *The Naga resistance movement: Prospects of peace and armed conflict* (Delhi: Regency, 2001), pp. 47–52.

[71] Asoso Yunuo, *The rising Nagas: A historical and political study* (Delhi: Vivek Publishing, 1974).

[72] NAI, External 7(31)-NEFA/56.

The lack of a road network worthy of the name further curtailed the Indian state's capacity to impose law and order. Frontier officers had not taken long to understand this. Fürer-Haimendorf had long before concluded that, '[T]he tribesmen's awe of fire-arms is offset by the realisation that Government parties cannot move fast, that they depend for transport on tribal porters, and that their lines of communications are extremely precarious [whereas tribals themselves can move fast]'.[73]

Deeper tensions explain this apparent ineptitude in road or airstrip construction. Infrastructure building involved a variety of strategic considerations, not easily reconcilable. As India's strategy in NEFA was to establish political authority over the borderland's inhabitants, roads were meant to enable contact with local communities in a way favourable to the administration – or so frontier officials hoped. In practice, the development of infrastructure presented a conundrum. Roads would certainly alleviate the need for porterage – the crux of tribal alienation in the hinterland – and tip the balance of power in favour of the state. But at the same time, their construction required a huge human investment that could only be provided by local populations, road building being even more labour-intensive than porterage. In other words, the accelerated expansion of the physical reach of the state could only be made at the risk of 'emotional integration'.[74]

Working with Local Populations

The dilemma was a major one. Compelled to work 'always in advance of its real resources in men and material', the Indian administration found that expansion and consolidation depended on its ability to elicit the participation from local inhabitants.[75] The state's 'information order' – the acquisition of formal and informal knowledge necessary to make sense of the eastern Himalayas[76] – relied heavily on indigenous knowledge. Local inhabitants knew the existence of paths between different valleys, like those that could be taken by heavily laden administrative parties. They knew where population centres lay or where to find water. And they knew the existence, extent, and nature of Tibetan or Chinese influence in the upper valleys.

[73] Christoph von Fürer-Haimendorf, 'Anthropology and administration in the Tribal Areas of the North East Frontier', *Eastern Anthropologist*, 3:1 (1949) (p. 10).
[74] K.L. Mehta, *In different worlds: From haveli to headhunters of Tuensang* (New Delhi: Lancers, 1985), pp. 125–127.
[75] NAI, External 7(31)-NEFA/56 (Points for AG's discussion on the expansion programme).
[76] Christopher Bayly, *Empire and information: Intelligence gathering and social communication in India, 1780–1870* (Cambridge: Cambridge University Press, 1996).

The possibility to maintain a presence in these places, remote from an Assamese or Indian perspective, was also predicated on local manpower. Outposts needed to be reached and re-supplied; yet, given the near absence of roads and the haphazardness of airdrops, the reach of the Indian state went in many places only so far as the feet and backs of tribal men and women would take it. By refusing to porter beyond a certain point, to certain villages, or at certain times, local inhabitants could hinder state expansion. Overgrown paths, drowned bridges, and ramshackle government buildings needed to be cleared, rebuilt, repaired if the administration's efforts at consolidation were to bear fruit. More often than not, it was the people living in their vicinity who were best able to do so.

Administrative tour diaries offer myriad instances of the importance of tribal labour and informants in the state-making process. Obtaining and retaining the services of tribal porters while on tour was a constant preoccupation well into the 1950s. Unless an agreement could be found on the length and direction of the journey, and on the rate of pay, tribal porters might refuse to show up or to proceed further, when they did not simply turn on their heels and go home. Colonial officers had regularly resorted to summons, intimidation, and punishment, whether by fining villages or doubling the number of porters to be supplied, but were forced to concede that negotiating was a far more efficient way to fulfil a mission. Moreover, the question of porterage threatened various communities' cooperation in other matters.

That this negotiation at all happened stemmed from an officer's ability to find intermediaries among the inhabitants of NEFA. Official tour diaries bring to the fore a frontier employee drawn from the indigenous population: the *dobashi*, or interpreter. As their title bears out, the first task of these men was to translate between the Assam Rifles' platoon or the touring officer and the inhabitants. Even if they spoke a local idiom, officers could not hope to speak the multiplicity of languages and dialects native to the eastern Himalayas. No less than four interpreters accompanied Peter James, who spoke Minyong fluently, on his tours of the Adi areas when he was the Abor Hills Political Officer.[77]

These men were not just a conduit for understanding. It was the *dobashi* who announced a government party's impending passage, ascertained whether a village could be entered, and settled the number of porters, their duties, and their rate of pay; it was the *dobashi* who collected

---

[77] Itanagar, APSA, NEFA Secretariat (1946), Tour diaries of PLS James for August 1945–December 1946. For some insights into an interpreter's life, see *Boken Ete*, ed. by Ete.

information and explained it to his superiors; and it was the *dobashi*, finally, who was responsible for communicating official policy to the inhabitants and for conveying their reaction to his superiors. These men were eventually titled Political Interpreter or Jamadar, highlighting their central role.

A second point of contact between NEFA officers and local villages or communities were the *gaonburas* – village 'chiefs' or 'headmen' who, unlike the *dobashi*s, were supposed to stay permanently in a given locality. *Gaonbura*s selected and sent out porters, organised path clearing between their village and the next, and prepared temporary campsites for the touring party. Many of the early tours of the 1940s focused on figuring out who the local strongmen and their followers might be, and on forging or renewing relations with them.

This was done through several interlinked practices, starting with the drinking of *apong* – a fermented rice beer consumed under various names among many eastern Himalayan communities – and, after India's independence, the invitation of important chiefs and authorities to Republic Day celebrations.[78] The officer recognised a *gaonbura* by giving him a red coat, which would become the symbol of his authority, and by distributing 'political presents' of salt, yarn, or tea (Figure 3.1).[79] Dating back to colonial times, the handing out of political presents grew noticeably after 1947, very likely to compensate for *posa*, which had been banned.[80] Red coats are still, to this day, worn by certain indigenous authorities.

In part, these rituals and appointments were clumsy attempts by state agents to paper over the impossibility of controlling their encounter with NEFA's inhabitants. Despite their 'frontier mind' training and the constant search for ethnographic clues, touring officials struggled to make sense of the cultural and political environment they were entering. Social and political organisation patterns; webs of friendship, alliances, or enmity; cultural worldviews

---

[78] Tawang notables witnessed Delhi's festivities on the first Republic Day after Tawang's takeover. The practice was henceforth made annual and extended to other tribes. APSA 1952, Confidential reports by Nari Rustomji, p. 19; Itanagar, APSA, NEFA Secretariat (1960), Tribal invitees from NEFA to witness the Republic Day Celebrations 1961 P57/60.

[79] Itanagar, APSA, NEFA Secretariat (1952), Supply of red cloth, S/6/52; Itanagar, APSA, NEFA Secretariat (1953), Tour diary of Area Superintendent Sagalee, P-57/53, pp. 2–3; Oshong Ering. Interview with the author, 11 February 2014, Pasighat (Arunachal Pradesh); Short Interview with G.T. Allen; Itanagar, APSA, NEFA Secretariat (1955), Tour diaries of Major S.M. Krishnatry, p. 17.

[80] Delhi, NMML, Elwin Papers (1957), Giving of political presents, S. No. 114.

Figure 3.1 Distribution of political presents in Adi areas, c. 1958
© Arunachal Pradesh Department of Information and Public Relations
(DIPR)

all resisted easy reading – on account both of their sheer complexity
and variety and of local reticence.[81] Conversely, Indian officials'
foggy understanding of identity and power dynamics lent itself to
being used by some individuals for their own advantage. Thus, the
Apatani traders who were the main linkage with the Assam plains
were most often from the lower classes, whose social position could
benefit from forging a relationship with an official who mistook them

[81] Itanagar, APSA, NEFA Secretariat (1957), Tour diary of HS Butalia, APO Subansiri,
R-139/57; S.M. Krishnatry, *Border Tagins of Arunachal Pradesh: Unarmed expedition, 1956*
(Delhi: National Book Trust, 2005), p. 54

for notables.[82] Men who became interpreters were perhaps in the best position to shape officials–inhabitants' encounters. Their control of communication channels meant they could overshadow their superiors. Some interpreters were so 'well versed with the rules of the game', remarked an official, that they 'would only have to grasp the frequency of topic and ... would, on [their] own heat, then rattle off the entire speech'.[83]

The Paradox of Vulnerability

Available sources hint that local people reacted to Indian state expansion attempts in a wide variety of ways, from outward hostility to friendly welcome, from aloofness to watchful curiosity. Officials were predisposed to view the eastern Himalayas as composed of bounded, coherent ethnic groups – 'the' Apatanis, 'the' Nyishis – acting all of a piece vis-à-vis the state: the former supposedly peaceful and thus better disposed towards the state than the latter, for instance. In fact, the grainy picture that emerges from tour diaries cannot be rendered through an ethnic lens. People's attitudes towards an outpost or a touring party evolved across time and space. They hardly mapped onto externally perceived ethnic boundaries and affiliations. Individual Indian officials' behaviour mattered, but the contingencies of micro-level politics (between individuals, clans, families, or villages) seemed just as important, if not more. And they were themselves linked to tribal world views, of which local officials had but a faint notion.

The complexity of local reactions to Indian authorities can be glimpsed during the short-lived expansion efforts of the 1910s. It was because one Mishmi chose, for his own reasons, to report Zhao Erfeng's advance that Indian authorities heard of his conquest of Dzayül, but other Mishmis only reluctantly gave information on the subject. Nor can Williamson's murder and the subsequent Abor Mission of 1911–1912 be reduced to an all-out struggle between the British and the Adis as a whole. While the centenary of Poju Mimak, the 'Anglo-Abor War', was commemorated in 2011, the collective memory of the conflict is not uniform among Adis.[84] Some consider it an anti-colonial mass struggle, some stress that only some villages, or some specific tribes, took part in the subsequent conflict. Others highlight that Williamson had not, in fact, been disliked during his

---

[82] London, SOAS, Fürer-Haimendorf Papers (1945), Diary, Camp Duta, May 1944–February 1945, PP MS 19, Box 4 (11 May 1944).

[83] Krishnatry, *Border Tagins*, p. 25. Also Yeshe Dorjee Thongchi. Interview with the author, 8 February 2014, Itanagar (Arunachal Pradesh).

[84] 'Souvenir of Anglo-Abor War memorial released', *Arunachal Times*, 17 August 2011.

prior visits to the foothills. And while many villages fought the advance of the party, others, like the big Galo village of Kombong, cautiously accepted its arrival and, after the Galo interpreter intervened, even welcomed it.[85]

When colonial officials set out for the Subansiri three decades later, they did so not just to evaluate Tibet's influence in the region but because some Apatanis had requested protection against the nearby Nyishi settlements of Licha and Likha. The two villages kept aloof, but other Nyishis soon flooded in to get their own grievances redressed. When it came to providing porters or information, however, several communities showed much ambivalence towards the colonial officer's presence. Linia, a Nyishi settlement economically interdependent with two Apatani villages, accepted to send porters but refused to proceed to the Palin and Upper Khru valleys, arguing that locals would defend their trade blocks by force. And when, a year later, another British officer approached Linia, half of the village ran away: their Apatani partners had apparently spread the rumour that the party was coming to burn their houses. As for the Nyishis living north of the Apatani plateau, some tried to scare off the exploring officer through elaborate threats and displays of force, while others adopted 'conspiracies of silence' when confronted with probing questions, professing ignorance and being 'purposely evasive' about what lay ahead.[86] Many groups and individuals carefully managed the information they revealed, not always to hinder a party but to direct it in a direction they favoured.

Some people chose to accept state officials proactively. In 1944, the last British official in the Siang Basin had found a camp of fifty temporary houses awaiting him near Bene Village, with 'an absolute army of gams [headmen]' and villagers from the surrounding Galo area ready to welcome him.[87] A similar reception took place in Leyak in 1952, when a party first visited the village. The official's surprise was great: Leyak was powerful, remote, and, above all, Nyishi (Bangni) – a tribe that the administration expected to be hostile. Instead, villagers came forward to greet him, 'extremely pleased that government had come to their area, as they had never seen anyone before'.[88]

---

[85] George Dunbar, *Frontiers* (Delhi: Omsons Publications, 1984 [c.1932]), pp. 150, 163, 165.

[86] New Delhi, NAI, External Affairs Proceedings (1945), Tour diaries of Capt Davy in the Dafla hills, 241-CA/45.

[87] APSA, James tour diaries August 1945–December 1946, p. 9.

[88] Itanagar, APSA, NEFA Secretariat (1952), Tour diary of Political Officer Sela, P-29/52, pp. 6–7. For a third instance, see Itanagar, APSA, NEFA Secretariat Files (1955), Tour diary and tour notes of S.M. Krishnatry, APO Subansiri, P/43/55, pp. 15–23.

This kaleidoscope of reactions can only be understood by exploring the context in which NEFA's inhabitants faced state expansion and their motivations in this encounter. Several factors consistently stand out. Villagers ready to accept the sojourn of a government party often did so in the hope of settling a dispute with others to their advantage. Officers regularly reported that locals with a grievance against a man or a village farther ahead were swelling their party's numbers.[89] Philip Mills wryly noted that 'the only reason the Apa Tanis welcomed the advent of Government . . . was that, being an astute people, they hoped we would put their chestnuts out of the fire for them and realise [their claims] from the [Nyishis]'.[90] More generally, ties with the *sarkar* could be a useful resource in intra-tribal politics.

Another major reason for countenancing state presence was to avail oneself of the benefits of trade. Bene, the village that so enthusiastically welcomed Peter James in 1944, had strong links with the plains of Assam, and its prosperity partly depended on the strength of these links. Villages suffering from food scarcity or economic isolation, especially if another community imposed it, were more likely than others to welcome the opening of an outpost.[91] The opportunity to obtain specific items through trans-regional commerce likewise played a part. Guns, which were mainly obtained from the plains and had come to play a significant role in the hunting practices and socio-economic hierarchies of the Sadiya Frontier Tract, were in high demand. Obtaining them, as well as ammunition, was easier if one had a link with the PO.[92]

A doctor's skill could be an equally powerful draw. Even in the midst of the Abor Mission of 1912, Adi women were turning to the expedition's doctor to check their ailments or deliver their babies. The Monpas, who hosted Frederick Bailey around the same time, were disappointed to find out he had not brought a doctor with him.[93] While not universal, the frequency of this attraction for medical treatment played a significant role in opening the possibility for a tension-free encounter, and eventually the

[89] APSA, P/43/55, p. 9.
[90] BL, IOR L/PS/12/3120 (Report on Tour to Eastern Daflas and Apa Tani, November–December 1945), p. 8.
[91] APSA, James tour diaries August 1945–December 1946, pp. 9, 32; APSA, P/43/55, pp. 2, 5, 20, 39.
[92] APSA, James tour diaries August 1945–December 1946, pp. 21, 31; Itanagar, APSA, NEFA Secretariat Files (1955), Tour diary of P. Nand, Base Superintendent Karko, p. 3; K.C. Johorey and Sudha Johorey. Interview with the author, 15 March 2014, Gurgaon (Haryana).
[93] Dunbar, *Frontiers*, pp. 150, 163, 165; F.M. Bailey, *No passport to Tibet* (London: Hart-Davis, 1957), pp. 241, 258.

establishment of an outpost.[94] Within a few months of Fürer-Haimendorf's arrival in the Apatani valley, more and more Nyishis and Apatanis were consulting the government surgeon. Some patients received his visits on a daily basis, and others even asked for 'cosmetic surgery'. The doctor had forged 'such a reputation by sowing together torn noses or ears that today even [Nyishi] women from Toko come to be operated on'.[95] The exploration of the Palin Valley in the late 1950s, meanwhile, took on a smoother turn after the PO managed to cure a man so sick that his funeral was being prepared.[96] In the circumstances, shortages of medical officers or of medicines were of particular concern to touring officials.[97]

Small details – singing or drinking together, playing with youths, distributing sweets, having a woman among the party – helped to create a measure of trust.[98] There was also the pull of sheer curiosity. Many people just wanted to see what the members of these strange parties looked like, at least when they were relatively small groups. Some equipment, practices, and artefacts were particularly intriguing. Cameras exerted a certain fascination, even if it did not extend to having one's picture taken. Wristwatches, bangles, or radios could prove another source of popular interest and puzzlement.[99] So were planes, initially. A PO's initially tense encounter with Nyishis and Apatanis during the Second World War was thus suddenly broken by the sighting of two planes in the sky.[100] But, by the mid-1950s, the 'government carts' had lost the power to impress.[101]

The interpreter's identity, origins, and personality were more decisive. Kombong's cautious decision to host an Abor Mission column in 1914 was due to the fact that the Galo interpreter accompanying the party hailed from a nearby village. Elsewhere, the inhabitants' initial suspicion

---

[94] In the 1920s, a frontier official thus forged a link with a young Sherdukpen notable by relieving him from his migraines. Eleanor Bor, *Adventures of a botanist's wife* (London: Hurst & Blackett, 1952), pp. 64–65.

[95] London, SOAS, Fürer-Haimendorf Papers (1945), Diary of Fürer-Haimendorf's first tour to the Apa Tani Valley, 1944–45, PP MS 19, Box 3, p. 123b.

[96] Itanagar, APSA, NEFA Secretariat (1957), Tour diary of Sri S. Loveraj, APO Nyapin, 155/57 (28 November entry). See also APSA, P/43/55, p. 23.

[97] APSA, James tour diaries August 1945–December 1946, p. 31.

[98] Ibid. (pp. 10, 11, 26); Verrier Elwin, *The tribal world of Verrier Elwin: An autobiography* (New York: Oxford University Press, 1964), pp. 255–256; Krishnatry, *Border Tagins*, pp. 47–48.

[99] K.C. Johorey and Sudha Johorey. Interview with the author; SOAS, PP MS 19, Box 339; Cambridge, CSAS, FP Mainprice Papers (1936–1949), 'Paul, 1943 Diaries', Box I, Part I, p. 94; Elwin, *An autobiography*, pp. 255–256, 271; APSA, P/43/55.

[100] Ursula Graham Bower, *The hidden land* (London: John Murray, 1953), pp. 20–21, 25–26.

[101] Elwin, *An autobiography*, pp. 255–256.

disappeared when they realised that the government interpreter was a friend of theirs. But the *dobashi*'s presence could also prove a double-edged sword, if unpopular or from a rival group.[102]

Indigenous worldviews and shifting local dynamics thus influenced individual and collective attitudes towards the NEFA administration. There were men who joined a touring officer in the hope of settling a grievance with a community to be met en route; the villages that barricaded themselves due to cultural taboos around disease; the porters who refused to go beyond the last settlement with whom they had friendly relations; the villages that let the PO enter their homes but refused to provide information on communities farther ahead lest the latter retaliate; or the communities who welcomed an outpost's creation because they hoped these would ease the trade blocks imposed by more powerful neighbours. Linia's Apatani partners spread rumours that Fürer-Haimendorf was returning to burn the village because they were busy preparing a festival, and feared that they would lose their trade monopoly with Linia's Nyishis if other Apatani porters accompanied the officer there.

Neighbouring Nyishis welcomed Mills but warned him against exploring further inland: accompanying a touring officer further north would enable them to conduct trade and obtain compensation for raids by their more powerful neighbours, but they also risked retaliation for introducing the *sarkar*, once the latter had left. To sway them, the administration had to show that it would be able to stay and be of use.[103] NEFA's inhabitants were hence 'fundamentally balanced in their appreciations of the costs and benefits of acquiescing to the government's terms'.[104]

For populations living under some degree of Tibetan influence, such appreciations also rested on an assessment of what the new rule would entail compared to Lhasa or local Tibetan power holders. The eastern Himalayas had been the target of the Tibetan state's 'civilising projects'. Its non-Buddhist inhabitants were derogatorily called *lhopa* ('barbarians'), and the term 'Monpa' originally designated a range of populations whose main commonality was geographic remoteness from Tibetan centres and supposed civilisational backwardness.[105] Subjected to tribute

---

[102] Graham Bower, *The hidden land*, pp. 16–18; APSA, Tour diaries of Major S.M. Krishnatry, 1955, p. 17; APSA, P/43/55; Itanagar, APSA, NEFA Secretariat (1955), Tour diary of APO I Taliha, Hipshon Roy, P/41/55, p. 5.

[103] NAI, External 241-CA/458–9 March, 13 March 1945.

[104] Christian Tripodi, 'Negotiating with the enemy: "Politicals" and tribes 1901–47', *Journal of Imperial and Commonwealth History*, 39:4 (2011), 589–606 (p. 590).

[105] Françoise Pommaret, 'The Mon-Pa revisited: In search of Mon', in *Sacred spaces and powerful places in Tibetan culture: A collection of essays*, ed. by Toni Huber (Dharamsala: Library of Tibetan Works and Archives, 1999), pp. 52–73 (pp. 52–62).

and corvée labour by Lhasa's powerful Sera Monastery, the non-Buddhist people around Pemakö readily accepted Indian administration as a protection against their northern neighbours, provided outposts would stay year-round. This conversely antagonised the Membas, who played an important role in tribute collection. Other Buddhists did not necessarily oppose Indian expansion. The Sherdukpens and Dirang Dzong Monpas extended their cooperation to the Indian outpost and even accepted to pay a house tax, likely because it compared favourably with their tribute to the *dzongpöns*.[106] In northern Kameng, many Tawang Monpas adopted a more circumspect attitude towards Indian officials for much of the 1940s.[107] Yet Tawang's takeover seems to have been on the whole peaceful.

How can we reconcile James Scott's contention that the inhabitants of Asia's highlands had consciously cultivated an 'art of not being governed' with this willingness to countenance state presence in their midst?[108] The answer might be that, rather than possessed of an innate drive to escape the state, NEFA's inhabitants were adverse to *a certain kind* of state presence – a presence based primarily on the use of violent coercion or the constant possibility for it and precluding local agency.

Even before the 1940s, relations between a touring official and the people encountered could take a peaceful form – provided the former did not go about with an armed escort. Williamson had not encountered resistance during his early forays in the Siang Basin, when he travelled in small company and unarmed, but when he decided to get the support of a large military squadron in 1911 in a bid to push up to the border, the decision cost him his life.

From the inhabitants' perspective, a state presence that *might* be acceptable was, by contrast, one that required their cooperation and could thus be malleable to their own needs, priorities, and purposes; it was also, by the same token, a state presence that could bring with it some concrete benefits, material or otherwise. This did not mean everyone in a given community, let alone a tribal group, had the same attitude towards an

---

[106] Itanagar, APSA, NEFA Secretariat (1940), Tour diaries of the APO Pasighat for November 1940–April 1944; London, BL, IOR (11 January 1944–2 February 1948), Fortnightly reports on the Assam Tribal Areas, November 1943–November 1947, IOR/L/PS/12/3117; New Delhi, NAI, External Affairs Proceedings (1946), Fortnightly reports in the Assam tribal areas for 1946, 315-CA/46; APSA, James tour diaries August 1945–December 1946; Mizuno and Tenpa, *A study of Monpa*, p. 53 (Interview with Pema Gombu).

[107] Itanagar, APSA, NEFA Secretariat (1945), Tour Diary of Political Officer Balipara, February 1944–November 1945, pp. 1–2.

[108] James C. Scott, *The art of not being governed: An anarchist history of upland Southeast Asia* (New Haven, CO; London: Yale University Press, 2009).

officer's arrival. Some individuals, starting with interpreters, had much greater scope to negotiate with the state.

After the mid-1940s, instances in which POs were treated with hospitality rose. Significantly, the communities concerned lived south of the Assam–Tibet trade watershed and had particularly been affected by the Second World War, due to wartime shortages and lucrative wartime work. The leverage they had derived from it had made them particularly skilled at negotiating with external actors, for example in refusing to settle for mediocre porterage pay and conditions. For these communities, engaging with the state could be profitable and necessary – provided it suited their own purposes.

In several instances, people began to make active demands on state authorities. After the war, Adi groups closer to the plains developed their village *kebang* into regional councils and eventually set up a pan-Adi council to advise the local PO on administration. In this case, the Officer had encouraged the move; at other times, tribal demands came ahead of government intentions. At the turn of independence, a large number of Adis gathered in Pasighat to discuss their hopes and stress their demands. They requested an administrative commitment to bringing peace and educational facilities and asked for political representation – something that India's constitution makers told them they were not ready for.[109] This 'very clear desire ... for representation' in several parts of NEFA forced Indian lawmakers to adapt – many Khamtis and Singphos were also asking for an MP.[110] In 1951, the Representation of the People Act accordingly instituted a nominated parliamentary representative for NEFA.[111]

The Politics of Prior Access

Coupled with relief and rehabilitation efforts after the earthquake, the paradox of vulnerability explains why an increasing number of people accepted Indian state presence after 1950. Yet, a third dynamic was also at play. There is an important nuance between accepting state presence and actively requesting it. When Leyak's Bangni villagers extended their hospitality to a surprised Indian officer in 1952, they had arguably noted that greater or prior access to the state was now an important factor in determining one's leverage, both vis-à-vis the state and towards other

---

[109] Itanagar, APSA, NEFA Secretariat (1947), Formation of Abor Tribal Council A-508/47.

[110] *The framing of India's constitution: A study*, ed. by B. Shiva Rao, 5 vols (New Delhi: Indian Institute of Public Administration, 1968), Volume III, pp. 703–705.

[111] New Delhi, NAI, Home Affairs Proceedings (1954), Nomination of members to the House of the People or Council of States representing NEFA in Assam, 73/4-Public.

inhabitants. Once NEFA authorities had a foothold in several areas, people in closest contact with them found themselves at an advantage, both to shape state presence and to make demands on it. This had initially given a disproportionate leverage to foothills communities. Campaign for political rights and welfare facilities in the Adi foothills during 1947–1948 had induced frontier authorities to focus their limited development initiatives after 1947 on them. As administrative headquarters moved inland and the number of centres increased, leverage partially shifted to groups located nearby. Increasingly, power relations revolved around the boundary between those who did have ties to government structures and those who did not, or not to the same extent. For more isolated groups, accepting and engaging with the NEFA administration was a way not to be on the losing side rather than the sign of a burning desire for Indian rule. Acting on this, some actively invited the state in.

Sometime in late 1950, a strange letter landed on the desk of the Lohit PO. Presenting himself as the headman of the Lisu village of Khomong, the sender announced his readiness to pay poll tax. The PO was astonished. That the purported headman volunteered to be taxed was surprising enough, but the official had not even known that the Khomong plateau was inhabited! An enquiry revealed that the Lisus came from the Sino–Burmese borderlands and had crossed the border sometime around 1947, to settle an area deserted by the local Singphos.

This small community's decision to migrate and their offer to pay poll tax hints at a shrewd understanding of what negotiating with the state could bring. Not only were the Lisus aware that India had little capacity or energy to prevent population movement in its Assam–Burma borderlands but they protected themselves by obtaining a Burmese laissez-passer. By voluntarily revealing themselves to Indian authorities – who had barely explored Khomong and hardly knew which jurisdiction it belonged to – and declaring themselves ready to become taxpayers, the Lisus portrayed themselves as peaceful and useful candidates for residence in NEFA. In doing so, they pre-empted being expulsed, the only 'foreigners' allowed to remain beyond the Inner Line being subject to tax. Their initiative succeeded. Not only were they granted the right to remain in India but within a year they had successfully established themselves in the much more prosperous Chowkham area.[112]

Often however, frontier officials struggled to grasp the values and multiple, changing contingencies shaping tribal attitudes towards

---

[112] Itanagar, APSA, NEFA Secretariat (1950), Settlement of 200 Lichus at Khomang GA-118/50.

them – and this failure of understanding could have serious consequences. One morning in 1948, Apatanis attacked the Kure outpost in
the Subansiri. Armed only with bow and arrows, they did not reach it in
time to catch the Assam Rifles contingent unaware. The garrison opened
fire, killing three men. Survivors fled back to their village, destroying the
outpost's granary along the way. The Assam Rifles responded by burning
down the houses and granaries of the suspected attackers' home villages,
shooting two more men in the process.

Written archives elide the events of Kure Chambyo ('the attack on
Kure'), but the shock in Shillong must have been great. Since the first
Western visits to the plateau in the late nineteenth century, Apatanis had
been romanticised as a civilised people whose isolation had not prevented
them developing an extraordinary agrarian culture. They were also
deemed peaceful, in contrast to their Nyishi neighbours. Yet, together
with the diaries or memoirs of officials working in the Subansiri prior to
Kure Chambyo, oral history gives us important clues as to the importance
of the attack's circumstances.[113]

The Apatanis who had welcomed Indian officials had done so on the
premise that they would help settle their disagreements with the Nyishis
but stay away from their own internal affairs. The invitation had come
from specific villages and individuals; if the rest accepted the outpost, it
was perhaps because of the possibility to trade more widely thanks to
colonial presence and the fact that porterage paid well during the Second
World War.

Within a couple of years, however, the Subansiri PO began adjudicat-
ing intra-Apatani disputes on the request of certain inhabitants. Not only
did this anger those who opposed government interference but the justice
dispensed was perceived as favouring those who had better access to the
state – the villages on whose territory the official's camp was located, and
from which his Political Interpreters hailed.[114] It is also possible that,
because of their fuzzy understanding of Apatani social hierarchies, Indian
officials relied on individuals not considered as the real authority holders
in their community, offending local notables.[115] Moreover, key advantages of the outpost's presence soon disappeared. The end of the war
caused army airdrops to stop, causing a rise in porterage even as the

---

[113] Stuart Blackburn, 'Colonial contact in the "hidden land": Oral history among the
Apatanis of Arunachal Pradesh', *Indian Economic and Social History Review*, 40:3
(2003), 335–365 (pp. 343–352).
[114] Stuart Blackburn, *Himalayan tribal tales: Oral tradition and culture in the Apatani Valley*
(Boston; Leiden: Brill, 2008), pp. 133–145.
[115] SOAS, PP MS 19, Box 4 (11 May 1944).

activity stopped being lucrative. Finally, the Assam Rifles garrison had just been reinforced (albeit with a view to settle Nyishi feuds).[116] In short, Kure Chambyo happened at a time when the conditions for countenancing state presence had lapsed for a significant number of Apatanis. The general silence of government sources about the incident makes it difficult to assess its impact on the NEFA administration's expansion policy. Yet the role that coerced porterage and the recourse to local food sources had played in triggering the attack likely played a part in convincing frontier officers that the airdropping of all outposts' requirements was preferable from now on, no matter how dangerous and inefficient.

Five years later, a far greater clash occurred. In October 1953, an exploratory government party was attacked at a place called Achingmori, deep in the un-administered Siang–Subansiri border-lands. Forty-seven people were murdered and dozens taken hostage.[117] The incident soon exposed the fragility of the post-colonial state's information order, and of its agents' position in the eastern Himalayas.

Speculation was rife after the massacre. Neither the perpetrators' identity nor their motivations were clear. At first, they were reported to be Nyishi. This changed soon afterwards: the people in question appeared to be Tagins, not Nyishis. One explanation for the incident relied on the trope of tribal violence, putting the massacre on the count of Tagin savagery.[118] Another, found in the Assamese media, denounced the attack as the result of the central government's con-tinued neglect of the eastern Himalayas.[119] Some observers provided a more circumstantial explanation: the touring PO had angered local Tagins by organising a military-like expedition through their terri-tory, employing coolies of a rival group in the process.[120]

---

[116] Blackburn, 'Colonial contact in the "hidden land"' (p. 358).

[117] Krishnatry, *Border Tagins*; Nari Rustomji, *Imperilled frontiers: India's north-eastern border-lands* (Delhi: Oxford University Press, 1983), pp. 132–135. The first casualty estimates were far higher: '70 killed in Abor Hills clash', *Amrita Bazaar Patrika*, 3 November 1953.

[118] 'Letters to the editor: NEFA administration (by "anthropologist")', *Assam Tribune*, 5 November 1953; NAI, External 241-CA/45. (Winter season 1944–1945, 1 December); Satyen Sen Gupta, 'Abors: Untamed tribesmen of India's Northeast Frontier', *Amrita Bazaar Patrika*, 7 November 1953. Yet, prolonged encounters with the Adis or the Nyishis had shown that neither tribe conformed to their alleged blood-thirsty nature. Nyishis had, for instance, rescued stranded pilots and brought them to outposts. NAI, 6/6-P/45 (Fortnightly report, late December 1944).

[119] 'Editorial: Abor Hills incident', *Assam Tribune*, 2 November 1953.

[120] 'Letters to the editor: What is wrong in NEFA', *Assam Tribune*, 1953; 'Editorial: The tragedy and after', *Assam Tribune*, 7 November 1953.

The multiplication of conjectures hinted at the NEFA administration's sheer lack of knowledge of the people it was encountering in the Siang–Subansiri borderlands. The very term 'Tagin' had scarcely been mentioned before in government sources. The people it was meant to describe had materialised as a single tribe under the administrator's gaze as largely due to the massacre; moreover, this characterisation was shaped by non-Tagins with older and closer contacts with Indian officials. In the circumstances, any interpretation of the roots of the Achingmori incident – and whether the government party had provoked it, either actively or because its presence gave inhabitants leverage in their relations with Achingmori's people – was mere guesswork.

The Indian government decided to immediately despatch half an Assam Rifles platoon to the Achingmori area. On 21 November 1953, Nehru was forced, for the first time, to make a parliamentary statement on NEFA policy and the handling of the crisis. To parliament members who wondered whether 'the Government would be justified in taking action because the [Tagins] lived in an un-administered area and they did not consider themselves as Indian citizens', he replied that this 'did not mean that [the area] was outside the territory of the Indian Union'. The government would punish the culprits without resorting to indiscriminate 'terror'.[121]

On the ground, however, the Tagin areas were treated 'almost as a war zone'.[122] The Tagin councils of elders were given an ultimatum to surrender the 'ringleaders' and release hostages to the Assam Rifles.[123] But when the party arrived after its three-week march, 'the only thing they could find were abandoned houses, chickens and pigs, which of course were slaughtered, and houses burnt'.[124] The population of most nearby villages had fled across the river. It took two months, the military canvassing of the entire area, and the arrest of many villagers,[125] to catch the leaders and release the hostages. Five Tagins were killed and another thirty-nine wounded during the operations.[126] Two of the leaders were

---

[121] 'No policy to strike terror in Abor Hills', *Amrita Bazaar Patrika*, 22 November 1953.
[122] Krishnatry, *Border Tagins*, p. 33.
[123] 'No decision for surrender yet by Daflas of Tagin area', *Amrita Bazaar Patrika*, 26 November 1950.
[124] Krishnatry, *Border Tagins*, p. 33.
[125] 'Troops leave for Tagin area: First phase of operations against tribesmen', *Statesman*, 29 November 1953; 'Army columns get into Tagin areas: No resistance from tribesmen', *Amrita Bazaar Patrika*, 9 December 1953; 'Expedition against Tagins: 3-Pronged advance towards Achingmori', *Assam Tribune*, 29 November 1953; '21 Tagins captured', *Times of India*, 18 December 1953.
[126] Krishnatry, *Border Tagins*, p. 33; 'Tagins at last submit to expedition party', *Assam Tribune*, 23 December 1953; 'Calm restored in Frontier Agency: Administrative centres established', *Times of India*, 29 January 1954.

eventually sentenced to life imprisonment, the others to shorter terms.[127] To ensure that the area would from now on be under control, the NEFA administration quickly established two centres on either bank of the Subansiri.[128]

Ostensibly, the Indian state had used its military might successfully.[129] But in reality, the crisis underscored the limits of its law and order capabilities. Frontier authorities' capacity to respond quickly to the incident was low: military columns took three weeks to reach the site of the massacre, and they were then forced into a long hide-and-seek game with the local people, whom they hardly knew. An inordinate amount of time, effort, and money had been spent to achieve the mission's limited objectives – catching the massacre's leaders and releasing the hostages. What's more, mustering the required number of Assam Rifles must have been difficult: the force was increasingly tied up in Tuensang and the Naga Hills District. The scale of the Achingmori massacre and the intensity of public scrutiny required a big punitive expedition, but replicating it would be difficult. If Achingmori had proved anything, it was that the state was inefficient at imposing itself in the eastern Himalayas – and that trying to do so would result in both antagonising the population and endangering the Indian state's own resilience.

In contrast, some officials had noticed that their efforts to establish relations with local inhabitants were more successful when they shed the 'escort complex' and acknowledged some vulnerability.[130] Going on tour unescorted was far more effective, felt Fürer-Haimendorf in the 1940s, because 'the very fact that no one else is about works in them the feeling that they are responsible for you, and they show themselves far more helpful, than when they carry loads, but see you surrounded by *sepoys*', and 'a small camp, consisting of a tent and two shelters for servants and interpreters, can also be much closer to the village, or indeed inside the village'.[131]

In 1956, two years after Achingmori, an official called Captain Krishnatry was sent back into the Tagin areas to establish outposts in the northern Subansiri. He followed Fürer-Haimendorf's advice: not only did he travel without an Assam Rifles escort but his wife accompanied him. Tagin *gam*s acted as intermediaries along the way. In approaching

---

[127] NAI, External 4(19)-P/55 (June report).

[128] 'Administration plan for Achingmori', *Statesman*, 12 December 1953; NAI, External 4(19)-P/55 (April report).

[129] Rustomji, *Imperilled frontiers*, p. 134.

[130] New Delhi, NAI, External Affairs Proceedings (1943), Claim by the Tibetan government that Tibetan subjects settled in Bhutan should be repatriated to Tibet. Measures taken to stabilize the MacMahon Line, 63/X/43 (Weightman, 11 January 1944).

[131] SOAS, PP MS 19, Box 4, p. 23 (4 March).

the Nas and the Mras who lived around the Tsari Mountain, the party carefully presented the outpost as a government attempt 'not to burden them with administrative demands ... [but] to study their problems, to help them out unless they did not want to'.[132] His wife proved an opportunity to encounter and engage with local women. Krishnatry eventually succeeded in establishing outposts at Limeking and Dinekoli, near the McMahon Line.

Later visits to the areas around Achingmori in the late 1950s further underscored the benefit, for state agents, of admitting to vulnerability in their relations with local inhabitants:

There was at first some apprehension that I had come to make further enquiries about the Achingmori tragedy. At a remote village ..., the leaders did not come to see me for a considerable time, though I was immediately surrounded by a large crowd of people. But presently the Chief, ... marched up in grim silence ... He obviously did not care greatly for what he saw. I could feel him drinking me in – the undistinguished features, the spectacles, the worn-out coat, frayed and baggy trousers, the muddy boots. Is that all, he seemed to say, that they have to offer? ... I would have to put on my little act, which in my opinion is worth a whole platoon of Assam Rifles as a safety measure. I removed my dentures. There was a roar of interest and excitement from the crowd. I put them back. Another roar. After I had conducted this humiliating performance several times, there was at last a reaction. The Chief's lips began to twitch, and he finally broke into a hearty laugh. Pointing to his greying hair, he declared, 'I am an old man too', and soon he was sitting beside me very affably ... by the time I left he was happy and content, and he was certainly almost vociferous in his demands for a fuller development of the area.[133]

Thus, insofar as the attempts of Indian authorities were successful from the mid-twentieth century onwards, these had much to do with the paradox of their vulnerability – a weakness that rendered their entrenchment precarious unless local people acquiesced to it, but which also made this acquiescence more likely. But, as Achingmori and Kure Chambyo showed, this paradox rested on a fragile balance, made all the more precarious because a further precondition for tribal cooperation was what the NEFA administration could offer them. In the aftermath of the Achingmori massacre, development-centred initiatives would acquire unprecedented importance.

[132] Krishnatry, *Border Tagins*, pp. 21, 2, and 23.
[133] Elwin, *An autobiography*, pp. 265–266.

4 The Art of Persuasion
Development in a Border Space

The NEFA administration was in an uncomfortable position in late 1953. The media's interest had been temporarily revived by Achingmori and they were casting a harsh light on its policies. Critical editorials had appeared, arguing that local tribes had 'a claim on the Indian Government as much as any other people for their development and welfare. This [was] a test and a challenge to the talent and leadership [of] new India.'[1]

These statements betrayed the added weight of debates surrounding the place and fate of indigenous communities in independent India. With the country's 'nationalist vocabulary' recast around national unity and development, the 'uplift' of its Scheduled Tribes – a constitutional responsibility of central and provincial governments – had become a means of fulfilling overarching national goals.[2] A Commissioner for Scheduled Castes and Scheduled Tribes had been appointed in 1951 and a pan-Indian Conference on Tribes and Scheduled Areas held a year later.[3] As the largest tribal region in India, NEFA was under particular scrutiny.

On the ground, the situation called for a reflection on the fundamentals of state expansion. Achingmori showed that semi-military expeditions and punitive promenades were prone to backfire, in addition to being costly and inefficient. NEFA officials did not have to look far to guess the potential consequences of continuing in this vein. In the Patkai, the Naga independence movement was increasingly militant. Delhi saw the

---

[1] 'Abor attacks one hundred years back: How British Govt was forced to pay tribute', *Amrita Bazaar Patrika*, 7 November 1953.
[2] Rochana Bajpai, *Debating difference: Minority rights and liberal democracy in India* (New Delhi: Oxford University Press, 2010).
[3] New Delhi, NAI, Home Affairs Proceedings (1950), Appointment of a Commissioner for Scheduled Castes and Scheduled Tribes and Staff for his office, 74/6/50-Public. The conference was attended by about 200 people, from tribal MPs to social workers, scholars, and officials. For Nehru's opening speech, see *Selected works of Jawaharlal Nehru – Second series*, ed. by S. Gopal (New Delhi: Jawaharlal Nehru Memorial Fund, 1996), XVIII, pp. 370–377.

phenomenon as the result of economic and political neglect. For the 'problem' to be solved, counter-insurgency would have to be conjugated with hearts-and-minds policies.[4] To stamp out Naga insurgency in Tuensang and prevent any repeat of that scenario among other ethnic groups, the development of NEFA became a priority.[5]

The use of development as a state-making tool in the eastern Himalayas was in itself nothing new. The notion had gradually gained credence among NEFA officials since the Second World War. A Medical Department had been founded in 1951, and, after a rapid recruitment campaign, several dispensaries had been built and anti-malaria measures launched.[6] In 1952, 'model villages' settled with earthquake victims had been built near Pasighat, and a community project started among the Khamtis of Chowkham.[7] These first projects formed the basis of what would become the key development structure in NEFA: the National Extension Schemes (NES). The first two had been founded a few months before Achingmori among the Noctes of Tirap, and at Ziro in Apatani territory.[8] Yet these development initiatives were still in their infancy, and they coexisted with the coercive state vocabulary long in force in the eastern Himalayas.

Achingmori and the Naga conflict brought to a head long-standing administrative discussions on how to consolidate India's hold over the eastern Himalayas. For the rest of the 1950s, the emphasis would be on expressing state presence in benevolent terms. Recognising the paradox of vulnerability was the first expression of that change. Yet, while frontier authorities' weakness made their implantation among the people of the eastern Himalayas acceptable, it was not in itself sufficient to make it advantageous to them. Rather, it was by establishing itself as the provider of tangible goods and benefits – as it had done after the 1950 earthquake – that the Indian state would

---

[4] One million rupees were quickly sanctioned 'for beneficial purposes' in the Naga areas, and another three to compensate Second World War damages. Jawaharlal Nehru, *Letters to Chief Ministers, 1947–1964*, ed. by G. Parthasarathi (New Delhi: Jawaharlal Nehru Memorial Fund, c.1985–), pp. 413–414.

[5] An editorial warned that while Achingmori might have been 'a local tribal outburst with little yet discernible political motive', it was a 'different [manifestation] of the same fundamental malady [as in Naga areas] and, as such, demand[ed] the same psychological approach'. 'Editorial: Assam tribes', *Amrita Bazaar Patrika*, 16 December 1953.

[6] R.N. Koley, *East Siang in the last fifty years (1947–1997)* (Pasighat: District administration, East Siang, c. 1997).

[7] Tarun Kumar Bhattacharjee, *The frontier trail* (Calcutta: Manick Bandyopadhyay, 1993), pp. 64–66.

[8] New Delhi, NMML, Elwin Papers (1954), Confidential reports on the NEFA 1952–4, S. No. 111; Itanagar, APSA, NEFA Secretariat (1953), Inauguration of 2nd Community Development Block at Namsang, CP-132/53.

legitimise and justify its presence, and thus entrench itself in the eastern Himalayas.

The Choice of Tribal Development

Within a few months of Achingmori, a momentous decision was taken. NEFA would not have one Adviser but two. Where the Adviser to the Governor would remain responsible for administrative expansion, his new colleague would implement a development strategy tailored to NEFA. Nehru himself designated the man for the task. An Englishman who had only recently been granted Indian citizenship, he was an ex-priest – a vestige from his early years as a Christian missionary in India – who had spent decades amongst the tribes of central India, committing himself to 'defending the aboriginal'. His name was Verrier Elwin.[9]

The appointment had a great resonance in Indian political circles, and not just because the incumbent was no career bureaucrat. Elwin had been a major protagonist of the 'Tribal Question' during the late 1940s. Rejecting assimilationist or civilising stances, this self-taught anthropologist vehemently argued that tribal communities needed protection from acculturation, conversion, and economic exploitation by the Indian 'mainstream'. This had done little to endear him among Indian nationalists and Christian missionaries. As for anthropologists, many accused Elwin of isolationism.

The perspective of a transfer of power had mollified Elwin. Determined to remain in independent India, he had declared that tribes already in contact with the rest of India's population would have to adapt. Only the 'real primitives' would require strict protection, but this protection would have to be enforced by the state. Meanwhile, Indian constitution makers had decided that certain tribes, starting with those in Assam, deserved specific safeguards indeed. This had enabled Elwin to become a naturalised citizen and even Deputy Director of India's Anthropological Survey. His long-term dream was to use anthropology as 'a scientific basis to policies aimed at the poor and the vulnerable', especially in tribal areas.[10] Nehru was to give him an opportunity to do just that, in NEFA.

In 1957, a small book prefaced by Nehru himself landed in Indian bookshops: *A Philosophy for NEFA*. Signed Verrier Elwin, the book was a precis of government principles and policies for the incorporation of the largest tribal region in India. What the frontier administration envisioned

---

[9] Ramachandra Guha, *Savaging the civilized: Verrier Elwin, his tribals, and India* (New Delhi: Oxford University Press, 2001), p. 123.
[10] Ibid. (p. 183).

was neither assimilation nor isolation but a comprehensive 'middle-way' that would bring 'the best things of the modern world to the tribes, but in such a way that these will not destroy the traditional way of life, but will activate and develop all that is good in it.' The aim, argued Elwin, was to understand 'what, from their point of view, is the best thing for the people of NEFA' and to implement it.

Within these overarching parameters, the administration would ensure material and social progress by fostering economic and agricultural self-sufficiency and installing law and order, while 'striving for a renaissance of art, music, beauty, colour, the joys and graces of living'. Frontier officials would take care not to create 'an inferiority complex' among the tribes. Nehru called it 'help[ing] the tribal people to grow according to their own genius'.[11]

All this was ultimately but a means to an end:

to see as the result of our efforts a spirit of love and loyalty for India, without a trace of suspicion that Government has come into the tribal areas to colonise or exploit, a full integration of mind and heart with the great society of which the tribal people form a part and to whose infinite variety they may make a unique contribution.

In other words, the NEFA 'Philosophy' was truly a state-making and nation-building endeavour, one of almost mystical proportions. Elwin presented it as 'the Prime Minister's gospel' and declared himself the Indian state's 'missionary' in the tribal Himalayas.[12]

On the face of it, the strategy of tribal developmentalism that would dominate state expansion in the 1950s was an ideology-driven plan, devised at the top of the Indian state to integrate NEFA into India. Elwin had been parachuted from above to apply a pre-forged solution to the Tribal Question to NEFA. This top–down process seemed further in evidence in the Five-Year Plans elaborated for the eastern Himalayas in the course of the decade, echoing those implemented elsewhere in India.

Yet, beneath the grand rhetoric, the NEFA Philosophy was also an adaptive strategy driven by the constraints and challenges frontier officials had long encountered on the ground. Its great lines had already emerged when Elwin was appointed, through daily interactions between frontier officials and local communities. Elwin himself might be the talented spokesman of the philosophy but he would often be absent from NEFA.

The significance of Elwin's appointment as Nehru's adviser on tribal issues was rather that, from now on, NEFA officials would have a direct

[11] Verrier Elwin, *A philosophy for NEFA*, 1st edn (Shillong: North-East Frontier Agency, 1957), pp. 9, 1, 51–54, 11.
[12] Ibid. (p. 9 and preface, respectively).

link to the topmost echelons of the Indian state. It was often tenuous, for Nehru had other preoccupations. But it was enough. From 1953 onwards, the lack of finance that had plagued the implementation of the first Five-Year Plan loosened up. Elwin's high profile in the media and strong ties to Nehru enabled frontier administration to neutralise the Finance Ministry's attempts to curb expenses. Tribal development would now come into its own.

The NEFA Philosophy in Action

Education and health care, the oldest welfare activities, remained priorities. The opening of dispensaries and the recruitment of medical personnel accelerated, mobile health units were sent to remote areas, and health campaigns were conducted, especially against goitre and leprosy. The Healthcare Department expanded its field of activity by undertaking medical propaganda, malaria surveys, and nutrition and sanitation campaigns (Figures 4.1 and 4.2).

Schools opened at an increasing space. By 1955–1956, NEFA counted 113 primary schools, 13 middle schools, and 3 high schools.[13] The style and curriculum of education in NEFA was the object of extended discussions. In 1954, a Conference on Basic Education for NEFA decided on educational priorities for the agency. Yet the teachers had to be trained first. Basic Education could only be implemented after 1957.[14]

A new discourse of agricultural improvement and food self-sufficiency simultaneously took root. British Indian officers had thought of NEFA as an agricultural frontier, classifying tribes hierarchically on the basis of agricultural technology, and noting the existence of any zone suitable to settled cultivation in their tour reports; this had failed to yield any results.[15] From the late 1940s onwards, settled cultivation, particularly wet-rice agriculture, formed the thrust of development efforts. The hope was that, as people learnt its techniques, they would progressively turn away from the primitive practice of shifting cultivation. Village workers were trained and appointed to promote it among local communities, demonstration farms founded, and 'model villages' used to experiment in terrace agriculture or new crops.[16]

---

[13] London, BL, Elwin Papers (1957), 'Ten years' progress in NEFA: A brief account of administrative and development activities in NEFA since independence' (Independence Day 1957), Mss Eur D950/84, pp. 32, 37–38.

[14] NMML, Elwin Papers, S. No. 111.

[15] London, BL, Miscellaneous papers relating to the North-East Frontier of India (1946), Tour diary of I. Ali, PO Balipara Frontier Tract, Mss Eur D1191/7.

[16] NMML, Elwin Papers, S. No. 111. Even today, it is in the former 'model villages' such as Mirem that terrace agriculture is most entrenched. Tamo Mibang, *Social change in*

Figure 4.1 Health chart created by the administration for Monpa
communities, 1960
© Arunachal Pradesh DIPR

These objectives aligned with the overall push for agricultural revolution that was taking place across India at the time, inspired by postcolonial 'high modernism'.[17] Assam's settled districts, while not a key
target for the creation of an intensive, capitalist agriculture, were an
important part of this scheme; a key agricultural frontier of the British

Arunachal Pradesh (the Minyongs) 1947–1981 (Delhi: Omsons Publications, 1994), pp.
122–123.

[17] James C. Scott, *Seeing like a state: How certain schemes to improve the human condition have
failed* (New Haven; London: Yale University Press, 1998), chapter 8.

Figure 4.2 The Roing hospital, Lohit
© Arunachal Pradesh DIPR

Empire, they appeared as the one region of India where there was still room for permanent agricultural colonisation.[18]

In NEFA, the objectives of agricultural self-sufficiency were more complex. Apart from improving the well-being of local communities, its achievement would enable larger and more self-reliant concentrations of administrative staff and reduce the cost of delivering supplies. Ultimately, it would lessen the tribes' economic reliance on Tibet and ensure greater control over the border.

[18] B.H. Farmer, *Agricultural colonisation in South and South East Asia* (Hull: University of Hull, 1969), pp. 6–14.

'Self-sufficiency' was accordingly replicated in other spheres of human activity. Craft centres serving both as training and production sites were opened across the agency. Some were multidisciplinary, others focused on particular crafts: weaving, cane work, hat making, sericulture, carpentry for instance.[19] Trainees were to go back to their village to use that skill for its benefit, or to remain at the centre as fully fledged workers. Through craft making, the administration aimed both to decrease trade with Tibet and to inject 'more colour' and 'more beauty' into tribal culture.[20]

'More colour, more beauty' was not an afterthought; it was the rhetorical core of the NEFA Philosophy. When it was decided to include tribal decorative elements in public buildings, a horrified Elwin realised that almost no one knew what tribal communal buildings really looked like. A well-administered, properly developed NEFA could only be achieved if its administration was in possession of precise and extensive knowledge about its people.

The notion had old colonial antecedents. Private and government ethnographers, explorers, or surveyors had played an important role in laying the ground for the annexation of the highland regions of colonial Assam. This had also given north-eastern India a long genealogy of government officials-cum-ethnographers. The challenge of acquiring sufficient knowledge about the eastern Himalayas bore strongly on the minds of Indian authorities in the 1940s, swaying their choice of J.P. Mills and Fürer-Haimendorf (one a Naga Hills official turned amateur ethnographer, the other a professional anthropologist) as frontier officials. Under Elwin's leadership – and there lay the strongest impact of his appointment – NEFA authorities would build a home-grown research apparatus that, without reaching the elusive goal of truly 'knowing the country', would soon have a major influence on state-making.[21]

In 1956, a Research Department was founded to enable frontier administration to 'move on both fronts, cultural and developmental'.[22] Anthropological research would help tailor government initiatives among given tribal groups, while inspiring 'self-respect' among them, for

[19] NMML, Elwin Papers, S. No. 111; Delhi, NMML, Elwin Papers (1956), Comments on ATA's reports, 1954–59, S. No. 133; Delhi, NMML, Elwin Papers (1961), Cottage Industries Training-cum-Production Centre, 1957–61, S. No. 46.

[20] New Delhi, NMML, Elwin Papers (n.d.), The policy of the Govt of India for the administration of NEFA, S. No. 166, p. 24.

[21] Delhi, NMML, Elwin Papers (1956), Correspondence with K.L. Rathee Financial Adviser NEFA, 1955–56, S. No. 2. The expression 'knowing the country' comes from Christopher Bayly, 'Knowing the country: Empire and information in India', *Modern Asian Studies*, 27:1 (1993), 3–43.

[22] Delhi, NMML, Elwin Papers (1956), Report of the Ministry of External Affairs, 1955–56, S. No. 110 ('A note on the political and administrative problems of the NEFA'), p. 73.

instance by emphasising the value and administrative use of their mother tongue.[23]

From ethnographic photography to linguistic research, from gazetteers to anthropological studies, the NEFA Research Department's priorities encompassed nearly every aspect of human activity. A General Culture Branch was in charge of anthropological work, museums, photography, and art production; a Historical Research Branch wrote gazetteers, maintained libraries, and conducted historical research; a Philology Branch prepared dictionaries, phrasebooks, or textbooks. A Statistical Section and Publicity Officers completed this elaborate structure.[24]

Within a year of its founding, the Research Department had become a fundamental component of the NEFA state apparatus. Philologists, librarians, curators, and research associates had been hired.[25] Government artists were preparing posters, calendars, and textbooks. By 1958, seven monographs on individual tribes were in print, along with books on mythology, games, dances, art – and the ubiquitous *Philosophy for NEFA*.

The cultural policy that sprang out from these research activities was wide ranging. A stream of illustrated songs' and folktales' booklets came out for use in local schools. Dances, music, and games were particularly encouraged. Touring officers were directed to ask for them and to reward them with political presents. Villagers were enjoined to build dancing grounds. Local games were promoted in schools, villages, and crafts centres.[26] Cultural centres, libraries, and museums were established in each division to 'present the tribal culture in its dignity and beauty ... [and] exhibit samples of the best folk art [of] India in order to inspire people'.[27] By the late 1950s, the Research Department was almost a state within a state, giving a new meaning to the notion of 'ethnographic state'.[28] Under the guise of welfare and development, Indian authorities were gradually entrenching themselves across much of NEFA.

[23] Nari K. Rustomji, *Verrier Elwin and India's north-eastern borderlands* (Shillong: North-Eastern Hill University Publications, 1988), p. 54.
[24] Delhi, NMML, Elwin Papers (1962), Orders and clarifications by K.L. Mehta concerning the Adviser for Tribal Affairs, 1956–62, S. No. 126.
[25] *Research in Arunachal, 1951–76* (Shillong: Directorate of Research, Arunachal Pradesh, 1978), pp. xxii–xxiii.
[26] NMML, Elwin Papers S. No. 133.
[27] *Lok Sabha Debates 1959 (Vol. XXVIII)* (New Delhi: Lok Sabha Secretariat, 1959), pp. 11257–11258.
[28] Nicholas B. Dirks, *Castes of mind: Colonialism and the making of modern India* (Princeton, NJ; Chichester: Princeton University Press, 2001).

Routinising the State

State-making was nowhere more in evidence than in the routine acts and rituals surrounding Community Projects and NES blocks, whereby a specific area of NEFA was selected for all-round development. Agriculture, health care, education, sanitation, and cottage industry initiatives concentrated there, on the assumption that this would enhance their individual impact. In economic terms, this was a localised 'big push'.

This was also a big push of the state. By gathering all development activities into one 'block', frontier authorities made a demonstration of *everything* the Indian state could do for the eastern Himalayas' inhabitants. Blocks would extend and represent its reach and its concern for people. Nehru hoped to see 'the entire Agency [covered] by NES blocks during the next ten years'.[29]

In late 1953, the Assam Governor personally inaugurated the second development block at Namsang, in Tirap. Senior frontier officials, tribal leaders, and local Noctes and Singphos all gathered to attend festivities carefully planned by NEFA's top bureaucrats. The day-long programme included a guard of honour, tree planting and village clearing, community feeding, tribal dances, and a cinema show. Especially revamped for the occasion, the village announced the new order to come; an exhibit on education, agriculture, and health proclaimed the promise of development and celebrated tribal culture; and a collective meal emphasised the links between a benevolent frontier administration and society, even as the Governor's presence asserted the authority of the Indian state.[30]

Welfare schemes assisted the writing of surveys and the collection of statistics. The NEFA section of the 1951 census had consisted of wild estimates that could not, by any stretch of the imagination, be likened to statistics. They were later found so greatly overestimated that development and administrative programmes had to be rethought.[31] The surveys conducted to delimit and plan NES blocks became a means to gather a wealth of information about an area and its people, from the number and size of villages to their generational and gender distribution, from land use statistics to rainfall and trade data or occupational profiles.

---

[29] Delhi, NMML, Elwin Papers (1955), Lectures and Notes on NEFA, 1953–55, S. No. 149 (Note on the NEFA by Nehru, 28 August 1955), p. 9.
[30] APSA, CP-132/53. Also NMML, Elwin Papers, S. No. 111 (Reports for 1952, October–November).
[31] Itanagar, APSA, NEFA Secretariat (1955), Enumeration of population in NEFA areas, R/13/55 ('Preparation of Census Data', P.N. Luthra).

Thematic surveys were later begun – on malaria, for instance, or nutrition.[32] These statistics were still far from scientific. Many were based on estimates, for people '[did] not like to give out facts'. Administrators contented themselves with obtaining 'figures . . . as accurate as possible without upsetting the sentiments of the people'.[33] When the time came for a new census in 1961, the impediments to an intensive population survey remained. There was no divisional statistical organisation and political staff were too overworked to fulfil what was an immense task. Many villages had never been surveyed, many more were semi-permanent, and the names of many settlements remained unknown; out of an estimated 3,500 villages, only 196 had local government officials.[34] How to distinguish and name the different tribes also remained unclear.[35] But an embryo of a crucial aspect of governmentality had been created.

Development and welfare schemes also made a mundane practice systematic: inspections. Touring was a crucial component of the relation-ship between tribal populations and the state, but officers and subordinate staff remained few in number, and their ability to conduct regular inspections was limited. By contrast, the creation of the various development branches quickly led to the recruitment of medical, agricul-tural, or crafts inspectors and sub-inspectors. Not only did this sheer multiplication of touring officials increase the frequency with which tribal communities encountered the state but, because such inspectors were locally based, they could cover more of the surrounding territory and diverge from usual itineraries. These appointments notwithstanding, touring officers of any rank or capacity were required to partake in the ritual of diary making and give their opinion on everything, whether it belonged to their sphere of interest or not. Encounters with a low-rank inspector one week, the Chief Medical Officer the other, and perhaps the Governor at some point constructed the state as a complex, top–down hierarchy. Whereas the lonely PO on tour in the 1940s had represented a very flat vision, the NEFA administration was beginning to acquire the

[32] Itanagar, APSA, NEFA Secretariat (1955), Survey report for the Ziro NES block NES-II 4/55; New Delhi, NAI, External Affairs Proceedings (1957), Survey of NEFA, 21(1)-NEFA/57; BL, Mss Eur D950/84.
[33] APSA, NES-II 4/55 (PO Subansiri to NEFA Director, Planning, 10 January).
[34] Delhi, NMML, Elwin Papers (1961), Census 1961, 1959–61, S. No. 118.
[35] Itanagar, APSA, NEFA Secretariat (1956), Preparation of tribal maps of the various states of India, R-101/56. On the opacity of ethnic and cultural denominations in the eastern Himalayas, see Françoise Pommaret, 'The Mon-Pa revisited: In search of Mon', in Sacred spaces and powerful places in Tibetan culture: A collection of essays, ed. by Toni Huber (Dharamsala: Library of Tibetan Works and Archives, 1999), pp. 52–73.

'topography of stacked, vertical levels' so integral to perceptions of the state.[36]

Raising the Stakes of Access

The most powerful way in which development blocks led to the entrench-ment of the state was by creating a spatial boundary between the terri-tories and populations that were covered and those that were not. Ever since administrative expansion had started in earnest, being the first individual or community to come into contact with Indian authorities had represented an advantage. Frontier developmentalism reinforced this by raising the stakes of access at the individual and collective level.

Earlier on, access had meant influencing a touring official to settle a feud in one's favour. Now it meant convincing him to implement a welfare scheme in one's own community rather than elsewhere; being chosen as a contractor for a bridge-building scheme; receiving a plethora of political gifts; or being sent on an all-expenses paid trip to Delhi. The areas for early development blocks were all selected on the basis of existing infrastructure and the welcome of the population. Daporijo was chosen over Doimukh because of the 'natural enthusiasm and inclination to work of the people'.[37]

The politics of access was most evident in the foothills. Adi regional councils were particularly apt at negotiating with government. In 1961, the Minyongs demanded an immediate shift of the Pangin administrative centre to one of their villages, Boleng. They gave added weight to their demand by using the self-help logic of the administration: all the Minyongs in Boleng were ordered to construct a helipad. Interestingly, this demand was voiced shortly after the community formed a Minyong-only *kebang*, distinct from pan-Adi councils. This differentiation between groups that lived in close interaction may well have been a direct response to development schemes, for which they now competed.[38]

Groups with the longest and strongest history of contact with govern-ment schemes and officials were often the most vocal in their dealings with frontier administration. The Padams and the Idu Mishmis of the Lower Dibang Valley made a series of complaints to their PO. These ranged from problems regarding engineering works – bills were not

---

[36] James Ferguson and Akhil Gupta, 'Spatializing states: Toward an ethnography of neo-liberal governmentality', *American Ethnologist*, 29:4 (2002), 981–1002 (p. 983).

[37] APSA, NES-II 4/55 (Datta to External Affairs Under-Secretary, 30 March 1956), pp. 27–28.

[38] Tamo Mibang, 'Bogum-bokang-kebang', *Yaaro moobang: A land of peace, prosperity and happiness*, 1 (2001), 26–29 (p. 28).

settled on time – to agricultural schemes – staff were accused of sloth, seeds were not sent on time – and education – the small, dispersed schools were replaced by two central ones upon popular request.[39] But groups that had not been prioritised by expansion could prove equally assertive. Villages in different parts of the Nyishi country seized the opportunity of a rare PO visit in 1954–1955 to express their frustration at the government's neglect of them, asking for an outpost and agricultural implements to begin wet-rice cultivation.[40] People around Achingmori demanded that all development contract works be given to their clan members.[41]

By the late 1950s, the most consistent demand alongside development schemes and schools was to get a job in the administration. Increasingly, government office became the main route to wealth and social status. If schools and craft centres eventually became popular, it was because they were seen as avenues towards these government jobs.[42]

The politics of access also operated at the individual level. This was done through a figure that remains anonymous throughout government archives: the Village-Level Worker. Initially meant to supplement agricultural staff, these workers soon became an integral part of the NES block model. It was agreed to appoint an average of ten workers per block, and one worker for every six to eight villages in non-block areas.[43] Tasked with monitoring the agricultural well-being of a community, mediating conflict, and reporting to higher authorities, Village-Level Workers became the link to the state in areas without privileged access to it.[44]

Unlike other development and administrative posts, the principle for village workers was to privilege local people for recruitment. Such appointments served to give a direct stake to tribal people in the burgeoning state apparatus, yet since there was only a limited number of positions, they fuelled the politics of access. The principle worked as a mechanism of balance of power between the old generation of tribal strongmen – on whom frontier administration had relied earlier on – and the new one of school graduates – whom it now promoted, and from which most village workers' posts were filled (Figure 4.3). There are hints

[39] NMML, Elwin Papers S. No. 133 (Puri to Development Commissioner, 19 March 1956).
[40] Itanagar, APSA, NEFA Secretariat Files (1955), Tour diary and tour notes of S.M. Krishnatry, APO Subansiri, P/43/55, pp. 5, 17.
[41] Itanagar, APSA, NEFA Secretariat (1955), Tour diary of APO I Taliha, Hipshon Roy, P/41/55, p. 1.
[42] NMML, Elwin Papers S. No. 133.
[43] New Delhi, NAI, External Affairs Proceedings (1957), Compendium of the Senior Officers Conference 1957, 3(13)-NEFA/57, pp. 108–109.
[44] Barmati Dai. Interview with the author, 12 February 2014, Pasighat (Arunachal Pradesh).

Figure 4.3 The new generation, c. 1958
© Arunachal Pradesh DIPR

that tribal communities were well aware of this. Tatan Mize recalls how, freshly arrived as a Village-Level Worker, he found out that the community's *gaonbura* had built his living quarters two miles from the village, and refused to move them.[45]

The line dividing those with easy access to administrative and development institutions from the others was reinforced in the late 1950s, when the administration decided to change its development strategy. Dismayed that only 18 per cent of the 5,000 people employed by frontier administration were tribal – most of them from other parts of Assam rather than from NEFA – the Planning Commission representative

[45] Tatan Mize, 'A part of my past life', *Yaaro moobang: A land of peace, prosperity and happiness*, 1 (2001), 21–25 (p. 23).

asked Rustomji and Elwin to change course.[46] Instead of spreading development schemes geographically by using the infrastructure of the existing seventy administrative centres, the new goal became to intensify activities around divisional headquarters and within existing NES blocks.[47] The number of prospective development blocks was reduced: the proposal to open forty NES blocks in the second plan period was reduced to eighteen blocks, and the objective to have the whole of NEFA covered by them was postponed till the end of the third plan.[48]

Tensions and Contradictions

The NEFA Philosophy gave Indian authorities the rationale and tools to recast their relationship with tribal populations in a constructive way, taking advantage of the latter's demand for the tangible goods and advantages state presence could procure. But the process was far from smooth.

Food self-sufficiency was still a dream by the end of the 1950s: 'near-starvation conditions' prevailed in some areas, and, in 1958, NEFA still imported 120,600 maunds of rice.[49] Together with the newly created Naga Hills Tuensang Area, it airlifted 8,500 tons of food, but airdrops were endangered by air force commitment in the Naga Hills.[50]

Development and cultural schemes suffered from a host of tensions and contradictions. The promotion of wet-rice cultivation bore unclear dividends. Early administrative policy had staunchly favoured it, espousing the blanket disapproval of shifting cultivation across India.[51] Yet, three years after the earthquake, the food situation in model villages was deplorable. Workers lived on one meal a day, and, once relief operations stopped, many men and women abandoned wet-rice cultivation in favour of traditional means of subsistence.[52] Even in areas where settled agriculture had taken root, the situation had not necessarily taken a turn for the better.

---

[46] Delhi, NMML, Elwin Papers (1957), Correspondence with Shri Sivaraman on the visit of a team of officers from Planning Commission and Central Ministry to NEFA, S. No. 10, pp. 8–9.

[47] NAI, External 3(13)-NEFA/57.   [48] NMML, Elwin Papers S. No. 10, pp. 7–17.

[49] New Delhi, NAI, External Affairs Proceedings (1958), Flights in NEFA, 10(2)-NEFA /58; New Delhi, NAI, Food & Agriculture Proceedings (1959), Supply of rice to Naga Hills, and NEFA, 54(3)C-59 Basic Plan II.

[50] NAI, External 10(2)-NEFA/58 (Summary report of discussions of 10 June 1958).

[51] Madhav Gadgil and Ramachandra Guha, *This fissured land: An ecological history of India* (Delhi; Oxford: Oxford University Press, 1993).

[52] Itanagar, APSA, NEFA Secretariat (1953), Food relief for the Community Project area, CP-30/53, p. 49.

People were fed, but malnutrition was rife: vegetable growing had disappeared.[53]

Had old tour reports been read more carefully, the administration might have guessed that shifting cultivation was more than a default choice. In 1945, an official had been

struck by the fact that the [Nyishi] ... is *by choice* a forest cultivator. In several places we came upon land which was clearly suitable for wet rice cultivation, indeed in some places rice had been cultivated in the past but the terraces had *been allowed* to fall down and the land had been abandoned.[54]

Indeed, shifting cultivation had many intrinsically attractive aspects: a greater variety of food types, higher calorie yield, greater resistance to epidemics, and lower manpower-per-hour ratio.[55] The frontier administration gradually came to understand this and began to promote wet-rice cultivation alongside it.[56]

But the major reason that food production expanded so slowly was that frontier communities faced too many competitive demands on their labour: public works, village works, porterage, training, and agriculture.[57] The administration preferred to see the dependence on outside supplies through the prism of tribal lethargy. Badly affected by opium addiction, the Mishmis were criticised for their 'apathetic attitude towards hard labour and dull resignation to the inevitable'.[58] Addiction certainly played a role in this, but the fact was that the Mishmis had to attend to many different and time-consuming tasks and, therefore, preferred to drop some of them.

These contradictions permeated all spheres of tribal activity. Elwin noted the challenge of encouraging the population to undertake self-help development work without seeing their own constructions fall into disrepair.[59] Other measures were counterproductive. Sanitation, supposed to be a characteristic of model villages, was often 'conspicuously absent' from them. A normal feature of Adi houses, latrines had not been built in those of the new village of Balek – officially to make it

[53] Itanagar, APSA, NEFA Secretariat (1958), Tour diary of LRN Srivastava, Assistant Research Officer, Siang, R-58/58.

[54] New Delhi, NAI, External Affairs Proceedings (1945), Tour diaries of Capt Davy in the Dafla hills, 241-CA/45 (Exploration and political work in the Dafla Hills, Winter 1944–45, 6 December), emphasis added.

[55] Victor B. Lieberman, 'A zone of refuge in Southeast Asia? Reconceptualizing interior spaces', *Journal of Global History*, 5 (2010), 333–346.

[56] NMML, Elwin Papers S. No. 133.

[57] Delhi, NMML, Elwin Papers (1961), Correspondence with Secretary, Scheduled Tribes Commission regarding his visit to NEFA, 1961, S. No. 135.

[58] *Lohit Valley Brochure* (n.s.: [NEFA Secretariat] c. 1965), pp. 40–41.

[59] New Delhi, NAI, Home Affairs Proceedings (1956), Elwin's notes on visit to Bomdila and Tawang, 4(5)-NEFA/56.

cleaner. Yet, as people disliked going to the jungle, the end result was a dirtier village.[60]

As for school attendance, it could be far beneath reported enrolment figures, and many teachers did not speak local languages.[61] Meanwhile, craft centres often failed to fulfil their purpose; much of the production was substandard and unsuited for highland life,[62] and most trainees gave up the skill they had been taught after returning to the village. Finally, tribal accounts hint that against official policy, tribal land was sometimes appropriated without compensation to the villagers, while greedy contractors deforested the foothills to send timber off to Assam.[63]

NEFA's inhabitants were not inactive in the face of these fault lines. Schemes or policies well accepted or demanded in one village could be resisted or evaded in others. Different groups and individuals could adopt contrasting attitudes. Often, this was because of dynamics internal to their social, economic, and cultural environment (which was not necessarily apparent to Indian authorities). Some thought ahead of development schemes. In Tuensang, many Konyaks raised complex questions regarding agricultural methods, from crop rotation and improved varieties of crops to best soil practices. These techniques went far beyond the administration's objectives, yet their initiative prompted the Agricultural Officer to recommend a programme of research and trial to support 'more intelligent and progressive farmers'.[64]

Elsewhere in Tuensang, the mood was more cynical: 'The people regard[ed] roads as being made for the use of officials ... they [came] to build them because they want[ed] the money and because of contracts.'[65] Villages increasingly demanded payment for any work done. Moreover, the presence of non-tribals outside the administrative ranks, particularly outside contractors, seldom elicited their approval.[66] Attempts to replace them with forest cooperatives linked to tribal councils in the foothills were made in the early 1960s.

---

[60] APSA, R-58/58.
[61] Delhi, NMML, Elwin Papers (1954–1957), Report by Elwin on tour in the Wancho sub-division of Tirap, S. No. 138 (Teju to Roing, November 1955), pp. 37–38.
[62] NMML, Elwin Papers S. No. 135.
[63] Oshung Ering, 'The changing phases of Pasighat', *Yaaro moobang: A land of peace, prosperity and happiness*, 1 (2011), 1–6 (p. 5).
[64] Itanagar, APSA, NEFA Secretariat (1952), Tour notes of Agricultural Officer, January 1952, Agri-7/52, p. 16.
[65] New Delhi, NMML, Elwin Papers (1959), Correspondence with K.L. Mehta, 1954–59, S. No. 7 (Elwin to Mehta, Bombay 16 September 1955).
[66] NMML, Elwin Papers S. No. 133 (Elwin to Mehta, 16 September 1955).

NEFA officials felt that these attitudes threatened the pace, durability, and effectiveness of development schemes; they also worried that they would create a government tribal class above and segregated from their local communities. Elwin lamented the lowering of standards of *dobashi*s in eastern NEFA – lazy, undisciplined, un-influential, and prone to using their position to help themselves freely in villages visited.[67] He also warned against the introduction of 'the evils of class system':

[Tribals] are becoming a 'cooly class'. In some places tribals identify themselves as forming part of the Administration and feel proud by just becoming a permanent porter or a 'chaprasi' [a junior office worker]. A tribal peon or an interpreter thinks it below his dignity to carry a small bag just because his officers consider it so and he expects a porter to carry it for him.[68]

Yet there was logic to this tribal adaptation. In a context where state presence had first manifested itself through relief and rehabilitation and was still driven by the provision of development and welfare schemes, the tendency to relate to it primarily through the provision of tangible goods and assets was perhaps inevitable. Further, the speed and pattern of development in the hills limited economic opportunities for individuals, and movement on the other side of the Inner Line was discouraged, so government employment was the easiest and most rewarding path to social mobility and wealth. Administrative propaganda itself participated in making the government-employed man or woman the benchmark against which the future of NEFA was to be measured (Figure 4.4).

Frontier administration was seldom self-reflective about this. There are no signs that it pondered whether trying to secure, at all costs, even a lowly government job was a sensible cost–benefit calculation given how difficult it was to tend one's field and build government roads at the same time. Instead, it resisted tribal demands for petty disputes to be referred to Political Officers rather than village authorities and fulminated against the tendency to rely on political gifts and relief for subsistence.[69] Some previously influential people now in the process of being sidelined were neither so naïve nor inactive about these changing configurations of power. The *gaonbura* of the Konyak village of Chingmei, for instance, obstructed the work of wet-rice cultivation led by the interpreters and even destroyed the new crop.[70]

[67] NMML, Elwin Papers S. No. 135 (Along the Patkoi in Tirap, December–January 1956), pp. 86–87.
[68] NMML, Elwin Papers S. No. 133 (S.R.K. Iyengar, 'A note on the classless nature of tribal society and the impact of administration on the same').
[69] Ibid. (Jayal to Haldipur, 11 May 1958); APSA, CP-30/53.
[70] APSA, Agri-7/52, pp. 15–16.

Figure 4.4 Verrier Elwin (seated, 3rd from the right) and other senior officials, 1958
© Arunachal Pradesh DIPR

The Nation in Limited Time-Space

Beyond its state-making aspect, the official aim of welfare, development, and cultural protection was to 'make [NEFA's tribes] feel at one with India, ... [make them] realise that they are part of India and have an honoured place in it'.[71] This conception of development as the way to Indian-ness belonged to an intellectual genealogy of 'developmental nationalism' in which nation, state, and development were deeply intertwined. The earliest incarnations of Indian nationalism had been articulated not around the celebration of national culture but around a systematic economic critique of colonial rule, deemed responsible for

[71] Nehru, *Letters to chief ministers* (29 October 1952), p. 151.

the dislocation of India's society and economy and its mass poverty. The attainment of freedom did not just mean abolishing colonial rule; it also meant unleashing productive forces and creating an egalitarian society in preparation for a re-forged Indian nation.[72] State involvement was considered central to this developmental nationalism; 'national backwardness and lack' required and legitimised state intervention in the economy, and the state itself was represented as 'a subject of needs'.[73] Building the state and building the nation appeared to go hand in hand.

In practice, state-making was only partially accompanied by nation-building. Part of the problem was that the NEFA Philosophy assumed that the eastern Himalayas' integration into an Indian nation would necessarily – indeed, automatically – follow from economic betterment and a revived tribal culture. Nurturing a sense of national belonging did not, therefore, need theorisation or systematic planning. In contrast to the long discussions on how to fine-tune development schemes, improve the acceptability of state presence, and preserve 'tribalness', strategic reflections on how to raise 'NEFA's awareness of its being India' were largely absent.[74]

As a result, nation-building initiatives remained fragmented, peripheral, and contingent. Government publicity officers and artists put up posters, charts, and calendars in administrative or training centres, and pictures of Gandhi and Nehru adorned the walls of local schools. But the emphasis was on 'produc[ing] a psychological climate designed to cure the inferiority complex which is such a danger to all peoples coming for the first time in contact with the outside world',[75] rather than on 'selling ... India to NEFA'.[76] Official art presented idealised visions of the proud, authentic tribal or the eastern Himalayas' pristine nature; neither the changes brought about by the administration nor scenes from elsewhere in India were included. The emphasis was on creating a sentiment of unity between the frontier tribes themselves.[77]

---

[72] *Developmental and cultural nationalisms*, ed. by Radhika Desai (London: Routledge, 2009); Manu Goswami, *Producing India: From colonial economy to national space* (Chicago: University of Chicago Press, 2004); Sumit Sarkar, 'Nationalism and poverty: Discourses of development and culture in 20th century India', *Third World Quarterly*, 29:3 (2008), 429–445.

[73] Srirupa Roy, *Beyond belief: India and the politics of postcolonial nationalism* (Durham, NC; London: Duke University Press, 2007), p. 110.

[74] New Delhi, NMML, Elwin Papers (1961), Differing views on publicity set up in NEFA, 1954–61, S. No. 128 ('On NEFA publicity' 20 February 1954), p. 2.

[75] Delhi, NMML, Elwin Papers (1957), Correspondence with Ministry of External Affairs about Research Fellowships, 1956–57, S. No. 5 (Note on the various points raised by the ministry).

[76] NMML, Elwin Papers S. No. 128, p. 2.

[77] London, BL, Elwin Papers (1958–1963), NEFA calendars, Mss Eur D950/85.

Where state-making was enacted both in the everyday and the exceptional, the nation was presented not as a part of daily life, but as restricted to special occasions. Performing the nation rested on the cele-bration of Republic and Independence Day in administrative centres and development blocks. Flag hoisting, dances, games, feasts, illuminations, fireworks, and Hindi movies – not to forget countless speeches by senior officers, notables, and interpreters – made for all-day jamborees, meant to expand the mental and emotional horizons of NEFA's inhabitants and to enact their connection with Indian administration.[78]

Their nature as nation-building exercises was reinforced by the annual participation of certain tribals in the flamboyant Republic Day parades in Delhi. From 1953 onwards, a few carefully chosen tribal leaders and strongmen were sent to the capital as special guests of the Prime Minister, along with troops of dancers. Exhibitions of local arts and crafts were also organised for the occasion.[79] These initiatives helped reinforce the Indian state's relationship with tribal elites and highlighted the 'simul-taneous time' inhabited by NEFA and the rest of India: these special guests were witnessing the parades in the capital on the same day that, back in NEFA, tribal people feasted.[80]

For all the merriment they entailed, these public celebrations still belonged to the realm of the exceptional. They took place on two days of the year only, and the potential for a tribal to attend one of them was dependent on his or her being relatively close to an administrative centre of development block. Moreover, while some communities regularly sent members to the capital, others might not even have heard of the Delhi parades. Available information suggests that a significant portion of the tableaux and dances selected by NEFA administration were themed around NEFA's Buddhist tribes, or conversely around Naga war dances and institutions.

Spatial and cultural imbalances can also be seen in the list of guests for 1953, all of whom were from Sela Sub-Agency (Kameng) and two-thirds from Tawang itself. In other words, some communities were showered with attention when others received hardly any. The effect on the Monpas was not necessarily productive either. By 1956, frontier administration instructed that 'people from Tawang should, under no circumstances, be

---

[78] Itanagar, APSA, NEFA Secretariat (1956), Republic Day celebrations in the Divisions P107/56; Itanagar, APSA, NEFA Secretariat (1956), Republic Day celebration 1957 P98/56 (PO Tuensang to Mehta, 18 December 1956), p. 64.

[79] APSA, P98/56 (Defence Ministry to Adviser to the Governor, 28 March 1956).

[80] Nehru, *Letters to chief ministers* (Letter dated 27 January 1953), pp. 225; Benedict Anderson, *Imagined communities: Reflections on the origin and spread of national-ism*, revised and extended edn (London: Verso, 1991), pp. 6, 37.

pressed to go to Delhi' and prohibited 'large dancing parties or uneducated delegations who are merely bewildered by the whole business'. From now on, only educated people would attend.[81]

Visits by Indian 'VIPs', such as Assam governors or key central officials, had the same taste of exceptionality. While they drew big crowds and mentioned 'India' more often than frontier officers, their visits were circumscribed in time, and limited to a few areas – mainly the headquarters and the foothills – of a territory the size of Austria.[82] Belonging to an Indian nation was a temporary experience, restricted to set and clearly defined dates – a pleasant but ephemeral feeling, which receded afterwards and remained forgotten until the next big event.

NEFA authorities did make decided attempts to reshape the politics of belonging in the eastern Himalayas, but these centred on the Indian state, narrowly embodied in the NEFA administration, rather than on India as nation: '[T]he tribes [should] regard themselves as one with ourselves', argued Rustomji.[83] The guiding concept was that a united, cohesive 'NEFA family' embracing both frontier staff and local population in a sort of emotional symbiosis.[84] Elwin put it most succinctly: 'We are to guide our children.'[85]

To anchor frontier staff in NEFA, the number of transfers out of the Agency was curbed, and married couples began to be hired.[86] The administration also sought to elaborate a lingua franca to bring frontier inhabitants together, as well as with the staff. From the mid-1950s onwards, Hindi was introduced as a second language in most of NEFA – until then, schools had mainly taught Assamese.[87] The policy apparently met with noticeable success in the higher reaches of the frontier such as the Monpa areas.[88] But in this part of India located hundreds of miles away from the Hindi-speaking belt, the natural association of the language was not the nation, but officialdom.

---

[81] APSA, P98/56 (A note on future policy regarding Republic Day parties to New Delhi).

[82] 'Nehru assures help to all frontier tribals', *Assam Tribune*, 23 October 1952.

[83] Delhi, NMML, Rustomji Papers (1963), Broadcasts, tour notes, articles, etc (1959–1963), S. No. 8 ('The curtain lifts'), p. 15.

[84] The words re-occur throughout administrative correspondence. See, for example, New Delhi, NMML, Elwin Papers (1955), Change of designation of political officers, S. No. 119.

[85] Delhi, NMML, Elwin Papers (1957), Report by Verrier Elwin on tours 1954–57, S. No. 138 (Teju to Roing, November 1955), p. 44.

[86] NMML, Elwin Papers S. No. 5 (Note on the various points raised by the Ministry); NMML, Elwin Papers S. No. 119 (Mehta to Kaul, 12 December 1955).

[87] Indira Miri, *Moi aru NEFA [NEFA and I]* (Guwahati: Spectrum Publications, 2003).

[88] New Delhi, NAI, External Affairs Proceedings (1955), Reports on NEFA, 4(19)-P/55 (Report for March 1955); New Delhi, NAI, External Affairs Proceedings (1956), Elwin's notes on visit to Bomdila and Tawang, 4(5)-NEFA/56.

Figure 4.5 Rustomji dancing with Abor warriors at Along, 1959
© Arunachal Pradesh DIPR

Above all, it was by adopting external signs of 'tribalness' that forms of belonging embedding the frontier state with local populations could be precipitated. There was a subtle equilibrium to achieve. Local authorities hoped to assert their authority over tribal communities through developmentalism, yet they also needed to blur the boundary between state and society by presenting the former as externally akin to, and understanding of, the latter.[89] Put differently, the NEFA administration had to 'look tribal' in order for the population to identify with it – even as, in practice, opportunities for this population to enter its ranks were few.

[89] New Delhi, NMML, Elwin Papers (1963), Elwin's appointment, 1956–63, S. No. 31 (Nehru to Chaliha, 1 August 1959).

Elwin and Rustomji attempted to find a balance by making the mastery of a local language a key duty of frontier staff, encouraging the wearing of tribal dress and constructing houses or offices in adherence with 'improved' tribal aesthetic and construction principles, as well as local building materials. Rustomji was seldom seen without his tribal jackets, and government buildings began to sport sitting platforms, hearths, bamboo or stone structures, curtains from local fabric, and paintings by tribal artists. Touring officials were encouraged to drink rice beer with the population and to partake in tribal feasts and ceremonies, and common activities were organised, such as football matches between local youth and Assam Rifles (Figure 4.5).

Like other aspects of the NEFA Philosophy, these attempts seldom met unmitigated success, and the strategy worked better in some places than others. Despite constant directives on the subjects, the linguistic abilities of frontier staff generally remained suboptimal. The directives on wearing tribal dress were more successfully implemented, but those on tribal-style buildings were ineffective.[90] Few of them followed the principle of 'grow-[ing] out of the landscape', and cement, mortar, or unpainted roofs disfigured settlements.[91] Radio broadcasts regularly took local staff to task for not following or understanding the NEFA Philosophy.

A Philosophy of Isolation

The NEFA Philosophy constructed the state as the go-between between tribal communities and the nation at large, protecting the former from the world. Frontier authorities continued the colonial practice of restricting physical interaction between the eastern Himalayas' inhabitants and 'settled' India, and even enhanced it. In 1951, lowland portions of the Frontier Tracts were transferred to Assam state jurisdiction, solving the NEFA administration's long-standing struggle to adjust the Inner Line to its sphere of jurisdiction. Controlling private Indian citizens' presence became easier – especially as, bar the Socialist leader Ram Manohar Lohia, the parliament and the pan-Indian press did not question limitations on freedom of movement. In fact, the only parliamentary question on these provisions was about *reinforcing* the Inner Line, by reducing the number of permits granted per year.[92]

---

[90] NAI, External 4(5)-NEFA/56; NMML, Elwin Papers S. No. 5 (Note on the various points raised by the Ministry).

[91] New Delhi, NMML, Elwin Papers (1960), Housing and colonies for tribals, 1959–60, S. No. 73.

[92] *Collected works of Rammanohar Lohia*, ed. by Mastram Kapoor, 9 vols (New Delhi: Anamika Publishers, 2011), IV, pp. 95–101; *Lok Sabha Debates 1958 (Vol. XV)* (New

To have this assurance, the frontier administration carefully managed the flow of information between NEFA and the rest of the country. Elwin cautioned against heavy engagement with the national press. Too great a spotlight on NEFA could generate rising numbers of Inner Line permit applications, and their rejection would become problematic. It might also disturb tribal lifestyles and open the administration's policy to criticism. The press was already too focused on the Naga conflict; preserving NEFA from its enervating presence was urgent.[93]

Maintaining hegemony over the constitution and dissemination of NEFA-related knowledge became a core administrative principle. Under Elwin's leadership, the NEFA Research Department successfully kept external scholars at bay. A party or two might visit every year, but few were allowed beyond the foothills.[94] The administration much preferred for outside researchers to use materials from '[government] scientists'[95]. From 1957 onwards, external institutions and visitors had to swear not to publish anything without first consulting frontier administration, which would further scrutinise their work prior to publication.[96]

Meanwhile, NEFA authorities tried to keep the press at arm's length by subtly channelling the amount and type of information available to it. Under normal circumstances, this was not particularly difficult. Compared to Kashmir or the nearby Naga Hills, the eastern Himalayas seemed quiet enough. While the Assamese media regularly covered NEFA – often in critical terms, for the area's administrative separation from Assam in spite of their constitutional union aroused much resentment – the pan-Indian press dedicated little space to it on its pages. When it did, it was primarily to transcribe the parliamentary speech of an External Affairs official, a government press note, or an officer's broadcast. Senior frontier officials such as Elwin or Rustomji also regularly wrote in the press.[97] When external events such as the Assam earthquake

Delhi: Lok Sabha Secretariat, 1958) (9 April 1958), p. 9080; *Lok Sabha Debates 1959 (Vol. XXVIII)* (31 March 1959), p. 8724.

[93] NMML, Elwin Papers S. No. 128 (Elwin note on NEFA publicity, 20 February 1954), p. 4.

[94] New Delhi, NMML, Elwin Papers (1957), Papers regarding the visit of an anthropological scholar to NEFA, 1955–57, S. No. 131.

[95] Delhi, NMML, Elwin Papers (1961), Correspondence with UNESCO, 1955–61, S. No. 17 (8 February 1957).

[96] NMML, Elwin Papers S. No. 5; Delhi, NMML, Elwin Papers (1962), Correspondence with the Department of Anthropology Calcutta and Madras University, 1956–62, S. No. 18 (Mehta to Acharya, 1 March 1957), p. 27. See also Delhi, NMML, Elwin Papers (1959), Correspondence with Minister for Planning and Development, Assam 1956–59, S. No. 11 (Elwin to All AROs, 3 March 1956).

[97] London, BL, Elwin Papers (1956), Miscellaneous newspaper cuttings, c. 1937–56, Mss Eur D950/31; London, BL, Elwin Papers (1958), Newspaper articles by Elwin on tribal people, the tribal problem etc, c. 1950–58, Mss Eur D950/27.

or Achingmori generated interest in NEFA, frontier authorities pre-empted critiques and unofficial investigations by opening up temporarily.[98]

A *modus vivendi* of sorts was gradually established between frontier administration and the national press. Small press parties representing various Indian journals were periodically allowed beyond the Inner Line to gain 'some insight into the state of affairs there'. These tours were sponsored by the central Press Information Bureau and their agenda was carefully set by frontier authorities, who also escorted participants throughout their journey.[99] Notwithstanding continued criticism from the Assamese press, this enabled the frontier administration to attract the goodwill of India's most influential media and tell the story of advancing NEFA, without losing control over what information filtered through nor over contacts between 'outsiders' and tribal populations.

These peculiar information flows had multiple consequences for the carving of a place for NEFA on India's mental maps. First, mutual awareness between the frontier and the rest of India was characterised by flux and reflux. The frontier appeared in the news mostly in the wake of inexplicably brutal or sudden events. Second, the space of the frontier was primarily comprehended through its physical rather than human quali-ties. Often, NEFA's inhabitants were not mentioned at all. But when they were, it was in disembodied terms or, indeed, by stressing the unity of the 'simple and often rugged sons of mountains fastnesses [*sic*] from the Himalayan ranges' with their environment.[100]

Equally importantly, ties to the plains were declining, further reifying boundaries between tribalness and non-tribalness, between hills and plains – dichotomies inherited from colonial representations and prac-tices of rule. Even with the Inner Line, there had been relatively important amounts of commercial, cultural, and religious interaction between the plains and the hills in colonial times – as the economic hardships experi-enced by NEFA populations during the Second World War testified. Assam officials had even organised events bringing together the inhabitants of the agency and those of settled districts. For the silver jubilee of George V in 1935, a thousand highlanders had descended to the plains, where they had feasted on the customary rice beer.[101]

---

[98] 'Quake devastation in Himalayan hills region: Probe into situation in deep interior of the mountain', *Amrita Bazaar Patrika*, 21 September 1950.

[99] See for instance 'Journey to NEFA I: Among the tribal people of the NEFA (by J.M. Mukherjee)', *Amrita Bazaar Patrika*, 1 February 1956.

[100] 'The Dogras and tribal groups in our army', *Times of India*, 30 July 1950.

[101] London, BL, Indian Civil Service memoirs (Assam) (1977), Memoir – Edward Francis Lydall, Mss Eur F180/4, 13–16.

Other important gatherings had been organised by the frontier administration after independence. During a two-day exhibition at Sadiya in 1949, 2,000 people from both hill and plains admired 'hand-made articles of the type made by the tribal people, but of improved design' as well as exhibits from the Assam Sericulture Department, the local women's association, and the local girls' high school.[102] Even more ambitious were the Hills and Plains Festivals held in Shillong until 1954, during which 500 artists and performers from all over Assam were invited to perform traditional dances (NEFA sent about 200 artists).[103] This was unity performed in limited space-time, and in exceptional rather than routine circumstances, but unity performed all the same.

These linkages gradually disintegrated over the course of the 1950s. The transfer of the plains portions of NEFA to Assam in 1951 played no small part in the process, but other dynamics were at play. The linked strategies of preventing de-tribalisation and promoting self-sufficiency contributed to cutting off existing ties. Movement from the hills to the plains was now discouraged. Elwin strongly opposed the Sherdukpens' seasonal migration to Missamari, which he held responsible for that community's decline since it spread diseases and discouraged them from agriculture.[104] Existing trade routes progressively died out: the traditional Apatani journeys to the plains to buy cattle became superfluous once husbandry projects were introduced.[105] Hills and Plains Festivals also ceased.

Not all these changes resulted from a deliberate desire to insulate the uplands' cultural and economic world; some were merely the indirect results of overall principles, particularly increasing local food production. Nor were all these policies successful. Yet, in any event, the cultural and economic distance that came as a by-product of the 'middle-way' philosophy contributed to insulating the 'real tribals' in NEFA from the rest of Assam – including the tribal communities of the plains.

The isolation was reinforced by a confrontational relationship between Delhi and the provincial government in Assam. Though constitutionally part of the state, NEFA was administered separately from its settled districts and outside the purview of its elected government. In due course, the eastern Himalayas were meant to fully integrate Assam, but this goal increasingly disappeared from the agenda of frontier administrators over the course of the 1950s.

---

[102] 'Two-day exhibition at Sadiya', *Assam Tribune*, 13 March 1949.
[103] 'Hills and Plains Festival: Artistes and athletes to join in large numbers', *Assam Tribune*, 11 December 1953.
[104] NAI, Home 4(5)-NEFA/56.
[105] London, SOAS, Fürer-Haimendorf Papers (1945), Diary of Fürer-Haimendorf's first tour to the Apa Tani Valley, 1944–45, PP MS 19, Box 3.

Frictions between Delhi and Assam governments dated back to India's Partition. This original mistrust was unexpectedly reinforced by the earthquake: the challenge of relief and rehabilitation left Nehru and other central actors with the impression that Assam authorities could not shoulder big responsibilities, like taking care of their highland regions.[106] Moreover, the growth of separatist movements across the latter, starting with Naga areas, led Delhi to see Assamese chauvinism as a major impediment to India's stability.

Tension over NEFA itself abounded. The NEFA administration's gradual shift from Assamese to Hindi as a lingua franca fuelled resentment in Assam, while provincial criticism of the NEFA Philosophy hardened frontier officials against a merger. Although a State Reorganisation Commission decided to keep the map of Assam unchanged in 1956, in practice the tide had clearly turned against the effective incorporation of NEFA into Assam.

Good Things, Bad Things

While nourishing the eastern Himalayas' inhabitants 'own genius' informed cultural or developmental policies, what 'being' and 'living tribal' meant was remodelled in the process. Officially, the administration was preserving tribal pride, culture, and traditions, and reviving them where they were endangered. Instructors were appointed to teach dance and song, which Elwin hailed as characteristically tribal activities.[107] In Kameng, he enjoined that everything should be done

> to revive the tradition that every village should have its band and its set of masks for the remarkable pantomimes that the Monpas and Sherdukpens do so well ... [we] should first enrich village life and then provide luxuries for the tourist trade. We are not to keep our people as museum specimens; we should equally avoid the danger of turning their finest products into museum specimens.

Elwin also recommended books on Buddhism for the Bomdila library, and the building of a leprosy home at Tawang in the local style, complete with its own *gompa* (monastery).[108] A 1958 booklet encouraged

> the playing and development of *indigenous games* in the schools of NEFA. A number of games are common to the whole of NEFA, but more are known

---

[106] Bérénice Guyot-Réchard, 'Reordering a border space: Relief, rehabilitation, and nation-building in northeastern India after the 1950 Assam earthquake', *Modern Asian Studies*, 49:4 (2015), 931–962.

[107] NMML, Elwin Papers S. No. 133 (K.L. Mehta Note, Camp Bomdila 9 April 1956).

[108] NAI, Home 4(5)-NEFA/56.

only over a limited area and yet are so greatly enjoyed . . . that it would be a pity not *to popularise them over a wider field.*[109]

Among the Wanchos of Tirap, the administration sought to revive faltering woodcarving traditions by promoting toy making, which would also provide the community with some income.

These visions of tribalness were highly selective. If the Wanchos were abandoning woodcarving, it was because the social context in which it took place was disappearing: headhunting had ceased.[110] Post-colonial administration asserted that developmental and cultural welfare strategies should consist in 'doing away with certain bad things', and raids and headhunting had henceforth been banned across NEFA.[111] Efforts concentrated on the two areas where both practices were prevalent: the Nyishi country and the Patkai. Other policies included using the *kebang* to discourage child marriage among the Galos.[112]

The administration's stance was not always so severe. Rice beer, which had important social and nutritional functions among the people of NEFA, was not banned. Instead, the sale of distilled liquor was stopped, and local spirits such as the Adi *apong* were promoted.[113] Another significant compromise concerned slavery. While keen on 'insisting that no one born in a free India can be born other than free', the administration tried to eradicate it gradually, mixing economic incentives and forced releases.[114] The justification was that local slavery practices were not racially based nor necessarily exploitative, and that freeing slaves could upset the economic and social well-being of both the freeman and his ex-owner.[115] Equally importantly, it could alienate tribes over which government authority was still weak.[116] Similar tensions were discernible in administrative initiatives on opium, which included conducting propaganda against its cultivation and consumption and attempts to curb smuggling routes, but coexisted with the monthly deliverance of opium

---

[109] Marion D. Pugh, *Games of NEFA* (Shillong: NEFA, 1958). Emphasis added.

[110] Delhi, NMML, Elwin Papers (1963), Extension of the appointment of Elwin as Adviser for Tribal Affairs, 1954–63, S. No. 152.

[111] NMML, Elwin Papers S. No. 149.

[112] Itanagar, APSA, NEFA Secretariat (1953), Annual administration report on the Abor Hills District for year ending 30 June 1953, P-46/53.

[113] Itanagar, APSA, NEFA Secretariat (1958), Tour notes of senior officers, PC-71/58, p. 2; APSA, P-46/53.

[114] NMML, Elwin Papers S. No. 5 (Note on the various points raised by the ministry).

[115] NAI, External 241-CA/45 (Davy's FO, 29 January 1945).

[116] Delhi, NMML, Elwin Papers (1957), Tour notes of Dr Verrier Elwin, 1954–57, S. No. 139; Itanagar, APSA, NEFA Secretariat (1957), Tour diary of SN Banerjee, APO Nyapin, R-97/57.

passes and limited amounts of the drug to 'addicts' in government shops.[117]

Not all manifestations of tribalness were equal, then. But beyond the disappearance of practices that prevented the consolidation of the Indian state's political legitimacy, other processes of selection were taking place. By limiting interaction with the rest of India, NEFA authorities were unravelling the dynamic, hybrid political economy and cultural ties that had linked the eastern Himalayas and the Brahmaputra valley, sequestering them from the national mainstream.

This progressive reification of the tribal/non-tribal boundaries was compounded by a simultaneous process of (re-)creation, of tribalisation. 'Doing away with certain bad things' had a corollary: 'introducing certain good things'.[118] By that, the administration did not solely mean welfare schemes; both for its own sake and to enable deeper state penetration, cultural engineering permeated frontier policy. Dance and songs were particularly useful and malleable tools in this regard. Appalled to find that Tirap's dancing traditions were dying because of their war-related ritual character, Elwin recommended separating dance from ritual and introducing agricultural dances from other areas. The old war dances could be redirected to signify the struggle against poverty, disease, or hunger.[119]

Sending in dance experts from the Siang Valley among the Mishmis served an ever-deeper function: the lack of songs and dance among them left 'no doubt that psychologically all branches of Mishmis are *lacking in a social sense*. They have a very strong sense of family and clan, but it is always the clan rather than the village that matters.' Igniting a broader Mishmi sense of community was a prerequisite for the build-up of development institutions, and hence of state presence:

although the Mishmis can make such good houses they have no idea of making a village and apparently no inclination to do so ... It is this fact that makes plans for development in these desolate and thinly-populated valleys so difficult.

Although it never formed a policy matter, 'villagisation' was an important aspect of the reconfiguration of the frontier at the time. Through dance and songs, the Mishmis could potentially forge broader human ties that would convince them of the benefits of living in tighter communities. Yet

---

[117] Itanagar, APSA, NEFA Secretariat (1953), Nari Rustomji – Confidential reports on the North-East Frontier Agency for 1953, p. 9; Oshung Ering, *The lingering memories* (Pasighat: Siang Literary Forum, 2005), p. 49.

[118] NMML, Elwin Papers S. No. 149, p. 24; S.L. Kalia, 'Sanskritization and tribalization', *Bulletin of the Tribal Research Institute*, 2:4 (1959), 43–53.

[119] NMML, Elwin Papers S. No. 138 ('Along the Patkoi in Tirap', December–January 1956).

Figure 4.6 Radio programme, c. 1956–1957
© Arunachal Pradesh DIPR

to do this, Elwin suspected that their traditional laws of landownership –
whereby the first settlers of a site owned all the land they marked out for
shifting cultivation, and could expel any later settlers – would first have to
be circumvented. Some aspects of tribalness had to be excised in order for
others to be born.[120]

The Problem of Dress

The vision of tribalness deployed in the NEFA Philosophy was thus both
selective and deeply normative. The 'problem of dress', which occupied

---

[120] NMML, Elwin Papers S. No. 139 ('In the desolate Khamlang Valley', November 1957).
Emphasis added.

an entire chapter of the *Philosophy for NEFA*, was the best testimony to this.[121] On one of his first tours of the Patkai, Elwin had been horrified to find Wancho women covering their naked bodies at the sight of a government official; many had also abandoned their hand-woven skirts to wear mill cloth. Meanwhile, many men sported black coats, 'foreign' hats, and electric torches and safety pins in lieu of ornaments. One elder even donned an old Chinese silk dressing gown.[122] Following that visit, senior frontier officials began to draw up a directive on dress.

Discussions around the directive highlight the interlinked fates of tribalness envisioned by the administration. Some changes were considered inevitable. Full or partial nakedness was doomed: 'even without any mockery, it is inevitable that tribals will wish to cover their nakedness when they visit administrative centres or descend to the plains.' The administration should rather focus on convincing women not to be ashamed of being naked, concluded senior officials.[123]

Yet, if change was predetermined, the administration needed to steer it. This meant reviving and enhancing weaving and ornament-making traditions. Unlike most other crafts, taught only in locales where they had traditional currency and could be made with local materials, weaving was promoted all across NEFA and independent weaving units established. Such centres aimed to increase local cloth production and enhance the beauty of indigenous textiles. In contrast to their Apatani neighbours, weaving was not much practised among the Nyishis, and their production was seen as lacking in patterns. A conference hence decided to use simpler Apatani patterns in Nyishi crafts centres, and to encourage them to devise their own designs based on 'simple natural objects'.[124]

To be successful, the administration had to answer two related questions: how should it get NEFA's population to abandon non-traditional clothes and garments, and why did an increasing number of tribal people wear them in the first place? Some thought the roots of the problem lay in people's desire to identify with state officials, to stand out and display one's wealth amongst fellow villagers, and to please the administration. In Tirap, interpreters, peons, *gam*s, and well-off individuals had all begun to wear 'the plains type of dress'. Mill cloth, small mirrors, berets, felt hats, and Khasi caps were means of displaying one's proximity to the state by means of identification as well as one's greater purchasing powers in

[121] Elwin, *A philosophy for NEFA*, Chapter 3.
[122] NMML, Elwin Papers S. No. 138, p. 5.
[123] NMML, Elwin Papers S. No. 133 (Deputy Adviser's note on ATA's Tirap, Report of 1954).
[124] Delhi, NMML, Elwin Papers (1961), NEFA Sudhar-Kendra, TEZO, 1956–61, S. No. 69, p. 60.

a time of monetisation. In the Wancho village of Rusa, peak caps became a hierarchical marker; the chief, his brother, and the interpreter wore them. Firearms served an equally important social purpose: the use of cartridges as body ornaments or house decorations marked one's ability to source modern weapons.[125]

The administration found itself in a diplomatic conundrum. It could only with difficulty pretend to impose a purified standard when the very relations of power expressed through dress largely stemmed from its arrival. Rather than imposing a standard type of dress, NEFA officials arranged uniforms for school children and interpreters – the two populations over which they had a measure of direct control, and whose dress could influence others.[126] Kilt or aprons 'in line with tribal tradition and properly woven and decorated with cowries' were chosen.[127]

In an echo of Gandhian dislike for it, eradicating the white mill cloth produced in the plains became a policy leitmotif. Weaving centres and 'tribal' shops were established to provide NEFA's inhabitants with the necessary amenities of life without harming Himalayan cottage industries or the 'beauty' of tribal life, and officials began to hold weekly bazaars in administrative centres.[128] Mill cloth was removed from the list of political presents and altogether banned. The administration also tried to dislodge the Marwari traders located near or even beyond the Inner Line. Seen as 'the advanced post of civilisation' in colonial times, they were now considered major agents of de-tribalisation and exploitation.[129]

These efforts were unsuccessful. The ban on mill cloth faltered: local production could not fulfil the demand for cloth, and few tribal clothing articles compared with mill cloth for warmth. As for government depots, they struggled to compete with private shops, more attractive and comfortable. Where European-style government stores seemed uninviting with their counters and lack of sitting space, *kaiya* stalls offered inviting raised platforms where people could casually sit, make their purchases, and gossip – and with Marwari merchants who were often quicker at mastering local languages than administrative staff.[130] In Pasighat, some Adi girls who had studied in Assam began wearing saris and high heels.[131] Underneath this

---

[125] NMML, Elwin Papers S. No. 133.   [126] NMML, Elwin Papers S. No. 2.
[127] NMML, Elwin Papers S. No. 133 (Rustomji Note, 19 April 1956).
[128] APSA, P-46/53; NMML, Elwin Papers, S. No. 111.
[129] Basil C. Allen, *Assam district gazetteer*, 10 vols (Calcutta: Baptist Mission Press, 1905), VIII: Lakhimpur. A visitor to NEFA at the turn of the 1950s noted the large number of Punjabi and Marwari shops in places such as Tezu and Pasighat. J.D. Baveja, *Across the golden heights of Assam and NEFA* (Calcutta: Modern Book Depot, 1961), p. 53.
[130] Delhi, NMML, Elwin Papers (1963), Regulation and control of shops and encouraging the sale of local craft goods in them, 1955–63, S. No. 116.
[131] Baveja, *Across the golden heights*, p. 69.

failure, however, lay the fact that NEFA's inhabitants were negotiating these tensions between development and tribalness in their own ways.

The Nine Lives of Tribalness

Just as they sought to mitigate the tensions brought about by developmentalism, and to reshape them to their advantage, Mishmis, Hrussos, or Padams responded in imaginative ways to the vision of tribalness to which the administration subscribed, resisting its prescriptive, rigid understandings of their identity.

Reactions to the promotion of weaving as a quintessential tribal craft were particularly strong. While considerable efforts were deployed to give life to crafts and weaving centres, in many cases attendance and production were low. For many tribal communities who possessed a long-standing weaving tradition, sending a girl away to train in an art she already mastered, often to a higher degree than the teacher, was a waste of time. If it was to persuade them, the administration had to do better than that: several communities expressed the desire to 'learn on shuttle looms and other machines whereby they can produce wider cloth and learn designs besides their own'. The same complaint could be heard in a letter to Nehru by a group of Mishmis, who protested that 'trainees are allowed to weave their respective clothes only, not the dresses of the different tribes'. They particularly disliked the prohibition on weaving *mekhela chador* (the traditional dress of Assamese women) and other Assamese garments, but also constraints on their movement and professional occupation. Through their protests, some people insisted on a dynamic process of learning and adaptation, against the administration's static vision of tribal identity.[132]

From 1960 onwards, the arrival of a new generation of school-educated young men in the lower reaches of the administration meant that such indigenous understandings could find their place in official policy. Oshong Ering, a young Area Superintendent from Pasighat, criticised administrative insistence on some 'tribal' patterns of architecture. Visiting the hostel of a local school, Ering was disturbed to find fire hearths in the middle of the rooms. Hearths were deemed a crucial feature of tribal habitations, and their inclusion into new buildings had become a matter of policy. Ering appreciated the intention behind it, but he doubted whether the choice of the hearth to embody tradition was

---

[132] Delhi, NMML, APCC Papers (1956), Sadiya District Congress Committee, 1955–56, Packet 23, File No. 12 (Letter to Nehru by different Mishmis, 11 December 1955), pp. 20–23.

practicable: it made for congested, dirty, and dangerous rooms; the smoke and ashes were a health hazard; and parents did not seem too fond of them.[133]

While not always answered, these various complaints generally found their way into subsequent administrative discussions. They do not seem to have overly worried frontier officials, with one exception: the tribal girl. In this particular case, development and tribalness seem not only badly adjusted, but in contradiction to one another. Elwin noted with concern that Tangsa girls – the beautiful, clean, well-dressed Tangsa girls – had become 'subject to a number of external influences which have thoroughly disturbed them'. What Elwin meant was that they were almost all fluent in Assamese, and sometimes in Gurkhali, and travelled freely to Assam state areas or to neighbouring Singpho territory to take part in the harvest or in local markets. Worse, some had even married non-Tangsas, including Assamese and Chinese men. The time was not far off when they would marry staff, and when agricultural production would collapse because of their reluctance to continue shifting cultivation.[134] Elwin later concluded that 'if the younger girls are not to be unsettled and drift to the towns in search of an easier and more exciting life, it is ... essential to lift from them part at least of the heavy, tedious and dirty burden of jhum [shifting] cultivation'.[135] In the meantime, girls' education should be set aside.[136] Tribal women were the last protection against de-tribalisation.

If they had such an issue with the dealings of tribal girls, it was perhaps because of Elwin and the NEFA administration's ultimate ambivalence. To a large extent, they remained trapped in the language of primitiveness despite their romantic vision of the emancipated tribal. Elwin and Nehru decried the use of the words 'primitive' or 'uplift' but they regularly let these words slip into their own language. 'On the whole, the tribes in the NEFA are more primitive than others', Nehru wrote.[137] These semantic slips were not mere trifles. By reverting as a last resort to the language of tribal irrationality or primitiveness when faced with developmental or cultural failures – regarding the use of doctors or some people's reluctance to work, for example – the frontier administration maintained some sense of relative security in the midst of the considerable challenges it

---

[133] Delhi, NMML, Elwin Papers Miscellaneous correspondence, S. No. 39 (Ering to Elwin, 29 September 1960), pp. 25–26.

[134] NMML, Elwin Papers S. No. 13875–78.

[135] Delhi, NMML, Elwin Papers (1964), Correspondence with Dr B.S. Guha, 1954–64, S. No. 9 ('Wet rice and the Abor women'), pp. 141–144.

[136] NMML, Elwin Papers S. No. 135 (Undated note by Elwin).

[137] NMML, Elwin Papers S. No. 149 (Note by Nehru, 28 August 1955), p. 6.

faced on a daily basis. Yet doing so also crystallised the image of the primitive native. Tribal communities responded to this not with passivity, but on their own terms, demanding forms of welfare and development suited not to a primordial tribalness, but to their values, their aspirations, their inner power struggles.

Part III

1959–1962

5   A Void Screaming to Be Filled
Militarisation and State–Society Relations

Indian state-making had seemingly found its pace over the course of the 1950s. By January 1959, NEFA counted sixty-one administrative centres. Indian authorities had also completed the first motorable road between a Frontier Division headquarters (Bomdila) and the rest of the world.[1] In Tibet, however, a major crisis was coming.

Shortly after the Monlam festival, PRC authorities in Lhasa invited the Dalai Lama to a cultural show. He accepted – reluctantly, for the representation would take place in a PLA camp and his bodyguards had been asked not to escort him. At sunrise on the day of the performance – it was the 10th of March 1959 – thousands of Tibetans began to block the entrances of the Norbulingka palace, where the Dalai Lama had retired for the warm season. Under no circumstances should their leader enter the Chinese camp, pleaded the crowds: the invitation was a trap to kidnap him.

The Dalai Lama promised not to attend the play, but unrest continued to rise. The crowds attacked two senior Tibetan members in the PRC administration on their way to the palace; one of them was beaten to death and his body dragged around the centre of Lhasa. Shouts like 'The Chinese must go, leave Tibet to Tibetans' could be heard across the capital, and anti-PRC demonstrations were being planned.[2]

Stranded inside the Norbulingka, the Dalai Lama's government found itself unable to control the situation. Protesters wanted it to endorse their actions, calls for the restoration of Tibetan independence were multiplying, and anti-Chinese agitation was spreading to other parts of Tibet. PRC authorities had not intervened yet, but it seemed only a matter of time. Mortar shells had landed just outside the Norbulingka.

The Dalai Lama and his entourage chose to flee. Having consulted the state oracle, the leader took off his distinctive glasses, put on the

---

[1] Itanagar, APSA, NEFA Secretariat (1959), Summary of activities in the administration during 1959 P49/59.
[2] The Dalai Lama, *My land and my people: Memoirs of His Holiness the Dalai Lama* (Delhi: Srishti, 2012 (1977)), pp. 171–172.

weather-beaten clothes of a Tibetan soldier, and left Lhasa with his family and a group of high officials. By the time PRC officials noticed his disappearance, he was in Lhoka, where Khampa guerrillas shielded him. At Lhotsé, a fortress sixty miles away from the NEFA border, the Dalai Lama declared renewed independence of the Tibetan government.

On 20 March 1959, ten days after the start of the protests, the Chinese set out to retake control of Lhasa. Fierce fighting broke out. The protesters' ranks had been swelled by remnants of the Tibetan army, but their energetic defence could not make up for the PLA's numerical advantage and superior firepower. Within days, the Norbulingka and the Potala were under Chinese control. Corpses littered the streets of the capital. At least 4,000 people had been arrested. Repression would soon spread across Tibet, forcing the Dalai Lama and thousands of Tibetans into exile.[3]

This mass rebellion against PRC rule makes it tempting to see China and India's state-making in Tibet and the Himalayas as diametrically different. In fact, a closer look at the PRC's policies in Tibet in the 1950s reveals commonalities between the two processes. In consolidating their presence in Tibet, Chinese authorities faced challenges not dissimilar to those encountered by their Indian counterparts south of the Himalayan range, and, in some aspects, the way they apprehended and tackled them echoed the latter's initiatives. Considering the contradictions of Indian state-making, the fact that state expansion generated comparatively less resistance on the southern side of the McMahon Line was due to a range of contingent factors. What's more, the Lhasa uprising and its aftermath were about to threaten the fragile edifice of state–society relations in NEFA.

'Liberating' Tibet

The settlement of the 'Tibet issue' had been set into motion well before the end of the Chinese Civil War.[4] Given its geographic location and the Cold War context, the PRC leadership considered the Tibetan plateau of great strategic importance. They also felt that annexing Tibet was essential to ensure the new regime's legitimacy and standing, both at home and

---

[3] Tsering W. Shakya, *The dragon in the land of snows: A history of modern Tibet since 1947* (London: Pimlico, 1999), pp. 195–211.

[4] In early July 1949, Liu Shaoqi wrote to Stalin to announce that the Chinese Civil War neared its conclusion: 'Only the control of Taiwan, Hainan, Xinjiang, and Xizang [Tibet] will by then [winter 1949–1950] remain unresolved'. *Chinese Communist foreign policy and the Cold War in Asia: New documentary evidence, 1944–1950*, ed. by Shu Guang Zhang and Jian Chen (Chicago: Imprint, 1996) (Memorandum, 4 July 1949), p. 119.

abroad. China, they insisted, was an indivisible state whose 'nationalities', which included the Tibetans, had no right to secede. Tibet had
been separated from the Chinese 'motherland' only through foreign
imperialism. If Mao and other CCP leaders had once talked of allowing
self-determination or forming a 'China Federation', such ideas had progressively been abandoned after the Communist Long March and the war
with Japan.[5]

When the Dalai Lama formally accepted the Seventeen Point
Agreement in late 1951, the PRC leadership's immediate plans came to
fruition. Tibetans would now 'return to the family of the motherland'.[6]
Beneath the victory, however, Communist China faced important constraints in concretising the incorporation of Tibet into its territory.

Mao had favoured a full military invasion of Tibet. Yet it became clear
that moving and supplying the necessary troops – even just as far as
Chamdo in western Kham – would be extraordinarily difficult. As Qing
generals or Republican warlords had experienced, the rugged, road-less
spaces of Tibet hampered the projection and maintenance of state power.
Moreover, the Korean War was draining the PLA's resources and
deepening China's diplomatic isolation. As a result, the PRC was forced
to combine military assault with diplomatic activism.[7]

The 'peaceful liberation' strategy recognised the importance of
winning over Tibetans, including local elites – a 'United Front' tactic
already implemented in other minority areas that had more to do with the
CCP's historical experience and the legacy of Han-centric nationalism
than with Marxist doctrines or Soviet precedents.[8] Their weak 'material
base' in Tibet notwithstanding, CCP authorities had few illusions about
the 'social power' they could exert.[9] The party's Tibetan membership was
exceedingly small, Tibet had few Han residents, and almost no one spoke
Mandarin.[10] Forging links with Tibetan society was essential.

The PRC began by patiently wooing the inhabitants of eastern Kham
and Amdo – another ethno-linguistic region of Tibet that was beyond

[5] Jian Chen, 'The Chinese Communist "liberation" of Tibet, 1949–51', in *Dilemmas of
victory: The early years of the People's Republic of China*, ed. by Jeremy Brown and
Paul Pickowicz (Cambridge, MA; London: Harvard University Press, 2007), pp.
130–159 (pp. 130–138); Xiaoyuan Liu, *Frontier passages: Ethnopolitics and the rise of
Chinese Communism, 1921–1945* (Stanford: Stanford University Press, 2004), chapters
4–5.
[6] Seventeen Point Agreement, quoted in Shakya, *The dragon in the land of snows*, p. 450.
[7] Michael M. Sheng, 'Mao, Tibet, and the Korean War', *Journal of Cold War Studies*, 8:3
(2006), 15–33.
[8] Liu, *Frontier passages*.
[9] Mao, quoted in Shakya, *The dragon in the land of snows*, p. 93.
[10] Melvyn C. Goldstein, *A history of modern Tibet, Volume 2: The calm before the storm,
1951–1955* (Berkeley: University of California Press, 2007), p. 22.

Lhasa's secular reach – prior to 1950. The two regions were a complex terrain of political contestation. Kham had been the subject of both Lhasa and Guomindang's state-making attempts, in turn colliding with the efforts of the local warlord, Liu Wenhui, to prop himself up. Guomindang authorities had benefited from self-rule movements fighting for 'Kham for the Khampas' against Liu's and Lhasa's encroachments.[11]

Like their predecessor, CCP leaders set out to court indigenous power holders in Kham and Amdo. Attendance to monastic ceremonies enabled party cadres to connect with them and to recruit monks to translate CCP manifestos. These were distributed in areas still uncontrolled, to spread a core message: Communist China would respect Tibetan culture and religion and work to improve living conditions. The CCP skilfully used cultural differences and political dissensions within Tibet, propping up the Panchen Lama – who challenged the Dalai Lama's leadership – and harnessing tense relations between Khampas and Lhasa to bring it to the negotiation table.[12]

PRC authorities wanted to see Tibet fully incorporated into China, but their immediate need was to obtain the quiescence and cooperation of its inhabitants. The Seventeen Point Agreement was drafted accordingly. The PRC was to respect Tibet's 'national regional autonomy' under the Dalai Lama-led government and leave the inhabitants' social, cultural, and religious beliefs undisturbed. Communist authorities pledged not to enact any socialist reforms without the agreement of the local government.

In October 1951, thousands of PLA soldiers entered Lhasa. They had been chosen carefully. The soldiers who attacked Chamdo were neither the fittest nor the best located for the purpose, but they had an excellent record working in hostile territory and penetrating new regions and knew how to survive with little logistical support. They had been trained not just in high-altitude warfare or survival skills, but also in United Front methods. They had learnt the basics of the Tibetan language, taken classes on Buddhism and Tibetan customs, and were instructed to respect property and behave kindly towards the population. Do not take 'even one needle from the masses', orders read.[13]

[11] Peng Wenbin, 'Frontier processes, provincial politics and movements for Khampa autonomy during the Republican period', in *Khams Pa histories: Visions of people, place and authority*, ed. by Lawrence Epstein (Leiden: Brill, 2002), pp. 57–84.

[12] Shakya, *The dragon in the land of snows*, pp. 34–37; Melvyn C. Goldstein and Gelek Rimpoche, *A history of modern Tibet, Volume 1: The demise of the Lamaist state, 1913–1951* (Berkeley: University of California Press, 1989), pp. 640–641.

[13] Goldstein and Rimpoche, *A history of modern Tibet, Volume 1*, pp. 643–644; Goldstein, *A history of modern Tibet, Volume 2*, pp. 30–31. These orders directly followed from 'Three Rules' of discipline practised in the Red Army. William Wei, '"Political power grows out

As in Amdo and eastern Kham, the PRC authorities despatched to Tibet strove to win over the people of newly conquered areas. Movies extolling the valour of the PLA and the joys of life under the CCP were screened, often with success given their novelty effect. The PLA sent dancing and singing troops to remote areas as 'visiting artists'. Lhasa and Shigatse's aristocratic and monastic elites were treated to lavish banquets and performances. A Tibetan-medium primary school was launched for Lhasa's upper-class children. CCP authorities encouraged the development of youth and women's organisations and collective sports, and used religious festivals to cultivate the goodwill of the masses and the elites. Monlam celebrations became the occasion to distribute alms to the monasteries and reassure the crowds who flocked to Lhasa for the occasion that their religion would be respected.

Presenting the CCP as a benevolent regime and the PLA as a virtuous, protective force was crucial. Their presence in the first years of occupation was precarious (some troops were close to starvation, and their numbers might not be sufficient to maintain control), and it generated considerable apprehension among major sections of the population. PLA soldiers were being harassed on the streets of Lhasa. Satirical songs circulated around the capital, expressing the doubts and fears of many inhabitants.

It did not help that the very presence of PRC cadres and troops destabilised Tibet's economy and threatened its agricultural supplies. In Lhasa, a town of just 30,000 inhabitants, the arrival of 8,000 PLA soldiers put huge stress on public facilities and accommodation, and above all on grain supplies – with inflation as a further consequence. Tensions were rife between Communist authorities and the two Prime Ministers tasked to deal with them, who had opposed accepting the Seventeen Point Agreement. Some non-elite Tibetans had formed an anti-Communist organisation, the People's Representatives.

In the early 1950s, PRC authorities in Tibet had to temporise, avoiding overt confrontation with the Dalai Lama's government and power holders across Tibet. But they simultaneously tried to displace traditional power structures. They overwhelmed Tibetan authorities with technical work, minted a special currency to compete with *tangka*s (Tibetan coins), and created a Military District Headquarters to incorporate Tibet into PRC military structures. Successful attempts were made to co-opt various Tibetan elites, including high officials, into these parallel administrative

of the barrel of a gun'": Mao and the Red Army', in *A military history of China*, ed. by David Andrew Graff and Robin Higham (Cambridge, MA: Westview, 2002), pp. 229–248 (p. 235).

structures: as Tibet's big landholders, monasteries and aristocrats benefited from the pressures on food and land generated by Chinese presence.

In April 1952, a violent incident in Lhasa proved an opportunity to dismiss the two Prime Ministers and rein in the People's Representatives. For the next three years, PRC authorities in Tibet prioritised improvements in self-sufficiency, mobility, and infrastructure. A grain procurement bureau was established, and two roads were built to connect Lhasa to China. By employing many Tibetan farmers, roadworks spread the cash economy and created an embryo of wage labour in local society. The use of trucks, the spread of a newspaper culture, and the installation of small hydroelectric plants were all meant to present the PRC as a modernising force.

The consolidation of Chinese presence in Tibet was boosted when the Dalai Lama attended the National People's Congress in Beijing in late 1954, where a constitution prohibiting secession was passed. He also participated in flamboyant Tibetan New Year celebrations, and met Mao for the first time. The operation was a great success for Communist authorities: the Dalai Lama went back to Lhasa with positive feelings about Mao and the 'progress' of the PRC.

The visit paved the way for the set-up of the Preparatory Committee for the Autonomous Region of Tibet (PCART). The new body would replace both the Dalai Lama's government and the Tibet Military Commission, paving the way for reforms and administrative integration. PRC leaders assured the Tibetan authorities they would be consulted, and denounced Han officials' errors and abuses of power. When the PCART was finally inaugurated in April 1956, the atmosphere between Chinese and Tibetans seemed more upbeat. CCP leaders hoped that soon, party supremacy would smoothly succeed the rule of the Dalai Lama.[14]

Towards Rebellion

In eastern Kham, however, revolt was brewing. Unlike Dalai Lama-held regions, the area did not benefit from the Seventeen Point Agreement's guarantees. In the early 1950s, PRC authorities had nevertheless exempted it from communist reforms such as rent reduction or land collectivisation. Autonomous districts had been created and a few Tibetans co-opted into local party and government institutions. The official justification was that minority areas were socially and

[14] Shakya, *The dragon in the land of snows*, pp. 92–130.

economically backward, but the decision also betrayed the uncomfortable position of party cadres in regions about which they knew little and where they needed to work with local secular and religious elites. Indeed, monasteries, chieftains, or big traders continued to hold greater sway.[15]

Initially, the hearts-and-minds policies of CCP cadres in eastern Kham and Amdo had had some success. Their overtures in preparation for Tibet's annexation had convinced some inhabitants to stay neutral in the conflict between Lhasa and Beijing. Some had even helped China's advance.[16] Yet, by the mid-1950s, fears were growing that eastern Kham would not be spared socialist reforms – especially as the region was about to be merged into reformed Chinese provinces. Vibrant trade with Han areas exposed locals to the spectacle of forced collectivisation elsewhere in the PRC, and the party cadres' assurances that reforms would be different in Tibetan areas fell on deaf ears. Attempts at land reforms had started in some localities, where they were met by staunch non-cooperation and outbreaks of violence.

Khampa hostility increased when PRC authorities decided to retrieve all the guns held by civilians. The bearing of arms played an important role in Khampa society, and the number and quality of weapons available had grown since the Second World War. When government orders for the voluntary surrender of arms failed, party cadres began using increasingly coercive tactics, even stripping Buddhist altars of their weapons.[17]

Armed resistance broke out shortly afterwards, in 1955–1956. Taken by revolutionary zeal, Kham and Amdo party cadres used Mao's nationwide call to hasten collectivisation to launch socialist reforms at full speed.[18] Besides redistributing land and forming mutual aid societies, they tried to sedentarise the nomads. The result was a wave of spontaneous and uncoordinated uprisings. PRC authorities responded by sending the PLA to crush them.

By the start of 1957, repression had led many Khampas to escape to the PCART. There, some organised themselves into a pan-Khampa resistance movement, the Chushi Gangdruk. As revelations about the

---

[15] The CCP had initially retained the Guomindang province of Xikang, which covered eastern Kham and chunks of Amdo. It was merged into Sichuan and Yunnan in 1955. The rest of Amdo was incorporated into Qinghai and Gansu.

[16] Goldstein and Rimpoche, *A history of modern Tibet, Volume 1*, pp. 640–641; Shakya, *The dragon in the land of snows*, pp. 36–37, 40; June T. Dreyer, *China's forty millions: Minority nationalities and national integration in the People's Republic of China* (Cambridge, MA: Harvard University Press, 1976), p. 87.

[17] Shakya, *The dragon in the land of snows*, pp. 138–139.

[18] Benno Weiner, 'The Chinese Revolution on the Tibetan frontier: State building, national integration and socialist transformation, Zeku (Tsékhok) County, 1953–1958' (unpublished PhD dissertation, Columbia University, 2012), pp. 332–397.

extent of the destruction in eastern Kham travelled with guerrillas and refugees, disquiet grew in the PCART. The insurgents were now petitioning the Tibetan government for advice and assistance, but the Dalai Lama worried that if they entertained their pleas for help, revolt might spread to areas under Lhasa's control. The whole of Tibet would be engulfed in Chinese repression.

PRC authorities initially temporised. They perhaps counted on long-held prejudices against Khampas in central Tibet, and on the resentment that their presence – which represented a second demographic and economic upheaval – was causing in Lhasa and elsewhere. Blaming the Guomindang and exiled Tibetans, they did not detain the refugees but restricted the circulation of CCP-sponsored Tibetan newspapers from Kham and Amdo, which were openly advocating the eradication of Buddhism.

When this failed to stem restiveness, they reorganised the PCART's administration to include more Tibetan cadres and promised to shelve reforms for five years. Tibetan officials were sent to Chushi Gangdruk strongholds to enjoin surrender while propaganda was conducted to convince people that the reforms had pure motives, and that their pace in Tibetan areas outside of the PCART would be lowered. This failed to stop the spread of the Chushi Gangdruk. Growing in strength and boldness, the movement had the CIA's clandestine support and links with Taiwan. The Cold War was becoming entangled with older conflicts in Tibet.[19]

By late 1958, the attempts of the Dalai Lama's government to chart a neutral course between the PRC and the insurgents, whom many Tibetan officials secretly admired, were increasingly desperate. CCP authorities were pressuring the Dalai Lama's government to eradicate the Khampas themselves, and these orders came with an increasingly explicit threat: should the revolt spread to Lhasa, all-out repression would ensue.

In this 'peculiar situation, in which neither the traditional Tibetan Government nor the Chinese had much control over the course of events in Tibet', Monlam 1959 loomed. The festival had long served as an occasion to express anti-Chinese sentiments. What's more, the young Dalai Lama was about to take his final theological examination, a juncture at which his predecessors had traditionally assumed the reins of power. It was in this context that the Lhasa uprising erupted.[20]

---

[19] Shakya, *The dragon in the land of snows*, chapters 5 and 6; Xiaoyuan Liu, 'Entering the Cold War and other "wars": The Tibetan experience', *Chinese Historical Review*, 19:1 (2012), 47–64.

[20] Shakya, *The dragon in the land of snows*, pp. 180–184.

The Tibet Question

Supporters of Tibet's independence tend to idealise the historical Tibetan polity as a fundamentally sovereign national entity, a Shangri-La brutally destroyed through military might in 1950–1951. Chinese nationalist discourses fetishise the date in a different light: the signature of the Seventeen Point Agreement marked Tibet's rightful return into the Chinese body politic and liberated it from centuries of serfdom and backwardness at the stroke of a pen.

Against these problematic narratives, a nuanced historiography of Tibet's relationship with China is coalescing. The recent de-politicisation of the Mao era has energised scholarship on the early PRC and its engagement with minority 'nationalities'. Although researching Tibet's historical and contemporary relationship with China remains challenging, it has become possible to start revisiting the decade prior to 1959.[21]

The consolidation of PRC rule over Tibetan areas was a drawn-out process that was neither linear nor spatially even. If the Dalai Lama-held areas were annexed in 1950–1951, Communist penetration into Amdo and eastern Kham predated it. Even in the PCART, histories of Tibet after 1950 focus on the experience of Lhasa and a few other regions. In many areas, including some of the trans-McMahon Line regions, the arrival of the PLA and party cadres took longer.

Moreover, while the history of Tibet after 1950 cannot be seen as the 'liberation' presented in state-sponsored Chinese historiography, neither can it be framed around the oppression–resistance paradigm. Tibetan reminiscences say that PLA forces initially behaved well and that many people aspired to *some form* of change.[22] Relations between Tibetans and PRC authorities were a shifting mixture of coercion, adaptation, negotiation, contestation, acceptance, cooperation, and overt or covert resistance.[23]

The PRC authorities' goal was to turn China from an empire to a nation, a project whose intellectual and political genealogy straddled

---

[21] Weiner, 'The Chinese Revolution on the Tibetan frontier', pp. 41–42.

[22] Dawa Norbu, *Red star over Tibet* (London: Collins, 1974); Kunga Samten Dewatshang, *Flight at the cuckoo's behest: The life and times of a Tibetan freedom fighter (as told to his son Dorjee Wangdi Dewatshang)* (Delhi: Paljor, 1997), p. 91. See also the interviews collected by the 'Tibet Oral History Project', www.tibetoralhistory.org/interviews.html (accessed 27 January 2015), particularly by Cho Lhamo, Sonam Tsomo, Gyurme Chodon, and Dhondup (alias).

[23] Shakya, *The dragon in the land of snows*; Goldstein, *A history of modern Tibet, Volume 2*; Melvyn C. Goldstein, *A history of modern Tibet, Volume 3: The storm clouds descend, 1955–1957* (Berkeley: University of California Press, 2013); Weiner, 'The Chinese Revolution on the Tibetan frontier'.

the ostensible divide between the imperial, Republican, and Communist eras.[24] Like other non-Han regions, Tibet was an important part in this project. In the last years of the Qing, imperial officials such as Zhao Erfeng had conducted annexation and Sinicisation campaigns. The Republican leader Sun Yat-sen had opposed the Qing, but his ideal of China as a 'republic of five nationalities' sought to naturalise the territory conquered by the dynasty as historical China. Even during the internal fragmentation and instability of the warlord period, prominent Republican intellectuals sought to re-imagine Tibet as part of a Chinese nation, casting Khampas as primitive co-nationals in need of civilisational transformation.[25] Chiang Kai-shek had conducted campaigns of assimilation and formed institutional structures to deal with national minorities.[26]

There were major tensions in all these projects – tensions that the Chinese Communist regime would also experience in Tibet. PRC authorities proclaimed that China was a unitary nation-state, soon to become fully socialist. But that nation-state's geo-body proceeded directly from Qing conquests – the conquests of an empire, and a foreign one at that. Empire would somehow have to be 'erased'.[27] And yet, at the same time, the very challenges encountered by CCP officials in ethnic minority areas – as indeed by many Republican and Nationalist power holders and intellectuals before them – led them to adopt tactics and strategies directly taken from the imperial repertoire in order to manage the situation.[28]

---

[24] Kirk W. Larsen, 'The Qing Empire (China), imperialism, and the modern world', *History Compass*, 9:6 (2011), 498–508. This is not to say the project was consensual: Chinese federalist movements also existed in the 1920s. Prasenjit Duara, *Rescuing history from the nation: Questioning narratives of modern China* (Chicago; London: University of Chicago Press, 1995), chapter 6.

[25] Yudru Tsomu, 'Taming the Khampas: The Republican construction of eastern Tibet', *Modern China*, 39:3 (2013), 319–344.

[26] Hsiao-ting Lin, *Modern China's ethnic frontiers: A journey to the west* (London: Routledge, 2011).

[27] Peter C. Perdue, '"Erasing empire, re-racing the nation: Racialism and culturalism in imperial China"', in *Imperial Formations*, ed. by Ann Laura Stoler, Carole McGranahan, and Peter C. Perdue (Santa Fe, NY: School for Advanced Research Press, 2007), pp. 141–169. The process is still at play today, for instance in the vigorous efforts of nationalist Chinese historiography to push ever further back the date at which Tibet became an integral part of China. Elliot Sperling, 'Tibet and China: The interpretation of history since 1950', *China Perspectives*, 3 (2009), 25–37.

[28] James Leibold, *Reconfiguring Chinese nationalism: How the Qing frontier and its indigenes became Chinese*, 1st edn (New York: Palgrave Macmillan, 2007); Uradyn Bulag, *Collaborative nationalism: The politics of friendship on China's Mongolian frontier* (Lanham, MD; Plymouth: Rowman & Littlefield, 2010); Weiner, 'The Chinese Revolution on the Tibetan frontier'.

Starting with Tibet's 'peaceful liberation', the tools adopted by PRC authorities for much of the 1950s were meant to incorporate the region through a 'battle concerning the hearts of the Tibetan people' and so gradually to socialise them into the Chinese nation.[29] United Front tactics and strategies were central to the enterprise. Instead of fostering a class struggle, the party-state sought to work through the elites – as imperial patterns directed – using their influence and authority to penetrate and convert local societies and give legitimacy to the new regime. Socialist transformation was postponed in favour of policies meant to raise local production and standards of living.[30] Instructions were to adapt state policies to local situations.

Big efforts were made to find Tibetan cadres and give their Han counterparts the cultural and linguistic skills needed to understand the regions they were sent to and forge relationships there. The work teams sent into rural areas were instructed to work through local power holders and discontented segments of society and to undertake small-scale initiatives, from entertaining people to solving local problems and providing health care – giving them an opportunity to boost their local standing and propagandise the area. Knowing their lack of knowledge about Tibet and minority areas, PRC authorities fostered research about them, before and after arriving in a new region.[31]

Armed forces played a central role in this United Front strategy. The PLA was not just a military force, it was also a means to a political end: social and national revolution. Its ancestor, the Red Army, had stood out from other Chinese warring forces with its discipline, fervour, and good behaviour – playing a significant role in winning Han Chinese for the CCP.[32] The Red Army was reorganised into the PLA in the early stages of the Civil War, through the mass enrolment of peasants in CCP-held areas. The birth of the PRC led to its reorganisation and modernisation but not to its emancipation from the CCP and its political goals. Placed under the direct control of the Party Central Committee, the armed forces were tightly associated to the party-state's political and socio-economic work and spent a huge proportion of their time on

---

[29] Jian Chen, 'The Tibetan rebellion of 1959 and China's changing relations with India and the Soviet Union', *Journal of Cold War Studies*, 8:3 (2006), 54–101 (p. 63).

[30] Weiner, 'The Chinese Revolution on the Tibetan frontier'.

[31] Dreyer, *China's forty millions*, pp. 63–137. This was part of a broader ethnographic enterprise on the part of PRC authorities. Thomas S. Mullaney, *Coming to terms with the nation: Ethnic classification in modern China* (Berkeley, CA; London: University of California Press, 2012).

[32] William Wei, '"Political power grows out of the barrel of a gun": Mao and the Red Army', in *A military history of China*, ed. by David Andrew Graff and Robin Higham (Boulder, CO: Westview, 2001), pp. 229–248 (pp. 233–236).

non-military projects. Indeed, they were meant 'to serve as a model for Chinese society'.[33]

In minority areas such as Tibet, the PLA's role was at once military, administrative, political, cultural, and socio-economic. As an instrument of revolution and national unification, it was troops who were to give the example of the positive, modernising, uplifting nature of the new regime, and it was the PLA's work teams who were sent to new areas to 'do good and make friends'[34] – establishing 'tent schools', delivering treatment, or undertaking social welfare initiatives.[35]

This strategy collapsed in the late 1950s, eventually leading to the uprisings of 1959. Chinese authorities' policies towards Tibet were inherently contradictory. The United Front strategy emphasised consultation and voluntary change, but in practice coercion was never far away, and often exerted. Although it cultivated indigenous elites, the CCP was fundamentally hostile to them; in the longer run, its demands on them amounted to undermining their own power base.[36] The guarantees given to the Dalai Lama-held areas under the Seventeen Point Agreement could be reneged upon, whereas Tibet's incorporation into the PRC was final.[37] PRC authorities outwardly respected Tibetan Buddhism and patronised its leaders and institutions but were deeply anti-religious underneath.[38] Likewise, Han leaders' chauvinism and sense of superiority showed beneath the surface of the rhetoric of equality.[39] And the PLA's presence, despite attempts to present it as a benevolent, positive force, was disruptive and potentially threatening.

Should we see the PRC's policies as duplicitous attempts to consolidate control until 'conditions were ripe' for a forcible transformation of Tibet, or as the outcome of a genuine belief that Tibetans would peacefully and voluntarily choose the road of nation-building once the advantages of belonging to China became clear? Scholarship is divided on the matter. A recent work argues that the conflagration was due to factionalism within the Communist administration of Tibet and to the revolutionary impatience of party cadres, who refused to wait longer for national

[33] Dennis J. Blasko, 'Always faithful: The PLA from 1949 to 1989', in *A military history of China*, ed. by David Andrew Graff and Robin Higham (Boulder, CO: Westview, 2001), pp. 248–284 (pp. 249–254). See also Bruce A. Elleman, *Modern Chinese warfare, 1795–1989* (London: Routledge, 2001), pp. 255–257; Odd Arne Westad, *Decisive encounters: The Chinese Civil War, 1946–1950* (Stanford, CA: Stanford University Press, 2003), pp. 109–114.
[34] Quoted in Dreyer, *China's forty millions*, p. 98.
[35] Weiner, 'The Chinese Revolution on the Tibetan frontier', p. 114.
[36] Ibid.; Shakya, *The dragon in the land of snows*.
[37] Chen, 'The Tibetan rebellion of 1959' (p. 61).
[38] The Dalai Lama, *Memoirs of His Holiness*, pp. 117–118.
[39] Weiner, 'The Chinese Revolution on the Tibetan frontier'.

integration and social change and decided to do without the mediation of local elites.[40]

Sino-Indian Echoes

Communist China's ultimate goals and struggles in Tibet were in fact not that dissimilar to that of its neighbour in NEFA. Nehruvian India too faced the challenge of a transition from empire to nation. Like the PRC, its territorial imagination and ambitions were built upon the claims of a foreign empire, but this territorial legacy was highly uneven in frontier regions (not to say shallow). Projecting and maintaining state power were not straightforward matters. Nor had nation-making processes that had accompanied or sprung against colonialism in other parts of India really touched the eastern Himalayas prior to 1947.

Independence did not lead to the abandon of imperial techniques and strategies in NEFA; on the contrary, they were crucial to the Nehruvian state's efforts to incorporate the region. Independent India authorities retained key aspects of British colonial practice in north-eastern India, from restricting and screening interaction between NEFA and the rest of the country to the touring official serving both as judge and law enforcer, and to the reliance on local intermediaries to expand and entrench state presence. Both the Inner Line and red coats still exist today.

Frontier authorities conversely did away with *posa*, but they simultaneously generalised, increased, and regulated the granting of political presents, first initiated in colonial times. And if the vocabulary of punitive promenades was replaced by the discourse of development in NEFA at the turn of the 1950s, the latter had its roots in the last few years of British rule. The 'developmental nationalism' of the Indian freedom was only one of the factors that led to its emergence: late colonial efforts to improve legitimacy, as well as pragmatic reactions to frontier conditions, were also at play.

In this and in other respects, the post-colonial NEFA administration was noticeably different from its British predecessor in the eastern Himalayas. To begin with, it was a proper administration. And yet, its workings recalled imperial techniques of rule in other contexts. In a sense,

---

[40] Ibid. Melvyn Goldstein also argues that the CCP leadership were conscious that nation-building worked best through persuasion and gradual conversion; the conflagration in Tibet occurred due to the impatience of local Chinese authorities. But Chen Jian or Tsering Shakya see promises of administrative autonomy or religious cultural freedom as a way for the Chinese regime to bide its time until it was in a more comfortable position in Tibet. Chen, 'The Tibetan rebellion of 1959'; Shakya, *The dragon in the land of snows*; Goldstein, *A history of modern Tibet, Volume 2*.

the size and influence of the Research Department within frontier admin-istration represented the culmination of the ethnographic state. The sanctuarisation of tribal-ness under the NEFA Philosophy had a complex genealogy that linked it to the colonial idea of tribes and non-tribals.

India and China alike were experiencing the tribulations of an attempted transition from empire to nation, in other words. A transition made all the more contradictory and incomplete by the fact that the 'process of empire' not only continued, but was seen as necessary to bring forth the nation in NEFA and Tibet – an ideal of 'unity in diversity' in India, of multiple 'nationalities' in China.[41] Frontier authorities on both sides of the Himalayas sought to hire staff specifically trained to work in minority or tribal areas, and to maintain a tight relationship between research and administration. They courted indigenous power holders and used health care and entertainment to build support. The adoption of United Front policies or a NEFA Philosophy, purportedly to liberate Himalayan and Tibetan people from colonial 'neglect' or foreign 'imperi-alism' and bring them into modernity and the nation, stemmed at once from adaptability and a belief in their own benevolence. In all this, Nehruvian and PRC authorities were trying to '[tap] into the heritage of the former empire's techniques of rule in the service of nationalism'.[42]

Why then did state–society relations in NEFA improve over the 1950s when tensions simultaneously grew in Tibet? One hypothesis is that the PRC faced greater odds in its attempts to incorporate Tibet. In Lhasa-held areas, Communist China's authorities were dealing with another state, with a long (if fraught) history and a developed institutional and ideological apparatus, reinforced by thirty years of *de facto* indepen-dence – starting with a standing army. By contrast, the Himalayan socie-ties Indian authorities encountered had for the most part experienced state formation only indirectly.

They were also far more fragmented than Tibet, where, despite fric-tions between vibrant regional identities, Buddhism provided a common sense of belonging and a clear demarcation with the rest of the world.[43] Nor was there something approaching China's Han majority in India. The representatives of the Indian state in NEFA were very diverse in

---

[41] David Ludden, 'The process of empire: Frontiers and borderlands', in *Tributary empires in global history*, ed. by Christopher Bayly and Peter Fibiger Bang (New Delhi: Palgrave Macmillan, 2011), pp. 132–150.

[42] Bulag, *Collaborative nationalism*, p. 67.

[43] Chinese Republican and Nationalist leaders had therefore tried to harness support in Tibetan areas through a Buddhism-friendly policy. Gray Tuttle, *Tibetan Buddhists in the making of modern China* (New York; Chichester: Columbia University Press, 2005).

origins. Elwin was a lapsed Englishman and Christian, Rustomji a Zoroastrian Parsi from Bombay, his deputy a half-Gujarati half-English Muslim from Hyderabad. A significant proportion of frontier staff came from other hill areas of Assam: senior administrators felt that their linguistic, cultural, and physical affinities with Himalayan people would make them more acceptable to the latter. Ralengnao Bob Khathing, the official sent to take over Tawang, was a Naga.

These factors alone cannot explain the divergent evolution of the situation in Tibet and NEFA. The secular authority of the Dalai Lama's government extended but to a portion of the Tibetan plateau and the surrounding highlands before 1951, and general (let alone united) resistance against China's presence took years to coalesce and was not predetermined. And it was precisely resistance against the PRC that forged a new, more encompassing sense of Tibetan identity.

Although they resembled each other in certain important aspects, Chinese and Indian expansionisms were far from identical. These differences likely played a major role in shaping state–society relations on either side of the McMahon Line. Unlike the PRC's, India's expansion into the eastern Himalayas had not been led by military canvassing of the region. The semi-military Assam Rifles were present on the frontier but in comparatively small numbers – especially since the war in nearby Naga areas kept the staffing of outposts below official instructions. In this, the situation in NEFA was noticeably different from that on the Tibetan plateau. There, the presence of the PLA meant that the coercive power of the state could never be concealed, regardless of attempts to present it as a benevolent, positive force. The very presence of thousands of troops in Tibet, and the huge pressures this entailed on local resources, was a major cause of tensions.

Chinese and Indian authorities alike felt the importance of building transport infrastructure in the regions to incorporate, but the former proved far more apt at realising their plans. Yet, in the process, they requisitioned huge numbers of local men and women and imported workforce from the outside. NEFA authorities conversely struggled to build roads throughout the 1950s, both for lack of engineers and because, faced with the resentment the recourse to local labour (or import of external workers) created among the inhabitants, they decided to supply their outposts by air wherever possible.

Moreover, the resources of NEFA remained comparatively untapped. While sawmills produced timber out of the forests at the foot of the hills, there is little available evidence that they exploited those farther inland. Nor did India open mines or build hydroelectric plants in the 1950s, as the PRC did in Tibet. The lack of transport infrastructure likely played a part in this. The NEFA Philosophy also influenced this by prioritising the retention of a pristine tribal-ness, promoting cottage industry rather than industrialisation or mining. In short, the Indian state was comparatively weaker and less extractive.

One should not characterise this as an opposition between a democratic India and an authoritarian PRC. Notwithstanding the absence of political representation in NEFA at the time or the brutality of the Nehruvian state in the nearby Naga Hills, the contours of India's incorporation of NEFA were above all the result of an excessively fragmented state whose top authorities often looked elsewhere, unlike China's. This is not to say that the Chinese party-state was a monolith – far from it.[44] Over Tibet specifically, CCP and PRC authorities experienced internal tensions and disagreements. The Northwest and Southwest Bureaus fought over the administration of Tibet, and local party officials could act of their own accord and against their superiors' intentions. But still, Tibet stood higher on the list of PRC priorities than NEFA for India, if only because it made up a huge proportion of its territory and because of China's posture in the Cold War.[45]

That the real momentum of Indian state-making began with the 1950 earthquake is also significant. By expanding through relief and rehabilitation, NEFA authorities were able to forge the beginnings of a constructive relationship with the eastern Himalayas' inhabitants. The earthquake had also struck south-eastern Tibet. In Kongpo, Pomé, and Pemakö, the disaster destroyed Buddhist monasteries and buried roads under landslides, while a village slid into the Tsangpo. In Dzayül, at least 780 people died. The earthquake was felt in Lhasa, Yunnan, and Sichuan. But it would take months, if not years, for the PLA to arrive in affected regions.[46] Not only would it not be able to harness the catastrophe for propaganda purposes, but the tremors would be interpreted in Lhasa as portent of a political cataclysm to come: annexation by China.[47] Yet, if Indian state-making had benefited from an unforeseen contingency in 1950, another external event was about to fragilise it.

---

[44] Jing Huang, *Factionalism in Chinese Communist politics* (Cambridge: Cambridge University Press, 2000).

[45] Goldstein, *A history of modern Tibet, Volume 2*, pp. 422–453; Sulmaan Wasif Khan, 'Cold War co-operation: New Chinese evidence on Jawaharlal Nehru's 1954 visit to Beijing', *Cold War History*, 11:2 (2011), 197–222 (pp. 60–62, 86–88).

[46] Ian Baker, *The heart of the world: A journey to Tibet's lost paradise* (London: Souvenir, 2006), pp. 110–111, 307; US Geological Survey, 'Historic Earthquakes: Assam-Tibet 1950', *Earthquake Hazards Program* (n.d.) http://earthquake.usgs.gov/earthquakes/world/events/1950_08_15.php (accessed 9 April 2015).

[47] Hugh Richardson, *Tibet and its history*, 1st edn (Oxford: Oxford University Press, 1962), p. 181.

Ripples of 1959

When the Dalai Lama's party had fled Lhasa on 17 March 1959, it had hoped to negotiate with the Chinese from within Tibet. But the safe haven provided by the Lhotsé fortress proved to be short-lived. The Dalai Lama had done his best to play the soldier, but word of his escape had filtered out, and he was quickly recognised. Staying in Tibet meant risking his capture by Chinese troops, now rushing towards Lhotsé, and execution or life imprisonment for his companions. On 31 March 1959, the Dalai Lama therefore approached the tiny Chutangmu outpost in north-western Kameng and requested asylum. Forewarned, the Tawang PO had sent his assistant to welcome him. The leader of Tibet had gone into exile.

News of the Dalai Lama's escape precipitated NEFA onto the national and international scene. For three weeks in April 1959, the media looked eagerly towards Kameng. The Dalai Lama was making his slow descent to the plains, holding blessing ceremonies and talks with Indian officials along the way. Pictures of Tawang and Bomdila, where he rested, were splashed on the front pages. Readers were treated to descriptions of the Monpas' enthusiastic welcome and religious devotion. The Tawang monastery became famous. Popular attention culminated when the Dalai Lama crossed the Inner Line into Assam on 18 April. Two hundred press correspondents from twelve countries had congregated at the entrance of Tezpur, the town's inhabitants in tow. Even Achingmori and the 1950 earthquake had not generated such publicity (Figure 5.1).[48]

Eventually, the Dalai Lama left Assam for Mussoorie in north-western India. Nehru welcomed him there and offered him political asylum. For NEFA authorities, this had been a perfect opportunity to showcase their progress – starting with the new and probably still shining motor road that the Dalai Lama had taken from Bomdila onwards.[49] Yet the excitement soon acquired darker undertones: China and India's diplomatic relations were rapidly deteriorating.

The two countries' relationship had ostensibly been constructive in the early 1950s. Although Nehru and other Indian nationalists had once been close to the Guomindang in the name of Pan-Asianism, the Cold War

---

[48] 'Dalai Lama having rest at Tawang monastery', *Amrita Bazaar Patrika*, 7 April 1959; 'Tawang: Where the Dalai Lama had a breathing spell', *Times of India*, 12 April 1959; 'Press correspondents converging on Tezpur', *Amrita Bazaar Patrika*, 15 April 1959.

[49] Verrier Elwin, 'A journey in north-east India', *Sunday Statesman Magazine*, 9 August 1959. Even the *Assam Tribune* had muted its criticism of the NEFA administration. 'Achievements of NEFA administration: Remarkable progress during last five years', *Assam Tribune*, 22 May 1959.

Figure 5.1 The Dalai Lama journeys through NEFA after escaping
Tibet, 1959
© Arunachal Pradesh DIPR

provided grounds for cooperation between India and the PRC.[50] The two
countries shared a dream of being recognised as regional powers and
a fierce opposition to American imperialism, which they saw as the
main force preventing Asia – and specifically themselves – from coming
into its own. Cooperation was essential to combat US hegemony.[51]

Domestically, the two countries had unspoken reasons to maintain
good relations. Although independent India had inherited the British

---

[50] Brian Tsui, 'The plea for Asia – Tan Yunshan, Pan-Asianism and Sino-Indian relations',
China Report, 46:4 (2010), 353–370.
[51] Khan, 'Cold War co-operation'.

India's para-diplomatic missions and direct relations with the Dalai Lama's government, the PRC did not openly denounce them. The regime was diplomatically isolated as a result of the Korean War.[52] It also needed Delhi's goodwill to secure its hold over Tibet, notably to ensure steady supplies of crucial goods: it was far easier to reach the plateau from India than from China.[53]

Meanwhile, Nehru preferred to treat the Sino-Indian boundary as a settled matter, in no need of discussion. Given the PRC's logistical problems in Tibet, raising the question of its ambiguous position vis-à-vis India's sovereignty in the Himalayas did not seem urgent. Indeed it could backfire: there was no need to remind China of the fragility of India's presence in NEFA.[54] Nehru had opted to build good relations with Beijing, hoping to negotiate greater autonomy for Tibet. India was among the first countries to recognise and establish diplomatic relations with the PRC, and it supported its international recognition and integration into the United Nations.

Sino-Indian diplomatic relations reached their zenith in April 1954 when Nehru and Zhou Enlai, the Chinese Prime Minister, signed a bilateral agreement proclaiming their 'peaceful coexistence'. Mutual respect for territorial integrity and sovereignty, non-interference in each other's domestic affairs, non-aggression, and equality would govern China and India's interaction, presenting the world with an alternative to power politics. The Panchsheel Agreement, as it became known in India, was also a treaty on 'Trade and Intercourse between Tibet Region of China and India'. India retained its three trade agencies in Tibet but handed over its postal, telegraph, and telephone network; it also agreed to withdraw its military escorts, relinquish land, building, and rest houses, and stop treating anyone but its own agents in its hospitals in the country. The PRC obtained the right to open three trade agencies on Indian territory. Nehru thought the agreement at least preserved Tibetan autonomy and enshrined the PRC's tacit acceptance of the McMahon Line – and so would keep Chinese authorities and forces away from India's borders. In fact, independent India had abandoned the special rights in Tibet it had inherited from its British predecessor and, through the agreement's title, tacitly acknowledged Chinese sovereignty over it.[55]

---

[52] Huei Pang Yang, 'Helpful allies, interfering neighbours: World opinion and China in the 1950s', *Modern Asian Studies*, 49:1 (2015), 204–240.

[53] K.C. Johorey and Sudha Johorey. Interview with the author, 15 March 2014, Gurgaon (Haryana).

[54] Srinath Raghavan, *War and peace in modern India* ([Basingstoke]: Palgrave Macmillan, 2010), p. 239.

[55] John W. Garver, *Protracted contest: Sino-Indian rivalry in the twentieth century* (New Delhi: Oxford University Press, 2001), pp. 51–52. For the text of the agreement, see

It is doubtful that a genuine spirit of Sino-Indian brotherhood ever truly existed. Nehru's positive attitude towards the PRC amounted to 'defense by friendship'.[56] As for the PRC, India's status as British India's successor state made it an object of mistrust and condescension. Delhi's protestations that it would not seek to interfere in China's domestic matters were received with scepticism.[57] Beijing also knew that India's insistence that there was no territorial dispute was meant 'to force us into implicitly acknowledging and legitimizing their occupation [of Tawang]'. They had no intention of doing so. Internally, sections at least of the Chinese leadership wanted the abolition of the Simla agreement and India's withdrawal from Tawang and the Siang Valley.[58]

The ink on the Panchsheel Agreement was barely dry when Nehru's qualms returned. Chinese maps had surfaced that showed a boundary alignment different from the McMahon Line and its counterpart in the western Himalayas, the Ardagh–Johnson Line. The Aksai Chin, a high-altitude desert on the edge of Ladakh, and most of NEFA were marked as Chinese territory. Delhi informally raised the matter with Beijing, who nonchalantly replied that these were but out-of-date Guomindang maps. Within a couple of years, the PRC's ambitions in the Himalayas became clearer. In 1957, it completed an important highway between Xinjiang and Lhasa, dramatically improving connectivity between Tibet and China. The road passed through the Aksai Chin.[59] Maps and Aksai Chin road aside, the PRC was wont to curtail the activities of Indian traders in Tibet, now that its supply situation had improved.[60]

'Agreement between the Republic of India and the People's Republic of China on trade and intercourse between the Tibet region of China and India' (originally reproduced in *Renmin Ribao* (*People's Daily*), 30 April 1954), *History and Public Policy Program Digital Archive* (29 April 1954), http://digitalarchive.wilsoncenter.org/document/121558 (accessed 27 April 2015).

[56] Michael Edwardes, 'Illusion and reality in India's foreign policy', *International Affairs*, 41:1 (1965), 48–58 (p. 49).

[57] Chinese Foreign Ministry, 'Cable from the Ministry: "Report on negotiations regarding the Tibet issue between China and India" (Original File: Chinese Foreign Ministry Archives (PRC FMA), 105-00011-02, 42–44. Obtained by Dai Chaowu and translated by 7Brands.)', *History and Public Policy Program Digital Archive* (24 December 1950), http://digitalarchive.wilsoncenter.org/document/114749 (accessed 27 April 2015).

[58] Chinese Foreign Ministry, 'Cable from Zhang Jingwu: "On issues of relations between China and India in Tibet" (Original File: PRC FMA 105-00032-23, 76–81. Translated by 7Brands)', *History and Public Policy Program Digital Archive* (21 October 1953), http://digitalarchive.wilsoncenter.org/document/114754 (accessed 27 April 2015).

[59] Raghavan, *War and peace in modern India*, pp. 244–247. Indian intelligence officers in fact already knew about the road, but its public opening forced them to react.

[60] China had implemented checks on the activities of Indian traders present in Tibet as early as in April 1958, when it stopped accepting payments in silver dollars to force Indian traders desiring to stay in Tibet to use Chinese paper currency. *Lok Sabha Debates 1958 (Volume XV)* (New Delhi: Lok Sabha Secretariat, 1958), pp. 2812–2816.

China too harboured growing suspicions towards its neighbour. After 1951, a sizeable community of elite Tibetans had re-centred itself on Kalimpong, a small town on the Sikkim–West Bengal border that was the biggest centre of Indo-Tibetan trade. These *émigrés* included prominent statesmen and aristocrats as well as members of the Dalai Lama's family. They were later joined by growing numbers of Khampa refugees and fighters. By the mid-1950s, the diaspora was actively seeking Indian, Guomindang, and American support against the PRC. In 1956, it unsuccessfully tried to get the Dalai Lama to remain in India, where the leader had attended the 2,500th anniversary of the Buddha's birth. Whether or not the Indian government supported these activities is unclear – Delhi had tried to curb *émigré* activities in 1954, and Nehru strongly counselled the Dalai Lama to return to Lhasa to find a *modus vivendi* with PRC authorities. But for China, the presence of many powerful Tibetan dissidents on Indian soil was duplicitous. Nehru's proposed visit to Tibet was indefinitely postponed by Beijing.[61]

Two years later in 1958, the Chinese Foreign Ministry and other departments formed a commission to look into the PRC's boundaries. In itself, this was 'a confession of ignorance' regarding the country's borderlands. After some preliminary research, the commission concluded that at least 1,400 kilometres were in dispute with India – starting with the NEFA–Tibet border. But more information was needed before the matter could be taken up with India.[62]

In January 1959, Zhou Enlai finally informed Nehru that the PRC considered its boundary with north-eastern India to be un-delimited.[63] From its perspective, the Simla Convention had been nothing but an imperialist ploy to humiliate and weaken China. Tibet was an integral part of its territory and had no right to conduct (let alone conclude) international negotiations. Without a Chinese signature, the convention was null and void – and the McMahon Line illegitimate.[64] A few months later, India's decision to grant asylum to the Dalai Lama enraged Beijing. Sino-Indian relations were about to descend into open hostility.

The first concrete sign of the deterioration in the relationship was the decline of long-distance trade between India and Tibet. Between

---

[61] Shakya, *The dragon in the land of snows*, pp. 119–120, 142–177.

[62] Sulmaan Wasif Khan, *Muslim, trader, nomad, spy: China's Cold War and the Tibetan borderlands* (Duke, NC: UNC Press, 2015), pp. 29–30.

[63] Srinath Raghavan, 'Sino-Indian boundary dispute, 1948–60: A reappraisal', *Economic and Political Weekly*, 41:36 (2006), 3882–3892 (p. 3887).

[64] Xuecheng Liu, *The Sino-Indian border dispute and Sino-Indian relations* (Lanham, MD: University Press of America, 1994), pp. 54–59. Quoted in Steven A. Hoffmann, 'Rethinking the linkage between Tibet and the China–India border conflict: A realist approach', *Journal of Cold War Studies*, 8:3 (2006), 165–194 (p. 168).

February and March 1959, import–export volumes collapsed. PRC authorities banned Indian and Tibetan currencies and imposed progressively greater restrictions on Indian traders' travels and activities. Their movement in Tibet was severely limited, free exchange facilities disappeared, and repatriating capital became difficult. Merchants were prevented from bringing home their unsold wares, and exports of raw materials became subject to Chinese approval. India implemented its own measures. While setting up custom posts on its north-western borders, it banned the export to Tibet of grain, wood, steel products, sugar, and cloth in quick succession from April 1959 onwards.[65]

A growing sense of unease gripped Indian public opinion. Disquietingly, old maps marking NEFA and parts of Ladakh as Chinese territory were still in circulation, and the PRC persisted in publishing them. Hitherto largely absent from border areas, the PLA was deployed along the McMahon Line and across from Nepal and Bhutan.[66] Indian academics and politicians began to denounce 'Red China's grand strategy in South Asia'.[67] Meanwhile, PRC media were whipping up anti-Indian propaganda. Was the situation morphing into a security crisis? The answer came soon enough.

On 25 August 1959, Chinese troops seized Longju, a small garrison post established by India in the Subansiri. The outpost had been established but a few months before, one of several meant to quietly reinforce the presence of Assam Rifles on the border.[68] The PLA felt it was India that was trying to build a federation in the Himalayas and took this as a provocation to force Beijing into acknowledging the McMahon Line: Longju was just north of its cartographic alignment.[69] Delhi initially denied reports about the clash, but

[65] 'Indian currency declared illegal in Tibet', *Amrita Bazaar Patrika*, 7 August 1959; 'Indian merchants in Tibet: Chinese put more restrictions', *Amrita Bazaar Patrika*, 21 August 1959; New Delhi, NAI, External Affairs Proceedings (1960), Smuggling of controlled items of goods to Tibet, 1/6/NGO/60-Part.I; ibid.

[66] M. Taylor Fravel, *Strong borders, secure nation: Cooperation and conflict in China's territorial disputes* (Princeton, NJ; Oxford: Princeton University Press, 2008), pp. 78–79.

[67] 'Concern felt over Indo-Tibet border: Publication of old maps persisted in by China', *Times of India*, 8 May 1959; H.V. Kamath, 'A Himalayan federation? Red China's grand strategy in S. Asia', *Amrita Bazaar Patrika*, 6 August 1959. Also Satyabarta Goswami, 'China's expanding horizon in the Tibetan border lands', *Amrita Bazaar Patrika*, 19 April 1959.

[68] If the Indian Chief of General Staff at the time is to be believed, tensions first built up when, in response to an Indian official's conferring of a red coat to a Longju elder, Chinese forces stationed nearby began to patrol more heavily in the area – following which occupants of the newly built Assam Rifles outposts intensified their own patrols. Lt-Gen B.M. Kaul, *The untold story* (Bombay: Allied Publishers, 1967), p. 232.

[69] PLA General Staff Department, 'Report: "Behind India's second anti-China wave" (Original File: PRC FMA 105-00944-07, 84–90. Translated by 7Brands)', *History and Public Policy Program Digital Archive* (29 October 1959) http://digitalarchive.wilsoncenter.org/document/114758 (accessed 27 April 2015).

India's military weakness vis-à-vis the PRC could no longer remain hidden.[70] The outpost had been easily overwhelmed, revealing the absence of strong Indian positions on the Subansiri border. Only one other outpost existed, Taksing. Like Longju, it was but a few months old.[71]

Central authorities could neither retake Longju nor reconnoitre the surrounding territory. Nehru's professed readiness to use force if bilateral talks failed flew in the face of the PLA's entrenchment.[72] Chinese troops were digging mines and building airfields around Longju, underscoring their claim that the outpost lay in their territory.[73] On 8 September, another letter from Zhou Enlai confirmed the seriousness of the dispute: the PRC rejected the McMahon Line and considered the western Sino-Indian boundary to be unmarked. To make matters worse, a former Governor of colonial Assam concurred: the McMahon Line '[did] not exist and never ha[d] existed'.[74]

Chinese forces nevertheless withdrew from Longju that November. This was hardly an Indian victory. The PLA had relocated only three miles north and re-occupying the outpost would cause another confrontation. India could not afford such a 'fairly major undertaking'.[75] Instead, an alternative outpost was established seven miles to the south.[76] 'Incursions' continued. Indian authorities counted 105 Chinese violations of NEFA and Ladakh's airspace between December 1959 and December 1960. The PRC responded with its counter-accusations. Nehru confessed that India was neither in the position of definitively identifying Chinese aircraft in NEFA nor in that of sending nearby jets to force them to land.[77] The implications were chilling. India's territorial and aerial sovereignty could not be defended.

---

[70] 'No Chinese incursion in Kameng Division', *Assam Tribune*, 27 August 1959; 'MPs' concern over Chinese in NEFA', *Amrita Bazaar Patrika*, 28 August 1959.

[71] APSA, P49/59, p. 24.

[72] 'No fresh incursion into NEFA', *Amrita Bazaar Patrika*, 1 September 1959; 'Use of force against China not ruled out', *Amrita Bazaar Patrika*, 6 November 1959.

[73] 'NEFA border post reinforced', *Amrita Bazaar Patrika*, 15 September 1962; 'Chinese dig mines all around Longju', *Assam Tribune*, 15 November 1959.

[74] '"McMahon Line does not exist": Former governor's view', *Times of India*, 4 September 1959.

[75] G.S. Bhargava, *The battle of NEFA* (New Delhi: Allied Publishers, 1964), p. 75.

[76] APSA, P49/59, p. 24.

[77] Chinese Foreign Ministry, 'Presentation of diplomatic note to India concerning Indian military personnel's encroachment on Chinese territory' (Original File: PRC FMA 106-01397-03, 10–11. Translated by Anna Beth Keim), *History and Public Policy Program Digital Archive* (21 April 1962) http://digitalarchive.wilsoncenter.org/document/114498 (accessed 27 April 2015); 'No instructions to shoot down alien planes: Premier's statement in Rajya Sabha', *Times of India*, 2 December 1959.

The Indian government now faced intense pressure to undertake a 'forward policy' in NEFA. The country's military strategy needed a complete makeover, argued the press and many politicians. To many, 'the "cartographical conquest" proclaimed by the Chinese ... [was] now being translated into real, physical conquest'.[78] Some Indian leaders responded with their own brand of expansionism. The socialist leader Ram Manohar Lohia declared that the Indo-Tibetan border should run much further north than its current alignment, enclosing the entire Tsangpo Valley and the sacred Mount Kailash within Indian territory. For good measure, he argued that Tibet was 'about 80 percent India and 20 percent China'.[79] Lohia's hawkish pronouncements participated in a growing popular consensus in India: firmness was the only way to deal with the PRC.[80] In 1950, NEFA had been considered a military backwater. Now it was India's weakest link.

Cartographic Anxiety and Its Effects

This 'cartographic anxiety' had a momentous consequence: the militarisation of the Indian Himalayas.[81] The weeks after Longju set the tone. NEFA was placed under the military control of the Eastern Command, and after a top-level meeting of army officers, operational headquarters were set up in Assam. By November, four additional army commands had been allocated to the sector. Military authorities began deploying troops and organising army bases and transport supply lines in NEFA and Assam, supported by central police battalions. Cuts in the defence budget were cancelled, and Delhi prioritised the funding of the arms industry.[82] Eventually, the Assam Rifles themselves were partially re-militarised, their operational deployment in NEFA and the Naga Hills entrusted to the Indian army. Released from administrative tasks, they were tasked

---

[78] 'Editorial: NEFA', *Amrita Bazaar Patrika*, 30 August 1959.
[79] *Collected works of Rammanohar Lohia*, ed. by Mastram Kapoor, 9 vols (New Delhi: Anamika, 2011), Volume IV (Press statement: 'Himalayan India: Some non-party and non-controversial suggestions', May 1960).
[80] 'Defence of NEF territory: MPs satisfied by Nehru's statement', *Assam Tribune*, 29 August 1959; 'Editorial: Need for firmness', *Assam Tribune*, 13 September 1959.
[81] Sankaran Krishna, 'Cartographic anxiety: Mapping the body politic in India', *Alternatives: Global, Local, Political*, 19:4 (1994), 507–521.
[82] 'Entire NEFA border is placed under army control', *Times of India*, 29 August 1959; 'Four new army commands under Jorhat HQ', *Assam Tribune*, 4 November 1959; 'Airstrips in NEFA: Construction to be taken up soon', *Assam Tribune*, 28 November 1959; 'Roads and air strips in NEFA: Proposals submitted', *Times of India*, 4 January 1960; New Delhi, NAI, External Affairs Proceedings (1962), Deputation of CRP battalion to NEFA, NI-1(2)/62; 'Cut in defence budget to be restored', *Times of India*, 9 February 1960.

with pushing up to the border as fast as possible.[83] A military adviser to the Assam Governor was appointed to liaise between the army head-quarters, the state government, and local administrations. The new Assam Governor was himself a career soldier.[84]

With militarisation now an official policy in NEFA, state presence became subordinated to it. The notion of security underpinning tribal developmentalism had been a broad one; security would proceed from a developed and contented population. From late 1959 onwards, the 'systemic entanglement' between development and security radically changed.[85] Development and welfare initiatives were made ancillary to military imperatives.

Infrastructural build-up testified to this evolution. NEFA's engineering programme had been much lauded after the Dalai Lama's escape: 300 miles of roads built since the First Five-Year Plan, including one completed just in time to save the great leader! Now it was cast as the root of India's strategic vulnerability in the eastern Himalayas: NEFA had *only* 300 miles of roads, most of them fit for use only in fair weather. As for motorable roads, the only one of note going into the hinterland was the one ... taken by the Dalai Lama.

More imperative than ever before, the improvement of transport and communications in NEFA adopted an unambiguous military rationale. In May 1960, the central government established a Border Roads Organisation (BRO) to build defensive roads to India's northern borders. Though a civilian institution, its employees acted as engineers to the armed forces. Indeed, they were deployed by the Defence Ministry. During its first three years, the BRO was entrusted to complete a road plan of no less than 1.2 billion rupees. The NEFA administration was pressed to contribute. It was to build 88 miles of roads, 157 miles of porter tracks, and several airfields in 1961–1962, using Rs 226,900,000 especially allocated for the purpose.[86]

NEFA authorities had other pressing matters on their hands: they were in the midst of a refugee crisis. From April 1959 onwards, Communist repression forced thousands of Tibetans to flee to India. For those from Lhasa and eastern Tibet, the shortest, safest route at their disposal was that which led into NEFA. It was also a region where the Chushi

[83] New Delhi, NAI, External Affairs Proceedings (1961), Procedure for applying Army Act and Rules to army personnel seconded to Assam Rifles, 1(8)-NEFA/61.
[84] 'Military adviser to Governor: Major-General Das appointed', *Times of India*, 3 October 1959; 'Editorial: New governor', *Assam Tribune*, 14 October 1959.
[85] Mahnaz Z. Ispahani, *Roads and rivals: The political uses of access in the borderlands of Asia* (Ithaca, NY; London: Cornell University Press, 1989), p. 214.
[86] 'Border road plan to cost Rs 120 crores', *Times of India*, 11 May 1960; 'Road construction in NEFA', *Times of India*, 12 July 1962. See also Kaul, *The untold story*, pp. 243–245.

Gangdruk were still active, though the guerrillas too would soon be forced to escape. Caught by the PLA before they could cross into safety, some refugees were forcibly sent back home, where they found their possessions gone, distributed around; but many more succeeded in crossing the border.[87]

Assam Rifles checkpoints – whose depletion due to the Naga conflict had not yet been offset by the military forward policy – found themselves overwhelmed. Refugees were arriving through Mago, through Bumla, through Monigong, through dozens of other routes. Among them was a man who had played a key role in the Dalai Lama's escape: the Chushi Gangdruk leader Kunga Samten Dewatshang. A terrible trek through a snow-covered pass had taken him and his family to the Kameng border, where NEFA officials at first hesitated. For the tiny border outposts, letting refugees in had political implications; it also meant disarming them and feeding them. The Dewatshang family was eventually allowed to cross into NEFA. Indian officials organised a distribution of *tsampa* (roasted barley flour) at a nearby Monpa village, and airdropped more food at Tawang, where hundreds of refugees camped in the open.[88]

Numbers are hard to ascertain, but within two months of the Dalai Lama's escape, the Kameng and the Subansiri divisions hosted 8,000 refugees. An additional 5,000 people had sought safety south of the McMahon Line.[89] Indian authorities intensified their efforts. One million rupees were sanctioned for relief purposes in August 1959.[90] NEFA officials organised jeep transport for women, children, and the disabled and built temporary transit camps for the refugees.[91]

By the time the Dewatshang family reached Bomdila, long thatched houses had been built to accommodate refugees, and planes were coming to drop as much food and essential items as weather could permit. The administration enlisted mule owners among the refugees to transport food to Bomdila from the nearest road head, providing the Dewatshang with much-needed cash. Refugee camps were organised in the plains, like at Missamari in the Kameng

---

[87] See 'Tibet Oral History Project', www.tibetoralhistory.org/interviews.html (accessed 27 January 2015). Especially the interviews of Tashi, Cho Lhamo, Tenzin Namgyal, and Dhondup.

[88] Dewatshang, *Flight at the cuckoo's behest*, pp. 143–148.

[89] Today's estimates speak of 85,000 persons fleeing Tibet at the time. United States Committee for Refugees and Immigrants, *World Refugee Survey 1998 – India* (1998), www.unhcr.org/refworld/docid/3ae6a8be8.html (accessed 19 October 2012).

[90] '2,396 Tibetans enter so far: Majority may not go back', *Assam Tribune*, 12 August 1959.

[91] 'Khampa warrior bands pouring into India', *Times of India*, 16 May 1959.

foothills.[92] But these camps soon filled up. As they hosted many more people than their barracks could accommodate, cholera, measles, and dermatitis spread.[93]

NEFA officials changed tactics. Instead of sending refugees to the foothills, whose climate and living conditions bewildered them, they dispersed them across various parts of the Indian Himalayas, including NEFA. There, they would participate in local development schemes, furthering India's purposes in the process. Thousands of refugees were rehabilitated in the Tawang–Bomdila region; they were also numerous near Gelling, in the Siang. The External Affairs Ministry organised their rehabilitation via frontier administration, appointing Tibetan interpreters as well as rehabilitation and medical officers. Working schemes were launched, with a preference for crafts production and roadwork. Border Road Camps were organised to house refugees. Yet not all of them were resettled in the hills. Bhalukpung, a site located just on the Inner Line between NEFA and Assam, was perhaps the biggest camp of all. There, hygiene and living conditions continued to be calamitous, and daily life was a struggle.[94]

A Fragilised Philosophy

The struggle extended to NEFA's inhabitants. Indian state-making in the eastern Himalayas had been re-articulated around military presence. On any given month, NEFA's inhabitants now witnessed numerous visits by various senior army officers, from the Engineer-in-Chief to the Eastern Command's Chief of Staff. Thousands of jawans arrived, and with them BRO and Central Reserve Police staff, army engineers, road workers, and military storekeepers. NEFA's ethnoscape changed. The new representatives of state power looked 'foreign' in a different way than administrative officials, who were preferably from other north-eastern tribes or

[92] Dewatshang, *Flight at the cuckoo's behest*, pp. 151–152; 'More Tibetans enter India – Difficult situation in Kameng', *Assam Tribune*, 25 April 1959; 'Tibetan refugees in Kameng include many dignitaries', *Assam Tribune*, 4 May 1959.

[93] Interview with Tsering Tashi (Interview #35). Interviewed by Martin Newman on 27 June 2007 (held at the Tibet Oral History Project), www.tibetoralhistory.org/inter views.html (accessed 27 January 2015).

[94] Itanagar, APSA, NEFA Secretariat (1961), Press notes issued by administration PC-17/ 61, p. 97 (Rehabilitation of Tibetan refugees in NEFA); Itanagar, APSA, NEFA Secretariat (1961), Tour notes of officers visiting sites for settlement of Tibetan refugees in NEFA Agri-7/38/61. Interview with Rashid Yusuf Ali. Interviewed by Rebecca Gnüchtel on 19 October 2006.

Assamese. Army battalions were Dogra, Sikh, or Kumaoni, and road workers were often Nepali or Tibetan refugees.[95] Tribal development had meant that the state was primarily represented by civilian personnel, development officers, and staff. Locally, the key link between the government and the people was the Village-Level Worker, a local man. Now their visibility was diminishing, threatened by the overwhelming presence of armed men and their auxiliaries. Despite ideas of employing local tribal youths as auxiliary armed forces, attempts in this direction had never materialised.[96] This was perhaps because, while NEFA was to be defended against an external aggressor, this imperative was primarily defined as defending its territory rather than its people. Since the Indian army failed to offer local people opportunities to integrate into it, it remained a more or less foreign body on the frontier – a fact that would soon turn into a recurring popular grievance. State presence in NEFA was being reinforced, but it was also becoming more jarring.

Militarisation contradicted the NEFA Philosophy in more ways than one. By letting the army in (or indeed, refugees), Delhi forsook the cardinal principle that the region not be flooded by outsiders. Just a year before, External Affairs officials had stressed their desire 'not to disturb the normal trend of tribal life by introducing large numbers of outsiders'.[97] Nehru had ordered to cut down expenditure on NEFA, and Elwin had been preparing a proposal for the reduction of frontier staff, suggesting retrenching the number of Assam Rifles.[98] This now seemed a major mistake: NEFA was a 'void screaming to be filled'.[99]

The way state authorities approached indigenous inhabitants also evolved. Touring increasingly moved away from 'the former pioneering days' of the lonely, *dim dam* (fly)-bitten officer. His successors were treated to 'well furnished and comfortable Circuit Houses, electricity, sanitary fittings, station wagons – all these ... unheard of and undreamt of in the frontier ten years ago'.[100] Ostensibly this was an improvement. Officials

---

[95] Itanagar, APSA, NEFA Secretariat (1960), Monthly confidential reports from POs, Sup-4/55/60-Part II (Report for May 1960). The 1962 war was later praised as an example of India's many ethnicities fighting together against the enemy. Bhargava, *The battle of NEFA*, pp. 102–108.

[96] New Delhi, NAI, External Affairs Proceedings (1953), Notes by T.N. Kaul, N/53/1395/105 (29 April 1953).

[97] *Lok Sabha Debates 1958 (Vol. XV)*, p. 9418.

[98] New Delhi, NMML, Elwin Papers (1959), Correspondence with K.L. Mehta, 1954–59, S. No. 7 (Elwin to Ken, 28 February and 4 July 1958).

[99] 'Chinese influence on border tribes', *Times of India*, 18 October 1959. Also Itanagar, APSA, NEFA Secretariat (1962), Development activities in border areas PC-14/62 ('note on the development of border areas').

[100] Delhi, NMML, Rustomji Papers (1963), Broadcasts, tour notes, articles, etc. (1959–63), S. No. 8, p. 55.

could now tour in decent conditions, and could therefore tour more and more often.

But these new, well-oiled touring mechanics threatened a crucial facet of the relationship between officials and local people. Early *mibong* (frontier officers) relied on their own two feet, and they had to make do with makeshift camps or cabins on the edge of a village. Perforce, they depended on tribal porters who could always drop them, and they were at a disadvantage when walking on NEFA's steep tracks. All this had made them seem less threatening to frontier populations. Their endurance might even have been a cause for empathy. Years after his retirement, some Adis still talked admiringly of 'Jembo's' stamina (Peter James, APO in the 1940s).[101] Jembo's successors did not make similar efforts. Some were even prone to postponing a tour should their route not include sanitary fittings.[102] And now that circuit houses and roads permanently marked the countryside, the inhabitants were constantly reminded of state presence.

Despite the misgivings of Elwin and other senior frontier officials, NEFA's development had clearly been put 'on a war footing'.[103] Important socio-economic transformations followed. Given the overriding need to supply the troops stationed in the interior of NEFA, directives prohibiting the entry of external traders became ineffective. More and more 'businessmen' settled beyond the Inner Line, where they made large profits. Small towns mushroomed across the agency, particularly around administrative and army headquarters. By 1962, Tezu hosted 3,000 people. Its officers' colony spread all over a hillock, with administrative offices at their foot, and its high school hosted 200 students from across the Lohit Division. Beside its hospital, cattle upgrading centre, and agricultural farm, it also had a Lokpriya Bardoloi Museum. A *pakka* (permanent) bazaar had been opened, the first of its kind in NEFA.[104]

Tibetan, Bhutanese, and Sikkimese stalls lined the roadsides in Bomdila, and Kameng villagers now came regularly to barter amongst themselves or sell to the government staff. The new weekly bazaar was a great success. One of its shops bore the Dewatshang name. The family, who had succeeded in avoiding the Missamari camp, had gradually found

---

[101] Delhi, NMML, Elwin Papers (1956), Comments on ATA's reports, 1954–59, S. No. 133 (Jayal to Haldipur, 11 May 1958). Peter James is still, today, the name most often mentioned by Adis.

[102] NMML, Rustomji Papers S. No. 8, p. 55.

[103] NMML, Elwin Papers S. No. 7 (Elwin to Mehta, 28 February 1958).

[104] 'NEFA tribesmen no longer in isolation: Large influx affects way of life', *Times of India*, 11 January 1961; Parag Chaliha, 'A trip to Tezu', *Assam Tribune*, 28 January 1962; 'Assam governor's tour in NEFA area', *Assam Tribune*, 19 February 1962.

their feet in NEFA. They were slowly constituting a trading network like the one they had had in Tibet (albeit on a smaller scale) and had built themselves a small two-roomed house of bamboo and timber.[105] For most of the Tibetan exiles now living around Bomdila, however, life was probably harder, and centred on road camps.

The normalisation of frontier settlements into towns was soon on NEFA's administrative agenda.[106] Urbanisation was both positive and disruptive for government consolidation. Tezu and other towns quickly overflowed with population, causing massive accommodation shortages. Also, there were never enough buildings to host administrative, welfare, and military facilities. Since solving the problem required extra workers, the influx of outsiders accelerated (Figure 5.2).[107]

For some, these new imperatives constituted an advantage. Some tribals from the Assam districts pleaded to be settled on arable land on the NEFA side of the Inner Line. This was the case of a group of Deoris, who pushed their claim 'as measure of our rehabilitation being flood victims of 1950 great earthquake and landless people'. To make their case, they sent a whole series of requests, the preparation of which must have taken up much time. This was a time when the administration was torn between the desire not to settle 'outsiders' on the frontier and the need to feed Indian troops stationed there. The Deoris built their case in direct reference to this dilemma. Presenting themselves as agents of agricultural progress and productive expansion, they argued that they would 'show our tribal brethren the method of good cultivation and its prosperity will benefit to all brothers and sisters living in the area'. They went on to stress their natural affinity with the NEFA tribes, buttressing their claim by attaching supportive letters from Singpho and Khamti villages. They had already been contacted and did not object to their demand. As a finishing touch, the Deoris argued that not being able to retreat beyond the Inner Line would cause them to lose their tribal nature. Their argumentation displayed consummate understanding of the new, conflicting priorities of frontier authorities and of how to use them to one's advantage. On 25 January 1961, their demand was approved.[108]

---

[105] Dewatshang, *Flight at the cuckoo's behest*, pp. 154–158.

[106] Itanagar, APSA, NEFA Secretariat (1962), Extension of town development act in parts of NEFA 1/PC-157/62.

[107] See, for instance, Itanagar, APSA, NEFA Secretariat (1962), Long-term requirement of Kalimpong goods by border CPO depot Sup/4/131/62, p. 25 (PO Subansiri to NEFA Commissioner, 23 June).

[108] Itanagar, APSA, NEFA Secretariat (1960), Settlement of tribal families of Saikhowa Mauza at Lalungpathar and other places in NEFA, Rev 2/60, pp. 15–19 (Landless Khamyang people to PO Lohit, 8 October 1960, People of Kolowlowa to PO Tirap, and People of Nampong and Nigru to PO Lohit, 10 October 1960).

Figure 5.2 The Bomdila administrative headquarters, c. 1959
© Arunachal Pradesh DIPR

State–Society Relations under Stress

Overall, the ways in which the independent Indian state showed itself to
the population it pretended to govern had not taken a turn for the better.
The new prevalence of armed forces gave it a military aspect that NEFA
authorities had constantly sought to downplay since the early 1950s. This
coercive element acquired salience almost immediately. In January 1961,
a year into the arrival of armed forces, the civilian administration decided
to take stock of the 'problems arising from the location of the army in the
interior' of NEFA. The conclusions were unsettling. Not only was militarisation generating a massive, general stress on the eastern Himalayas'

fragile resources, it also relied on a widespread recourse to forced, or at least coerced, labour.

Land, food, and forests were the most affected resources. The need to station thousands of jawans and build support infrastructure necessitated extensive occupation of land, preferably flat. This meant requisitioning NEFA's already scarce arable land, made even more precious by the spread of wet-rice cultivation. The army's need for land did not stop there. It also included making space for firing ranges and defence installations. As a result, food shortages plagued both civilians and the military. Moreover, fuel reserves were being depleted at an alarming rate, the result of an abnormal consumption of local resources. The army's reliance on forests over which NEFA populations had a special claim was particularly problematic.[109] A seemingly less negative impact of militarisation concerned work opportunities for tribal populations. The new expansion momentum had increased the number of jobs available, in particular for interpreters and *jamadars*.[110] A model school was built at Rupa to 'fit [tribal students] as leaders in any sphere of life', and frontier administration now acknowledged that 'the ultimate aim ... [was] that all the services should be manned by the NEFA tribals themselves'.[111]

Yet job creation had mainly one face: reluctant labour. The lack of transport infrastructure generated a huge demand for road workers, builders, and above all porters. Again, the phenomenon was not fundamentally new. Labour extraction, and porterage in particular, had always been the major thorn in the side of the Indian state's attempts to establish itself firmly yet peacefully on the frontier. But the issue was now more vexed than ever. The state's hunger for manpower was unprecedented, and it tied up almost the entire population: by 1961, each adult in NEFA spent at least one-sixth of his or her time on government work. What's more, tribal communities were asked to contribute this increasing labour even as they were pressured to give up their land and step up agricultural production.[112]

The dynamics through which jobs on the periphery of government had become the major factor in social status and mobility on the frontier were simultaneously destabilised. In a context of militarisation, the scope for agency for those who held government jobs was more restricted. Moreover, the rehabilitation of Tibetan refugees exacerbated the politics

---

[109] New Delhi, NAI, External Affairs Proceedings (1961), Problems arising from the location of the army in the interior, 12(2)-NEFA/61 (Note, 20 May 1961).

[110] Itanagar, APSA, NEFA Secretariat (1962), Opening of administrative centres and checkposts on border areas of Kameng, 1 PC-54/62.

[111] APSA, PC-14/62 ('note on the development of border areas').

[112] APSA, 12(2)-NEFA/61 (Secret report on NEFA, January 1961).

of access in areas where they were resettled. Getting a government job was more competitive than ever. With their 'Tibetan tailors, *momo*[dumplings]-restauranteurs, Lamas, traders and craftsmen', Bomdila and Tawang were turning into 'miniature Gangtoks' (the capital of Sikkim). Although life remained hard for most of them, some refugees were taking up government positions that the Hrussos, Bangnis, or Buguns had become accustomed to holding. 'Even the Monpas, as they become more politically conscious, may come to feel that the Tibetans have been allowed too much freedom in their area and that their own interests have not been sufficiently safeguarded', argued Rustomji, who had resumed his position as Adviser to the Governor:

we have a fair number of Tibetans in various Government institutions, such as the crafts centres, schools and hospitals. This is all to the good, as we have a responsibility to rehabilitate Tibetan refugees as early as possible. We have to be very careful, however, that we do not create a situation of tension for the future.

But tensions were already there: some local officials were 'practically compelling the tribal people to porter loads or present themselves as road labourers'. The corrosive impact of such practices was worsened by the fact that civilian administration had based its rhetoric of expansion and friendliness precisely on a promise that forced labour would not be imposed. 'You are asking us to improve our cultivation and at the same time are taking from us the only land on which improvements can be made', protested Daporijo's inhabitants. Tirap villagers pointed out that the bridges they had built 'in self-help' mainly benefited government staff.[113] Monpa road workers appealed 'again and again that they should not be requested to continue working on the road during the period of cultivation'. Dirang's inhabitants were even clearer: they requested not to be asked for labour anymore.[114] Across NEFA, the complaints were the same.

The situation caused great alarm among frontier authorities, who felt that 'the people in the border areas [should not be] given the scope of entertaining any grievance against the Administration'.[115] Finding ways to preserve their working relationship with local inhabitants while accommodating the army's demands was not easy, however.

---

[113] Ibid. (Appendix to Rustomji's tour note on visit to Tawang). See also APSA, Sup/4/131/62.
[114] APSA, 12(2)-NEFA/61Rustomji's tour note on visit to Tawang and appendix, April 1961.
[115] Itanagar, APSA, NEFA Secretariat (1963), Compensation for use of cultivable land by the army, GA-98/63 (Biswas, 9 May 1963).

To mitigate the adverse impact of militarisation, the frontier administration championed a 'completely self-contained' military presence on the frontier.[116] The army was to be entirely self-sufficient in its agricultural needs, resorting to airdropping if necessary; crop and fuel production schemes such as eucalyptus groves were to be started; and troops were ordered not to camp near villages or to visit them to buy goods.[117]

Figure 5.3 Roadwork in the Lohit Division, c. 1961
© Arunachal Pradesh DIPR

[116] APSA, 12(2)-NEFA/61 (Report on the NEFA for January 1961 and Assam Governor to Foreign Secretary, 3 May 1961).
[117] See respectively: APSA, Sup-4/55/60-Part II; APSA, 12(2)-NEFA/61 (Rustomji to Mehta, 4 May 1961); 'NEFA tribesmen no longer in isolation: Large influx affects way of life'.

Land acquisition was a special preoccupation. The NEFA administration pushed for a general principle of compensation for cultivable land by the army. But, understandably, farmers were often reluctant to part with their land, especially if the loss of the anticipated harvest was not also compensated. Local officials were keen not to ignore this resistance. The issue caused never-ending discord between civilian and military authorities. POs complained that the army disregarded the procedure for releasing land, failing to inform them of their requirements and earmarking or requisitioning land without their consent. Moreover, the armed forces refused to pay more for land than elsewhere in India; indeed, they threatened to requisition all the land they needed outright.[118]

Some senior NEFA officials, like the Development Commissioner, decided to come to terms with the army's demands. His colleagues on the ground did not see it that way. Chakma, PO at Daporijo in the Subansiri, resisted any compromise: unless and until the army acceded to people's demand for a higher rate of compensation, he would prevent any land from being requisitioned. His dogged persistence won the day.[119]

Yet, as a rule, digging heels against India's military command bore little fruit. Civilian authorities had to find other ways to protect state–society relations. To alleviate the recourse to forced labour – which risked to 'turn the dice' much more than the few cases of soldiers or tuskers behaving badly, many officials felt[120] – the NEFA administration set up a professional porter corps and expanded its Animal Transport Section. But morale was low, and it was difficult to recruit local men when this still meant persuading them to leave their fields.[121]

NEFA officials simultaneously tried to socialise the armed forces into local ways. Each division prepared explanatory brochures to teach the jawans about the inhabitants, their relationship to land, forest, and rivers, NEFA's administrative set-up, and the state of communications. They also directed troops to read a selection of more specialised books on the region. One of these brochures, 'Subansiri welcomes you', concluded with 'Dos and Don'ts': don't abuse a tribal – don't give too many

---

[118] APSA, 12(2)-NEFA/61 (Note, 20 May 1961).
[119] APSA, GA-98/63 (Luthra, 31 May 1963).
[120] APSA, 12(2)-NEFA/61 (Appendix to Rustomji's tour note on visit to Tawang).
[121] New Delhi, NAI, External Affairs Proceedings (1959), Grant of convoy duty allowance to drivers and sardars of Animal Transport Sections in NEFA, 12(13)-NEFA/59; NMML, Elwin Papers S. No. 133 (Jayal to Haldipur, 11 May 1958); APSA, Sup/4/131/62, p. 33.

presents – don't laugh at them – don't break their taboos – don't refuse food or beer.[122]

If the NEFA administration could only hope to influence the army, it retained a measure of control over Assam Rifles. Reiterating self-sufficiency as the ultimate goal, it directed each outpost to

> try their best to make the local population feel that they are all one and that they belong to the same family. This is more important for Assam Rifles to have such an attitude as this Force has been employed for a very long period in these areas, and ... will continue to be in the area for a long time to come ... Even a small effort will go a long way in making the local population feel the sincerity of our purpose of being in the area for their interest.

Platoon commanders were to devise practical ways of participating in development work and social functions in the local community. The stress was on contributing to local agricultural and welfare schemes – school and hospital construction, farms, sharing of military medical staff with local civilians – and on social miscegenation. Neighbouring villages were invited to annual functions and festivals and allowed to borrow the local battalion's pipe band for their own ceremonies.[123]

In one known case, this could not diffuse the situation. When a group of students decided to watch a free movie in Ziro on Independence Day 1961, the outing degenerated into a clash with passing motor vehicles. Four people were arrested, causing unrest in the local high school. More students were arrested, the school was closed, and the alleged leaders of the unrest were banned from readmission.[124] The reality of tensions caused by militarisation could not be discounted.

Rustomji warned his superiors not to play with fire. If the Naga conflict was any benchmark, even a huge army could waste itself trying to hold the mountainous terrain around Assam. NEFA was many times bigger than Nagaland, even more mountainous, and far less well connected. The conclusion was clear: 'We just cannot afford ... a situation where our tribes would resent our presence amongst them and decide to resist us.'[125]

[122] New Delhi, NMML, Verrier Elwin Papers (1960), 'Subansiri welcomes you': A brochure written for the use of Army officers, S. No. 154.

[123] Itanagar, APSA, NEFA Secretariat (1962), Participation of Assam Rifles in local development work PC-11/62.

[124] APSA, Sup-4/55/60-Part II; 'Student unrest in NEFA: Closure of school creates much resentment', Times of India, 12 December 1960.

[125] APSA, 12(2)-NEFA/61 (Appendix to Rustomji's tour note on visit to Tawang).

6 Salt Tastes the Same in India and China
A Different Kind of Security Dilemma

The Indian army had after 1959 planned an 'in-depth' defence for NEFA. Small check points along the border would symbolise Indian sovereignty and send early warnings of a Chinese invasion, which a second, more substantial line of outposts would slow down. The bulk of Indian forces would position itself from the border, on key mountain passes and north–south valleys. Taking advantage of overextended Chinese supply lines, the jawans would then mount a strong counteroffensive.

These plans had not been fully implemented when, in November 1961, the Indian government changed its mind. The army would now defend the McMahon Line itself, leaving no strategic gap unoccupied. The same went for Ladakh, near Kashmir, where troops were to patrol as far as the Indian-backed Ardagh–Johnson Line and outposts to be established in what was still no-man's-land.

Ever-growing fears about China's territorial aims lay behind this more assertive forward policy. In April 1960, Zhou Enlai had visited Delhi to discuss the border dispute. In a press conference, he had unofficially suggested that China would accept the McMahon Line in return for India dropping its claim to the Aksai Chin. Nehru, under huge pressure from public opinion and political circles, took it as a ploy to force India to accept that the whole Sino-Indian boundary was undefined. The PRC would get the Aksai Chin in exchange for a promise it could easily rescind. His answer was unequivocal: there would be no territorial 'horse-trading'.[1]

Border talks were 'a long time dying' over the next two years.[2] Ostensibly, teams of Indian and Chinese officials had been appointed to examine the evidence for their contradictory territorial claims and produce a joint report. In practice, the PRC had widened its claim to Ladakh

[1] Steven A. Hoffmann, *India and the China crisis* (Berkeley: University of California Press, 1990), p. 87.
[2] London, SOAS, Moraes Collection (1945–1974), Newspaper clippings and typescripts of columns, articles and tour articles, PP MS 24/03 ('Chou–Nehru talks drag on', 24 April 1960).

and the Aksai Chin, and the PLA resumed patrolling in the no-man's-land. Indeed, it established itself closer to its new claim line – one of its outposts was just four miles away from an Indian one – and Chinese road building in the region was proceeding apace.[3]

If intelligence reports were correct, military build-up was also under way north of the McMahon Line. A road fit for one-ton trucks ran from Tsona to the PLA's headquarters in Lhoka. A two-way road linked the latter to Chayül, to the east. As for Dzayül, it would soon boast two road connections to the Chamdo–Lhasa highway. Telegraph lines were being extended south of the Tsangpo River, the PLA had moved into Pemakö, and Chinese check points and barracks were appearing along the border.[4]

Indian authorities saw their forward policy as a defensive and circumscribed response to Chinese expansionism, but from the PRC's perspective it was the Indian army's actions that were threatening. Domestically and internationally, the early 1960s were an extremely volatile time for China. Its rift with the Soviet Union was deepening, and the country reeled from the catastrophic effects of the Great Leap Forward. Moreover, both the United States and Taiwan were now actively helping Tibetan guerrillas. China also suspected India of giving a helping hand: were the CIA, the Guomindang, and the Khampas not using Kalimpong as a base?[5] Its sensitivity to international threats – perceived or real – thus exacerbated, the CCP leadership was particularly concerned with Indian activism in the Himalayas.[6]

The realisation that the cartographic McMahon Line was often blind to local topography had led the Indian army to rectify its alignment by posting troops in areas along the actual watershed or the highest Himalayan crest – without discussing this with China. The Longju confrontation had resulted from such a unilateral readjustment. In Ladakh, new outposts were to be placed in locations where they could tactically dominate over PLA positions. This was seldom achieved, but, in one case

---

[3] Hoffmann, *India and the China crisis*, pp. 92–102.

[4] New Delhi, NAI, External Affairs Proceedings (1961), Intelligence reviews from army headquarters, 5/9/R&I/61; New Delhi, NAI, External Affairs Proceedings (1961), Reports (other than annual) from Lhasa (Tibet), 6/35/R&I/61.

[5] Indian authorities knew about pro-Tibetan CIA activities on its territory, but whether Nehru truly helped them prior to the 1960s is still debated. See John Kenneth Knaus, *Orphans of the Cold War: America and the Tibetan struggle for survival* (New York: Public Affairs, 1999); Kenneth Conboy and James Morrison, *The CIA's secret war in Tibet* (Lawrence, KA: University of Kansas Press, 2002); John W. Garver, 'Review essay: India, China, the United States, Tibet, and the origins of the 1962 war', *India Review*, 3:2 (2004), 171–182; Melvyn C. Goldstein, *A history of modern Tibet, Volume 3: The storm clouds descend, 1955–1957* (Berkeley: University of California Press, 2013).

[6] Allen Whiting, *The Chinese calculus of deterrence: India and Indochina* (Ann Arbor, MA: University of Michigan Press, 1975).

at least, jawans established an outpost across the supply lines of a small Chinese position, cutting it from the rear. Other newly established outposts could, from a Chinese perspective, threaten the Aksai Chin road that linked Tibet to Xinjiang and the rest of the PRC.[7]

By spring 1962, the military situation along the Sino-Indian border increasingly resembled a security dilemma. China and India's efforts to improve their military presence and territorial control over NEFA and Ladakh echoed against one another, causing yet more infrastructural and military build-up on either side of the Himalayas. Yet, the spiral of outpost creations, intrusive patrols, and diplomatic acrimony was but the most ostensible form of escalation. An older struggle around the identities, habits, and actions of Himalayan people was accelerating – a struggle in which India and China saw each other as a subversive shadow state.

The Trouble with Mobile Subjects

As Indian public opinion turned stridently anti-Chinese after 1959, the NEFA administration battled increasing media criticism. Elwin and other frontier administrators were accused of keeping India's north-eastern frontier in a dangerous vacuum, in a naïve and culpable oblivion of the PRC's designs over it.[8]

In reality, NEFA authorities had long been acutely conscious of China's nearby presence. After all, it was Tibet's takeover by the PRC that had generated the decisive momentum for state expansion. The PLA had appeared north of the McMahon Line in the last months of 1951. Dzayül, which had not seen Chinese soldiers since the 1910s, soon had a network of military camps, headquarters, and garrisons, including two near the Indian border. Around the same time, troops began to arrive north of Tawang.[9] The move was likely linked to India's takeover and to orders to disperse troops towards Tibet's borders, offsetting the pressure on Lhasa.

In response, a special kind of Political Interpreter was appointed in NEFA border areas: Tibetan Agents.[10] Unlike Tibetan-speaking

---

[7] Hoffmann, *India and the China crisis*, pp. 69, 97–98, 104.

[8] Elwin already had to defend himself in 1958. New Delhi, NMML, Elwin Papers (1959), Correspondence with K.L. Mehta, 1954–59, S. No. 7 (Elwin to Mehta, 4 July 1958).

[9] New Delhi, NAI, External Affairs Proceedings (1952), Tibet policy: Top secret notes on India and China, 7(1)P/52 (Fortnightly review of Sino-Tibetan intelligence, late December 1951).

[10] New Delhi, NAI, External Affairs Proceedings (1955), Reports on NEFA, 4(19)-P/55; Itanagar, APSA, NEFA Secretariat (1952), Tour diary of Tibetan Assistant Tawang, P-184/52; Itanagar, APSA, NEFA Secretariat (1955), Tour diary of Assistant Tibetan Agent Kibithoo P-82/55.

interpreters who had earlier on built relationships with the Monpas, Membas, or Sherdukpens, these officials were also responsible for tracking trans-border Chinese activities. By assessing the strength of PRC troops or the extent of infrastructure construction, they provided Delhi with a wealth of information – intelligence that would become even more precious once PRC authorities began imposing a stranglehold on Indian missions in Tibet.[11]

Just as important were the other aims of border surveillance: watching population movements and reporting any Chinese welfare and development initiatives. Delhi's belief that China would not seek to invade India militarily seemed to be comforted by the PLA's activities across the McMahon Line in the early 1950s. Chinese troops were still absent from most border areas, and the Dzayül and Tsona garrisons spent less time on military training than on building basic infrastructure and growing food for themselves. Having arrived on foot, entirely dependent on local porters and pack animals, they were isolated, poorly supplied, and subjected to the unknown rigours of the Himalayan winter. In these circumstances, the cooperation of local inhabitants was essential.[12]

NEFA authorities watched how, from 1952 onwards, their PRC counterparts tried to forge a relationship with the inhabitants of south-eastern Tibet. Within a few months of their arrival in Dzayül, Chinese troops built a school for local children. They publicly contributed to the organisation of New Year celebrations in the valley and tried to interfere as little as possible into local lives. Echoes of these initiatives reached NEFA, where they were duly and warily noted.

Most worrying for Indian authorities was the situation in Monyül, now partitioned by the McMahon Line. Tibetan traders visiting Tawang were spreading word that the region's occupation would be 'as easy as [a] morning walk' for the PLA, and that Bhutan would soon have to choose between India and China. There were also strong possibilities that a lama just arrived at Mago, north of Tawang, was a Chinese spy. Intelligence services had reported the presence of five such spies in Monyül, and the man was trying to 'dominate [the Monpas'] religious minds with the idea that they are closely linked with Tibet at least on religious grounds and are inseparable from it'.[13]

---

[11] New Delhi, NAI, External Affairs Proceedings (1960), Payment of arrears of rent to G.T. Phunkhang for Gyantse land, 8(17)EAD/60; NAI, External 6/35/R&I/61 (Report for May).
[12] NAI, External 7(1)P/52 (Fortnightly review of Sino-Tibetan intelligence, late December 1951).
[13] Ibid. (Reviews for January 1952).

True or not, reports of such propaganda fed into some long-held fears among Indian authorities. Colonial officials had viewed cultural, religious, and economic ties between the people of the Himalayan slopes and those of Tibet as an inherent threat to Indian sovereignty and legitimacy. In a region where trade was a key channel of power – a channel harnessed by Assam authorities themselves – the red-and-black border of quality Tibetan wool that some northern Nyishis wore on their coats, the yaks reared by people in the north-eastern Subansiri, the brocades Mechuka's Membas favoured, were all taken as signs that even where Lhasa had no visible political control, its pull effect was still great. Wartime forays in the Subansiri had revealed that the non-Tibetan people living north of the Sippi Valley, well south of the plateau, did all their trade with it; their southern neighbours accordingly called the area *Agla Nieme*, Near Tibet. Colonial officials had taken it as proof that the de facto international boundary in the Subansiri was not the McMahon Line but the southern edge of *Agla Nieme*.[14]

British Indian authorities had been even more concerned that, should the opportunities offered north of the border prove greater, NEFA's inhabitants might pack their bags and go. Their qualms were far from unfounded: locals often moved when confronted with an oppressive or otherwise unacceptable polity. The Meyors of Walong had settled there around 1943–1944 to escape poverty in nearby Dzayül, prompted, it seems, by the local *dzongpön*s' heavy taxation.[15] Their neighbours, who shared similar 'Tibetan' cultural traits, had immigrated from Monyül several generations ago. One day, so their tale went, a cruel *dzongpön* ordered the people of Tsona to flatten a mountain that kept his fortress in perpetual shadow. Villagers worked and worked, never receiving a wage for their labour, until they abandoned this impossible task. When the *dzongpön* came to inspect the work, they murdered him and escaped Monyül, finding refuge among the Mishmis.[16]

---

[14] London, BL, IOR (1929–1947), Assam: Annual reports on Frontier Tracts IOR/L/PS/ 12/3114 (Report by J.P. Mills for the year ending 30 June 1945).

[15] Ambika Aiyadurai, 'The Meyor: A least studied frontier tribe of Arunachal Pradesh, northeast India', *Eastern Anthropologist*, 64:4 (2011), 459–469 (p. 460). A Tibetan refugee tells a similar story of people fleeing to Bhutan to escape high taxation. Interview with Sonam Tsomo (Interview #45M). Interviewed by Rebecca Novick on 13 April 2010 (held at the Tibet Oral History Project), www.tibetoralhistory.org/interviews.html (accessed 27 January 2015).

[16] Itanagar, APSA, NEFA Secretariat (1954), Information of special nature on the Lohit area, R-64/54 (Extract from tour diary of Sawthang La, May–July 1954), p. 23. The Membas of Pemakö and the Lishpas of the Dirang area have similar tales. See respectively: Kerstin Grothmann, 'Population, history and identity in the hidden land of Pemakö', *Journal of Bhutan Studies*, 26 (2012), 21–52 (pp. 30–31); Kazuharu Mizuno

People's capacity to escape a state that did not suit their needs was the source of major anxieties for the latter, and had historically fuelled tensions between neighbouring polities in the eastern Himalayas. Back in 1943, it was the Tibetan government's attempts to repatriate Monpas living in Bhutan that spurred colonial India's decision to vindicate the McMahon Line. In British eyes, this was primarily a sly attempt to wrest Monyül from India. Yet Lhasa's aggressiveness rather betrayed the exasperation and powerlessness of a government that had constantly tried to keep 'its' population in place – and failed. The initial Tibeto–Bhutanese repatriation agreement, in 1799, had some desperate undertones:

In future the Tibetan and Bhutanese authorities should exercise strict control over their subjects in order to prevent them from leaving their homes [They] should also administer justice over their respective subjects without any partiality and look after the interests of their subjects, so that there may be *no cause for [them] to run away*. On the other hand, all the subjects should also live in their homes quite contentedly and should faithfully carry out the obligations of the law and taxes of the Government. They must not continue to follow *the bad habit of deserting their homes on even a minor cause of complaint*. In the event of one or two persons acting foolishly, in the same way as the offspring of animals do, by running away from their home, the authorities concerned must not give any assistance, but, on receipt of a request, steps should be taken to hand them over to the rightful government.[17]

A hundred and fifty years and three bilateral agreements later, Tibetan authorities were in no better position. In 1943, headmen around Tsona and Tawang refused to pay taxes, arguing that their productive capacities had declined due to population loss.[18] Despite repeated orders and the threat of physical and economic punishment, people continued to 'indulge in the bad practice of migrating'. Attempts at bilateral negotiations had often ended with Lhasa reluctantly conceding that people who had emigrated before a certain date would never be recovered.[19]

In this, Himalayan populations showed a careful appreciation of what the presence of a certain state could bring them, especially compared to that of another polity. Back in 1910, the inhabitants of Dzayül had taken

---

and Lobsang Tenpa, *Himalayan nature and Tibetan Buddhist culture in Arunachal Pradesh, India: A study of Monpa* (Berlin: Springer, 2015), p. 10.

[17] New Delhi, NAI, External Affairs Proceedings (1943), Claim by the Tibetan Government that Tibetan subjects settled in Bhutan should be repatriated to Tibet. Measures taken to stabilize the MacMahon Line, 63/X/43 (Order by Surkhang Depon in 1826). Emphasis added.

[18] New Delhi, NAI, External Affairs Proceedings (1943), Lhasa weekly letters, 62/X/43 (12 September).

[19] NAI, External 63/X/43 (Order by Kalon Shatra in 1852).

Zhao Erfeng's conquest – at Lhasa's expense – with equanimity. In contrast to the parts of Kham where mass uprisings took place, Qing authorities had neither had time to move many troops into Dzayül nor to launch radical plans for demographic and cultural change or agricultural and economic exploitation. Europeans visiting the region at the time noted that the Dzayülis had good reasons not to oppose Chinese presence: 'The Chinese, although to our minds cruel and ruthless, in some ways treated the population better than the Tibetan government itself did. They took rather less in taxes and, equally important, they paid for their "ula" [*ulag*, corvée labour].'

Some inhabitants looked even further. A Rima villager intimated that he and others would be even happier under British rule, for 'they had heard that the people in Assam are well governed and lightly taxed'.[20] It was perhaps on a similar reasoning that the Mishmi chief Tungno declared himself a British subject and went all the way to Sadiya to alert British authorities of China's conquest of Dzayül. Thirty years later during the Second World War, Dzayülis still had a 'high opinion of British administration', reportedly. They even reacted positively to 'a rumour spread by Mishmis that Dzayül had been given to the British who would shortly come to administer it'. Local traders were said to dislike the heavy taxation imposed by Lhasa's tax collectors, whereas India perceived no such levy.[21]

Around the same time, Dzayül's *dzongpöns* protested about the presence of 'runaways' near Walong. The Sadiya PO was less than enthusiastic about repatriating Tibetan subjects. Their migration might cause Lhasa a loss of revenue and labour but it certainly worked to India's advantage: thinly populated, the Walong area needed migrants.[22] Lest a rift with Lhasa occur, Delhi instructed local officials to discourage settlement and to conciliate the *dzongpöns*, yet the Meyors' continued presence in the northern Lohit Valley hints that frontier authorities did little to enforce these orders.[23]

[20] Perhaps because 'from what they had heard of other places they did not expect this [good treatment by the Chinese] to last'. F.M. Bailey, *China–Tibet–Assam: A journey, 1911* (London: Jonathan Cape, 1945), p. 98.

[21] New Delhi, NAI, External Affairs Proceedings (1945), Reports relating to Tibet received from DIB, 114/CA/45 (Report no.4.45).

[22] New Delhi, NAI, External Affairs Proceedings (1945), Proposed settlement of Tibetans in the Walong area on the North East Frontier, 230-CA; New Delhi, NAI, External Affairs Proceedings (1946), Meeting between the Assistant Political Officer, Lohit Valley, and Rima Dzongpön, 49-NEF/46.

[23] Itanagar, APSA, NEFA Secretariat (1950), Tour Diary of Assistant Political Officer Lohit, B.C. Bhuyan, GA-12/50.

In the absence of relevant Chinese and Tibetan sources it is difficult to ascertain the existence of this pro-British inclination, let alone its depth; these pieces of wartime intelligence might well have been intended to further the arguments of the PO, who was at that very moment proposing to annex Dzayül.[24] That some Dzayülis at least might have favoured just such an annexation cannot be discounted, however. These reports came at a time when Lhasa authorities were taking steps to reinforce their territorial control and modernise the Tibetan state, including by raising more taxes; geographically peripheral, agriculturally rich, and close to Chinese Xikang, Dzayül would have been particularly affected by their efforts. Moreover, Indian sources mention many other instances – in India's favour *as well as* against it – of individuals', groups', or families' propensity to evaluate one state in the mirror of another. Finally, Khampas had several times before 1900 chosen, or even called in, Chinese imperial authorities in order to escape Lhasa's rule.[25] One should envision the possibility that, just as their forebears had initially welcomed the Qing as an improvement over local Tibetan authorities, the Dzayülis of 1945 felt that a seemingly less intrusive or extractive state – for now, India – might better suit their interests.

China's Shadow

Tibet's 'peaceful liberation' exacerbated the link between people's mobility and state anxieties. By 1952, Indian authorities feared that cross-border dynamics between Dzayül and the Lohit Valley were turning to their disadvantage. Intelligence reports stressed that while the PRC had begun various development schemes around Rima, there was no corresponding effort on the Indian side of the McMahon Line:

the NEFA administration is doing its best but its limited resources are incommensurate with the vastness of the problem and, therefore, compared to what the Chinese seem to have already achieved, our progress so far has been small. It is extremely important that the situation should be faced realistically and that NEFA be endowed with adequate resources to launch similar large scale development schemes on our side *so that the border tribals may not look towards the Chinese for their salvation.*[26]

---

[24] New Delhi, NAI, External Affairs Proceedings (1946), Ratification of the McMahon Line below Rima, 307-CA/46 ('Settlement of the McMahon Line', 12 September 1945).

[25] Xiuyu Wang, *China's last imperial frontier: Late Qing expansion in Sichuan's Tibetan borderlands* (Lanham, MD: Lexington Books, 2011).

[26] NAI, External 7(1)P/52 (Fortnightly review of Sino-Tibetan intelligence, late December 1951). Emphasis added.

The implication was clear. If India could not provide the people of NEFA with the facilities or goods they increasingly demanded, it risked losing them to China.

Figuring out PRC policy vis-à-vis border populations became a constant preoccupation for Indian officials. Often derived from information given by locals who had travelled across the McMahon Line for personal purposes, the reports of Tibetan Agents became crucial tools to set and revise the standards of India's own state-making activities. These adjustments were to protect the relationship between NEFA authorities and Himalayan people and ensure the latter's cooperation, quiescence, and allegiance. Rooted in the continued agency of local populations vis-à-vis Indian state expansion, the undercurrent of anxiety that lay beneath the development and welfare schemes undertaken in the name of the NEFA Philosophy was exacerbated by China's nearby presence.

In 1955, the Assistant Tibetan Agent for Kibithoo returned from the Lohit Division with disquieting information. Chinese authorities had launched an important infrastructure programme in Dzayül, presenting it as an effort to supply border people with foods and necessities through airdrops: if roads and airfields were built, 'all kinds of goods [would] come to Rima, and local people [could] purchase goods at a much lower price'. Dzayülis were accordingly asked to cooperate in road construction.[27] Most worrying was the PLA's role as an agent of frontier development. Its troops played a big part in the government road construction programme, and still managed 'to help in the raising of crops and to participate in other beneficent activities in the area'. 'We cannot afford the luxury of keeping such a large body of [Assam Rifles] standing by only for the maintenance of law and order', concluded External Affairs officials; their task in 'clearing up the political situation in Tuensang' or 'expanding the administration right up to the border' notwithstanding, it was essential to involve the Rifles in development activities.[28]

China's shadow affected cultural and development schemes in NEFA in a myriad ways. Officials worried about the efforts of PRC authorities to project a benevolent attitude towards cultural and religious symbols. Surely nothing good could be expected from the dissemination in the eastern Himalayas of PRC-printed photos of Buddhist leaders and famous monasteries, or of maps found in the possession of travellers sent to NEFA – maps that showed most of the agency as coming under Chinese jurisdiction.[29] Even the charts on yak rearing prepared by PRC

[27] NAI, External 4(19)-P/55 (Sawthang La to APO Hayuliang, 3 April 1955).
[28] Itanagar, APSA, NEFA Secretariat (1962), Participation of Assam Rifles in local development work PC-11/62 (Kaul to Mehta, 8 February 1955).
[29] NAI, External 4(19)-P/55.

authorities were worrying. 'Extremely well-done' and culturally sensitive, they 'would certainly make a considerable impression' in Tawang if circulated there.[30]

Concerns about the circulation of people and artefacts caused NEFA authorities to launch several attempts to undermine cross-border interaction in the 1950s, especially in Monyül and the Lohit Valley. Tibetan *dzongpöns* had been forced out of Tawang in 1951 and the monastery was now led by Monpas, but Buddhist figures from the plateau retained huge influence in Monyül. As the Qing Empire had once experienced, cutting off the 'silken threads' of Tibet's religious authority was much harder than removing the 'yoke of gold' of its secular administration.[31] The visits of Tibetan lamas therefore aroused strong suspicion among Indian authorities. Banning them from NEFA was neither possible – the boundary was too porous – nor expedient – the risk of antagonising the Monpas was too great. Instead, Indian officials tried to monitor comings and goings by instituting a permit system for travellers from Tibet. Those who reported their presence could, at the Assam Governor's discretion, be granted relatively generous lengths of stay. Tibetans wishing to attend the fairs in the foothills or the shrines of Assam were closely watched by Indian authorities. So were petty officials who crossed the border to settle personal business or to meet the PO. In the Lohit–Dzayül corridor, Indian authorities initially adopted a sterner approach: Tibetan travellers were henceforth to be prevented from using this route to Assam.[32]

Frontier administration simultaneously tried to stamp out secular Tibetan taxation from NEFA. Efforts in this direction predated India's independence, but intensified after 1951.[33] While Indian authorities were ready to countenance the continuation of monastic tribute in Monyül for the sake of state–society relations, they extended no such privilege to the local *dzongpöns*. A year after India's takeover in Tawang, it became evident that Tibetan tax collectors still visited, so the administration put outposts near the key mountain passes. By June 1952, the Tsona *dzongpöns* struggled to perceive taxes south of the border.[34]

Attempts to insulate Monyül from trans-McMahon Line areas went further. While PRC authorities tried to replace Tibetan currency in Tibet,

---

[30] New Delhi, NMML, Verrier Elwin Papers (1961), Correspondence with T.N. Kaul, 1953–61, S. No. 8 (Elwin to Kaul, 7 August 1956).

[31] Scott Relyea, 'Yokes of gold and threads of silk: Sino-Tibetan competition for authority in early twentieth century Kham', *Modern Asian Studies*, 49:4 (2015), 963–1009.

[32] NAI, External 7(1)P/52; Itanagar, APSA, NEFA Secretariat (1951), Permission to visit Gelling by Tibetans P-53/51.

[33] Itanagar, APSA, NEFA Secretariat (1946), Tour diaries of PLS James for August 1945–December 1946.

[34] NAI, External 7(1)P/52.

Indian officials did the same in NEFA. Reasons to do so were both political and practical. The first few months of Tawang's occupation had been trying for Indian authorities. The rupees brought by their representatives were useless: Monpas were ready to porter or otherwise work against payment but refused to accept anything but Tibetan currency. Lest Tawang's new authorities find themselves without food and accommodation, Indian representatives in Sikkim and Tibet had had to search high and low to obtain Rs 150,000 in Tibetan currency from the Bhutan Maharajah and Tibetan wool traders.[35] The Monpas' exclusive preference for Tibetan currency was thus a double hindrance. Not only did it undercut the idea of India's sovereignty over Tawang, it also threatened the very survival of its state presence in the region.

By 1954, Tawang's administrative canvassing had made giant strides.[36] Indian authorities devised several steps to increase the popularity of the rupee in the region. They could not count on time to displace Monyül's customary currency. Locals had too many practical reasons to favour it. The Monpas' main trade fair was at Tsona, in PRC territory, and the rigours of the Himalayan weather quickly wore out Indian rupee notes – a problem that did not exist with Tibetan *tangka* coins. A further hurdle was that banning their use under threat of punishment, as the local Tibetan Agent had tried to do in a proclamation, would likely have negative effects on the attitude of the Monpas.

Indian authorities settled on a more indirect policy. The trade depot recently established at Tawang began to accept purchases in Indian currency only and to sell articles that the Monpas traditionally bought from Tsona. To further compete with the Tsona fair, the PO organised a biannual fair on the Indian side of the border and found an Indian market for Tawang's cottage industries, like paper making.[37] Finally, the Indian authorities took a stern policy only for Chinese currency: people found in possession of PRC dollars upon returning from Tibet were fined.[38]

Displacing Tibetan currency thus went hand in hand with attempts to undermine trading ties between Tawang and Tibet by providing some crucial articles and goods on the Indian side of the border.[39]

[35] New Delhi, NAI, External Affairs Proceedings (1951), Occupation of Tawang by the GOI, 18(C)51.
[36] Itanagar, APSA, NEFA Secretariat (1955), Tour diary of Assistant Tibetan Agent Lumla.
[37] New Delhi, NAI, External Affairs Proceedings (1954), Circulation of Tibetan currency in Indian territory, N/54/2243/105.
[38] Itanagar, APSA, NEFA Secretariat (1957), Confidential report in NEFA for December 1957.
[39] Delhi, NMML, Elwin Papers (1957), Tour notes of Dr Verrier Elwin, 1954–57, S. No. 139 (Ramos, Pailibos, Boris tour, October–December 1958).

The Tawang PO banned the export of grain to Tibet, fining Tibetan traders found in possession of it.[40] The policy was particularly strong in the case of salt. The commodity played a key role in the lives of Himalayan people, and, as such, the provenance of an ethnic group's salt supply participated in regulating networks of influence and authority. 'There is no No-Man's-Land on the MacMahon Line, and salt from India or from China tastes the same',[41] declared an *Assam Tribune* reader likely connected to the NEFA administration in 1953: the eastern Himalayas' inhabitants would recognise the authority of the country that would fulfil their salt requirements. Indian authorities accordingly developed a salt policy to displace Tibet as a source of the precious condiment, offering it to remote communities and attempting to generalise its Assamese variety across NEFA.[42]

Despite this interference, cross-border interaction continued throughout the 1950s. Even in Tawang, which the NEFA administration most craved to insulate, the trade, pilgrimage, and monastic ties of the Monpas with Tibet continued. The town was packed with Tibetan traders in the summer months, come to profit from the lucrative export of local chillies to Tsona.[43] The salt trade remained similarly brisk, the NEFA administration proving unable to fulfil the population's requirements.[44] Every year on the fifteenth day of the first month of the Tibetan calendar, the Monpa village of Panchon was flooded with Buddhist devotees from all over Tawang, Tsona, and eastern Bhutan. They were there to worship at the Gorsam Chorten, a *stupa* famous throughout the region. Meanwhile, Panchon children still got their education from the Tsona *gompa*. In return, the village elders gifted loads of millet and other grains to the abbot. Under the NEFA administration's grain export ban, the latter practice should have been outlawed. Yet the local Tibetan Agent granted permission for the Panchon villagers to send their grain to the Tsona monastery, asking only that they start paying their due in cash or butter from 1958 onwards.[45] Indian authorities could not risk harming their standing among the Monpas for a few loads of grain.

---

[40] APSA, Tour diary of Assistant Tibetan Agent Lumla, 1955; APSA, Confidential report in NEFA for December 1957.

[41] 'Letters to the editor: What is wrong in NEFA', *Assam Tribune*, 1953.

[42] See, for example, New Delhi, NMML, Elwin Papers (1954), Confidential reports on the NEFA 1952–4, S. No. 111 (1952 report, p. 14 and 1953 report, pp. 23–24); NAI, External 4(19)-P/55 (January 1955).

[43] Itanagar, APSA, NEFA Secretariat (1957), Report on the NEFA for May–June 1957.

[44] NMML, Elwin Papers S. No. 139.

[45] APSA, Tour diary of Assistant Tibetan Agent Lumla, 1955 (March 1955).

The Seeds of Competition

Successful or not, the state-making efforts of NEFA officials had an unforeseen consequence: they fuelled a similar sense of vulnerability among their Chinese counterparts. If the PRC appeared threatening to Nehru and frontier authorities, its presence in Tibet in the 1950s was marked by frailties and deficiencies – weaknesses that were harnessed and exacerbated by Tibet's non-state actors, whether traders, nomads, dissidents, village dwellers, or spies. The actions and attitudes of people living along Tibet's international borders were of particular concern to Chinese authorities.[46] There, hearts-and-minds policies were even more necessary. For, in the vicinity of borders of the McMahon Line, people still had a time-tried option: crossing over.

In the wake of the Seventeen Point Agreement, the inhabitants of several parts of south-eastern Tibet had made insistent overtures towards India, asking it to expand its control over them before the arrival of PRC. As the PLA gave signs of entering Pemakö in 1952, Indian authorities got word that the local Membas accordingly planned to move south of the McMahon Line. In January, two headmen and a group of Pemakö villagers came to meet the Siang Division official at Gelling, in NEFA. The party declared that they had always thought Indian territory extended beyond the Zangchula Pass – so a former APO had said, they claimed – and were more than willing to accept Delhi's authority. A similar incident occurred hundreds of miles to the west. The villagers of Leh, south-west of Tsona, appeared one day at the Assam Rifles outpost of Chutangmu. They declared that they considered the McMahon Line to pass north of the village and requested India to extend its administration accordingly.[47] Khampas who had fled eastern Tibet in 1950 and established themselves in the northern part of Pemakö then tried to move further south, beyond the McMahon Line.[48]

To avoid an untimely diplomatic crisis with China, NEFA officials dismissed all these requests. The Siang PO told the disappointed Pemakö party that the border extended only to the Kebangla Pass and that they should 'gracefully submit to the new [Chinese] regime'; he then tried to discourage them from continuing to use the Siang Valley as a trade route between Tibet and Assam. Checkpoints in the area were bolstered to prevent immigration, and outposts elsewhere along the

---

[46] Sulmaan Wasif Khan, *Muslim, trader, nomad, spy: China's Cold War and the Tibetan borderlands* (Duke, NC: UNC Press, 2015).
[47] NAI, External 7(1)P/52 (Weekly review for 26 January 1952, and fortnightly reviews for late December 1951 and early January 1952).
[48] Grothmann, 'The hidden land of Pemakö' (pp. 36–37).

border received orders 'not to encourage or entertain' further requests to revise the boundary. As for Tibetan pilgrims visiting Assam, frontier officials were to monitor their return home.[49]

Despite these Indian policies, PRC officials near the McMahon Line had strong reasons to worry about developments in NEFA. Control over south-eastern Tibet had historically been crucial for Lhasa, and that importance likely remained after 1950. Kongpo's forests, almost the only ones on the plateau, provided the wood for the capital's buildings.[50] Dzayül was the rice bowl of Tibet, and its low altitude even made it suitable for tea production.[51] As for Pemakö and the northern Subansiri, they played an important part in Tibetan mysticism. Some of the most venerated sites of Tibetan Buddhist practice were there – the 'hidden land' of the Tsangpo's Great Bend and Tsari, the holiest of mountains, circumambulated every twelve years during the Rongkor Chenmo. As the greatest of all Tibetan Buddhist pilgrimages, the latter had been a key state-making opportunity for Lhasa.[52] Last but not least, a major route between Lhasa and China passed through Kongpo.

Just as Indian officials warily glanced over the border, they were thus being looked at by their Chinese counterparts. The two countries were turning into mutual shadow states. Beijing sent Delhi periodic signals of its watchfulness. In mid-1952, Zhou Enlai warned Nehru that if India built a road connecting Assam to Tibet, China would build its own road to the border.[53] Frontier administration needed no such reminder. To men on the spot, the PRC's proximity was a daily experience. Reports on northern NEFA were full of incidents and encounters: villagers from the Upper Lohit Valley bumped into PLA patrols in the dark of the night; a Kameng sub-inspector and constable had allegedly been kidnapped by PRC authorities; Chinese pictures of the Dalai Lama and the Panchen Lama were found in possession of Dirang Dzong villagers; and a Mishmi returned from Dzayül saying that the Chinese had gently but extensively questioned him about India's expansion in the Lohit.[54]

---

[49] NAI, External 7(1)P/52. In the Siang, the negative attitude of frontier officials was perhaps also shaped by the hostility shown by Adi groups to further Buddhist immigration into their land. Tour Diary by the APO Tuting for 1957, referred to in Grothmann, 'The hidden land of Pemakö' (p. 37).

[50] Kunga Samten Dewatshang, *Flight at the cuckoo's behest: The life and times of a Tibetan freedom fighter (as told to his son Dorjee Wangdi Dewatshang)* (Delhi: Paljor, 1997), p. 46.

[51] Israel Epstein, *Tibet transformed* (Beijing: New World Press, 1983), pp. 103–104.

[52] Toni Huber, *The cult of Pure Crystal Mountain: Popular pilgrimage and visionary landscape in southeast Tibet* (New York; Oxford: Oxford University Press, 1999), chapters 9–10.

[53] *Selected works of Jawaharlal Nehru – Second series*, ed. by S. Gopal (New Delhi: Jawaharlal Nehru Memorial Fund, 1996), XVIII, pp. 474–475.

[54] NAI, External 7(1)P/52 (16 February 1952 review); NAI, External 4(19)-P/55 (November report).

The Rongkor Chenmo pilgrimage fostered mutual anxieties. When thousands of men and women converged on the Tsari Mountain in 1956, the first time since Tibet's annexation, Indian and Chinese authorities grasped the significance of the event. PRC officials, who had long used medical treatment as a cheap and effective way of winning trust,[55] sent small medical teams to Tsari to tend to pilgrims.[56] India launched an entirely unarmed expedition towards the northern Subansiri that same year, founding an outpost at Limeking in the vicinity of the mountain.[57]

In the borderlands straddling the ill-defined McMahon Line, China thus stood dangerously close to India, and India to China. Border officials became pervaded by the thought that their initiatives towards Himalayan populations should always compete with – and indeed surpass – those of the other state.It was this feeling that led Indian intelligence services to urge Delhi to allocate more funds to NEFA in 1952. Should India's development schemes fail to keep up with those of the PRC, went the reasoning, tribals would turn to the latter for 'salvation'.[58] The fear of being compared permeated monthly confidential dispatches to Delhi. Reports like those for May and June 1957 did little to assuage NEFA authorities' qualms. The Chinese had succeeded in attracting several Mishmis to their border school in Dzayül; like the other children, they were taught in Tibetan and Mandarin and received free food, clothing, and accommodation. PRC authorities were making headway in their relations with the Idu Mishmis of the Dibang Valley, the least adminis-tered part of the Lohit Division. They had appointed a local man as interpreter and, thanks to him, had convinced some Idus to go on a big tour of China, all the way to Beijing. On their return, they had been presented with a rifle, two guns, and a pistol – prized items in Mishmi society. Further west, where the Tsangpo becomes the Siang, Bokars on either side of the McMahon Line were being courted through school creation or the granting of a monthly salary to village elders.[59]

[55] June T. Dreyer, *China's forty millions: Minority nationalities and national integration in the People's Republic of China* (Cambridge, MA: Harvard University Press, 1976), pp. 100, 115; Benno Ryan Weiner, 'The Chinese Revolution on the Tibetan frontier: State building, national integration and socialist transformation, Zeku (Tsékhok) County, 1953–1958' (unpublished PhD dissertation, Columbia University, 2012), p. 114.

[56] Huber, *The cult of Pure Crystal Mountain*, p. 170.

[57] S.M. Krishnatry, *Border Tagins of Arunachal Pradesh: Unarmed expedition, 1956* (Delhi: National Book Trust, 2005); NAI, External 4(19)-P/55 (Report for December 1955).

[58] NAI, External 7(1)P/52 (Fortnightly review of Sino-Tibetan intelligence, late December 1951).

[59] APSA, Report on the NEF Agency for May–June 1957.

Officials serving in NEFA's northern reaches devised hearts-and-minds tactics of their own to counteract Chinese shadowing own. One day in 1955, the Kibithoo Tibetan Agent, Sawthang La, happened to meet a Dzayüli carpenter in the Lohit Valley. Kamasha – for that was the carpenter's name – had been working on a *gaonbura*'s house when Sawthang La arrived, accompanied by a government surgeon. Due to local Mishmis' frequent visits to the Assam plains, malaria was quite common in the hamlet and the surrounding area. Witnessing people gathering around the doctor, Kamasha grew curious. Sawthang La explained that they were receiving anti-malarial treatment. Further impressed by the Tibetan Agent's distribution of medicines, salt, tea, and cigarettes, Kamasha asked to be given an injection and some tablets. Sawthang La happily obliged: ill or not, what mattered was that the carpenter's encounter with the NEFA administration would make for 'very good propaganda to the people beyond the border'.

Sawthang La's hopes were apparently confirmed. Sitting together by the fire that evening, Kamasha confessed being 'very much impressed with the work of [the Indian] Government'. Dzayül's Chinese authorities did send around doctors and interpreters to give free medical treatment, but unlike the NEFA administration they gave neither political presents nor seeds and agricultural implements for free. What's more, they perceived a 'grain tax' on Dzayülis, something the Mishmis told him Indian authorities did not do. Although 'the people in Rima area are very much improved since the occupation of the area by the Chinese', Kamasha reportedly observed, 'people who settled down within Indian territory are really fortunate'. India too could generate a pull effect.[60]

Heightened Fears

As India and the PRC sought to entrench themselves in the eastern Himalayas, their state-making efforts had become visible not just to each other, but also to the region's inhabitants. The boundary issue notwithstanding, both countries needed a stable, constructive relationship with the latter to fully control 'their side' of the Himalayas. Yet because they took place simultaneously, Chinese and Indian expansion efforts afforded indigenous people a bargaining space. From a state perspective, it seemed that Himalayan inhabitants always had the option to *choose* between two state-making projects. And there was plenty of historical evidence of people's propensity to move to more favourable political

---

[60] APSA, P-82/55 (Entry for 17 February).

climes. In their anxious proximity, the Chinese and the Indian state constituted each other's alternative – and, therefore, a threat. For much of the 1950s, mutual shadowing had nevertheless been relatively stable. Securing border areas competed with India's other priorities. When it came to deciding where to expand or consolidate, many NEFA officers felt that it made more sense to use their limited resources in 'the interest of the main blocks of population', often located farther away from the border, than to exhaust themselves trying to materialise the McMahon Line.[61] Chinese authorities, meanwhile, had not yet established themselves all along the border. In cases like Pemakö, they stayed at a distance; the decision might well have been spurred by the inhabitants' threat to move to India.

The events of 1959 upset this state of affairs. In the aftermath of the Lhasa uprising, both Chinese and Indian troops began to push their presence up to the McMahon Line. On the PRC side, the move betrayed problems beyond India's own forward policy: partly because of China's weak presence, the regions north of NEFA were a major stronghold of Khampa guerrillas in Tibet. Yet, by sending troops into Kongpo to defeat them, the PLA exacerbated India's fears of Chinese expansionism.[62]

Adding to Indian anxieties, the PRC had opened up boundary negotiations with two other Himalayan neighbours since 1959: Burma and Nepal. And they seemed to be going well. Upon gaining independence from Britain in 1948, Burmese authorities had found themselves in a similar position to Chinese and Indian ones – namely, having to impose themselves in border territories previously under indirect rule. The conditions were ripe for a shadowing security dilemma similar to that on the Sino-Indian border but for a key difference: Guomindang irregulars had entrenched themselves in the Sino-Burmese borderlands. The presence of a common enemy in their borderlands gave Burma and China an impetus to compromise, and eventually a boundary agreement was signed in January 1960 and a treaty that October. Meanwhile, the PRC had launched negotiations with Nepal, with which it shared a recognised customary boundary. Here too, they shared a goal in the borderland: neutralising Tibetan guerrillas now ensconced in remote

---

[61] Itanagar, APSA, NEFA Secretariat (1955), Expansion programme for Subansiri for 1955–56 P189/55, pp. 11–12.

[62] PLA General Staff Department, 'Report: "Behind India's second anti-China wave" (Original File: PRC FMA 105-00944-07, 84–90. Translated by 7Brands)', *History and Public Policy Program Digital Archive* (29 October 1959) http://digitalarchive.wilsoncenter .org/document/114758 (accessed 27 April 2015).

parts of Nepal. In both cases, negotiations also aimed to send a signal to India. Instead, these border talks only fuelled Indian fears.[63]

As bilateral relations soured, Indian authorities came to perceive the socio-economic networks and cultural traits of northern NEFA, and its inhabitants' 'Mongoloid' features, as an unacceptable liability. (Even today, Mongoloid phenotypes are not included in mainstream imaginaries of the 'Indian' face.)[64] Faced with China's boundary claims, government historians published pages upon pages to prove that the McMahon Line, notwithstanding its unquestionable legality, coincided with India's geographical and cultural limits. But the people of NEFA's interaction with Tibet put this neat story into question.

The uneasiness was palpable in some official publications. 'There [was] no doubt that the McMahon Line ... merely confirmed the natural, traditional, *ethnic*, and administrative boundary in the area', declared the External Affairs Ministry in 1962. Yet, almost in the same breath, it added: 'boundaries between any two countries are *not determined by ethnic affiliations* of people living in frontier regions. It is also possible that people of the same racial stock live on either side of a border.'[65] The contradiction had the taste of a confession.

For Delhi, the existence and complexity of cross-border ties provided Beijing with a dangerous advantage. In summer 1959, a PLA patrol ventured south of the Thagla Ridge, the topographic feature India saw as the international boundary in north-western Kameng. Indian authorities were incensed, but the PRC denied any incursion had taken place. On the contrary, it argued that the Thagla Ridge lay squarely within Chinese territory. Did Leh and Timang, two villages near Tsona, not have the customary right to use pasture lands located south of the Thagla Ridge? And, if so, was that not proof that Kameng's Khinzemane area actually lay *north* of the McMahon Line? India rejected the claim. While 'it [was] not uncommon for border villages on one side to use by mutual agreement pastures lying on the other side of the international boundary', protested Delhi, 'the exercise of this privilege cannot be regarded as evidence in support of a territorial claim'.[66]

---

[63] M. Taylor Fravel, *Strong borders, secure nation: Cooperation and conflict in China's territorial disputes* (Princeton, NJ; Oxford: Princeton University Press, 2008), pp. 85–93. On the negotiations with Nepal, see also Khan, *Muslim, trader, nomad, spy*, chapter 3.

[64] Jelle J.P. Wouters and Tanka B. Subba, 'The "Indian face", India's northeast, and "the idea of India"', *Asian Anthropology*, 12:2 (2013), 126–140.

[65] 'India-China border problem', ed. by Ministry of External Affairs – External Publicity Division (New Delhi: Government of India, [1962]) (pp. 1–2). Emphasis added.

[66] 'India's protest to China: Firm stand on McMahon Line', *Amrita Bazaar Patrika*, 11 September 1959.

India's defensiveness increased alongside older fears that NEFA's inhabitants might well choose to settle across the border or invite China in. H.V. Kamath, an opposition politician, returned from a tour of north-eastern India in late 1959 with ominous pronouncements. China planned no less than the creation of a Himalayan Federation. To do so, it was using all the means at its disposal to seduce local people with 'ethnic affinity and irredentism, economic allurement and hatred of the West besides, of course, ideological claptrap'. And the scheme might well work, argued Kamath:

the psychological assault will make a sizeable dent because of the prevailing anti-Indian sentiment [in the Himalayas] Nor is the economic offensive likely to fail in its effect on the terribly poor and backward people of the region, what with trade inducements, and the picture presented by the rapid agricultural and industrial development programme in neighbouring Tibet ... China is not so stupid as to launch a military attack ... Her *modus operandi* will, therefore, be infiltration, erosion and subversion, the weapons being mainly psychological and economic.

Kamath was particularly hawkish, but the *Times of India* echoed part of his diagnosis. 'All along the frontier there is a great awareness of Tibet', warned the daily; 'the tribesmen keep visiting ... and returning from there with armfuls of Chinese magazines which show in pictures the progress Tibet is making.'[67]

Senior NEFA officials too were increasingly worried: 'the entire border has not been receiving adequate attention from us, especially so far as education is concerned, due to communication and other difficulties', admitted a confidential note on the development of border areas from January 1962.[68] And now that the Indian army was moving into NEFA, the relationship civilian administrators had managed to establish with local tribes was already in full upheaval, and in places perhaps in danger. Should people living close to the McMahon Line deem it more advantageous, or less restrictive, to deal with Chinese authorities, India's hold over the eastern Himalayas would weaken – or worse.

PRC border officials were no less preoccupied with reinforcing their presence on the Himalayan frontier, and not just because of India. They too were now increasingly concerned that people declare their loyalty, clearly and definitively.[69] By 1961, the Khampas had been ousted from Kongpo and a quietness not seen since 1957 had seemingly returned to

---

[67] H.V. Kamath, 'A Himalayan federation? Red China's grand strategy in S. Asia', *Amrita Bazaar Patrika*, 6 August 1959; 'Chinese influence on border tribes', *Times of India*, 18 October 1959.

[68] Itanagar, APSA, NEFA Secretariat (1962), Development activities in border areas PC-14/62. 'A note on the development of border areas'.

[69] Khan, *Muslim, trader, nomad, spy.*

south-eastern Tibet. Yet the fact was that the PLA had not been able to prevent thousands of warriors from crossing into the safety of NEFA. Many of them had resettled on the southern side of the McMahon Line. Indian authorities had systematically screened and disarmed them, reportedly, but the strong Khampa presence in centres such as Tawang and Bomdila likely fuelled PRC concerns, especially since many dreamed of returning and the CIA backed anti-Chinese insurgents elsewhere.[70]

The PRC also had good reason to worry about the reaction of indigenous people towards its strengthened presence. The latter were not necessarily well disposed towards Khampas: a Chushi Gangdruk leader recalled struggling to convince people in Kongpo that he had not come to loot them, while Indian intelligence reported that some guerrillas had forcibly enrolled locals and collected fines from villages suspected of cooperating with the Chinese.[71] But, as the case of Lhasa shows, anti-Khampa feelings by no means meant support for the PRC.[72]

In northern Pemakö, many inhabitants renewed their request to settle in Tuting in the Siang. NEFA authorities again rejected their immigration proposal, lest it 'lead to international complications'.[73] When PRC authorities gave signs of moving into Pemakö around 1960, people decided to do without India's permission. They stopped their cultivation, packed their belongings, and – much to local POs' alarm – moved to NEFA.[74] By the time Chinese troops finally occupied it in 1961, Pemakö had lost the bigger part of its population. To convince the rest to stay, the PLA distributed salt and co-opted the young relatives of local notables now settled in NEFA.[75] But if the inhabitants of south-eastern Tibet were to stop seeing India as a place to escape impending 'democratic reforms', PRC authorities would somehow have to make their neighbour seem less attractive, including to the visitors from across the border who spread information about conditions in NEFA. China and India's state-making competition was about to escalate dramatically.

[70] 'Screening of Tibetan refugees', Times of India, 25 April 1961.
[71] Dewatshang, Flight at the cuckoo's behest, pp. 129–130; APSA, Report on the NEF Agency for May–June 1957.
[72] Tsering W. Shakya, The dragon in the land of snows: A history of modern Tibet since 1947 (London: Pimlico, 1999), pp. 173–174.
[73] APSA, Report on the NEF Agency for May–June 1957.
[74] Itanagar, APSA, NEFA Secretariat (1960), Monthly confidential reports from POs, Sup-4/55/60-Part II (Report for May 1960).
[75] NAI, External 6/35/R&I/61 (Special report on development of the other side of the northern border for June 1961); NAI, External 5/9/R&I/61 (Intelligence summary for September 1961).

Figure 6.1 Nari Rustomji is introduced to the Gams of Tuting,
October 1959
© Arunachal Pradesh DIPR

A Game of Shadows

The shop at Mechuka had not been there long. A few months perhaps, not more than a year. Its shelves were lined with all sorts of goods that villagers generally bought across the border, in Tibet: metal utensils, cutlery, and agricultural implements; blankets and clothes of thick Tibetan wool; yarn and raw wool for knitting; beautiful Tibetan bells, jewellery, and beads. There were also less familiar items, and even things that no Memba had ever seen: torches, locks, keys, even umbrellas. This was a 'fair-price shop', the Mechuka Tibetan Agent had explained, a shop specially established by the Indian government so that the Membas could easily find all they would need for their daily lives and more, and which would buy anything they cared to produce – all at a very advantageous price. There would be no more need to make the arduous trek to Tibet.

Mechuka was not the only locality to get a government emporium in the early 1960s: fair-price shops and border depots were appearing all across NEFA's northern reaches. A strangely hectic atmosphere seemed to reign among Indian administrative circles. From the Bhutan border to Limeking in the Siang and all the way to Anini in the Dibang Valley, schools, hospitals, and craft centres were popping up. Ambitious development schemes, normally initiated in the regions closer to Assam, were being earmarked for border areas. In 1960, Tuting, Bomdila, and Mechuka itself had become the first electrified settlements in the whole of NEFA. Two hundred workers were busy clearing a landing group for Mechuka, others were installing pigs and poultry farms, and Agricultural Officers were distributing sheep and goats. Indian authorities had financed improvements to the Mechuka *gompa*, in dire need of a renovation, and appointed Tibetan-speaking teachers in border schools. They were even building brand new monasteries.[76]

India's administrative presence along the McMahon Line was increasing accordingly. Siang officials were busy building airstrips in the border villages of Yatong and Yingkiong. 'In view of the increasing importance of the area following developments in Tibet', the Tawang Assistant Political Officer had been upgraded to Political Officer, putting him on an equal footing with his Bomdila-based colleague. For long the last expansion priority, the Subansiri boasted three new administrative centres, two of them created soon after the Longju incident of August 1959.[77] NEFA's border areas were fast turning into the prime focus of Indian frontier authorities.

Outpost creation, fair-price shops, and government-funded monastery construction served the same purposes: thwarting China's territorial

---

[76] Itanagar, APSA, NEFA Secretariat (1962), Long-term requirement of Kalimpong goods by border CPO depot Sup/4/131/62; APSA, PC-14/62; New Delhi, NAI, External Affairs Proceedings (1959), Proposal for the creation of an Engineering Division at Along, 16(16)-NEFA/59 (Durai to External Affairs Under-Secretary, 26 November 1959); Itanagar, APSA, NEFA Secretariat (1959), Summary of activities in the administration during 1959 P49/59, pp. 31–32; Itanagar, APSA, NEFA Secretariat (1962), Demarcation of divisional boundaries 1 P-42/62 (List of issues the different senior officers want covered); Delhi, NMML, Elwin Papers (1961), Correspondence with Secretary, Scheduled Tribes Commission regarding his visit to NEFA, 1961, S. No. 135 (Ramos, Pailibos, Boris tour, October–December 1958), pp. 149–150; Itanagar, APSA, NEFA Secretariat (1962), Border Areas Production Scheme, Ind-4/62, p. 34.

[77] APSA, P49/59, pp. 24–32.

claims and neutralising its power of attraction for NEFA's inhabitants. In the 1940s, colonial officials had advocated dispensing 'liberal funds ... [for] beneficent activities' as a means of displacing Tibetan influence.[78] This time as well, development activities were to serve Indian expansion against another state presence.

The logic, however, was slightly different. As long as the Bokars, the Membas, or the Mishmis continued to visit Tibet, 'fifth-column infiltration and ... indoctrination' could threaten India's territorial integrity. Concretising the McMahon Line not only hinged on military canvassing but also on the capacity of Indian authorities to reshape the human geography of NEFA's northern areas, to dissociate their inhabitants from Tibet while redirecting all existing trade and social flows towards India. The Sino-Indian border was to become reality through its embodiment in the bodies, the actions, and ultimately the thoughts of local inhabitants.

There was a problem, however: people could not by force be prevented from crossing the McMahon Line. Respecting the Panchsheel agreement of 1954 – which stipulated that borderlanders had the right to move freely across the Sino-Indian boundary – was not the problem: Beijing and Delhi had no compunction in disregarding its provisions for long-distance, professional trade as their relations soured. Rather, banning trans-border traffic was hardly possible because, although they had multiplied since 1959, Assam Rifles border checkpoints were undermanned and stranded in difficult terrain. Nor were NEFA's civilian authorities in favour of coercion, which might damage India's standing among border tribes and work to China's benefit. In these conditions, the only hope to stop populations from crossing was to give them incentives not to do so – by providing everything they might need or want.[79]

The proliferation of depots and stores such as the Mechuka fair-price shop was only the most visible effort to reconfigure the lives of border people. Indian authorities undertook to 'maintain regular supply of ... goods [normally acquired in Tibet] to the tribal people as and when required by them'. POs were asked to ascertain local needs so that the administration could order the purchase of the 'requisite quantity of goods'. These were then sold to border communities at heavily subsidised prices, decided by border officials so as to 'suit local conditions': 'tribal people on the border should not pay ... more than what they used to pay for them in Tibet'. The principle's ostensible benevolence had everything to do with the drive to overcome the greater attractiveness of Tibetan goods. To encourage the shift, officials discussed the reasons

---

[78] NAI, External 63/X/43 (PO Sikkim to Foreign secretary, 16 June).
[79] APSA, Sup/4/131/62, p. 53.

for the arrival of the army and Assam Rifles reinforcements with local communities, obtained their advice on lists of goods and pricing schemes, and took care to give 'benevolent name[s] in the local language' to border shops.[80] Since reducing exports to Tibet was the other priority, Indian authorities committed to buying the goods that people produced for sale or barter with trans-McMahon Line areas. Some officials hoped that the process would lead to the successful monetisation of tribal societies; even better, they hoped that as 'the people [would] gradually learn the value and use of money [they would] try to earn more money by way of porterage or contract work', solving a key administrative problem into the bargain.[81] These hopes were often dashed by people's reluctance to pay for goods in cash. To achieve their goal, border officials hence had to follow the rules of the game in the local economy: barter.

Attempts to divert trade flows away from Tibet required enormous efforts on the part of India's civilian administration. Many of the goods that border inhabitants required were unavailable in NEFA. If they were, they were not of a type or quality sufficient to entice them. Frontier officials had to go 600 miles to Kalimpong, the crucial centre of long-distance trade between Tibet and India and home to a big Tibetan community.

The scheme was time consuming and extremely costly, so NEFA officials tried to develop craft and production centres in border areas in parallel. This offered the quadruple advantage of minimising transport costs, employing local people, monetising the economy, and using local raw materials. In addition to farms and livestock rearing schemes, the administration introduced various crafts in border areas: silversmithy, clay modelling, carpet weaving. The aim was to create border communities who would not rely on access to their Tibetan economic hinterland for their subsistence, by transitioning to government-funded production centres and tribal cooperatives (initially subsidised through government loans and grant-in-aid) for trade and production.

The administration had a sizeable advantage in its attempt to replicate the Tibetan craft tradition on their side of the border: the know-how of Tibetan exiles themselves. It therefore focused its rehabilitation efforts on the creation of craft centres in refugee settlements. The objective was both to produce for the refugees' own use and to supply articles to border communities – thereby recreating the socio-economic networks that had tied many NEFA people to the Tibetan plateau *within an Indian geographic space*, insulated from Tibet itself. Tibetan exiles were to produce the crafts from home for border communities that were themselves in the

---

[80] APSA, Ind-4/62, pp. 11–12.   [81] APSA, Sup/4/131/62, p. 25.

process of losing contact with Tibet. We do not know if Indian authorities grasped the irony. Had they done so, this would have changed little to border development policies that, at their core, were meant to mirror those of PRC border authorities – in fact, to outcompete them.[82]

The Impossible Border

The trouble was that this game of shadows went both ways. China too was accelerating its efforts to win over border populations – in Tibet *and* in NEFA. Across the McMahon Line, development facilities, trade outlets, and cultural initiatives were flourishing. For each fair-trade shop or each Tibetan-language school put up by an Indian official, a corresponding facility seemed to be freshly built on the Chinese side. More than ever, Indian frontier authorities obsessed about development initiatives across the border. Pomé was witnessing the rapid build-up of welfare facilities and entertainment opportunities. By March 1962, the village of Tramo was equipped for telephone and wireless transmissions and boasted no less than three hospitals; visitors and inhabitants were treated to cinema shows and cultural performances. Alupu, across from the Dibang Valley, had a new border shop and a cooperative. So did Chingdong, across from Taksing in the Siang Division, and Sangacholing, across from Sarli and Huri in the Subansiri. PRC officials were specially posted to hasten development work in these various border areas; they also gave free treatment to outdoor patients and assisted villagers with irrigation work and road building.[83]

Even more unnerving for NEFA officials, such initiatives seemed clearly underpinned by an evaluation of their own welfare and development schemes. PRC officials stationed at Leh north of Kameng were questioning travellers about the division's border shops – what goods they sold, at what price, what did they not provide among the things people wanted. Longju had been turned into a large centre of propaganda directed at NEFA's inhabitants.[84] Far from being turned back, those who crossed the Sino-Indian border were treated to 'lavish entertainment, free

---

[82] APSA, Ind-4/62; APSA, Sup-4/55/60-Part II. On Kalimpong, see Tina Harris, *Geographical diversions: Tibetan trade, global transactions* (Athens, GA: University of Georgia Press, 2013).

[83] P.N. Luthra, 'NEFA People and the Chinese invasion', *The March of India*, July 1963, pp. 3–5. From late 1961 onwards, the end of Kongpo and Lhoka's pacification would have enabled the PLA to refocus on economic development. Fravel, *Strong borders, secure nation*, p. 182.

[84] Itanagar, APSA, NEFA Secretariat (1962), Development activities of the Chinese across the border PC-55/62L (Developmental activities of the Chinese in Tibet, Appendix, 18 November 1962).

board and lodging, expensive presents and very liberal barter terms'.[85] Indian authorities were certain of it: all along the McMahon Line, the Chinese were systematically trying to 'win over NEFA people with entertainment, baits, and courtesy'.[86] Some of these enticements had a more immediate intent: obtaining information or, even better, hiring people to spy across the border. Tribal travellers were questioned on their bona fides and on what they knew of developments on the other side of the McMahon Line; Tibetan refugees settled in NEFA were suspected of unknowingly harbouring Communist informants in their midst. (Many Tibetan refugees have sombre memories of arriving in India only to be suspected of being Chinese spies.)[87]

And yet, problematically, Indian authorities too needed such movement to maintain their intelligence networks in Tibet, let alone to conduct propaganda there. The same refugees screened by Assam Rifles to detect spies in their midst were also questioned extensively about happenings in the PRC.[88] The tensions between the two imperatives – ending populations' cross-border contact and obtaining enough information from the other side to be prepared, militarily and developmentally – were hard to solve. This double-edged situation affected border people themselves, subject to official suspicion yet able to manipulate the information they gave to either side.

The Sino-Indian contest for the allegiance of border people was hence fast accelerating. An anecdote from May 1962 is revealing in this regard. That spring, two Bangru hunters from the Subansiri decided to visit Chayül, across the McMahon Line. This was the ideal season to hunt wild sheep and musk deer. They had just arrived in the village of Gumla when a Chinese government interpreter came to meet them. Instead of ordering the two men to return to NEFA, he told them that if they took the time to go to the *dzong* (fortress) to meet the local Chinese officer, they would receive plenty of wheat flour, tea, cooked rice, vegetables, and even pork. The two men had not come to trade, but heavy snowfall had dashed their hopes of a good hunt; they went to the *dzong*. The interpreter had not lied. The Chinese officer and his wife came in person to greet them, and all the promised ingredients were offered to them for free. The officer then let them proceed on deeper into Tibet.

[85] APSA, Sup/4/131/62.   [86] Luthra, 'NEFA people and the Chinese invasion'.

[87] '150,000 Chinese troops along border of India', *Hindustan Standard*, 21 June 1960; Interview with Wangmo (Interview #67). Interviewed by Martin Newman on 4 July 2007 (held at the Tibet Oral History Project), www.tibetoralhistory.org/interviews .html (accessed 27 January 2015).

[88] NAI, External 6/35/R&I/61 (A special report on development of the other side of the northern border for June 1961).

The two men decided to make the most of their good fortune; they continued their journey until Lhotsé, where they bartered the goods they had acquired at a profitable rate. The loss from their cancelled hunting trip had been more than recouped.[89]

Even as PRC authorities tried to stop Tibet residents from entering India, they thus encouraged NEFA inhabitants to ignore the existence of the border. The Chinese officer's goal in hosting the Bangru hunters was not merely to obtain information about Indian activities across the border (which he did), but to impress the two men with the PRC's successful entrenchment in the old Tibetan power structures (he received them in the former seat of power, from which Lhasa's tax collectors had historically descended upon NEFA). He also displayed a seemingly effortless generosity in giving food and supplies not merely plentiful and varied, but of the sort that India could not easily provide. Finally, by granting them free and safe passage deeper into Chayül, he stressed that it was India that was restricting their interaction with Tibet; China was innocent. The intent seemed clear: to show that the PRC could provide more, better, and quicker, and all that without hindering the movement of the NEFA population, for trade or otherwise. In this context, India's attempts to materialise the McMahon Line floundered.

China and India's shadowing had tangible effects. In late 1959, the only school established by the Indian government in the Tagin regions of the Subansiri closed down after locals, observing Chinese educational facilities across the border, decided to send their children there.[90] NEFA authorities responded by intensifying development efforts on the Subansiri border. At Sarli and Huri, where administrative presence was a mere couple of years old, the local officer encouraged people to state their grievances and held dozens of public meetings and 'informal camp fires' to communicate about border shops. Such gatherings were also the occasion to convince people to open cooperatives and share testimonies about Chinese brutality, so that they would not cross the McMahon Line. Elsewhere, they monitored the articles of Chinese border shops, much like their PRC counterparts adjusted their stocks in function of what Indian stores provided.[91] 'The only way to solve the problem [of people crossing over for trade]', read a policy note, was to offer 'more attractive economic incentives than what the Chinese [were] providing'.[92]

---

[89] Itanagar, APSA, NEFA Secretariat (1962), Extracts from confidential reports on border trades and merchandise, Sup4/139/62, p. 3.
[90] 'Chinese influence on border tribes'.
[91] APSA, Sup/4/131/62 (Inspection note, Huri circle, P.P. Shrivastav); APSA, PC-55/62L.
[92] APSA, Sup/4/131/62, p. 53.

In such a tense context, the NEFA administration's ever-present staff and equipment shortages were more problematic than ever. Civilian border officials fought pitched battles to find buildings for shops and accommodation, or even to obtain enough furniture and office stationery.[93] To make matters worse, the army's arrival made the intricacies of decision-making more complex than ever between frontier staff, their Shillong superiors, and External Affairs officials. Schemes took months to be sanctioned and goods often arrived late, hampering the opening of border depots and administrative efforts to discourage trade.[94] In northern Kameng, villagers had stopped going to Tibet to get salt, but they were upset that the PO's promise to give them Indian salt instead had not been met (despite their offer to build an airstrip for the purpose). 'If we are to discourage the import of salt from Tibet, it is obviously our responsibility to make supplies available ourselves, and this we are not adequately ensuring', wrote Rustomji – who had returned as Adviser to the Governor – after witnessing the situation in April 1961.[95]

On 16 January 1962, NEFA's senior officials took several important decisions regarding border development strategy. From now on, they would arrange as many airdrops as necessary to fulfil the requirements and demands of border populations – no matter the cost. An official would specifically manage the purchase of 'Kalimpong goods', and the central government would commit to buying all the NEFA produce that was not naturally in demand elsewhere in India. The administration would try to sell these goods either to staff or to crafts emporium in Delhi and other big cities, but if articles could not be sold, they would purely and simply be written off.[96] Indian frontier authorities were ready to do whatever it took to keep NEFA's border populations on their side.

A comprehensive nation-building strategy was simultaneously devised for border areas. The escalation of Sino-Indian competition forced NEFA authorities to give more thought to their hitherto limited efforts in that direction. PRC authorities were reportedly spreading word across the border that the tribes of NEFA were ethnically akin to the Hans, who would shortly come to free them from India – while mustering support for this in Tibet itself.[97] 'In view of the international developments across the border', it was now deemed essential to provide people living close to

[93] Ibid.   [94] APSA, Ind-4/62.
[95] New Delhi, NAI, External Affairs Proceedings (1961), Problems arising from the location of the army in the interior, 12(2)-NEFA/61 (Rustomji's tour note on visit to Tawang).
[96] APSA, Sup/4/131/62, p. 25; APSA, Ind-4/62 (Minutes of policy meeting on 16 January 1962), pp. 10–13.
[97] P.B. Sinha and A.A. Athale, 'History of the conflict with China', ed. by India History Division – Defence Department (New Delhi: Ministry of Defence, 1992) (p. 60).

Tibet 'added opportunities [not just] for economic development but also *for social intercourse with a view to integration with the rest of the country'.*[98] Without such proactive policies, senior frontier officials worried that insulation from Tibet would not be sufficient to secure NEFA for India.

The focus was on tribal youth and their education. In a move that sparked fury in Assam, Hindi, hitherto taught only as a second language, replaced Assamese as the medium of instruction.[99] Annual tours took NEFA students across India 'so that they could realise that they are part and parcel of the great Indian nation and should take pride in its rich heritage, civilisation and culture'. These Bharat Darshan tours had been tried a few times before, but only haphazardly. Now they were systematic, and no expenses were spared for the purpose. The External Affairs Ministry sanctioned Rs 30,000 to send a group on a whirlwind trip to Guwahati, Lucknow, Delhi, Chandigarh, Simla, Agra, Bombay, and Calcutta. Local youth were sent to the interdivisional tournament at Along, which few of them had hitherto attended, and divisional sports tournaments were organised in addition.

The number of border schools grew in parallel. Investments were made to build or rejuvenate local schools, while a NEFA Youth Training Institute was started for teenage students unable to study in normal institutions. Schools began to depute eight of their best students each year to public schools in Shillong and elsewhere in India, with a view to train them for various technical and administrative jobs in due course.

Where education had hitherto been meant to foster the students' pride in their culture, it now also aimed to stress the advantages of belonging to India vis-à-vis China. The Youth Training Institute would be 'a model institution typifying in itself all the characteristics of an enlightened free socialistic democracy', which would also stress 'the characteristics and setbacks of totalitarian society, such as [the] use of force, [and the] absence of the fundamental freedoms and human rights'.[100] Which side of the McMahon Line was suffering was meant to be obvious.

The Sino-Indian security dilemma that materialised in the early 1960s was therefore not just a military one. In the eastern Himalayas at least, it also stemmed from China and India's shadow state relationship, itself tied to their uncertain relationship with local inhabitants. Garrisoning the

---

[98] APSA, PC-14/62 (Note on the development of border areas). Emphasis mine.

[99] Indira Miri, *Moi aru NEFA [NEFA and I]* (Guwahati: Spectrum, 2003); *The outlook on NEFA*, ed. by Assam Sahitya Sabha (Calcutta: Nabajiban, 1958).

[100] APSA, PC-14/62 (Note on the development of border areas). See also Itanagar, APSA, NEFA Secretariat (1961), Press notes issued by administration PC-17/61 (Reorientation of education programme in border areas of NEFA), p. 99.

Figure 6.2 Rustomji hosting a party of students about to undertake
a Bharat Darshan
© Arunachal Pradesh DIPR

border with ever-greater strength was insufficient for frontier authorities. Achieving security also meant securing the Monpas', the Mishmis', or the Dzayülis' exclusive attention and cooperation. Providing *more* facilities, *more* development, *more* goods than the other state was therefore crucial. Yet, just as military build-up on one side of the border called for more militarisation on the other, competitive state-making only fuelled India and China's mutual fears, compounded by their superficial understanding of local people. Spread by travellers, refugees, and even soldiers, tales and rumours of the other side flew back and forth across the NEFA–Tibet borderlands.[101]

By mid-1962, the *Hindi–Chini Bhai-Bhai* era had collapsed. The Trade Agreement of 1954 had lapsed, India refusing to renegotiate it. China was actively courting Bhutan, with which India had a special relationship. The Indian army was pushing its platoons up to the very edge of the McMahon Line, while the NEFA administration had decided to do its utmost to carry out its border development strategy. Meanwhile, the PRC was completing its occupation of Pomé and northern Pemakö, and senior PLA officials were seen reviewing the areas north of the Siang and Subansiri divisions. Chinese authorities in Tsona were reportedly proclaiming that they would soon eject India from Tawang, where they would work for the benefit of poor people.[102] The situation was fast escalating.

---

[101] Oshong Ering. Interview with the author, 11 February 2014, Pasighat (Arunachal Pradesh).

[102] B.N. Mullik, *My years with Nehru: The Chinese betrayal* (Bombay: Allied Publishers, 1971), pp. 334, 339; Sinha and Athale, 'History of the conflict with China' (pp. 76–77).

7   Open War

State-Making's Dress Rehearsal

On a foggy morning in November 1962, a party of Shimong Adis was returning from their annual expedition to collect aconite. The mood was joyous as they traced their way back to Yingkiong, in the north of the Siang Division. The group had successfully cajoled Jimu Tayang, the dangerous spirit of the mountains, into letting them gather mushrooms to fabricate poisoned arrows. A rousing celebration awaited them at home. No one was perhaps more exhilarated than Tarun Bhattacharjee, the young civilian official posted at Yingkiong; it was the first time he had been invited on such an expedition. The party had just arrived home when Bhattacharjee received an astonishing message from his superior: China had invaded.[1]

Six weeks earlier, on 8 September, PLA troops had surrounded Dhola, a small Indian outpost recently opened below the Thagla Ridge, in Kameng. Indian authorities rushed troops to Dhola. The outpost's location was nearly indefensible, but it was right on the trijunction with Tibet and Bhutan, and India would defend it at any cost.

While Chinese and Indian troops exchanged fire near the Thagla Ridge, Delhi minimised the seriousness of the situation. China might have crossed the McMahon Line but there was really no need to cancel the Defence Minister's trip abroad, much less the Prime Minister's. By 12 October a major skirmish had taken place, yet the Indian army was no closer to rescuing Dhola. In fact, many troops supposed to defend Tawang had been lost in an attempt to repel the Chinese. But if Delhi was to be believed there was still no cause for alarm. The intrusion was serious, conceded Nehru before boarding a plane to Ceylon, yet it was no more than that: an intrusion. The Chinese would be thrown out, and the 'steel gate' of the Himalayas would protect India.[2]

A week later, on 20 October 1962, the steel gate broke down. Around 5 a.m., the PLA began bombing the Thagla Ridge area. By the end of the

---

[1] Tarun Kumar Bhattacharjee, *Alluring frontiers* (Guwahati: Omsons Publications, 1988), pp. 126–130.

[2] 'China forced us to act: Their advance must be stopped – Nehru', *Amrita Bazaar Patrika*, 16 October 1962.

night, Dhola and two other outposts were overrun. On the opposite end of the Himalayas, Chinese forces had launched themselves against Ladakh, on the edge of the Aksai Chin. A full-scale war had begun.

To say Indian forces were unprepared is an understatement. On both the eastern and the western fronts, their positions were thinly spread and often small, only one platoon in some cases. The soldiers who manned them lacked equipment and had but summer clothing to protect them against the onset of Himalayan winter. Nor could clothes or weapons be delivered easily, given the lack of roads between forward posts and their supply base. Yet they were facing PLA troops who had benefited from a comprehensive programme of reorganisation and modernisation since 1950.[3]

Indian positions on the Aksai Chin fell in quick succession. Eventually, senior military officials ordered soldiers to withdraw beyond China's boundary claim. In NEFA, outposts on the route to Tawang could not resist either. Several hundred kilometres to the east, the tiny Kibithoo outpost fell on 22 October. Walong, the most important outpost in the Lohit, was under direct threat. Its garrison temporarily stalled the Chinese advance despite being greatly outnumbered. On 25 October, Longju and Asafila in the Subansiri came under attack. Meanwhile, the PLA had launched a three-pronged assault on Tawang. Poorly defended, the town had to be evacuated.

India's military High Command decided to regroup its forces on the Sela, a 4,170-metre-high mountain pass between Tawang and Bomdila. The Sela was considered NEFA's core defensive feature; as long as Indian forces held it, the PLA would not pass. For three weeks, the Sela indeed seemed impregnable. Yet on 18 November the safety valve disintegrated: Chinese troops had discovered a yak trail local herders used to avoid the difficult climb, and had simply bypassed the Sela. The bulk of Indian forces in the eastern sector were now encircled, and Bomdila under attack. It fell on the same day. The road to Tezpur in Assam – the road to India – was wide open.

The biggest shock was yet to come. On 20 November 1962, two days after conquering Bomdila, the PRC announced a unilateral ceasefire. In NEFA, its troops eventually withdrew north of the disputed border. But in the west, they had ousted India from the Aksai Chin plateau.[4]

---

[3] Dennis J. Blasko, 'Always faithful: The PLA from 1949 to 1989', in *A military history of China*, ed. by David Andrew Graff and Robin Higham (Boulder, CO: Westview, 2001), pp. 248–284 (pp. 250–254).
[4] Srinath Raghavan, 'A bad knock: The war with China, 1962', in *A military history of India and South Asia: From the East India Company to the nuclear era*, ed. by Daniel P. Marston and Chandar S. Sundaram (Westport, CT: Prager Security International, 2007),

Why did China go to war against India in 1962, and how could the latter have been so unprepared? In the years following the conflict, the answer seemed obvious enough: an expansionist, power-hungry PRC had betrayed India.[5] Such simplistic assessments have since given way to critical analyses of Delhi's foreign and military policies and, conversely, to an appreciation of Beijing's own threat perceptions.[6] Convinced that its new border posts were too small to provoke retaliation and that China would not risk American and Soviet intervention, the Indian leadership failed to see that the acceleration of military build-up could lead to open war.[7] Fraught civilian–military relations, multiple institutional failures, and a poor handling of intelligence reinforced India's complacency.[8]

China was in fact ready to attack. By mid-1962, the Sino-Soviet split was a distinct possibility, the Tawang crisis had stoked fears of invasion, and the United States was actively courting India, which also enjoyed good relations with Moscow.[9] The non-renewal of the Sino-Indian Trade Agreement of 1954 had led to a famine in parts of Tibet, and local Muslims were mobilising against PRC authorities.[10] Beijing felt that Delhi was trying, with Moscow and Washington's collusion, to grab extra portions of disputed territory while undermining PRC control over Tibet for its own benefit.[11] Domestic instability after the disastrous

---

pp. 157–174. For soldiers' and civilian officials' accounts, see John P. Dalvi and Frank Moraes, *Himalayan blunder: The curtain-raiser to the Sino-Indian War of 1962*, 2nd edn (Bombay: Thacker, 1969); Niranjan Prasad, *The fall of Towang, 1962* (New Delhi: Palit & Palit, 1981); D.K. Palit, *War in high Himalaya: The Indian army in crisis, 1962* (London: Hurst, 1991); K.P.S. Menon, *A diplomat speaks* (New Delhi: Allied Publishers, 1974); B.N. Mullik, *My years with Nehru: The Chinese betrayal* (Bombay: Allied Publishers, 1971).

[5] Margaret W. Fisher, Robert A. Huttenback, and Leo E. Rose, *Himalayan battleground: Sino-Indian rivalry in Ladakh* (New York: Praeger, 1963).

[6] Neville Maxwell notably accused the Indian leadership of having provoked China by refusing to renegotiate the McMahon Line's alignment and by pushing troops further and further into the Himalayas. Neville Maxwell, *India's China war* (London: Cape, 1970).

[7] Steven A. Hoffmann, *India and the China crisis* (Berkeley: University of California Press, 1990), parts 2–3.

[8] Yaacov Vertzberger, *Misperceptions in foreign policy making: The Sino-Indian conflict, 1959–1962* (Boulder, CO: Westview, 1984).

[9] Jian Chen and Kuisong Yang, 'Chinese politics and the collapse of the Sino-Soviet alliance', in *Brothers in arms: The rise and fall of the Sino-Soviet alliance, 1945–1963*, ed. by Odd Arne Westad (Washington, DC: Woodrow Wilson Center Press, 1998), pp. 246–284; Robert J. McMahon, 'U.S. policy toward South Asia and Tibet during the early Cold War', *Journal of Cold War Studies*, 8:3 (2006), 131–144 (pp. 139–141); Paul M. McGarr, *The Cold War in South Asia: Britain, the United States and the Indian subcontinent, 1945–1965* (Cambridge: Cambridge University Press, 2013), chapters 2–3.

[10] Sulmaan Wasif Khan, *Muslim, trader, nomad, spy: China's Cold War and the Tibetan borderlands* (Duke, NC: UNC Press, 2015), chapter 4.

[11] John W. Garver, 'China's decision for war with India in 1962', in *New directions in the study of China's foreign policy*, ed. by Alastair Iain Johnston and Robert S. Ross (Stanford, CA: Stanford University Press, 2006), pp. 86–130.

Great Leap Forward and Mao's tendency to envision the worst-case scenario exacerbated China's growing sense of vulnerability.[12]

A key dimension of the 1962 war has hitherto stayed buried, however. The conflict was preceded not just by military and diplomatic escalation between India and the PRC but by an older and increasingly tense shadowing contest to convince the eastern Himalayas' inhabitants that one state, and not the other, was the better alternative. Even before 1959, China and India's forced coexistence had led them to believe that the other side held irredentist views over the NEFA–Tibet borderlands, irredentism fostered through bio-politics. And the risk to see people vote with their feet was not theoretical: in China's Xinjiang, Kazakhs were fleeing en masse to the Soviet Union.[13]

The 1962 war did not halt China and India's tug of war for Himalayan people's allegiance and cooperation. In fact, it was its culmination. By invading NEFA, the PRC did not just aim to force a humiliated India to recognise its possession of the Aksai Chin. It also hoped to get, once and for all, the upper hand in their shadowing competition.

NEFA under Chinese Rule

On 23 October 1962, Tawang's military commander informed the PO that he would not be able to hold the town. Chinese troops were already at Bumla, and there were only two battalions to defend Tawang. The time had come to evacuate. As soldiers and officials abandoned northern Kameng, civilians braced themselves for the arrival of the PLA. 'What brutal treatment will be given to the inhabitants of NEFA by the Chinese' after the jawans' departure, worried Katon Borang, an Adi student.[14] Lt-Gen L.P. Sen, India's second most senior army official, had no doubt about the answer: 'white flag or no white flag, [the Chinese] would slaughter the whole lot, monks, Monpas and anyone else they found.'[15]

But when the civilian administration returned to Tawang after the war, they found no trace of such behaviour on the part of the occupant. Contradicting reports of its desecration, the PLA had left the Buddhist monastery intact. No women had been molested, no demands for porter-age had been made, and nothing had been taken without payment.[16]

---

[12] Allen Whiting, *The Chinese calculus of deterrence: India and Indochina* (Ann Arbor, MA: University of Michigan Press, 1975).

[13] M. Taylor Fravel, *Strong borders, secure nation: Cooperation and conflict in China's territorial disputes* (Princeton, NJ; Oxford: Princeton University Press, 2008), pp. 101–105.

[14] 'Letters to editor: Panic-stricken NEFA (by Katon Borang)', *Assam Tribune*, 25 October 1962.

[15] Prasad, *The fall of Towang*, p. 115.

[16] Oshong Ering. Interview with the author, 11 February 2014, Pasighat (Arunachal Pradesh); New Delhi, NAI, External Affairs Proceedings (1962), Return of civil

Dewatshang, the trader and former Chushi Gangdruk leader who had found asylum in NEFA, found his house completely undisturbed on returning to Bomdila after the ceasefire.[17] Far from subjecting NEFA's populations to countless atrocities as Indian decision-makers and public opinion had predicted, the PLA had shown remarkable restraint in the midst of a full-blown military assault.

In fact, Chinese troops did more than leave the population unharmed. During their occupation of NEFA, they 'deliberately adopted a policy of appeasement'. Monpas who had fled to the forest were told they could return, safe in the knowledge that their property would not be touched, their religion and customs respected, and their freedom of movement undisturbed. The PLA had only come to liberate them.[18] To show this was not mere propaganda, the occupant insisted on 'permitting the people of Tawang as well as other areas small freedoms and liberties ...', showering presents on [them ...], extolling the "easy and affluent" life under the Communist regime, ... [and importing] quite a large stock of fancy things'.[19] Tawang might be full of war debris, but it was also 'filled with memories of the Chinese' dancing with the locals.[20]

NEFA officials thought it particularly ominous that the PLA had not had recourse to compulsory labour, the practice at the heart of tensions between Indian authorities and local people. The Chinese had

made a demonstration of their attitude and approach to the tribal people; they have laid emphasis on the fact that they carry their loads themselves ... They have tried to demonstrate in other ways also that it is not their policy to lord it over the people as is sometimes the tendency amongst our officials.[21]

In contrast to their 'concerted efforts to woo and win the people',[22] invading troops had systematically destroyed, damaged, or removed what embodied or belonged to the Indian civilian government in NEFA. When the Dirang Dzong Officer returned to his offices after the war, he found

administration to NEFA, 49(4)/NI-62 (Rustomji note, 23 January 1963); Itanagar, APSA, NEFA Secretariat (1962), Fortnightly confidential report on NEFA for April, May, August, September–December 1962 (November and December reports).

[17] Kunga Samten Dewatshang, *Flight at the cuckoo's behest: The life and times of a Tibetan freedom fighter (as told to his son Dorjee Wangdi Dewatshang)* (Delhi: Paljor, 1997), p. 171.

[18] APSA, Fortnightly confidential report on NEFA for April–December 1962 (November report). Chinese troops did destroy some private property around Kibithoo, but only that belonging to people who had evacuated along with the administration. Malnourished Tibetan porters caught stealing local food supplies were immediately punished. Itanagar, APSA, NEFA Secretariat (1963), Relief and rehabilitation of evacuees in Lohit Frontier Division (Walong & Kibithoo areas), PCT-56/62.

[19] 'Chinese bait for Tawang people', *Assam Tribune*, 13 December 1962.

[20] Desmond Doig, 'Debris of war in Towang', *Statesman*, 1 February 1963.

[21] NAI, External 49(4)/NI-62 (Rustomji note, 23 January 1963).

[22] 'Chinese bait for Tawang people'.

them stripped bare of their belongings. The scene echoed that at the Tawang and Bomdila POs' residences: after serving as the PLA headquarters, they had been emptied of its furniture and works of arts, down to the curtains. The Bomdila PO even found explosives hidden in his chimney.[23] The Dirang hospital and dairy farm had had their wooden planks removed, the telephone poles on Kameng's main road had been uprooted, and expensive copper wire had been stolen. All governmentowned livestock in Bomdila had been eaten, and the Chinese had removed all engineering stores from Walong, including electric generators. Valuable equipment, such as medicines, blankets, and clothing, had been removed from Bomdila, as had been precious jewellery from the government-built monastery and museum. Mechuka, meanwhile, had lost its tables, its chairs, and its bicycles. Even Rabindranath Tagore's statue in front of the Bomdila Club had suffered its share of indignity: its nose had been chopped off.[24] An estimate spoke of Rs 2,500,000 of damages for Kameng alone.[25]

Through its wartime behaviour, China seemingly hoped to display its benevolence and state capacity towards native inhabitants. The PLA was trained as much in propaganda and political work as in military techniques. It was no coincidence that the Buddhist monastery built by the NEFA administration in Tawang was destroyed but the 'genuine' *gompa* left intact. Nor was the destruction of husbandry farms and electric structures, two key government schemes in border areas, random. By juxtaposing their solicitude to the population onto the violence, symbolic or real, meted out to the agents and the symbols of Indian state power, Chinese forces sought to prove that, whereas India was weak and could neither protect nor deliver to the population, the PRC not only could, but would do so.

The strength of the demonstration also lay in its embodiment in an aspect of frontier development both spectacular and vexing for Indian authorities: road building. Expanding transport infrastructure in NEFA had been a nightmare even after 1959. The Defence Minister had bitterly complained that the landslide-prone landscape resembled a nightmarish

---

[23] K.C. Johorey and Sudha Johorey. Interview with the author, 15 March 2014, Gurgaon (Haryana).

[24] NAI, External 49(4)/NI-62 (Confidential report, 25 January 1963); APSA, Fortnightly confidential report on NEFA for April–December 1962 (December report); 'Chinese troops near Senge Dzong', *Statesman*, 14 January 1963; Doig, 'Debris of war in Towang'; 'Chinese touch evident in Dirang', *Assam Tribune*, 6 January 1963.

[25] '3237 Indian prisoners still with Chinese', *Amrita Bazaar Patrika*, 20 February 1963. In Monigong and Mechuka, the Chinese reportedly carried away or destroyed Rs 1,500,000 of government property. *Lok Sabha debates 1963 (Volume XII)* (New Delhi: Lok Sabha Secretariat, 1963), pp. 5463–5464.

'chocolate pudding'.[26] By the time Indian officials returned to NEFA's border areas in early 1963, the PLA had left an enduring mark of its presence: new roads. North of Tawang, a shiny motorable segment of twenty-five miles led all the way to Bumla, close to the McMahon Line. The road from Tawang to Jang had been improved, a large bridge had been built on the Tawang Chu River, and another one repaired.[27] In one month, Chinese troops had succeeded in doing what Indian authorities had taken years to achieve. And they had done so without using tribal workers. As Rustomji 'drove almost up to Bumla without the least difficulty', his reflections were dark:

The Chinese must thus have impressed the tribal people of their competence in other fields than warfare. [They] will undoubtedly be making a comparison between the speed with which the Chinese have constructed this road and the comparatively slow progress of our own engineers.[28]

The PLA had not just humiliated India's military; it had shown it could build roads on 'chocolate puddings' at little cost for local inhabitants.

The end of the war did not end this demonstration of superiority. By announcing a unilateral ceasefire on 20 November, the PRC leadership projected military prowess and restraint. Two days after the announcement, 'the myth ... that Chinese troops were invincible in battle' was rushing through the Indian media like wildfire.[29] The implication was that Indian authorities had only been allowed back in NEFA thanks to China's magnanimity.

Having single-handedly decided the end of the conflict, China still had the upper hand. The immediate aftermath of the war was, it seems, carefully engineered to strengthen the comparison between the PRC's invincibility and India's comparative powerlessness and shallowness. Though the PLA proclaimed it would eventually retreat beyond the 'Line of Control' – in effect the McMahon Line – it pointedly delayed its departure, keeping the NEFA administration in the dark as to when and how far to return.[30] In practice, fighting continued: withdrawing Indian troops were fired upon.[31] General orders to return were only sent to the civilian

[26] Krishna Menon, *India and the Chinese invasion* (Bombay: Contemporary Publishers, 1963), p. 32.
[27] APSA, PCT-56/62 (Brief findings of Kibithoo tour by S.K. Kalra); P.B. Sinha and A.A. Athale, 'History of the conflict with China', ed. by India. History Division – Defence Department (New Delhi: Ministry of Defence, 1992) (p. 132).
[28] NAI, External 49(4)/NI-62 (Rustomji note, 23 January 1963).
[29] 'Chinese soldier: A robot in a padded coat', *Statesman*, 22 November 1962.
[30] 'Chinese lurk around Towang: Robbed foodbags on way to Tibet', *Amrita Bazaar Patrika*, 4 January 1963; 'Chinese continued to fire on Indians till December 3', *Statesman*, 25 December 1962.
[31] Sinha and Athale, 'History of the conflict with China' (pp. 375–376).

administration a week after the ceasefire and remained conditional.[32] When an apparent Chinese withdrawal was reported in Bomdila on 10 December, the civilian administration was barred from resuming its duties until armed police detachments had ascertained the absence of enemy troops. By 5 January 1963, the Indian flag was once again flying over Monigong in the Siang, but, on 17 January, Tawang was still occupied, despite a withdrawal announced for two days earlier. The local official only returned on 21 January, a full two months after the ceasefire.[33]

The PLA's presence remained palpable. More roads were being built close to the border, and the concentration of Chinese troops continued.[34] Some had retreated only a few miles beyond Indian administrative centres, over which they sent their planes. When the PO Kameng returned to Bomdila in mid-December 1962, the PLA was only twelve miles away, and its agents kept visiting the town. Indian police forces were instructed not to move around, lest they encounter obstruction.[35] In Dirang, Chinese troops stayed entrenched even as Indian soldiers were returning. They reportedly forced them to accept 'invitations' to their military camp for some supper, the jawans' pantries having been destroyed.[36] Indian intelligence services also feared that Chinese spies were still entrenched in NEFA.[37]

NEFA officials worried that the Chinese would find further ways to undermine their return, for instance by removing Indian equipment and possessions after officially handing them over.[38] As for prisoners of war, the PLA took its time to release them.[39] The evacuation of frontier officials had already dealt a blow to the façade of Indian sovereignty, and their ostensible failure to move back immediately after the PLA's departure, or to erase its shadow, only added cracks to the edifice. The disturbed circumstances of the NEFA administration's return and China's ostentatious watchfulness underscored India's lack of control, and hence of sovereignty, over the eastern Himalayas.

There was a final element to China's demonstration of superiority. Upon leaving the regions they had occupied, the PLA left a consistent message to NEFA's people: if negotiations with India failed, it would

---

[32] Itanagar, APSA, NEFA Secretariat (1962), Arrangements for relief accommodation for staff evacuated from Divisions, P/90/62 (wireless message, 28 November 1962).
[33] NAI, External 49(4)/NI-62 (AG to Foreign, 17 and 23 January 1963).
[34] 'Chinese massing in Tibet: More roads stab at Indian border', *Statesman*, 28 December 1962.
[35] NAI, External 49(4)/NI-62 (AG to Foreign, 30 December 1962).
[36] 'Chinese troops near Senge Dzong'.
[37] Sinha and Athale, 'History of the conflict with China' (p. 380).
[38] NAI, External 49(4)/NI-62 (Foreign to AG, 26 December 1962).
[39] '3237 Indian prisoners still with Chinese'.

return to liberate them.[40] 'Write and tell us if the Indians trouble you', departing troops reportedly told the Monpas after stressing India's military reverses. They even brought in a young Tibetan Lama to convince them that, 'in case they accepted the Chinese Administration', their religious practices and institutions would be respected.[41] Village chiefs were distributed weapons and equipment.[42] To these parting gifts, they added salt, cloth, and pictures of Mao. When the Tawang PO re-entered his ransacked residence after three months of exile, he found three abandoned soldier helmets awaiting him – dragons painted on them.[43]

War as Performance

The Sino-Indian war was not just a quick military conflict; it also resulted in the PRC's occupation, for several weeks if not months, of Indian-held territory. Looking beyond military history or diplomatic background to explore the behaviour of the PLA suggests a different picture of the war. By crushing its neighbour's 'illusions of grandeur', China had 'taught India a lesson', but not the obvious one.[44] The lesson was that it was the superior state, not merely the superior army – and it was primarily meant for borderland populations. For years prior to the war, Chinese and Indian authorities had used development schemes and the provision of welfare and trade facilities to undermine the credibility of the neighbouring state in the eyes of trans-border communities, to intimidate its representatives, and, most importantly, to tie the population on 'their' side of the border firmly to that territory and the local state. Yet by mid-1962, attempts to dissuade Himalayan populations from choosing the other state had gone awry. China and India were locked in a constant struggle to outdo one another. So PRC authorities resorted to another way to rehearse their greater state capacity: military invasion and temporary occupation.

War, then, was a performance, a demonstration meant for Indian leaders and public opinion, for international and domestic audiences, and, last but not least, *for the people living on either side of the McMahon Line.* The story it told was that of China's greater capacity and potential, and of India's corresponding weakness. PRC rule over Tibet was deeply

---

[40] APSA, Fortnightly confidential report on NEFA for April–December 1962 (December report).

[41] 'Chinese to lurk around Towang'.

[42] Sinha and Athale, 'History of the conflict with China' (p. 381).

[43] Doig, 'Debris of war in Towang'.

[44] Sarvepalli Gopal, *Nehru: A biography*, 3 vols (New Delhi: Oxford University Press, 1975–1984), Volume III, p. 230.

contested, and many exiles living in India dreamt of returning home triumphantly. For people on the Tibetan side of the border, China's wartime lesson was that India was not, and would never be, a viable alternative for them: how could it defend the Tibetans when it could not protect its own territory and abandoned its people?

The performance was also aimed at the people of NEFA. Occupation was meant as a window into the deficiencies of Indian rule, spelling out what its absence – and even, perhaps, permanent Chinese control – could mean for them. Through their magisterial handling of the war, benevolence, and promises to return as liberators should the inhabitants demand it, PRC authorities aimed to usher an anti-Indian resistance movement in NEFA. India's attempts to retake possession of the region would be greatly hampered, relieving China of its uncomfortable geographical promiscuity with India. PRC authorities' ideal scenario might even have gone further, envisioning a pro-China popular movement in NEFA – if not to annex the region, then at least to tie India's hands in the boundary issue. In short, the 1962 war was a dress rehearsal, experimenting and projecting a version of the future.[45]

One might object that this successful invasion ended with the PLA's unilateral withdrawal, but China had little to gain from staying in NEFA by force. If the eastern Himalayas are relatively easy to invade from the Tibetan plateau's elevated position, they are much harder to keep. The Indian army was now massing in the foothills. Besides, the PRC had overstretched its food and arms supply lines by going deep into NEFA.[46] Considering Tibet and China's food situation at the time, obtaining these supplies might not have been easy in the first place. It could only have gotten harder had the conflict lasted longer, and the PLA would have been unable to maintain its policy of not touching people's supplies.[47] Had it been able to stay, the PRC would likely not have done so without losing the reputation for invincibility and benevolence earned during the early stages of the conflict – yet this reputation was crucial to persuade NEFA's and Tibet's populations of its superiority.

Chinese authorities also had to reckon with the Cold War context. The Aksai Chin was empty and in any case linked to Kashmir, a territory disputed between India and Pakistan. It was important to

---

[45] Fiona McConnell, *Rehearsing the state: The governance practices of the exile Tibetan government* (Oxford: John Wiley, 2016).

[46] Sinha and Athale, 'History of the conflict with China' (pp. 155, 215, 373–375); G.S. Bhargava, *The battle of NEFA* (New Delhi: Allied Publishers, 1964), p. 116.

[47] New Delhi, NAI, External Affairs Proceedings (1961), Intelligence reviews from army headquarters, 5/9/R&I/61 (July report).

India, but not crucial.[48] NEFA was a much larger, and inhabited, piece of territory; given mainland India's already tenuous land link to Assam, control over it was vital for Delhi. Should the PRC seek to retain it through military might, it risked an unpredictable escalation that could cause the Soviet Union and the United States – who had just averted nuclear war during the Cuban Missile Crisis that October – to intervene. Nehru had made passionate calls for London and Washington's military assistance. Spotting an unforeseen opportunity to end India's non-alignment, Britain and the United States had promised deliveries of military equipment. By mid-November, their envoys were on their way to India.[49] Moscow, which had initially professed neutrality over the dispute, would soon declare its support for India's position. The PRC could not risk upsetting the Cold War status quo.

Above all, the invasion was meant to give China a definite upper hand in Himalayan state-making. Permanent military conquest was unnecessary in this context, and even damaging potentially. Crushing India's armed forces was sufficient to demonstrate to Tibet's populations that India could never be a safe or beneficial alternative. Conversely, a strategic but explicitly temporary withdrawal was necessary to preserve the fiction of Chinese benevolence towards tribal communities. It also maintained the PRC's image of a restrained power, giving it leverage in boundary negotiations with other neighbours, but also in post-war international mediation attempts with India.[50] The hope was arguably that this would settle the situation in Tibet while keeping the door to a pro-Chinese (or at least anti-Indian) movement permanently open. Beijing would secretly support precisely such resistance in nearby Nagaland, and elsewhere in north-eastern India, for the rest of the 1960s and early 1970s.[51]

---

[48] John W. Garver, *Protracted contest: Sino-Indian rivalry in the twentieth century* (New Delhi: Oxford University Press, 2001), chapter 3.

[49] Jian Chen, 'The Tibetan rebellion of 1959 and China's changing relations with India and the Soviet Union', *Journal of Cold War Studies*, 8:3 (2006), 54–101 (p. 98); Srinath Raghavan, *War and peace in modern India* ([Basingstoke]: Palgrave Macmillan, 2010), pp. 298–309; McGarr, *The Cold War in South Asia*, chapter 5. This failed to make India enter an alliance with Britain and the United States. Rudra Chaudhuri, 'Why culture matters: Revisiting the Sino-Indian border war of 1962', *Journal of Strategic Studies*, 32:6 (2009), 841–869.

[50] This is certainly how Beijing presented it to ambassadors from the Soviet block. 'Minutes of conversation between Chinese Vice Foreign Minister Zhang Hanfu and ambassadors from Socialist countries on Beijing's decision to unilaterally withdraw its forces (Original File: PRC FMA 109-03798-03, 11–14. Obtained by Dai Chaowu and translated by 7Brands)', *History and Public Policy Program Digital Archive* (21 November 1962) http:// digitalarchive.wilsoncenter.org/document/114775 (accessed 27 April 2015).

[51] Subir Bhaumik, 'The external linkages in insurgency in India's northeast', in *Insurgency in North-East India*, ed. by P. Phakem (New Delhi: Omeons Publications, 1997),

Moving Back In

Recourse to force had been a long-standing way of managing vulnerability on the part of China-based polities.[52] By orchestrating a limited but seamlessly executed conflict in their common borderland, the PRC aimed to get an unambiguous, permanent upper hand against its Indian shadow state. Prima facie, it had succeeded. India's armed forces had been military routed, and its frontier administration was in shambles. Across NEFA, dozens of administrative centres had been evacuated in the face of Chinese advance. Only Tirap had remained undisturbed. Most of the northern reaches of the Subansiri, Siang, and Lohit divisions had emptied out of their administrative staff, and in Kameng, the evacuation was almost total.[53] The exodus had continued even after the ceasefire.[54]

Condemned to wait on the sidelines for the end of Chinese occupation, the embattled NEFA administration had one opportunity to be proactive: relief. As the PLA swept through NEFA, thousands of inhabitants descended into the Assam plains; moving, temporarily or not, was an important strategy to sidestep or escape war in the region.[55] Faced with Tawang's impending fall, between 3,000 and 5,000 Monpas thus chose to leave their homes.[56] Thousands of Tibetan refugees fled as well. Three years after their first exile, the Dewatshang family was uprooted again. Others followed suit as the Chinese forced their way to Bomdila. Though officers tried to persuade the inhabitants to stay put,[57] streams of people came down from other parts of NEFA.[58] The inhabitants of Along and

---

pp. 89–100; Bertil Lintner, 'Missions to China by insurgents from India's Northeast', in *Indian and Chinese foreign policy in comparative perspective*, ed. by Surjit Mansingh (New Delhi: Radiant, 1998), pp. 433–438.

[52] Melvyn C. Goldstein and Gelek Rimpoche, *A history of modern Tibet, Volume 1: The demise of the Lamaist state, 1913–1951* (Berkeley: University of California Press, 1989); Philip A. Kuhn, *Origins of the modern Chinese State*, English edn (Stanford, CA: Stanford University Press, 2002); Charles Patterson Giersch, *Asian borderlands: The transformation of Qing China's Yunnan frontier* (Cambridge, MA; London: Harvard University Press, 2006); Hsiao-ting Lin, *Tibet and Nationalist China's frontier: Intrigues and ethnopolitics, 1928–49* (Vancouver: University of British Columbia Press, 2006); *The Chinese state at the borders*, ed. by Diana Lary (Vancouver: University of British Columbia Press, 2007).

[53] NAI, External 49(4)/NI-62 (AG to Foreign, 18 December 1962).

[54] New Delhi, NMML, APCC Papers (1957–67), Correspondence with government, Packet 30 File 14 (Bhagavati to Nehru, 14 January 1963), p. 190.

[55] James C. Scott, *The art of not being governed: An anarchist history of upland Southeast Asia* (New Haven, CO; London: Yale University Press, 2009), Chapter 5.

[56] Itanagar, APSA, NEFA Secretariat (1962), Rehabilitation of refugees in Kameng, CGA-207/62 (Minutes of the meeting at Bomdila, 27 October), pp. 9–10.

[57] Oshong Ering. Interview with the author.

[58] NAI, External 49(4)/NI-62; Itanagar, APSA, NEFA Secretariat (1962), Policy matters regarding the rehabilitation of evacuees, PCT-61/62; 'Exodus from NEFA continues',

Pasighat were flown down to Dibrugarh.[59] In total, an estimated 11,000 people evacuated.[60]

For civilian authorities this was a chance to demonstrate their enduring capacity to care for the population in spite of the defeat. Relief would alleviate India's relative weakness vis-à-vis China – say in military prowess or road building – by affirming its strength in the area in which its state capacity had historically been most efficiently embodied. The civilian exodus played to one of the relative strengths of the NEFA administration. It was in the context of post-earthquake relief operations that the first large-scale encounter with frontier populations had taken place in 1950. The resettlement of Tibetan exiles after 1959 had enhanced frontier officials' experience in these matters. Funds were specifically earmarked for relief and rehabilitation in the agency's budget.[61] This was the sort of crisis that India had experience in tackling.

No time was lost in launching relief measures. Authorities in Kameng, which bore the brunt of the assault, held an emergency meeting to organise help and shelter for people who were making their way down to the plains. Staging camps were organised on exit roads and transit camps established in the foothills, while evacuees were provided with free food rations, shelter, medical attention, and blankets.[62]

As the military crisis worsened, a general relief plan was devised. Transit camps in the foothills were reaching overcapacity and it was uncertain how far the Chinese would advance. To cope with the situation, the NEFA administration cooperated with the Assam government, which undertook to feed, clothe, accommodate, and transport all the evacuees to safe places.[63] Many were transferred to Guwahati, Nowgong, and other towns on the Brahmaputra's south bank, where they were mostly accommodated in school and college premises.[64] Several officials who had evacuated were appointed as *ex officio* liaison officers to spearhead the

---

Assam Tribune, 26 November 1962; 'Enemy agents active in Tezpur: NEFA tribals' painful trek to Assam plains', *Amrita Bazaar Patrika*, 29 November 1962.

[59] Barmati Dai. Interview with the author, 12 February 2014, Pasighat (Arunachal Pradesh); Oshong Ering. Interview with the author.

[60] NMML, APCC Papers Packet 30 File 14 (Bhagavati to Nehru, 14 January 1963), p. 190.

[61] Itanagar, APSA, NEFA Secretariat (1963), Rehabilitation of 48 families from Tezu Community Development Block affected by the Chinese aggression, PCT/44/63 ("PRE for 1963–64 and BE for 1964–65").

[62] APSA, CGA-207/62 (Minutes of the meeting at Bomdila, 27 October 1962), pp. 9–14.

[63] APSA, PCT-61/62, pp. 3–6.

[64] 'Relief of evacuees from Bomdila', *Assam Tribune*, 21 November 1962; 'Gauhati's warm reception to evacuees', *Assam Tribune*, 23 November 1962; 'More tribal evacuees from NEFA', *Assam Tribune*, 25 November 1962.

process; the rest of the staff was instructed to continue discharging their normal duties if possible, in addition to war-related tasks.[65]

To project the resilience of India's state capacity in spite of military discomfiture, authorities sought to recreate an atmosphere of normalcy and self-assured governance within the camps and in unoccupied parts of NEFA. Camps were supervised and manned by evacuee staff, if possible keeping them with the community of their posting. The Tawang arts and crafts centre had immediately reopened at Bomdila with the evacuated trainees; it then continued in transit camps. The administration took care to adapt food rations to people's taste and organised cinema shows and indoor and outdoor games within the camps; it also undertook a census to reunite families and villages.[66]

Even after the ceasefire, people kept arriving at transit camps on the edge of Assam.[67] Local officers had been instructed to tell the inhabitants that evacuating was a matter of personal choice but that, if they did choose to leave, the administration would commit to organise their rehabilitation outside of NEFA and bear the entire responsibility for it.[68] Given the general uncertainty about whether the conflict had really ended, Indian authorities began discussing the permanent resettlement of evacuees elsewhere in Assam and other mountainous parts of the country. Plans were made to resettle thousands of them in the Autonomous Districts of Assam, where they could reconstitute villages and find living conditions and constitutional protections similar to those they enjoyed at home.[69]

Chinese forces eventually deigned to give concrete signs of a withdrawal. Since the return of administration and the evacuees could now be countenanced, resettlement plans were abandoned. The time had come to move back in as quickly and as efficiently as possible, to repatriate evacuees, and to restore day-to-day administration.[70]

The problem was that, for all their efforts towards the evacuees, Indian officials had completely lost touch with a large proportion of the NEFA's inhabitants for weeks, if not months. The vast majority of the frontier's inhabitants – some 325,000 people – had remained where they were during the conflict. Apatanis and neighbouring Nyishis had refused to evacuate; several of their *gaonbura*s declared that, should the PLA come, they would fight back with their bows and arrows. Another group of

[65] APSA, PCT-61/62, pp. 3–6.
[66] APSA, CGA-207/62 (Minutes of the meeting at Bomdila, 27 October 1962), pp. 9–14.
[67] 'More evacuees pouring in', *Assam Tribune*, 27 November 1962.
[68] APSA, PCT-61/62 (Government of India, NEFA order), pp. 3–6.
[69] '15,000 Tribal evacuees come from NEFA', *Assam Tribune*, 28 November 1962.
[70] 'Return journey to NEFA starts', *Assam Tribune*, 3 December 1962; NAI, External 49(4)/ NI-62.

Nyishis came down to Charduar only to put their women and children into safety, before going back to defend their homes.[71] In the event, Chinese troops never came that far. But many of NEFA's people had directly or indirectly experienced Chinese state presence, and even more had witnessed the rushed departure of the Indian administration.

When frontier officials began making their way back to NEFA in mid-December 1962, it was therefore with understandable nervousness. Some worried that the civilian administration had withdrawn too fast, without waiting for a clear signal from the army.[72] In several places, notably in the Lohit Valley – where the Indian army had most successfully resisted – withdrawal had often seen the army destroy public property, such as bridges, lest it serve the enemy's purposes. Around Daporijo, this scorched earth policy had shocked the inhabitants.[73] Moreover, war had erupted after three years of upheaval, years during which militarisation had undermined the very foundations on which NEFA's inhabitants engaged with Indian authorities. In fact, the trade-off between agricultural production and porterage had worsened in the months prior to the war, threatening food sufficiency in several parts of NEFA.[74] In the circumstances, Rustomji and other officials had reason to fear they would not be welcomed with open arms.

And yet, when a government party reached Mechuka in early 1963, something different happened: 'people . . . came to us jumping and laughing and talked to us in the most amiable manner', reported a relived officer. 'They seemed to feel a great relief after the withdrawal of the Chinese. It is really gratifying that they . . . do not now have grievances against anybody. They do not go about complaining.'[75] In the Hrusso regions of southern Kameng, a junior officer also received, to his surprise, a good reception.[76] In Bomdila, the PO and his wife returned to find people waiting for them by the road.[77] Members of the Indian press – who had accompanied the couple – painted an atmosphere of enthusiastic welcome, where joy and relief mingled; the resumption of Indian administration was nothing less than 'the return of the parents to a child'.[78]

---

[71] APSA, P/90/62 (Telegram), p. 129.

[72] NAI, External 49(4)/NI-62 (Memo, 8 December 1962); APSA, Fortnightly confidential report on NEFA for April–December 1962 (December report).

[73] APSA, P/90/62 (PO Daporijo to ADGA, 20 November 1962).

[74] Itanagar, APSA, NEFA Secretariat (1962), Progress of construction work in Siang PC-127/62; Itanagar, APSA, NEFA Secretariat (1962), Fortnightly report – Agriculture and community development PC-38/62 (Raisinghani note, 20 September 1962).

[75] NMML, APCC Papers Packet 30 File 14 (Bhagavati to Nehru, 14 January 1963), p. 190.

[76] NAI, External 49(4)/NI-62 (Extract on re-entry into Buragaon).

[77] K.C. Johorey and Sudha Johorey. Interview with the author; B.G. Verghese. Interview with the author, 21 March 2014, New Delhi.

[78] 'Life smiles again in Bomdila', *Amrita Bazaar Patrika*, 1 February 1963.

One should be wary of such comforting narratives. Privately, government officials knew better than to take at face value any joviality displayed by the inhabitants. Returning from a tour of NEFA, a central government Minister reported that, for all the apparent goodwill, 'it will be also wrong to think that [people] have not felt it. A bad impression has, no doubt, been created. In a village near Pasighat one Adi cultivator told us that it was not proper for the people in authority to leave the people in those days of crisis.'[79] Rustomji had similar misgivings: 'the swift military success of the Chinese . . . has considerably weakened the confidence of the Monpas in our ability to protect them.'[80]

Indeed, the feeling that Indian authorities had abandoned the scene seemed widespread.[81] Why had they retreated from most of NEFA 'when there was no immediate danger to all the areas', asked some Adis? And why had the evacuation been so disorganised? At Karko in the Siang, the departing police unit had done such a good job of destroying their barracks that the village hospital caught fire. Elsewhere, it was a school and private houses that had been destroyed by BRO staff, yet tuskers had damaged really strategic equipment 'in such a perfunctory manner that the Adis could not accept it as a well planned scheme to put the Enemy in difficulty'. People also complained that the administration and the army had retreated without giving them the opportunity to participate in the resistance against the Chinese: they had not been offered a role in the military, let alone been given modern weapons.[82] Tuting's people had left their homes following an officer's warning that the PLA would bombard them, only to find themselves stranded in Yingkiong.[83] Beneath the outward 'welcome' then, other feelings were clearly at play (Figure 7.1).

An All-Too-Convincing Demonstration

Why did a majority of NEFA inhabitants accept the return of Indian authorities in 1962–1963 despite their disillusions and the PLA's good behaviour? In public, frontier officials stuck to a simple, comforting script: 'the spirit of NEFA is alive and astir in Tarun Bhattacharjee' and the people of Yingkiong, proclaimed Rustomji in an All India

[79] NMML, APCC Papers Packet 30 File 14 (Bhagavati to Nehru, 14 January 1963), p. 190.
[80] NAI, External 49(4)/NI-62 (NK Rustomji note, 23 January 1963).
[81] K.C. Johorey and Sudha Johorey. Interview with the author.
[82] NMML, APCC Papers Packet 30 File 14 (Bhagavati to Nehru, 14 January 1963), pp. 190–192. See also Nari Rustomji, *Enchanted frontiers: Sikkim, Bhutan, and India's north-eastern borderlands* (Calcutta: Oxford University Press, 1973), pp. 286–287.
[83] Oshong Ering. Interview with the author.

Figure 7.1 Indira Gandhi visiting Mechuka (Siang), 1963
© Arunachal Pradesh DIPR

Radio broadcast, and that, in turn, was because 'Mr Bhattacharjee speaks Adi like an Adi and has won the confidence and affection of the people'.[84] Yet in government reports and correspondence, Rustomji had his qualms.

Glowing, paternalistic reports of the Mishmis' or the Monpas' innate patriotism papered over the complex, ambiguous, and contingent reasons for which local inhabitants might envision the return of Indian administration. These were likely rooted in China's and India's competing yet substantively different state-making modes on the frontier, and their implications for the relationship between state and local society. The vision of the Chinese state that the PLA had projected during its

[84] Nari Rustomji, 'High praise for NEFA officers', *Statesman*, 28 December 1962.

occupation of northern NEFA was defined by military strength, if not invincibility; by extreme efficiency (in road construction); and by self-sufficiency (in fulfilling its food or labour requirements). By contrast, the Indian state appeared too vulnerable to either protect or provide for people.

The issue was that this did not have to be proven to NEFA's inhabitants. Vulnerability had defined the Indian state as it expanded in the 1950s, and people had accepted this expansion not in spite or in ignorance of this vulnerability, but partly because of it. It was vulnerability that prevented the Indian state from erecting itself as separate from local society and preserved the possibility for people's agency in accepting or manipulating when, how, and how far state penetration could go. And it was also vulnerability that enabled local communities to shape this state presence, and what it delivered.

The repression in Tibet further shaped people's assessment of the Chinese state. NEFA had been a major escape corridor for Tibetan refugees after 1959 – indeed the most important one. While the exiles often aroused the hostility of local tribes when they settled in their midst, their passage had exposed them to tales and evidence of the effects of Chinese rule.[85] The anguish of Katon Borang, the Adi student who had expected the worst from the PLA during the war, was rooted in his awareness of 'the inhuman treatment meted out to the Tibetans by the Chinese in recent years. It is a nightmare to the people of the area.'[86] That it was forced labour by Tibetans that permitted the PLA to build roads at breakneck speed must also have been apparent to some people at least. Just as second-hand knowledge of socialist reforms in Han regions had fuelled Khampa hostility against the PRC in the 1950s, NEFA's people had reason to question the PLA's display of benevolence.

The eastern Himalayas' inhabitants were not the helpless audience of China's dress rehearsal. Indeed, they had never been so at any point of its state-making competition with India. If a majority – though not all – decided to accept the returning Indian administration, it was likely because they had made their own interpretation of the Sino-Indian confrontation. And the conclusions they drew were not those hoped for by PRC authorities.

Arguably, the PRC's demonstration of invincibility, impeccable efficiency, and self-sufficiency had been *too convincing*. The benevolence

---

[85] Yeshe Dorjee Thongchi. Interview with the author, 8 February 2014, Itanagar (Arunachal Pradesh).

[86] 'Letters to editor: Panic-stricken NEFA (by Katon Borang).' Tibetan refugees were still entering NEFA in the months preceding the war. APSA, Fortnightly confidential report on NEFA for April–December 1962 (early October).

of such a strong state would depend on its leniency towards populations, not on its need to negotiate with them. Moreover, if occupation had shown local communities that China could deliver, and in very little time, it had also shown that they themselves had little control over what it delivered. The Indian state, by contrast, was fragile and imperfect: but its tensions, its vulnerabilities, its reliance on the population, and perhaps its focus on relief and rehabilitation offered more space to negotiate, criticise, and make demands.

In crucial ways, intended roles in the war performance – with Himalayan people as the audience, China as the hero, and India reduced to a bit part – did not work out. The audience actually took part in the rehearsal. Departing Chinese troops had insisted that, should the NEFA population wish so, they would come back to its rescue. Given its adversary's masterly demonstration in road-building matters and the powerless position into which it had been cornered, the odds seemed clearly stacked against India.

In this context, the fact that no popular unrest threatened the return of Indian authorities to NEFA after the war suggests that China lost the bet it had initiated. By attacking decisively, the PRC had hoped to dominate the state-making competition and conclude it to its advantage. Put differently, Chinese authorities wished to get rid of their Indian shadow state. Yet this concentrated test on how each country met their state-making and nation-building objectives backfired. China's grand rehearsal worked, but too well.

Should this not invite us to revisit the outcome of 1962? Viewed solely in terms of controlling strategic territory or settling the military aspect of the security dilemma in one's favour, the victory was unquestionably China's. India's military defeat could not have been clearer, and it shattered its leadership's confidence, destroying the non-alignment ideal and fundamentally undermining Nehru's own standing with public opinion and the state apparatus. The PRC also secured the Aksai Chin.

Yet, if the war really was an unambiguous disaster for India, why is it, as John Garver points out, that 1962 'remains China's forgotten war', hardly present in the literature published in the PRC? 'Is this because China's leaders feel that they miscalculated grossly in launching [it]?'[87] The answer is that, where the other goal of the war is concerned – resolving China's impossible coexistence with India – the PRC seemed to have tried and failed. Not only did popular resistance against Chinese rule in Tibet continue, but NEFA's people cooperated with returning

[87] John W. Garver, 'Review: India and the China crisis', *China Quarterly*, 129 (1992), 232–233 (p. 232).

Indian authorities. In that light, the narrative of the 1962 war as an unredeemable defeat for India suddenly loses its shine.

Mending the Wounds

This is not to say that India had won Himalayan 'hearts and minds'. There were strong signs that while the inhabitants of NEFA were ready to help returning Indian officials, their cooperation was conditional. Indian press reports celebrated the resumption of administration as the sign that local men and women could now 'continue their normal life, bearing the scar of the Chinese attack', yet a return to normalcy was hardly possible.[88] The restoration of administrative and development infrastructure to its pre-war conditions would not only take time, but, by its very nature, the conflict had radically altered the relationship between the Indian state and NEFA's inhabitants.

People had significantly contributed to the war effort. Many had sheltered and helped wounded or retreating soldiers; others had donated money, built airfields, cleared jungles, and knitted clothes for the armed forces. In the northern Subansiri, 2,000 Tagins – the same people the Indian press had characterised as bloodthirsty savages ten years before – had helped the army.[89] The wartime posters (see Figures 7.2 and 7.3), likely used for propaganda purposes among NEFA inhabitants after the war, depict various tribes tending to wounded jawans during the invasion. While the implication of candid patriotism is problematic, the depiction is comparatively more accurate than that in the second poster, which shows a sari-clad Mother India sheltering her tribal children from Chinese troops.

If people 'preferred' India over China in 1962, their criticism of the administration's wartime conduct and their emphatic tales of the PLA's good behaviour were implicit reminders that the preference was relative and far from settled. Indeed, it entailed a *commitment* on the part of the Indian state. Many strongly articulated how they understood this commitment. Returning officials were confronted with a long list of popular demands all across NEFA. These were not in themselves new. Tribals had long petitioned the administration with a variety of requests and representations – from demanding the reinstatement of a demoted officer whom they liked, to complaints about the quality of government-supplied

---

[88] 'Life smiles again in Bomdila'.
[89] NMML, APCC Papers Packet 30 File 14 (Bhagavati to Nehru, 14 January 1963), pp. 191–193.

Figure 7.2 Indian war poster no. 1, 1962
© Arunachal Pradesh DIPR / The British Library Board, Mss Eur D950/
86 (Colour Poster no. 3)

Figure 7.3 Indian war poster no. 2, 1962
© Arunachal Pradesh DIPR / The British Library Board, Mss Eur D950/
86 (Colour Poster no. 1)

rice and sugar.[90] But compared to the pre-war period, requests and petitions were far more varied, extensive, and precise.

Claims for wartime losses were among the first demands. Merchants wanted to be compensated for the loss of their mules, artisans for their tools, and villagers, in general, for their household goods, their damaged homes, their empty granaries. Long after the war, and notwithstanding bureaucratic tardiness, people continued to make claims for lost or damaged property to their local officials, sometimes individually, sometimes collectively.[91]

Relief and rehabilitation formed only part of more general demands. People requested communications adapted, and indeed meant, for local needs. Villagers specified the roads they wanted to see built or improved, demanded good airstrips and regular air services to the big administrative and population centres, and asked for phone and telegraph communications with Assam, as well as rapid mail delivery. Education constituted another key demand. Villages wanted subsidies or grants to build school buildings, free boarding and lodging for girls, allowances and stipends for staff children. Some demanded a geological survey and adequate facilities and implements for agricultural and weaving industries.[92]

Another widespread demand was that the Indian army recruit NEFA men, or at the minimum equip them with arms and ammunition to defend themselves. Equally strong were the calls for a reorganisation of the administration to increase popular control. People expressly demanded that their representative visit them more frequently and keep in constant touch.[93] Sections of the educated youth were rapidly organising, and some, like the Galo Students' Union, put the administration under increasing pressure to integrate its members into their ranks.[94] Some villagers took the initiative by rebuilding roads and bridge themselves, but the onus was now on India to improve its capacity to answer the aspirations of 'its' population for economic and educational well-being, as well as its greater participation in civilian and military administration.[95]

---

[90] Itanagar, APSA, NEFA Secretariat (1962), Tour notes of statistician Sup-4/99/62.

[91] APSA, PCT-56/62; Itanagar, APSA, NEFA Secretariat (1963), Chinese aggression – Compensation to Kameng staff and other people, PCT/47/63.

[92] NMML, APCC Papers Packet 30 File 14 (Bhagavati to Nehru, 14 January 1963), p. 194. See also 'Bomdila people's morale very high', *Assam Tribune*, 23 December 1962; K.C. Johorey and Sudha Johorey. Interview with the author.

[93] NMML, APCC Papers Packet 30 File 14 (Bhagavati to Nehru, 14 January 1963), p. 191. On the wish of some to join the Indian army, see Itanagar, APSA, NEFA Secretariat (1963), Recruitment of NEFA and Nagaland boys in the Indian army, GA/89/63.

[94] Itanagar, APSA, NEFA Secretariat (1963), Galo students conference at Along PLB-207/63; Itanagar, APSA, NEFA Secretariat (1963), Report on the Galo Students Union, GA-88/63.

[95] Oshung Ering, *The lingering memories* (Pasighat: Siang Literary Forum, 2005), p. 27.

NEFA officials keenly felt the need to respond to popular demands.[96] Their fear of losing legitimacy had been stoked by an incident at a place called Chayangtajo. When a police detachment had returned to this region of eastern Kameng in January 1963, local Bangnis killed them. Oral histories hint that the massacre had little to do with the war: Chayangtajo villagers had resented the local police's arrival in the region with the support of an interpreter from an enemy village.[97] But Indian authorities took it as evidence that the defeat had sowed seeds of political, pro-Chinese subversion. To erase the memory of Chinese soldiers carrying their loads themselves, argued Rustomji, Indian authorities would have to be 'equally radical, and reduce, if not eliminate altogether, our demands for porterage on the tribal people'.[98] His subordinates agreed. 'There is no doubt that if the welfare of the people and their whole-hearted support to the Government and loyalty is to be obtained, then we must bring a change in the administration setup in all the border areas.'[99]

Responding to popular concerns seemed all the more important given that the ceasefire had only meant the start of another Sino-Indian battle, diplomatic this time. At the Colombo Conference organised by the Non-Aligned Movement to discuss the dispute, PRC authorities vocally rejected the legal and topographical basis for the McMahon Line, and argued that that they had only attacked out of necessity.[100] In NEFA itself, PRC activities and propaganda across the McMahon Line retained their undermining potential.[101] In Huri in the Subansiri, where people felt left out of development schemes,[102] the administration even worried

---

[96] Available sources mention, without elaborating, that an incident was averted some time in 1963. New Delhi, NAI, Home Affairs Proceedings (1963), Appointment of a Security Commissioner, NEFA, 573(84)-63-NEFA (Yusuf Ali note, 6 September).

[97] An oral narrative explains that the Tajo clan chose to attack the local police battalion on 26 January 1963, on the first Republic Day after the end of the war. The rationale was that the force would be relaxing that day. Together with the villagers' skilful use of modern weapons, whose use they had mastered since 1959, the timing of the attack likely fuelled government interpretations of the incident as being a rejection of Indian rule. 'The Tajo CRPF battle at Chayangtajo', Story told to Rebecca Gnüchtel by Katuk Killo (with the assistance of Solung Sonam), July 2015. Available government sources are remarkably evasive on Chayang Tajo. See, for example, Itanagar, APSA, NEFA Secretariat (1963), Administrative pattern of NEFA – Reorganisation, PLA/32/66 (Memo 'Pattern of Administration in NEFA').

[98] NAI, External 49(4)/NI-62 (Rustomji note, 23 January 1963).

[99] APSA, PLA/32/66 (Note on upgrading the charges of the subdivisons of Tuting and Mechukha).

[100] New Delhi, NAI, External Affairs Proceedings (1963), Political reports (other than annual) from Peking, HI/1012(14)/63-II.

[101] New Delhi, NAI, Home Affairs Proceedings (1963), Administrative Pattern for NEFA, 573(16)-NI/63 (Minutes of the General Committee Meeting).

[102] AFSPA, PLA/32/66.

that people had been 'subverted by the Chinese'.[103] Finally, many officials felt a sense of debt towards NEFA's inhabitants.[104]

More than ever concerned with the quality of state–society relations and people's perception of India, NEFA authorities undertook several initiatives to generate 'beneficial political effects' in early 1963.[105] When they realised that people around Bomdila lacked even basic items after the war, they arranged special airlifts of salt and other essentials. They took steps to compensate tribes for any food eaten by the armed forces during the war, especially in areas that had helped civilian or military authorities. They granted house tax exemption in the areas subject to it, and they stepped up their pressure on the army to compensate for requisitioned land and property. *Ex gratia* relief was granted, for example for property damaged by the Chinese or looted. Other requests – such as the demand of Hrusso leaders to settle forty families in the foothills – were apparently considered favourably.[106]

Faced with central guidelines to limit compensation and relief, local officials again and again articulated the need to rehabilitate people for security reasons. 'It is the people who have been psychologically affected', wrote the Lohit PO in an attempt to get funds: 'Their confidence in us we must regain.' A few months later, he made a further plea: it was essential that Meyor evacuees, who had found their fields and granaries ransacked upon their return home, should be given free rations at least until March 1964. There would be 'serious political repercussions' if the Indian government refused, for '[t]he comparison of those looked after by the Chinese and those whom we urged to come down to the plains with us will be very unfavourable to us'.[107] Similar preoccupations led the administration to dispense political presents liberally during the tours of central politicians. So much so that, by the middle of 1963, funds earmarked for the purpose had been completely exhausted and more were requested.[108]

---

[103] Ibid. (Memo 'Pattern of Administration in NEFA').   [104] APSA, PCT-56/62.

[105] APSA, PCT-61/62 (T.S. Murty, Property losses during emergency, 23 July 1963), p. 171.

[106] NAI, External 49(4)/NI-62; Itanagar, APSA, NEFA Secretariat (1963), Compensation for use of cultivable land by the army, GA-98/63; APSA, PCT-61/62 (AG to POs January 1963, Property losses 23 July 1963, and Johorey to DC Darrang, 30 December 1962), pp. 157, 164, 171.

[107] APSA, PCT-56/62 (Issue of free rations to Walong & Kibithoo evacuees).

[108] Itanagar, APSA, NEFA Secretariat (1963), Relief and rehabilitation – Budget for 1963–64, PCT/48/63 (PO Siang to Assistant AG, 11 July 1963).

NEFA authorities knew that short-term solutions would not suffice. On the longer term, they tried to increase popular acceptance by accelerating development schemes, especially in border areas. They campaigned for scheduled flights between Assam and the various Frontier Divisions and went back on the imposition of stamp duties in NEFA, circumscribing them to a few urban areas and to specific goods only.[109] The Indian government also decided not to send back Tibetan refugees, most of whom had fled to Assam during the war, to the border regions where they had settled after 1959. Their presence near the McMahon Line not only seemed a security risk; it also angered local inhabitants – who, among other things, accused them of having looted their property during the war. Some, like the Dewatshang family, were allowed to remain at Bomdila and reopen their shops there. But most of the exiles were eventually resettled in Tirap or elsewhere in India.[110]

Indian authorities sought to display their ties with the people by adopting a much more proactive policy of employing them at various echelons of the administration and in the army. In the Siang, the administration organised pioneer forces and home guards after meeting with the Adi *kebang*s.[111] In regions where there were enough educated youth, measures were taken to appoint them as Base Superintendents, the start of a senior administrative career. Where this was not the case, appointing locals as fully fledged members of the administration was difficult, but given 'the rapidly moving tempo of events ... it might be undesirable to postpone delegating responsibility to our tribals'. To 'cut the ground from under complaints about devolution of power in NEFA being too slow', local notables were appointed as assistants to senior officers, with status and salaries equivalent to those of intermediate officials.[112] NEFA officials campaigned with central and military authorities to hasten tribal

---

[109] Itanagar, APSA, NEFA Secretariat (1962), Handing over notes of VV Mongia, PC/58/62; Itanagar, APSA, NEFA Secretariat (1962), Fortnightly report – Cooperative PC-38/62; AFSPA, PLA/32/66; Itanagar, APSA, NEFA Secretariat (1963), Operation of IAC service in NEFA, SIP/4/100/63; New Delhi, NAI, Home Affairs Proceedings (1962), Exemption from stamp duty of the tribals from NEFA, 40 (29-/62-NI).

[110] Dewatshang, *Flight at the cuckoo's behest*, pp. 170–174; APSA, PCT-61/62 (Telegram PO Bomdila to AG, 28 December 1962), p. 139; Itanagar, APSA, NEFA Secretariat (1963), Miscellaneous correspondence on settlement of Tibetan refugees in NEFA, PCT/12/63.

[111] NMML, APCC Papers Packet 30 File 14 (Bhagavati to Nehru, 14 January 1963), p. 192.

[112] Itanagar, APSA, NEFA Secretariat (1962), Appointment of tribal leaders as administrative officers, CGA-232/62.

recruitment into the armed forces, including if necessary by reducing the educational requirements in a context where few young men had yet benefited from a full education.[113] Finally, NEFA's first graduates were quickly promoted within the administration.[114]

The End of a Philosophy

In their effort to restore equilibrium in their relations with local inhabitants, NEFA authorities had to contend with another upheaval. Across India, the mood was of soul-searching. Who was responsible for the defeat, for the humiliation? Was it the former colonial authorities, like Olaf Caroe? Was it army leaders, like General Kaul, taken sick just before the war? Was it civilian authorities, like Krishna Menon, the hawkish Defence Minister? Was it intelligence officers, who had failed to appraise Delhi of the gravity of China's military build-up? Or even – dare one say it – Nehru himself?[115] And what about the smaller wartime debacles, like the frenzied (and unnecessary) evacuation of Tezpur in Assam?[116]

The controversy would last several decades. Indeed, it has not stopped. To many, it seemed that until 1959 the Indian state had remained culpably unaware of the existence of its north-eastern frontier; that it had taken the flight of the Dalai Lama and the Chinese seizure of Longju to wake up Delhi from its lethargy and force it to undertake a forward policy at breakneck speed; and that even this was too little, too late.[117]

The culprits for this vacuum were not hard to find: it was NEFA's civilian officials and their 'philosophy'. The Assam media accused Elwin and Rustomji of pursuing anti-Assamese, anti-national policies that kept

---

[113] APSA, GA/89/63; Itanagar, APSA, NEFA Secretariat (1963), Minutes of Senior Officers' Conference 1963, GA-69/63 (Luthra, 4 February 1964).

[114] Tokong Pertin, 'A tribute to "Head Makbo"', *Arunachal Times*, 7 May 2014.

[115] Caroe was taken to task over the non-concretisation of the McMahon Line after the Simla Convention. London, BL, Reid Papers (1959–63), Papers on the Naga independence movement and the dispute with China, Mss Eur E278/80 (Caroe to Reid, 7 January 1963). On the debate regarding civilian and military responsibilities, see Yaacov Vertzberger, 'Bureaucratic organisational politics and information processing in a developing state', *International Studies Quarterly*, 28:1 (1984), 69–95; Srinath Raghavan, 'Civil–military relations in India: The China crisis and after', *Journal of Strategic Studies*, 32:1 (2009), 149–175.

[116] Delhi, NMML, APCC Papers (1956), Sadiya District Congress Committee, 1955–56, Packet 23, File No.12.

[117] D.R. Mankekar, *The guilty men of 1962* (Bombay: Tulsi Shah, 1968); Lt-Gen B.M. Kaul, *The untold story* (Bombay: Allied Publishers, 1967); Prasad, *The fall of Towang*; 'Ex-IAF chief Tipnis blames Nehru for defeat in 1962 China war', *Times of India*, 20 November 2012.

NEFA militarily unprepared and isolated from the rest of India.[118] Reproaches fused from government and political circles. Ram Manohar Lohia, the socialist leader who had criticised the NEFA administration's Inner Line policy before the war, had finally been allowed on an escorted tour of the region after years of trying to enter the agency. He had come back with scathing remarks and radical proposals for its industrialisation, the eradication of shifting cultivation and 'social reforms'.[119] The agency's civilian authorities were taken to task over the evacuation and stood accused of harbouring a 'defeatist outlook', if not of being responsible for the 'low morale' and 'unreliability of the people', accused of collaborating with the occupant.[120]

While Elwin fiercely defended himself and his philosophy, Rustomji tried to tell his own version of the war, emphasising the heroism of the people and the staff.[121] For their part, POs objected to their negative characterisation. Yet, internally, frontier authorities knew that extensive changes had to be made. Not only did they have to answer the claim that they had not given due attention to nation-building and interaction between NEFA and the rest of India, they also felt that, insofar as a 'feeling of psychological separatism, if at all any', might reign in the region, it 'would only be as a result of our attitude and wrong approach'.[122]

Changing local patterns of government became a key concern. More than ever, the accent was on accelerating, and indeed completing, the consolidation of Indian state presence. Regions not yet explored or under firm control, like north-eastern Kameng or the upper Dibang Basin, were to be turned into independent subdivisions with their own officer and administrative staff. Border areas were upgraded into separate charges.[123] In an unusual joint session in mid-1963, NEFA and Assam officials agreed to cooperate more closely, to solve their boundary disputes, and to strengthen interaction between Assam and NEFA inhabitants.[124]

While officially still committed to the 'development of the people along the middle course', senior frontier officials decided to do away with the

---

[118] APSA, P/90/62 ('A policy vindicated'), p. 219; New Delhi, NMML, Verrier Elwin Papers (1963), Correspondence with Vishnu Sahay, 1963, S. No. 6 (Elwin to Sahay, 13 June).

[119] *Collected works of Rammanohar Lohia*, ed. by Mastram Kapoor, 9 vols (New Delhi: Anamika), pp. 113–123; New Delhi, NMML, Rammanohar Lohia (Roma Mitra) Papers (1963), Urvasiam se patra [Letter from NEFA], S. No. 1.

[120] NAI, Home 573(16)-NI/63; Mullik, *My years with Nehru: The Chinese betrayal*, p. 422.

[121] Rustomji, 'High praise for NEFA officers'.   [122] NAI, Home 573(16)-NI/63.

[123] AFSPA, PLA/32/66; NAI, Home 573(16)-NI/63; Itanagar, APSA, NEFA Secretariat (1963), Points for discussion by the PO Anini, GA-151/63.

[124] APSA, GA-69/63; AFSPA, PLA/32/66.

'philosophy' that Nehru, Elwin, and Rustomji espoused. Elwin died a year later in February 1964, Nehru just three months later. Rustomji was transferred to Bhutan. With NEFA now under military control, it was in Bhutan – whose king was a childhood friend – that he found scope to implement the 'hastening slowly' strategy.[125]

The time had come to accelerate all schemes, to boost agricultural production, and to cover NEFA with community development blocks and cooperatives, especially in border areas.[126] The decision was made to start harnessing the frontier's material resources that, to the exception of forests in the foothills, had largely been left unexploited.[127] Already in evidence by the early 1960s, the risk that changes in occupational patterns and educational levels would lead to a generational clash and drain the youth away from their villages was accepted. As for the cultural transformations that socio-economic change would bring, Indian authorities decided that they were unavoidable but that they would try to ensure the preservation of 'basic culture', until such time as tribals could revive the rest.[128] Core aspects of the NEFA Philosophy had been put to rest.

Nation-building received unprecedented importance. Under a Cultural Integration Scheme, the All India Radio launched expanded daily programmes 'purely meant for propaganda purposes among the rural folk of NEFA'. One of its segments included sending local inhabitants all the way to Shillong for a broadcast interview.[129] In border areas, a specific 'emotional integration' strategy was devised to counter PRC propaganda, from cinema and magic lantern sessions to the establishment of a special radio station. Gatherings and marionette shows ridiculing PRC leaders were regularly organised. People received medallions of prominent Indian personalities to compete with those of Mao in circulation.[130] Educational scholarships were granted to NEFA students wishing to study outside the agency, calendars began to display India's cultural and industrial achievements, and textbooks underlining Indian culture and history and NEFA's place in it were prepared.[131]

---

[125] Nari Rustomji, 'Bhutan Today', *Bulletin of Tibetology*, 3:2 (1966), 64–70.

[126] APSA, PCT-56/62; Itanagar, APSA, NEFA Secretariat (1963), Reorganisation of the NEFA Secretariat, ESTT/97/63; Itanagar, APSA, NEFA Secretariat (1963), Brief summary of activities of the administration during 1963, GA/207/63.

[127] Itanagar, APSA, NEFA Secretariat (1963), Establishment of tea estate in NEFA, PC/81/63; Itanagar, APSA, NEFA Secretariat (1963), Mineral Advisory Board, PC/62/63.

[128] NAI, Home 573(16)-NI/63 (Minutes of the General Committee Meeting).

[129] Itanagar, APSA, NEFA Secretariat (1963), Cultural Integration Scheme, R-6/63. (PC Dutta note, 22 January).

[130] NAI, Home 573(16)-NI/63 (Minutes of the General Committee Meeting).

[131] APSA, GA-69/63 (Speech by the Assam Education Minister); London, BL, Elwin Papers (1958–63), NEFA calendars, Mss Eur D950/85; Itanagar, APSA, NEFA

While the pre-1959 NEFA Philosophy rested on an artificial divide between the tribal and the non-tribal and between hills and plains, the post-1962 turn towards 'emotional integration' had its own puzzling elements. By the late 1960s, NEFA officials would be so keen 'to re-establish and strengthen the fact that historically and culturally [tribals] belong to India' that they would see India everywhere in their lives. Nyishi and Apatani dress styles would be deemed the exact replica of that of Rama and Lakshmana in the Ramayana, and the Noctes of Tirap identified as the lost cousins of South Indian priests – courtesy of a similar hairstyle. The goal of government research became 'to find out such similarities and try to identify the people, their religion and culture with the rest of the country'. This instrumentalisation would have momentous consequences on NEFA's religious landscape: Indian authorities would argue that local beliefs and practices needed to be 'improved', largely by the means of making them more like Hinduism.[132]

Sovereignty over People, Sovereignty over Territory

And yet, more than ever before, civilian state-making and nation-building had to contend with militarisation. In the post-war climate, central authorities launched decisive attempts to modernise their armed forces and reinforce their military presence in the Himalayas. The full militarisation of NEFA was deemed of the upmost priority. Soon after the invasion, civilian authorities lost control of the Assam Rifles, placed under the army's operational control, and a special NEFA Security Commissioner was appointed to liaise with the army and deal with security matters.[133] The 'disarmament' of frontier administration that had taken place after Achingmori ended, as many officers began once again to use armed escorts.[134] Militarisation and the drive to canvass the entire border led to the end of another old principle, that of not settling non-tribals in NEFA. Vijaynagar, a finger-shaped territory wedged into Burma, was settled with jawans.[135] Chakma and Hajong tribal refugees

Secretariat (1963), Papers to the Special Committee, Textbook (Minutes, 19 March 1969).

[132] Itanagar, APSA, NEFA Secretariat (1962), Policy directives issued by NEFA administration, R-36/62 (Minutes of the first meeting of the Research Forum, 17 January 1968).

[133] Mullik, *My years with Nehru: The Chinese betrayal*, pp. 480–483; New Delhi, NAI, Home Affairs Proceedings (1969), Passing of operational control of Assam Rifles deployed in NEFA from the army to the civil authorities, 13/25/69-PVII; NAI, Home 573(84)-63-NEFA.

[134] NMML, Elwin Papers, S. No. 6 (Elwin to Sahay, 6 August 1963).

[135] The administration had so far always rejected settling the frontier with soldiers. New Delhi, NAI, Home Affairs Proceedings (1963), Agricultural settlements in NEFA, 210(11)/63-NEFA; NAI, Home 573(16)-NI/63.

from East Pakistan (Bangladesh) were resettled in the lower hills of
NEFA. Towns like Bomdila became dominated by bunkers and
cantonments.[136]

In 1965, the primacy of the Indian state's military presence was underpinned by NEFA's transfer to the Home Ministry. Seven years later,
central authorities reaffirmed their plan to retain control over the region:
in 1972, NEFA was renamed Arunachal Pradesh and became a Union
Territory. Much to the anger of Assamese leaders, the region formally
ceased to be part of Assam. Central control continued even after
Arunachal Pradesh's transformation into a state, in 1987. Political and
administrative power continues to lie not so much with the elected state
government as with an informal nexus headed by Home Ministry authorities, working with the army and other military, police, and intelligence
units. Development remains subordinate to strategic imperatives.[137]

As in the early 1960s, militarisation destabilised the civilian administration's attempts to repair and protect its reputation among the inhabitants. NEFA officials, who felt the victims of second-rate treatment
compared to the armed forces, had to find ways to rehabilitate war-
affected people and promote development without treading on the army's
toes.[138] Mishmis already uprooted in the mid-1950s to form more manageable 'compact' villages were barred from going home after the
war: their land had been permanently requisitioned for defence purposes.
When the Adviser to the Governor visited them, they forcefully voiced
their need for governmental assistance to rehabilitate themselves once
and for all, but the civilian administration's subsequent requests for funds
to help them were curtailed.[139]

Cross-border interaction became more and more difficult. Military
build-up intensified, Indian authorities began to actively discourage interaction with trans-McMahon Line areas, and inhabitants who still insisted
on it had to get special permission from military and intelligence
authorities.[140] Entrenched habits and traditions, such as families' seasonal migration between Tawang and Tsona, became a thing of the past.[141]

[136] Yeshe Dorjee Thongchi. Interview with the author.
[137] Sanjib Baruah, *Durable disorder: Understanding the politics of northeast India* (Oxford:
Oxford University Press, 2007), p. 63.
[138] Itanagar, APSA, NEFA Secretariat (1963), Matters relating to the study of NEFA
students COOP/16/63.
[139] APSA, PCT/44/63.
[140] Alexander Aisher, 'Through "spirits": Nyishi tribal cosmology and landscape ecology in
Arunachal Pradesh, Northeast India' (unpublished doctoral thesis, University College
London, 2005), p. 67.
[141] Interview with Karma Wangdu (Interview #46M). Interviewed by Rebecca Novick on
13 April 2010 (held at the Tibet Oral History Project), www.tibetoralhistory.org/inter
views.html (accessed 27 January 2015). Some small-scale cross-border movement

Insofar as it forcibly separated communities on either side of the border and imposed an economic stranglehold on some of them, NEFA's civilian authorities had reason to worry about its effect on the state–society relationship – especially since, insofar as attempts to expand local infrastructure networks accelerated, they prioritised military needs. Fearful that the presence of roads close to the border would help China mount another invasion, the Indian Defence Ministry forbade their construction in the vicinity of the McMahon Line.[142] Taken for purely military purposes, the policy flew in the face of the desire expressed by border people for roads that would give them access to goods, benefits, and interaction with what was now to be 'their' world, India.[143] Thus, and although the process remains unclear for want of information, one may talk of an overall 'closure' of the Sino-Indian border after 1962 – though not an absolute one.

In the three years before the war, development-centric attempts to strengthen Indian state presence in NEFA had perforce contended with a novel strategy, militarisation. The defeat against China caused the latter logic to prevail, fully subordinating the civilian administration's activities to defence imperatives. The shift betrayed and heightened local tensions between two aspects of sovereignty: control over territory and control over people.

Traditional understandings of sovereignty as the 'unlimited and indivisible rule by a state over a territory and the people *in it*' not only tend to fetishise territoriality and the state; they also suppose that sovereignty over people proceeds from sovereignty over territory.[144] But in Tibet and the Himalayas, the reach of a given polity historically hinged on the subjects it controlled far more than on a territorially demarcated authority. It was for that reason that Monpa migration to Bhutan had so angered the Dalai Lama's government: Lhasa's rule stemmed from its ability to extract corvée labour.

Outwardly, the twentieth-century Indian state subscribed, like the Chinese one, to Western notions of sovereignty emphasising territorial control; but in practice, state agents long prioritised the achievement of

---

continues, however. Stuart Blackburn, 'Memories of migration: Notes on legends and beads in Arunachal Pradesh', *European Bulletin of Himalayan Research*, 25/26 (2003–2004), 15–60 (p. 19 and footnote 22).

[142] Itanagar, APSA, NEFA Secretariat (1963), Construction of important border roads in the NEF Agency, PC/130/63; AFSPA, PLA/32/66.

[143] Yeshe Dorjee Thongchi. Interview with the author; B.G. Verghese. Interview with the author.

[144] John Agnew, 'Sovereignty regimes: Territoriality and state authority in contemporary world politics', *Annals of the Association of American Geographers*, 95:2 (2005), 437–461. Emphasis added.

authority over people in the eastern Himalayas. Colonial officials had felt that the best way to enshrine British Indian sovereignty against Qing China was to ensure that the Mishmis or the Adis would have no 'intercourse with any Foreign Power other than the British Government', not to assume the actual administration of the region. Their successors in independent India too prioritised rule over people: tribal cooperation was a prerequisite for effective territorial control. And given that agency, the problem with China seemed more that it would draw locals in than that it would invade. Development and welfare schemes were more effective a strategy to bind people to the Indian state, and ultimately to bring about its territorial consolidation, than the stationing of troops at the border.

In other words, the 1950s appear as a period of vacuum in NEFA only if one restricts understandings of state power to military might. Moreover, insofar as militarisation was not the path taken in the eastern Himalayas at the start of India's independence, responsibility for the decision lay as much with the then defence establishment's disinterest in the region as with civilian frontier authorities.

At first glance, the scale of India's military defeat in 1962 shows that this decision was a fateful mistake. But let us envision the alternative: what would military build-up have achieved in NEFA, had it happened as soon as the PRC had annexed Tibet? It is not sure, to begin with, that this would have been sufficient to guard India against a Chinese military assault. Indeed, it might even have provoked an attack earlier. And even if a defeat of the scale of 1962 could have been averted through early militarisation, the cost of such a policy in terms of state–society relations would have been extremely high. (One need just think of the tensions that followed the arrival of the Indian army in 1959.) So high indeed that it could have prevented civilian Indian authorities from achieving the requisite measure of acceptance amongst the eastern Himalayas' inhabitants – and have made them open to supporting the Chinese.

Conclusion

The aim of this book was to suggest new ways to think about contemporary Sino-Indian relations, bringing to the fore the competitive dimension of Indian and Chinese state-making at the border and the role of the Himalayas' inhabitants in shaping them. Further research would help us better understand these processes. Should local-level sources for the Chinese side of the border become available, the specificities of PRC state-making in the border counties of today's Nyingchi and Shannan prefectures in the Tibetan Autonomous Region may be recovered with more precision than has been possible here. Greater accumulation of detailed ethnographic work on specific areas of Arunachal Pradesh would help delineate the micro-level politics at play in the eastern Himalayas – too often construed in binary national terms – and bring to the fore the inhabitants' own worldviews and perspectives. Finally, further research on how the low politics of Sino-Indian relations evolved-after 1962 would also be crucial.

The Persistence of State Shadowing?

Prima facie, escalation might seem less of a risk today than in the 1950s and 1960s, for India and the PRC have never again gone to war with one another. India continues to claim the Aksai Chin and China to call Arunachal Pradesh 'South Tibet' but, when a military clash occurred in 1987, they took pains to stop its escalation.[1] Armed stand-offs have occurred several times since then in the Himalayas yet have not been allowed to degenerate.[2] Various mechanisms have been put in place from the 1990s onwards to ensure this, from a 1993 Agreement on the

---

[1] Steven A. Hoffmann, *India and the China crisis* (Berkeley: University of California Press, 1990), pp. 232–233.
[2] Shishir Gupta, 'China, India in border skirmish ahead of Xi visit', *Hindustan Times*, 16 September 2014.

Maintenance of Peace and Tranquility along the Line of Actual Control to joint exercises in Ladakh.[3]

This prudence has much to do with China and India's need for one another. With booming economies and the world's two biggest domestic markets, their potential for economic exchange and partnership is vast, leading to a 'cooperation-cum-competition' dynamic.[4] Restraint despite continued military build-up and regular 'incursions' also betrays the lessons learnt, on both sides, from the 1962 war. Indian authorities embarked on a long-term plan to modernise and strengthen their armed forces after the conflict, but they likely do not wish to risk another military defeat: China retains its locational advantage and it still benefits from much better infrastructure in border areas.[5] For their part, PRC authorities might have learnt that while military victory secured them the Aksai Chin, war is not as malleable a state-making tool as thought.

Time, along with the war, has deepened the division of the eastern Himalayas into two halves. The erstwhile NEFA has become a full-fledged state: Arunachal Pradesh has its own capital and bureaucracy, headquartered in the specially created town of Itanagar. Hindi is now the lingua franca, and locals take advantage of the economic and educational opportunities offered in so-called 'mainland' India. Trade networks have been redirected away from Tibet – as authorities had hoped to do prior to 1962.[6] On the other hand, recent ethnographic work shows that the Indian army has progressively found a *modus vivendi* with Arunachal's inhabitants.[7]

This growing divide across the McMahon Line is accentuated by the gradual depopulation of border areas close to it. Many local communities

---

[3] 'Agreement on the Maintenance of Peace and Tranquility along the Line of Actual Control in the India–China Border Areas', 07 September 1993, http://peacemaker.un .org/chinaindia-borderagreement93 (accessed 2 April 2015); 'Laddaakh men bhaaratiya–ciin senaa ka pahla sanyukt abhyaas [First India–China military exercise in Ladakh]', *Dainik Jagran*, 8 February 2016.

[4] David M. Malone and Rohan Mukherjee, 'India and China: Conflict and cooperation', *Survival*, 52:1 (2010), 137–158; Jonathan Holslag, *China and India: Prospects for peace* (New York; Chichester: Columbia University Press, 2010).

[5] Abheet Singh Sethi, '82 Per cent of strategic roads along Sino-Indian border unfinished', *Economic Times*, 29 June 2015.

[6] Alexander Aisher, 'Through "spirits": Nyishi tribal cosmology and landscape ecology in Arunachal Pradesh, Northeast India' (unpublished doctoral thesis, University College London, 2005), p. 67. On politics and the re-diversion of Himalayan trade networks, see Tina Harris, *Geographical diversions: Tibetan trade, global transactions* (Athens: University of Georgia Press, 2013).

[7] Pallavi Banerjee and Xiangming Chen, 'Living in in-between spaces: A structure-agency analysis of the India–China and India–Bangladesh borderlands', *Cities*, 34 (2013), 18–29; Swargajyoti Gohain, 'Imagined places: Politics and narratives in a disputed Indo-Tibetan borderland' (unpublished doctoral thesis, Emory University, 2013).

had been socio-economic intermediaries between the plateau and the lower Himalayan slopes. Since the 1960s, their status and well-being have suffered from the loss of connections to Tibet, even as military-centric decisions have kept their areas logistically cut off from India and sidelined from development priorities – in stark contrast to the civilian administration's pre-war strategy. Indian authorities now fear that if they cannot stall it, this depopulation of border areas will fuel Chinese territorial infiltration.[8]

In Tibet, Chinese authorities have cancelled the 'tyranny of distance' that once hampered their rule. Railways, roads, and airports now reach all the border regions. Re-baptised Medog County, Northern Pemakö was the last part of the PRC without highway connections; the 2013 inauguration of a highway has ended this. Border regions and troops can now easily be supplied and monitored. Heavy immigration from Han-inhabited parts of China has been taking place.[9]

And yet, competitive state shadowing may be far from over in the eastern Himalayas. Well into the twenty-first century, the PRC faces intense popular resistance to its occupation of Tibet. Two to three thousand Tibetans flee to India every year.[10] As for India, enthusiastic claims that the 'Arunachalis' feel fiercely, unambiguously Indian are put in doubt by ethnographic research. The cooperative attitude of Tawang's inhabitants towards India appears pragmatic in nature.[11] Complaints continue to be voiced about the Indian state's failure to provide consistently and fairly for its citizens. 'From many places on the Indian side of the border', Arunachal's inhabitants can observe 'China's well-built concrete barracks, with roads connecting many of their border outposts'[12]. The sight makes the comparative underdevelopment of such transport and communications infrastructure all the more jarring for border inhabitants, frustrated by the consequent lack of health care, education, and trade facilities – and more generally in need of interaction with the

---

[8] Kerstin Grothmann, 'From a dominant power to a "Backward Tribe": The effects of Indian territoriality on Memba society of Mechukha' presented at the 4th Conference of the Asian Borderlands Research Network (December 2014); Sanjib Kumar Baruah, 'Govt to curb migration from areas near China', *Hindustan Times*, 27 June 2015; Nitin A. Gokhale, 'Why villages along China border need urgent attention', *ABP Live*, 27 June 2015.

[9] June T. Dreyer, 'Economic development in Tibet under the People's Republic of China', *Journal of Contemporary China*, 12:36 (2003), 411–430.

[10] Conservancy for Tibetan Art and Culture (CTAC), 'North American Tibetan community cultural needs assessment project: Findings and recommendations', (c. 2002) www .tibetanculture.org (accessed 7 June 2013).

[11] Banerjee and Chen, 'Living in in-between spaces'.

[12] Ajay Shukla, 'The Dalai Lama visit: New Delhi's message to Tawang', *Business Standard*, 14 November 2009.

rest of the world.[13] Finally, the post-1962 strategic settlement of civilians from outside NEFA in the region is causing worrying ripples in today's Arunachal Pradesh: the Indian Supreme Court's decision to grant citizenship to Chakmas and Hajongs (refugees from Bangladesh who were resettled in NEFA from the mid-1960s) has caused uproar and widespread mobilisation in the state.[14]

Indian authorities appear mindful of these tensions. The 2015 decision to grant Scheduled Tribe status to the Lisus of Vijaynagar was reportedly taken because central security authorities feared that unless they were heard, the community would be 'co-opted' by China – which continues to support Naga insurgents in north-east India.[15] A similar thought might have caused Delhi's quick U-turn on its decision to give special powers to the army in Arunachal's border districts with Assam, after local politicians and civil society organisations vocally protested.[16]

All this suggests that the friction of co-existence between China and India has evolved rather than disappeared – and that more research on the topic is therefore needed. Embedded as they are in multiple interactions, including cross-border ones, state-making and nation-building can never be linear, nor fully achieved, particularly in supposedly 'post-colonial' borderlands such as the eastern Himalayas. Instead, they are always at risk of unravelling and hence permanently in need of re-enactment.[17] The presence of the 'other country', the shadow state, gives local inhabitants a measure of leverage against state authorities – for instance in demanding autonomy.

This inchoate nature of state-making and nation-building is reinforced by the trade-offs and structural tensions that characterise these processes –

---

[13] Ishaan Tharoor, 'Beyond India vs. China: The Dalai Lama's agenda', *Time*, 5 November 2009; Jabin T. Jacob, 'The Sino-Indian boundary dispute: Sub-national units as ice-breakers', *Eurasia Border Review*, 2:1 (2011), 35–45 (p. 39).

[14] 'Arunachal people express dismay over SC verdict on Chakmas & Hajongs', *Northeast Today*, 26 September 2015.

[15] 'Long wait ends, Yobin's [*sic*] accorded ST status', *Arunachal Times*, 31 March 2015; Bertil Lintner, *Great Game east: India, China, and the struggle for Asia's most volatile frontier* (New Haven, CT: Yale University Press, 2015).

[16] 'Centre bows to pressure from Arunachal Pradesh, modifies AFSPA order', *Times of India*, 12 May 2015.

[17] On the networked, fragmented, relational nature of sovereignty, see for instance: Arjun Appadurai, 'Sovereignty without territoriality: Notes for a postnational geography', in *The geography of identity*, ed. by Patricia Yaeger (Ann Arbor, MI: University of Michigan Press, 1996), pp. 40–58; Stephen D. Krasner, 'Rethinking the sovereign state model', *Review of International Studies*, 27:5 (2001), 17–42; James Sidaway, 'Sovereign excesses? Portraying postcolonial sovereigntyscapes', *Political Geography*, 22:2 (2003), 157–178; John Agnew, 'Sovereignty regimes: Territoriality and state authority in contemporary world politics', *Annals of the Association of American Geographers*, 95:2 (2005), 437–461; Fiona McConnell, '*De facto*, displaced, tacit: The sovereign articulations of the Tibetan government-in-exile', *Political Geography*, 28 (2009), 343–352.

particularly in a context of finite state resources. Expanding towards the border as fast as possible, or consolidating state presence in more populated areas? Extracting revenue, labour, and resources, or forgoing them to avoid generating popular resistance? Putting the army in charge to secure the territory militarily, or minimising the state's coercive potential to ensure its acceptability? Banning trade and interaction across a new international border, or accepting it for the sake of precious intelligence? Building roads to abolish terrain and distance, but with what workforce – an imported one that would leave indigenous inhabitants feeling flooded, or a local one that would put too much pressure on communities' capacities? And then, building roads for whom: to help the military canvass territory, or to serve the needs of populations for economic and social interaction?

The paradoxical nature of the Chinese and Indian states, at once postcolonial and imperial, further increases the anxieties arising from state–society dynamics. Marked by the trauma of colonial subjugation, India and the PRC cannot conceive of imposing anything but the most absolute form of sovereignty and control in the Himalayas – even as the latter has been shown very difficult to achieve.[18] Yet it is precisely this absolutism that renders coexistence impossible, especially as it hinders visions of the Himalayan borderlands that, by accepting or even embracing local dynamics, could make for fewer tensions.[19]

As India and the PRC proclaim to work on their border dispute, speculation on the possibility of a resolution has been rife for years – largely on the assumption that the territorial status quo will just be officialised. But some analysts point out that resource-hungry China needs Arunachal far more today than in the 1950s, given the region's wealth in natural resources. This notwithstanding, it is not certain that solving the boundary dispute will enable China and India to coexist peacefully, as long as they retain their imperial nature in their common borderland. Tensions might persist, not merely because of China and India's geopolitical rivalry in the Asia-Pacific but also because mutual shadow state anxieties remain.

In fact, a new security dilemma has potentially emerged between India and the PRC in the twenty-first century, with significant risks for their relationship with the people of the eastern Himalayas. Faced with booming economies and growing water shortages, the two countries eye with appetite the tremendous hydraulic resources of the region, Asia's 'water

---

[18] Manjari Chatterjee Miller, *Wronged by empire: Post-imperial ideology and foreign policy in India and China* (Stanford, CA: Stanford University Press, 2013).

[19] Jacob, 'Sub-national units as ice-breakers'.

tower'. The Tsangpo-Brahmaputra is not among the world's longest rivers, but it is certainly one of the most powerful: only the Amazon and the Congo discharge more sediments.

PRC authorities are now building dams on the Tibetan plateau, upstream of South Asian countries. The first of several dams on the Tsangpo's Great Bend was completed in late 2015. Even more anathema to India, Chinese leaders dream of redirecting the Tsangpo to flow east into the Yangtze.[20] Meanwhile, Indian authorities are racing to dam their section of the eastern Himalayas, hoping not just to harness the untapped hydroelectric potential of Arunachal's rivers – the greatest in India – but also to reinforce their rights to them against China. A hundred-and-sixty or so memoranda of understanding to build dams in Arunachal have been signed.[21] In a context where legal regimes surrounding the use and sovereignty over international watercourses remains blurry, the China–India dynamic has acquired another factor of instability.

Whether or not China and India can concretise their hydraulic ambitions, their attempts to do so will remodel the very geography and environment of south-eastern Tibet and the eastern Himalayas. The consequences on biodiversity, on forest cover, on seismic risks, on sacred geographies, on the availability of agricultural (or indeed merely inhabitable) land, could be drastic. Many civil society organisations in Assam and Arunachal Pradesh are now actively mobilising against dams, whose benefits would mostly accrue to other parts of India.[22] Growing deforestation due to the timber industry might further fuel discontent.[23] For the PRC, this could exacerbate popular resistance to its rule over Tibet. For India, which has comparatively faced far less opposition to its incorporation efforts since 1962, the shift towards an extraction-centric policy could well endanger the status quo of state–society relations in Arunachal – especially if it takes the shape, as in Tibet, of disempowered

---

[20] Kenneth Pomeranz, 'The great Himalayan watershed: Agrarian crisis, mega-dams and the environment', *New Left Review*, 58 (2009), 5–39; Brahma Chellaney, *Water: Asia's new battleground* (Washington, DC: Georgetown University Press, 2013).

[21] Sanjib Kumar Baruah, 'Arunachal dams: Despite issues, govt collected crores', *Hindustan Times*, 30 April 2012; *Map of dams in Arunachal Pradesh*, International Rivers, Available: www.internationalrivers.org/resources/map-of-dams-in-arunachal-pradesh-7590 (accessed 1 July 2015); 'Scrap 15 of 44 dams planned across Siang in Arunachal: CWC report', *Hindu*, 15 February 2014.

[22] 'Independent People's Tribunal on dams in Arunachal Pradesh: Interim Report' (Itanagar: Independent People's Tribunal, 3 February 2008); Arnab Pratim Dutta, 'Assam's dam crisis', *Down to Earth*, 15 October 2010.

[23] Kazuharu Mizuno and Lobsang Tenpa, *Himalayan nature and Tibetan Buddhist culture in Arunachal Pradesh, India: A study of Monpa* (Berlin: Springer, 2015), pp. 123–124.

development.[24] Aspirations to 'exit options' might then surface.[25] If so, competitive state shadowing might remain the order of the day in the eastern Himalayas.

State-Making and International Relations

The dynamics of Sino-Indian tensions bring into sharp relief the difficulty of separating 'international relations' from state-making or nation-building in the border spaces where two countries physically meet – particularly two emerging, heterogeneous polities grappling with the integration of their fluid margins. China and India's relationship is but a particularly vivid instance of the entanglement between international relations and state-making. The birth of more than a hundred new countries over the last seven decades reflects a global process of decolonisation and the generalisation of the nation-state model. For a majority of these new states, building themselves means wrestling with a complex and contentious past, including the problematic legacies of often indirect or uneven colonial rule over diverse territories and people. It also means adjusting, or even redefining, relations with neighbouring polities – some of which face similar state-making or nation-building challenges. What is at stake, then, is to explore how international relations work on the ground as well as in diplomatic or top decision-making circles – and with what consequences.

To do so necessitates combining the study of interstate relations with the social, cultural, and political history of borderlands. These have long been ignored by mainstream scholarship for their lack of congruence with single area studies or national histories. A growing literature shows, however, that it is precisely this seemingly uneasy fit onto political and cultural maps of the world that makes them fascinating objects of enquiry. For it is there that states' anxieties about expansion and consolidation run highest, that their inner workings and contradictions come to light, and that the very meanings of state, nation, or territory can be

---

[24] Sanjib Baruah, *Hydropower, mega dams, and the politics of risk* (December 2012), www.india-seminar.com/2012/640/640_sanjib_baruah.htm [accessed 5 April 2015]; Raju Mimi, '"Power" house or powerless: A debate on dams in Arunachal Pradesh', *India Water Portal* (19 March 2014) www.indiawaterportal.org/articles/powerhouse-or-powerless-debate-dams-arunachal-pradesh (accessed 5 April 2015). On Chinese development policies in Tibet, see Andrew Martin Fischer, *The disempowered development of Tibet in China: A study in the economics of marginalization* (Lanham, MD; Lexington Books, 2014); Emily T. Yeh, *Taming Tibet: Landscape transformation and the gift of Chinese development* (Ithaca, NY: Cornell University Press, 2013).

[25] *Crafting state-nations: India and other multinational democracies*, ed. by Alfred C. Stepan, Juan J. Linz, and Yogendra Yadav (Baltimore: Johns Hopkins University Press, 2011), p. 44.

deconstructed.[26] From the perspective of two emerging states such as India and China, the fluid nature of their common borderland cannot be countenanced. It is an interstitial space that has to be conquered, all the more decisively because of each other's presence.

Looking at international relations from the ground up, and not just from above, can tell us much about the nature of global or regional political change. Stories centred on the corridors of power or the big geopolitical chessboard are more likely to clothe states with the garb of power or coherence, or to fall into a 'territorial trap'.[27] Stories based on the tangible, peopled spaces where countries meet on a daily basis are more likely to highlight their frailties, their inconsistencies, their insecurities. They can highlight the complex and evolving tensions not just between civilian and military authorities or between various ministries, but between various levels of administration. Clearly, the world inhabited by officials on the ground was not the same as that of their superiors in Delhi or Beijing.[28] They can also help us discern bottom-up dynamics, and how they intersect with, or contradict, top–down ones.[29]

Borderland perspectives also bring to the fore people whose existence otherwise remains but a footnote in studies of international relations, when they are not completely erased: borderlanders themselves. The lowly (and lonely) checkpoint guard, the villager, the sheepherder, the trader, the school-going child all observe and participate in the relations between China and India on a daily basis – even if it is to assert that their competition makes no sense to them. And this, in turn, means expanding our methodology beyond the archive of high politics to look at different types of sources, including local-level, private, or literary ones. Sources that could tell us something of these day-to-day encounters between states, when they spy on, browbeat, emulate, outdo each other. Sources that tell us something of the changing, blurry nature of sovereignty and legitimacy. Sources, finally, that can help us better grasp the interface between state and non-state actors in international relations – starting with the role of border populations.

---

[26] Willem van Schendel, *The Bengal borderland: Beyond state and nation in South Asia* (London: Anthem, 2005).

[27] John Agnew, 'The territorial trap: The geographical assumptions of international relations theory', *Review of International Political Economy*, 1:1 (1994), 53–80; John Agnew, 'Still trapped in territory?', *Geopolitics*, 15:4 (2010), 779–784.

[28] This still holds true for local Chinese authorities in Tibet today. Fernanda Pirie, 'The limits of the state: Coercion and consent in Chinese Tibet', *Journal of Asian Studies*, 72 (2013), 69–89.

[29] For a similar argument but from a political geography/anthropology perspective, see Jason Cons, 'Impasse and opportunity: Reframing postcolonial territory at the India–Bangladesh border', *Samaj*, 10 (2014), 1–14.

Maps

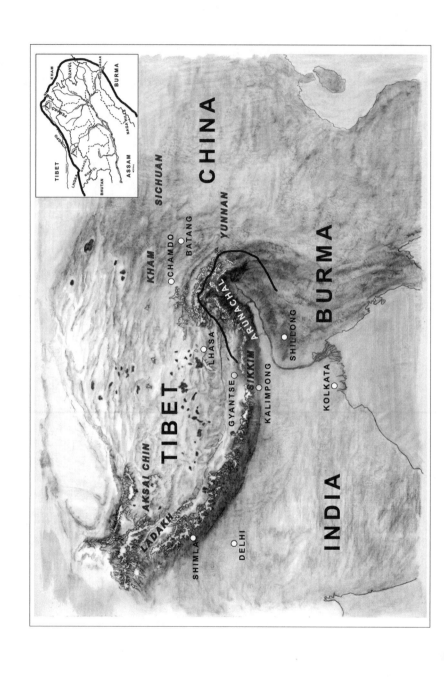

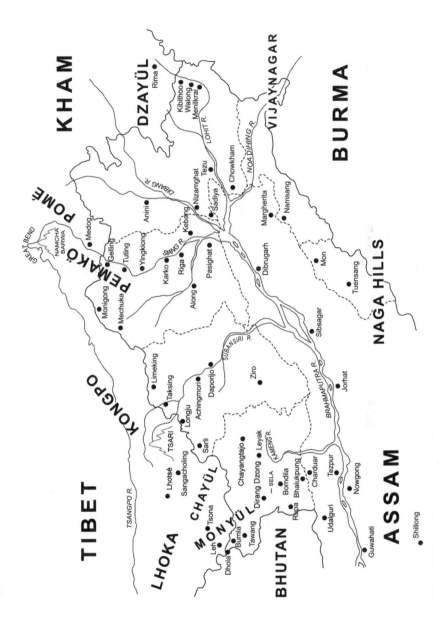

Map 2 Main places mentioned

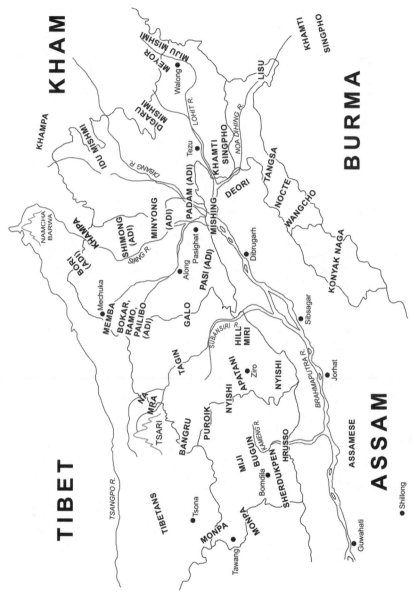

Map 2. Ethnic groups of the eastern Himalayas

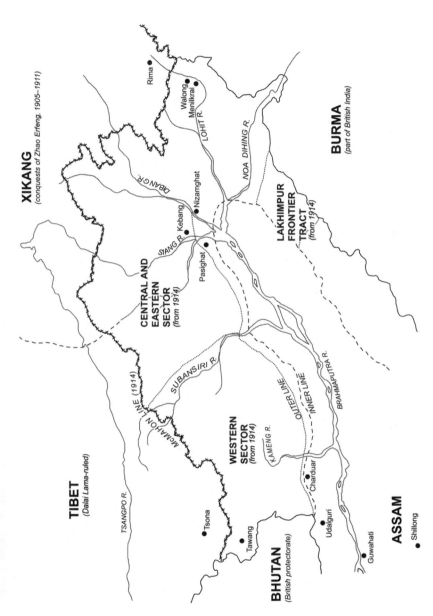

Map 4 The eastern Himalayas in the 1910s

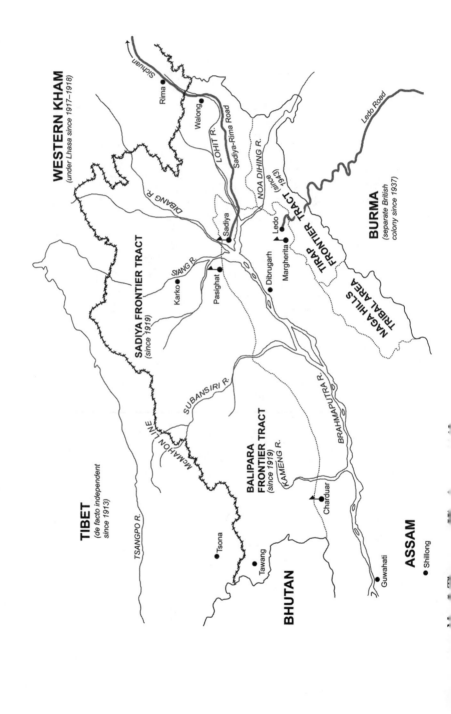

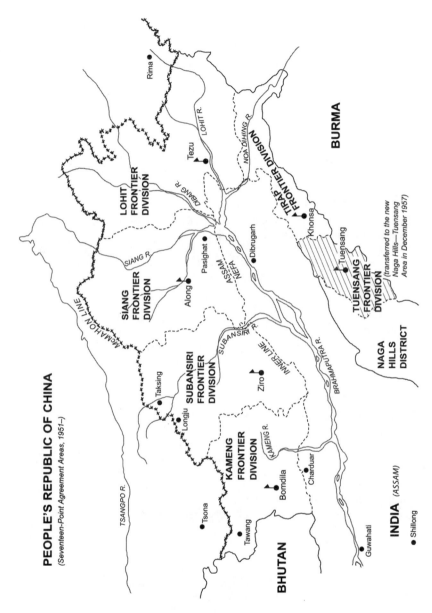

Map 6 The eastern Himalayas, c. 1955

Select Bibliography

Unpublished Official Records

Arunachal Pradesh

NEFA Secretariat Official Publications, Reference Library of the Arunachal Pradesh Research Directorate, Itanagar
NEFA Secretariat Records, Arunachal Pradesh State Archives (APSA), Itanagar

Assam

Assam Secretariat – General Department Files, Assam State Archives (ASA), Guwahati
Assam Secretariat – Tribal Areas Department Records (TAD), ASA, Guwahati

New Delhi

Foreign and Political Department Proceedings, Indian National Archives (NAI), New Delhi
Ministry of Education Proceedings, NAI, New Delhi
Ministry of External Affairs Proceedings, NAI, New Delhi
Ministry of Food & Agriculture Proceedings, NAI, New Delhi
Ministry of Home Affairs Proceedings, NAI, New Delhi
Ministry of States Proceedings, NAI, New Delhi
Secretary of the Governor-General Proceedings, NAI, New Delhi

United Kingdom

Dominions, Commonwealth Relations, and Foreign Office (DO) Records, UK National Archives (UKNA), Kew (London)
Foreign Office Records (FOR), Kew (London), UKNA, Kew (London)
India Office Records (IOR), British Library (BL), London
Prime Minister's Office Records (PREM), UKNA, Kew (London)

Official Publications

Arunachal Pradesh / NEFA

A Dictionary of the Taraon language, for the use of officers in the North-East Frontier Agency administration, Taraon-English–English-Taraon, with an introduction on the people and the language (Shillong: Philology Section, NEFA Research Department, 1963)

A phrase book in Idu (Shillong: North East Frontier Agency Research Department, 1962 [1963])

Elwin, Verrier, *A philosophy for NEFA. With a foreword by the Prime Minister of India*, 1st edn (Shillong: North-East Frontier Agency, 1957)

Democracy in NEFA (Shillong: North-East Frontier Agency, 1965)

Hornbill Magazine (Shillong: NEFA Secretariat, 1960–1969)

Khound, T.P., *NEFA on the march* ([Shillong]: Cultural Research Officer for the North East Frontier Agency, [1964?])

Lohit Valley Brochure (n.s.: [NEFA], c. 1965)

North East Frontier Agency, *A brief account of administrative and development activities in North-East Frontier Agency since independence* (Calcutta: A. Dhar, 1957)

Pugh, Marion D., *Games of NEFA* (Shillong: NEFA, 1958)

Research in Arunachal, 1951–76 (Shillong: Directorate of Research, Arunachal Pradesh, 1978)

Assam

Assam. Directorate of Information and Publicity, *The ninth year of freedom* (Gauhati: Tribune Press, c. 1956)

Assam. Directorate of Information and Public Relations, *Assam after independence: A review of Assam's achivements [sic] in the various fields of activities during the nineteen year-span of freedom* (Shillong: s.n., [1966])

Assam. Directorate of Information and Public Relations, *Assam, 1977: An exciting tale of Assam's triumphant journey (1947–77) from backwardness to modernity* (Gauhati: Assam Government Press, 1978)

India

A report on the measures of rehabilitation and reconstruction undertaken by the Government of India in the Naga Hills and Manipur State in 1944–45, in order to repair the ravages caused by the Japanese invasion of 1944 (Delhi?: s.n., 1949)

Census of India 2001, Arunachal Pradesh Data Highlights: Scheduled Tribes (2001)

Constituent Assembly Debates (1946–1950), http://parliamentofindia.nic.in/ls/debates/debates.htm

India. Administrative Reforms Commission, *Report of the Study Team on the administration of Union Territories and NEFA* (Delhi: [Manager of Publications], 1969)

India. Census Commissioner, *Census of India, 1951: Assam* (Delhi: Manager of Publications, 1953)

India. Commissioner for the Scheduled Tribes and Scheduled Castes, *Report for 1960–61* (Delhi: [Manager of Publications], c. 1961)

India. Commission on the Hill Areas of Assam. Government of Assam. Directorate of Information and Public Relations, *Summary of Pataskar Commission's report on the hill areas of Assam* (Shillong: Directorate of Information & Public Relations, 1966)

India. External Publicity Division – Ministry of External Affairs, *Prime Minister on Sino-Indian relations* (New Delhi: Ministry of External Affairs, 1961)

India–China border problem (New Delhi: Government of India [1962])

Chinese aggression: Prime Minister's Letter to Heads of States and their replies (New Delhi: Government of India, 1963)

India. History Division – Defence Department, *History of the conflict with China* (New Delhi: Government of India, 1992)

India. Ministry of Development of North-Eastern Region, 'North-eastern region Vision 2020: Vision statement' (May 2008), http://mdoner.gov.in/index2 .asp?sid=242

India. Ministry of Tribal Affairs, *National Tribal Policy* (2006)

India. Office of the Registrar General, *Census of India 1961: Assam* (Delhi: Manager of Publications, 1964)

India. States Reorganisation Commission, *Report of the States Reorganisation Commission* (Delhi: [Manager of Publications], 1955)

Lok Sabha Debates 1950–1963 (New Delhi: Lok Sabha Secretariat, 1950–1963)

People's Republic of China

Mao Zedong on diplomacy (compiled by the Ministry of Foreign Affairs of the PRC and the Party Literature Research Center) (Beijing: Foreign Languages Press, 1998)

Tibetan Government in Exile

Office of H.H. the Dalai Lama, *Tibetans in exile, 1959–1969: A report on ten years of rehabilitation in India* (Dharamsala: Bureau of H. H. the Dalai Lama, 1969)

United States

United States. Central Intelligence Agency, The Sino-Indian border dispute (1963)

Individual and Institutional Private Paper Collections

Cambridge

Cambridge, Centre of South Asian Studies (CSAS) (1936–1949), Mainprice (F.P.) Papers

Cambridge, CSAS (c. 1937–1969), Charles Pawsey Papers
Cambridge, CSAS (1940–1964), Meiklejohn Papers
Cambridge, CSAS (1944), Bor Papers, Small Collections Box 4
Cambridge, CSAS (1947–1958), Collins (J.W.) Papers

London

London, BL (1918–1964), Reid Collection, Mss Eur E278
London, BL (1924–1964), Verrier Elwin Collection, Mss Eur D950
London, BL (1929–1986), William G. (& Mildred) Archer Papers, Mss Eur F236
London, BL Miscellaneous papers relating to the north-east frontier of India (1944), Mss Eur D1191
London, BL (1948–1968), H F Burbidge: 'The War in Assam from the View of a District Police Officer', dated 24 October 1948; and R C R Cumming: 'The Police in Assam during the War of 1939–45', dated 10 October 1968, Mss Eur F161/32
London, BL (1930–1947), Indian Civil Service Memoirs: Assam, Mss Eur F180/3–7
London, School of Oriental & African Studies (SOAS) Archives (c. 1917–1990), Christoph von Fürer-Haimendorf Papers, PP MS 19
London, SOAS (1924–1958), J.P. Mills Collection, PP MS 58
London, SOAS (1950–1974), Frank Moraes Collection, PP MS 24

New Delhi

New Delhi, Nehru Memorial Museum & Library (NMML), All India Congress Committee Papers (AICC Papers)
New Delhi, NMML, Assam Pradesh Congress Committee Papers (APCC Papers)
New Delhi, NMML, Assam's say and suggestions (Memorandum by the Asom Jaitiya Mahasabha) (1950)
New Delhi, NMML, Omeo Kumar Das Papers (1919–1974)
New Delhi, NMML, Jairamdas Doulatram Papers (1924–1975)
New Delhi, NMML, Verrier Elwin Papers
New Delhi, NMML, Rammanohar Lohia (Roma Mitra) Papers (1963), 'Urvasiam se patra' [Letter from NEFA], S. No. 1
New Delhi, NMML, Bishnuram Medhi Papers, (1947–1968)
New Delhi, NMML, Sri Prakasa Papers (1908–1958)
New Delhi, NMML, Nari K. Rustomji Papers

Published Primary Sources

Indian Official Records

'Agreement on the Maintenance of Peace and Tranquility along the Line of Actual Control in the India–China Border Areas' (07 September 1993), http://peacemaker.un.org/chinaindia-borderagreement93

Allen, Basil C., *Assam District Gazetteers*, 10 vols (Calcutta: Baptist Mission Press, 1905)
Bose, Manilal, ed., *Historical and constitutional documents of north eastern India (1824–1973)* (Delhi: Concept Publishing Company, 1979)
Brochure of the Lohit District ([Shillong]: Research Branch: Lohit District, c. 1965)

Chinese Official Records

Cold War International History Project (CWIHP): Sources from Chinese Foreign Ministry Archives (PRC FMA). Available on the History and Public Policy Program Digital Archive, http://digitalarchive.wilsoncenter .org/collections
Zhang, Shu Guang and Jian Chen, eds., *Chinese Communist foreign policy and the Cold War in Asia: New documentary evidence, 1944–1950* (Chicago: Imprint Publications, 1996)

Published Private Papers

Lohia, Ram Manohar, *Collected works of Rammanohar Lohia*, ed. by Mastram Kapoor, 9 vols (New Delhi: Anamika Publishers, 2011)
Mansergh, Nicholas and E. W. R. Lumby, eds., *The transfer of power 1942–7*, 12 vols (London: H.M.S.O., 1970)
Nehru, Jawaharlal, *Letters to chief ministers 1947–1964*, ed. by G. Parthasarathi (New Delhi: Jawaharlal Nehru Memorial Fund, c. 1985–)
Selected works of Jawaharlal Nehru, Second Series, ed. by Sarvepalli Gopal (New Delhi: Jawaharlal Nehru Memorial Fund, 1994–)
Nehru's India: Select speeches, ed. by Mushirul Hasan (New Delhi: Oxford University Press, 2007)
Pant, Gobind Ballabh, *Selected works of Gobind Ballabh Pant*, ed. by B.R. Nanda (New Delhi: Oxford University Press, 1994–)
Patel, Vallabhbhai, *Sardar Patel's correspondence, 1945–50*, ed. by Durga Das, 10 vols (Ahmedabad: Navajivan Publishing House, 1971–1974)
Sardar's letters: Mostly unknown, ed. by Manibehn Vallabhai Patel and G.M. Nandurkar (Ahmedabad: Sardar Vallabhai Patel Smarak Bhavan, 1980–1983)
The collected works of Sardar Vallabhbhai Patel, ed. by Pran Nath Chopra (Delhi: Konark, 1990)

Memoirs, Diaries, Autobiographies

Arunachal Pradesh Pensioners' Welfare Association, *Reminiscences: Lest we forget* (Shillong: APPWA, c. 1999)
Bailey, F.M., *China–Tibet–Assam: A journey, 1911* (London: J. Cape, 1945)
No passport to Tibet ([s.n.], 1957)
Bardoloi, Gopinath, *Gopinath Bardoloi: Indian constitution and centre–Assam relations, 1940–1950*, ed. by Nirode Kumar Barooah (Guwahati: Publication Board, Assam, 1990)

Baveja, J.D., *Across the golden heights of Assam and NEFA* (Calcutta: Modern Book Depot, 1961)

Bhargava, G.S., *The battle of NEFA* (New Delhi: Allied Publishers, 1964)

Bhattacharjee, Tarun Kumar, *Alluring frontiers* (Guwahati: Omsons Publications, 1988)

Enticing frontiers (Delhi: Omsons Publications, 1992)

The frontier trail (Calcutta: Manick Bandyopadhyay, 1993)

Bor, Eleanor, *Adventures of a botanist's wife* (London: Hurst & Blackett, 1952)

Cooper, T.T., *The Mishmee Hills: An account of a journey made in an attempt to penetrate Thibet from Assam to open new routes for commerce* (London: H.S. King & Co., 1873)

The Dalai Lama, *My land and my people: Memoirs of His Holiness the Dalai Lama* (Delhi: Srishti Publishers, 2012 [1977])

Dalvi, John P. and Frank Moraes, *Himalayan blunder: The curtain-raiser to the Sino-Indian War of 1962*, 2nd edn (Bombay: Thacker, 1969)

Dewatshang, Kunga Samten, *Flight at the cuckoo's behest: The life and times of a Tibetan freedom fighter (as told to his son Dorjee Wangdi Dewatshang)* (Delhi: Paljor Publications, 1997)

Dunbar, George, *Frontiers* (Delhi: Omsons Publications, 1984 [c. 1932])

Elwin, Verrier, *The tribal world of Verrier Elwin: An autobiography* (New York: Oxford University Press, 1964)

Ering, Oshung, *The lingering memories* (Pasighat: Siang Literary Forum, 2005)

'The changing phases of Pasighat', *Yaaro Moobang: A Land of Peace, Prosperity and Happiness (Bilingual Magazine of the Adi Baane Kebang Youth Front, HQ Pasighat, East Siang)*, 1 (2011), 1–6

Ete, Liju, ed., *Boken Ete: An oddyssey* (Naharlagun: The author, 2011)

Fürer-Haimendorf, Christoph von, *Life among Indian tribes: The autobiography of an anthropologist* (Delhi; Oxford: Oxford University Press, 1990)

Galbraith, John Kenneth, *Ambassador's journal: A personal account of the Kennedy years* (London: Hamilton, 1969)

Graham Bower, Ursula, *The hidden land* (London: John Murray, 1953)

Hamilton, A., *In Abor jungles of north-east India* (New Delhi: Mittal Publications, 1983 [reprint])

Kaul, B.M., *The untold story* (Bombay: Allied Publishers, 1967)

Kaul, P.N., *Frontier callings* (Delhi: Vikas Publishing, 1977)

Kaul, T.N., *Diplomat's diary (1947–99): China, India and USA (The tantalising triangle)* (Delhi: MacMillan, 2000)

Kingdon-Ward, Jean, *My hill so strong* (London: Cape, 1952)

Knaus, John Kenneth, *Orphans of the Cold War: America and the Tibetan struggle for survival* (New York: Public Affairs, 1999)

Krishnatry, S.M., *Border Tagins of Arunachal Pradesh: Unarmed expedition, 1956* (Delhi: National Book Trust, 2005)

Mehta, K.L., *In different worlds: From haveli to headhunters of Tuensang* (New Delhi: Lancers Books, 1985)

Menon, K.P.S., *India and the Chinese invasion* (Bombay: Contemporary Publishers, 1963)

A diplomat speaks (New Delhi: Allied Publishers, 1974)

Miri, Indira, *Moi aru NEFA [NEFA and I]* (Guwahati: Spectrum Publications, 2003)

Mize, Tatan, 'A part of my past life', *Yaaro Moobang: A Land of Peace, Prosperity and Happiness (Bilingual Magazine of the Adi Baane Kebang Youth Front, HQ Pasighat, East Siang)*, 1 (2001), 21–25

Mullik, B. N., *My years with Nehru: The Chinese betrayal* (Bombay: Allied Publishers, 1971)

Norbu, Dawa, *Red star over Tibet* (London: Collins, 1974)

Palit, D. K., *War in high Himalaya: The Indian army in crisis, 1962* (London: Hurst, 1991)

Porter, A.W., 'Report on the expedition to the Hukawng Valley and Naga Hills (Burma), Season 1928–29' (Maymyo: Government Branch Press, 1929)

Prasad, Niranjan, *The fall of Towang, 1962* (New Delhi: Palit & Palit, 1981)

Rustomji, Nari K., *Enchanted frontiers: Sikkim, Bhutan, and India's north-eastern borderlands* (Calcutta: Oxford University Press, 1973)

    Imperilled frontiers: India's north-eastern borderlands (Delhi: Oxford University Press, 1983)

Sen, P.C., *Two decades in NEFA and Arunachal, 1954–76* (Morekupur: Dr Panu Chandra Sen, 2007)

Taring, Rinchen Dolma, *Daughter of Tibet* (London: John Murray, 1970)

Tayyebulla, Mohammad, *Between the symbol and the idol at last* (New Delhi; New York: Allied Publishers, 1964)

Thangsia, Z., *Memoirs of 1929–1992: An autobiography featuring NEFA and adjoining north-eastern states* (Shillong: Achula Darneichawng Sailo, 2004)

Tsarong, Dundul Namgyal, *In the service of his country: The biography of Dasang Damdul Tsarong, Commander General of Tibet*, ed. by Khenmo Trinlay Chödron (Ithaca, NY: Snow Lion, 2000)

Tsering, Tashi, Melvyn C. Goldstein, and William R. Siebenschuh, *The struggle for modern Tibet: The autobiography of Tashi Tsering* (Armonk, NY; London: M.E. Sharpe, 1997)

Tyson, Geoffrey, *Forgotten frontier* (Calcutta: W.H. Targett & Co., 1945)

Miscellaneous

Assam Sahitya Sabha, ed., *The outlook on NEFA* (Calcutta: Nabajiban Press, 1958)

Caroe, Olaf, 'The India–China frontiers: Review', *Geographical Journal*, 130 (1964), 273–275

Coupland, Reginald, *The future of India* (Oxford: Oxford University Press, 1943)

Doulatram, Jairamdas, *The people of the frontier* (s.n.: s.d., 1956)

Dutta, S. and B. Tripathy, eds., *Sources of the history of Arunachal Pradesh* (New Delhi: Gyan Publishing, 2008)

Elwin, Verrier, *North-east frontier in the nineteenth century* (Bombay: Oxford University Press, 1959)

Kingdon Ward, Francis, 'The Assam Himalaya: Travels in Balipara I', *Journal of the Royal Central Asian Society*, 25 (1938), 610–619

    'The Assam earthquake of 1950', *Geographical Journal*, 119 (1953), 169–182

Frank Kingdon Ward's Riddle of the Tsangpo gorges: Retracing the epic journey of 1924–25 in south-east Tibet, ed./additional material by Kenneth Cox, Kenneth Storm, Jr., and Ian Baker, 2nd edn (Woodbridge: Garden Art Press, 2008)

Koley, R.N., *East Siang in the last fifty years (1947–1997)* (Pasighat: District administration, East Siang, c. 1997)

Luthra, P.N., *Constitutional and administrative growth of the North-East Frontier Agency* (Shillong: North-East Frontier Agency, 1971)

Nehru, Jawaharlal, *The discovery of India* ([S.l.]: Meridian Books, 1945)

Pemberton, R.B., *Report on the eastern frontier of British India* (Guwahati: Department of Historical and Antiquarian Studies, 1991[1835])

Reid, Robert, 'The excluded areas of Assam', *Geographical Journal*, 103 (1944), 18–29

History of the frontier areas bordering on Assam, 1883–1941 (Delhi: Eastern Pub. House, 1983)

Rustomji, Nari, 'Bhutan Today', *Bulletin of Tibetology*, 3:2 (1966), 64–70.

Verrier Elwin and India's north-eastern borderlands (Shillong: North-Eastern Hill University Publications, 1988)

Sharma, S.K. and Usha Sharma, eds., *Documents on northeast India*, 11 vols (Delhi: Mittal Publications, 2005)

Shiva Rao, B., ed., *The framing of India's constitution: A study*, 5 vols (New Delhi: Indian Institute of Public Administration, 1968)

Subansiri, *Magazine of Doimukh High School*, First Year, First Volume (June 1962).

Le Tibet et la République Populaire de Chine: Rapport présenté à la Commission internationale de Juristes par le Comité juridique d'enquête sur la question du Tibet (Genève: Commission Internationale de Juristes de Genève, 1960)

Newspapers

Archives

Amrita Bazaar Patrika, Calcutta
The Assam Tribune, Guwahati
The March of India
The Statesman, Delhi and Calcutta
The Times of India, Bombay

Recent

The Arunachal Times
Asian Tribune
BBC Hindi (Hindi)
BBC News, London
Business Standard, Delhi
Daily News and Analysis

Dainik Jagran (Hindi)
DNA
The Economic Times
The Financial Times
Hindustan Standard
Hindustan Times
The Indian Express
Livemint (Hindustan Times)
The New York Times
Outlook
Reuters
Seven Sisters Post
The Telegraph
Time
The Wall Street Journal
Z-News

Audio-Visual Sources

1959 India, Newly arrived Tibetan refugees in the Missamari camp. British Pathé. 1959

F.P. Mainprice Photographic Collection, CSAS, Cambridge

Fürer-Haimendorf Photographic and Film Collection, SOAS, London (available online at http://digital.info.soas.ac.uk/cgi/c/Furer-Haimendorf/F%C3%BCre r-Haimendorf%20Collection_Homepage)

J.P. Mills Photographic Collection, SOAS, London (available online at http://digi tal.info.soas.ac.uk/cgi/c/J_p_mills/J%20P%20Mills%20Collection_Homepage).

Mackrell Collection (1942), CSAS, Cambridge

Naga Videodisc Collection, Digital Himalayas Archive, University of Cambridge / Yale University (available online at http://himalaya.socanth.cam .ac.uk/collections/naga/coll/4/xintroduction/detail/all/index.html)

NEFA Photographic Collections, Arunachal Pradesh Directorate of Information & Public Relations (IPR), Itanagar (Arunachal Pradesh)

Oral Sources

Interviews by the Author

Barmati Dai. Interview with the author, 12 February 2014, Pasighat (Arunachal Pradesh)

Oshong Ering. Interview with the author, 11 February 2014, Pasighat (Arunachal Pradesh)

K.C. Johorey and Sudha Johorey. Interview with the author, 15 March 2014, Gurgaon (Haryana)

Egul Padung. Interview with the author, 11 February 2014, Pasighat (Arunachal Pradesh)
Yeshe Dorjee Thongchi. Interview with the author, 8 February 2014, Itanagar (Arunachal Pradesh)
B.G. Verghese. Interview with the author, 21 March 2014, New Delhi

Second-Hand Interviews

The 26th January 1963 Tajo CRPF battle at Chayangtajo. Story told to Rebecca Gnüchtel by Katuk Killo (with the assistance of Solung Sonam), July 2015.
Interview with Rashid Yusuf Ali. Interviewed by Rebecca Gnüchtel, 19 October 2006, Shillong (Meghalaya)
Interview with G.T. Allen. Interviewed for the 'Oral Archive: Plain Tales from the Raj' series in 1972–1974 (held at the SOAS Archives, London)
Interview with Florence Meiklejohn. Interviewed by Mary Thatcher on 17 July 1979 (held at the Centre of South Asian Studies, Cambridge), www.s-asian .cam.ac.uk/archive/audio/meiklejohn.html
Interview with Dr Naik. Interviewed by Uma Shankar on 1 May 1973 (held at the Centre of South Asian Studies, Cambridge), www.s-asian.cam.ac.uk/archiv e/audio/naikd.html
Minnesota Tibetan Oral History Project, http://collections.mnhs.org/ioh/index .php/10000814
Tibet Oral History Project, www.tibetoralhistory.org/interviews.html
Tibetan Oral History Archive Project, Case Western Reserve University, http:// tibetoralhistoryarchive.org/

Secondary Sources

Published

'A true description of the Sino-Indian War in 1962', *Xizang Wenxue*, Supplement to no. 4 (1998)
Acuto, Michele, 'Edges of the conflict: A three-fold conceptualization of national borders', *Borderlands*, 7 (2008), www.borderlands.net.au/vol7no1_2008/acu to_edges.htm
Adshead, Samuel Adrian M., *Province and politics in late Imperial China: Viceregal government in Szechwan, 1898–1911* (London: Curzon, 1984)
Agha, Sameetah, 'Sub-imperialism and the loss of the Khyber: The politics of imperial defence on British India's North-West Frontier', *Indian Historical Review*, 40 (2013), 307–330.
Agnew, John, 'The territorial trap: The geographical assumptions of international relations theory', *Review of International Political Economy*, 1 (1994), 53–80
  'Sovereignty regimes: Territoriality and state authority in contemporary world politics', *Annals of the Association of American Geographers*, 95 (2005), 437–461
  'Still trapped in territory?', *Geopolitics*, 15 (2010), 779–784

Ahuja, Ravi, *Pathways of empire: Circulation, 'public works' and social space in colonial Orissa (c. 1780–1914)* (Hyderabad: Orient Blackswan, 2009)

Aiyadurai, Ambika, 'The Meyor: A least studied frontier tribe of Arunachal Pradesh, northeast India', *Eastern Anthropologist*, 64 (2011), 459–469

Alam, Aniket, *Becoming India: Western Himalayas under British rule* (New Delhi: Cambridge University Press (CUP), 2008)

Aldenderfer, Mark and Yinong Zhang, 'The prehistory of the Tibetan plateau to the seventh century AD', in *The Tibetan history reader*, ed. by Gray Tuttle and Kurtis R. Schaeffer (New York: Columbia University Press, 2013), pp. 3–48

Alexander, André, *The traditional Lhasa house: Typology of an endangered species* (Münster: LIT Verlag, 2013)

Anand, Dibyesh, 'The Tibet question and the West: Issues of sovereignty, identity and representation', in *Contemporary Tibet: Politics, development and society in a disputed region*, ed. by J.T. Dreyer and B. Sautman (London: M E Sharpe, 2006), pp. 285–304

'Strategic hypocrisy: The British imperial scripting of Tibet's geopolitical identity', *Journal of Asian Studies*, 68 (2009), 227–252

'Remembering 1962 Sino-Indian border war: Politics of memory', *Journal of Defence Studies*, 6 (2012a), 177–196

'China and India: Postcolonial informal empires in the emerging global order', *Rethinking Marxism*, 24:1 (2012b), 68–86

Anderson, Benedict, *Imagined communities: Reflections on the origin and spread of nationalism*, Revised and extended edn (London: Verso, 1991)

Antlöv, Hans and Stein Tønnesson, eds., *Asian forms of the nation* (Richmond: Curzon, 1996)

Aosenba, Dr, *The Naga resistance movement: Prospects of peace and armed conflict* (Delhi: Regency, 2001)

Appadurai, Arjun and Carol Breckenridge, 'On moving targets', *Public Culture*, 2 (1989), i–iv

'Sovereignty without territoriality: Notes for a postnational geography', in *The geography of identity*, ed. by Patricia Yaeger (Ann Arbor, MI: University of Michigan Press, 1996), pp. 40–58

Aris, Michael, 'Notes on the history of the Monyul corridor', in *Tibetan Studies in honour of Hugh Richardson: Proceedings of the International Seminar on Tibetan Studies*, ed. by Michael Aris and Aung San Suu Kyi (Warminster: Aris & Phillips, 1980), pp. 9–20

Hidden treasures and secret lives: A study of Pemalingpa (1450–1521) and the sixth Dalai Lama (1683–1706) (London: Kegan Paul, 1989)

Arpi, Claude, *1962 and the McMahon Line saga* (Delhi: Lancer, 2013)

Bajpai, Rochana, *Debating difference: Minority rights and liberal democracy in India* (New Delhi: Oxford University Press (OUP), 2010)

Baker, Ian, *The heart of the world: A journey to Tibet's lost paradise* (London: Souvenir, 2006)

Banerjee, Pallavi and Xiangming Chen, 'Living in in-between spaces: A structure–agency analysis of the India–China and India–Bangladesh borderlands', *Cities* (2012), http://dx.doi.org/10.1016/j.cities.2012.06.011

Barnett, Robert, ed., *Resistance and reform in Tibet* (Bloomington: Indiana University Press, 1994)

and Ronald Schwartz, eds., *Tibetan modernities: Notes from the field on cultural and social change* (Leiden: Brill, 2008)

Barpujari, H.K., *Problem of the hill tribes: North-east frontier. Vol. 3, 1873–1962, Inner Line to McMahon Line* (Guwahati: Spectrum, 1981)

Barrow, Ian J., *Making history, drawing territory: British mapping in India, c. 1756–1905* (New Delhi; Oxford: OUP, 2003)

Baruah, Sanjib, *India against itself: Assam and the politics of nationality* (Philadelphia: University of Pennsylvania Press, 1999)

Durable disorder: Understanding the politics of northeast India (Oxford: OUP, 2007)

Hydropower, mega dams, and the politics of risk (December 2012), www.indiaseminar.com/2012/640/640_sanjib_baruah.htm

Bateman, Joel, 'In the shadows: The Shadow Cabinet in Australia' (Australian Government – Department of Parliamentary Services, 2008)

Baud, Michiel and Willem Van Schendel, 'Toward a comparative history of borderlands', *Journal of World History*, 8 (1997), 211–242

Bayly, Christopher, *Empire and information: Intelligence gathering and social communication in India, 1780–1870* (Cambridge: CUP, 1996)

and Tim Harper, *Forgotten armies: The fall of British Asia, 1941–1945* (London: Allen Lane, 2004)

Bétéille, André, 'The Definition of Tribe', in *Tribe, caste and religion in India*, ed. by Romesh Thapar (Delhi: Macmillan, 1977), pp. 7–14

Bhattacharjee, J.B., 'The eastern Himalayan trade of Assam in the colonial period', in *Proceedings of the North-East India History Association, First Session* (Shillong: Singhania, 1980), pp. 174–192

Bhattacharya, Sanjoy, *Propaganda and information in eastern India, 1939–45: A necessary weapon of war* (Richmond, Surrey: Curzon, 2001)

and Benjamin Zachariah, '"A great destiny": The British colonial state and the advertisement of post-war reconstruction in India, 1942–45', *South Asia Research*, 19 (1999), 71–100

Bhaumik, Sarbari, 'Unsettled border', Himal South Asian (January 2011)

Bhaumik, Subir, 'The external linkages in insurgency in India's northeast', in *Insurgency in north-east India*, ed. by P. Phakem (New Delhi: Omeons, 1997), pp. 89–100

Bidwai, Praful, 'The panic of 1962', *Frontline*, 27 (4–17 December 2010), www.frontlineonnet.com/fl2725/stories/20101217272510000.htm

Bille, Franck, Gregory Delaplace, and Caroline Humphrey, eds., *Frontier encounters: Knowledge and practice at the Russian, Chinese and Mongolian border* (Cambridge: Open Book Publishers, 2012)

Billorey, R.K., 'Frontier trade, 1914–62: Case studies of two tribes of northeast India', in *Proceedings of the North-East India History Association, First Session* (Shillong: Singhania, 1980), pp. 193–202

'Oral history in north east India', in *Proceedings of the North-East India History Association, Second Session* (Shillong: Singhania, 1981), pp. 14–22

Blackburn, Stuart, 'Colonial contact in the "hidden land": Oral history among the Apatanis of Arunachal Pradesh', *Indian Economic and Social History Review*, 40 (2003), 335–365

'Memories of migration: Notes on legends and beads in Arunachal Pradesh', *European Bulletin of Himalayan Research*, 25/26 (2003–2004), 15–60

Himalayan tribal tales: Oral tradition and culture in the Apatani Valley (Boston; Leiden: Brill, 2008)

and Toni Huber, eds., *Origins and migrations in the extended eastern Himalayas* (Leiden: Brill, 2012)

Blasko, Dennis J., 'Always faithful: The PLA from 1949 to 1989', in *A military history of China*, ed. by David Andrew Graff and Robin Higham (Boulder, CO: Westview, 2001), pp. 248–284

Borang, Gindu, 'Trade practices of the Adis with special reference to Padams', *Yaaro Moobang: A land of peace, prosperity and happiness (Bilingual magazine of the Adi Baane Kebang Youth Front, HQ Pasighat, East Siang)*, 1 (2001), 14–18

Borland, Janet, 'Capitalising on catastrophe: Reinvigorating the Japanese state with moral values through education following the 1923 Great Kanto Earthquake', *Modern Asian Studies*, 40 (2006), 875–907

Bose, Mani Lal, *History of Arunachal Pradesh* (Delhi: Concept, 1997)

Botea, Roxana and Brian D. Taylor, 'Tilly tally: War-making and state-making in the contemporary Third World', *International Studies Review*, 10 (2008), 27–56

Brass, Paul R., 'The strong state and the fear of disorder', in *Transforming India: Social and political dynamics of democracy*, ed. by Francine R. Frankel and others (New Delhi: OUP, 2000), pp. 60–89

Brewster, David, *India's ocean: The story of India's bid for regional leadership* (London: Routledge, 2014)

Brown, Judith M., *Modern India: The origins of Asian democracy*, 2nd edn (Oxford: OUP, 1994)

Bruce Reynolds, E., 'Failed endeavours: Chinese efforts to gain political influence in Thailand during World War II', *Intelligence and National Security*, 16:4 (2001), 175–204

Bulag, Uradyn Erden, *Collaborative nationalism: The politics of friendship on China's Mongolian frontier* (Lanham, MD; Plymouth: Rowman & Littlefield, 2010)

Burbank, Jane and Frederick Cooper, *Empires in world history: Power and the politics of difference* (Princeton, NJ; Oxford: Princeton University Press, 2010)

Cederlöf, Gunnel, *Founding an empire on India's north-eastern frontiers, 1790–1840: Climate, commerce, polity* (Delhi: OUP, 2013)

Chakrabarty, Dipesh, Rochona Majumdar, and Andrew Sartori, eds., *From the colonial to the postcolonial: India and Pakistan in transition* (New Delhi; Oxford: OUP, 2007)

Chang, Jui-te, 'An imperial envoy: Shen Zonglian in Tibet, 1943–1946', in *Negotiating China's destiny in World War II*, ed. by Hans J. Van de Ven, Diana Lary, and Stephen R. MacKinnon (Stanford, CA: Stanford University Press, 2015), pp. 52–69

Chappell, David A., 'Ethnogenesis and frontiers', *Journal of World History*, 4 (1993), 267–275

Chatterjee, Partha, 'Development planning and the Indian state', in *The state and development planning in India*, ed. by Terence J. Byres (New Delhi: OUP, 1994), pp. 51–72

ed., *Wages of freedom: Fifty years of the Indian nation-state* (Delhi; Oxford: OUP, 1998)

The politics of the governed: Reflections on popular politics in most of the world (New York; Chichester: Columbia University Press, 2004)

Chatterjee Miller, Manjari, *Wronged by empire: Post-imperial ideology and foreign policy in India and China* (Stanford, CA: Stanford University Press, 2013)

Chatterji, Joya, *The spoils of Partition: Bengal and India, 1947–1967* (Cambridge: CUP, 2007)

Chaube, Shibani Kinkar, *Hill politics in northeast India*, 2nd edn (Hyderabad: Orient Longman, 1999)

Chaudhuri, Rudra, 'Why culture matters: Revisiting the Sino-Indian border war of 1962', *Journal of Strategic Studies*, 32 (2009), 841–869

Chelan, Linda, ed., *The Chinese state in transition: Processes and contests in local China* (London: Routledge, 2009)

Chellaney, Brahma, *Water: Asia's new battleground* (Washington, DC: Georgetown University Press, 2013)

Chen, Jian, *Mao's China and the Cold War* (Chapel Hill, NC: University of North Carolina Press, 2001)

'The Tibetan rebellion of 1959 and China's changing relations with India and the Soviet Union', *Journal of Cold War Studies*, 8 (2006), 54–101

'The Chinese Communist "Liberation" of Tibet, 1949–51', in *Dilemmas of victory: The early years of the People's Republic of China*, ed. by Jeremy Brown and Paul Pickowicz (Cambridge, MA; London: Harvard University Press (HUP), 2007), pp. 130–159

and Kuisong Yang, 'Chinese politics and the collapse of the Sino-Soviet alliance', in *Brothers in arms: The rise and fall of the Sino-Soviet alliance, 1945–1963*, ed. by Odd Arne Westad (Washington, DC: Woodrow Wilson Center Press, 1998), pp. 246–284

Christie, Clive J., 'Great Britain, China and the status of Tibet, 1914–21', *Modern Asian Studies*, 10 (1976), 481–508

Clancey, Gregory, 'The Meiji earthquake: Nature, nation, and the ambiguities of catastrophe', *Modern Asian Studies*, 40 (2006), 909–951

Clark, Gregory, *In fear of China* (London: Cresset Press, 1968)

Cohn, Bernard S., *Colonialism and its forms of knowledge: The British in India* (Princeton, NJ; Chichester: Princeton University Press, 1996)

Coleman IV, William M., 'The uprising at Batang: Khams and its significance in Chinese and Tibetan history', in *Khams Pa histories: Visions of people, place and authority*, ed. by Lawrence Epstein (Leiden: Brill, 2002), pp. 31–56

Comtois, Claude, 'Transport and territorial development in China 1949–1985', *Modern Asian Studies*, 24 (1990), 777–818

Conboy, Kenneth and James Morrison, *The CIA's secret war in Tibet* (Lawrence, KA: University of Kansas Press, 2002)

Cons, Jason, 'Impasse and opportunity: Reframing postcolonial territory at the India–Bangladesh border', *Samaj*, 10 (2014), 1–14

Dai, Yingcong, *The Sichuan frontier and Tibet: Imperial strategy in the early Qing* (Seattle: University of Washington Press, 2009)

Darwin, John, *The empire project: The rise and fall of the British world-system, 1830–1970* (Cambridge: CUP, 2009)

Dasgupta, Anindita, 'Remembering Sylhet: A forgotten story of India's 1947 Partition', *Economic and Political Weekly*, 43 (2008), 18–22

Dean, Karin, 'Spaces and territorialities on the Sino–Burmese boundary: China, Burma and the Kachin', *Political Geography*, 24 (2005), 808–830

Deepak, B. R., *India & China, 1904–2004: A century of peace and conflict* (New Delhi: Manak, 2005)

Desai, Radhika, ed., *Developmental and cultural nationalisms* (London: Routledge, 2009)

Dhar, Bibhas, *Transhumants of Arunachal Himalayas: The Pangchenpas and the Thingbupas of Tawang District* (Guwahati: Geophil, 2009)

Dicken, Peter and others, 'Chains and networks, territories and scales: Towards a relational framework for analysing the global economy', *Global Networks: A Journal of Transnational Affairs*, 1 (2001), 89–112

Dirks, Nicholas B., *Castes of mind: Colonialism and the making of modern India* (Princeton, NJ; Chichester: Princeton University Press, 2001)

Dodin, Thierry and Heinz Räther, eds., *Imagining Tibet: Perceptions, projections, & fantasies* (Boston: Wisdom Publications, 2001)

Donnan, Hastings and Thomas M. Wilson, *Borders: Frontiers of identity, nation and state* (Oxford; New York: Berg, 1999)

Dreyer, June T., 'Traditional minorities elites and the CPR elite engaged in minority nationalities work', in *Elites in the People's Republic of China*, ed. by Robert A. Scalapino (Seattle: University of Washington Press, 1972), pp. 416–450

China's forty millions: Minority nationalities and national integration in the People's Republic of China (Cambridge, MA: HUP, 1976)

'Economic development in Tibet under the People's Republic of China', *Journal of Contemporary China*, 12 (2003), 411–430

China's political system: Modernization and tradition, 8th edn (Boston; London: Longman, 2012)

Duara, Prasenjit, *Rescuing history from the nation: Questioning narratives of modern China* (Chicago; London: University of Chicago Press, 1995)

The global and regional in China's nation-formation (London: Routledge, 2009)

Dzuvichu, Lipokmar, 'Roads and the Raj: The politics of road building in colonial Naga Hills, 1860s–1910s', *Indian Economic and Social History Review*, 50 (2013), 473–494

Edney, Matthew H., *Mapping an empire: The geographical construction of British India, 1765–1843* (Chicago: University of Chicago Press, 1997)

Edwardes, Michael, 'Illusion and reality in India's foreign policy', *International Affairs*, 41 (1965), 48–58

Edwards, Penny, 'The tyranny of proximity: Power and mobility in colonial Cambodia, 1863–1954', *Journal of Southeast Asian studies*, 37 (2006), 421–443

Egreteau, Renaud, '"Are we (really) brothers?": Contemporary India as observed by Chinese diplomats', *Journal of Asian and African Studies*, 47 (2012), 695–709

Elden, Stuart, 'Thinking territory historically', *Geopolitics*, 15 (2010), 757–761

Elleman, Bruce A., *Modern Chinese warfare, 1795–1989* (London: Routledge, 2001)

Elliott, Mark, 'Frontier stories: Periphery as center in Qing history', *Frontiers of History in China*, 9:3 (2014), 336–360

Epstein, Israel, *Tibet transformed* (Beijing: New World Press, 1983)

Farmer, B.H., *Agricultural colonisation in South and South East Asia* (Hull: University of Hull, 1969)

Ferguson, James and Akhil Gupta, 'Spatializing states: Toward an ethnography of neoliberal governmentality', *American Ethnologist*, 29 (2002), 981–1002

Fischer, Andrew Martin, *The disempowered development of Tibet in China: A study in the economics of marginalization* (Lanham, MD; Plymouth, UK: Lexington Books, 2014)

Fisher, Margaret W., Robert A. Huttenback, and Leo E. Rose, *Himalayan battleground: Sino-Indian rivalry in Ladakh* (New York: Praeger, 1963)

Fiskesjö, Magnus, 'Mining, history, and the anti-state Wa: The politics of autonomy between Burma and China', *Journal of Global History*, 5 (2010), 241–264

Fong, Vanessa L. and Rachel Murphy, eds., *Chinese citizenship: Views from the margins* (London: Routledge, 2005)

Franke, Marcus, *War and nationalism in South Asia: The Indian state and the Nagas* (London: Routledge, 2009)

Frankel, Francine R. and Harry Harding, eds., *The India–China relationship: Rivalry and engagement* (New Delhi: OUP, 2004)

Fürer-Haimendorf, Christoph von, 'Anthropology and administration in the tribal areas of the north east frontier', *Eastern Anthropologist*, 3 (1949), 8–14

Himalayan barbary (London: J. Murray, 1955)

The Apa Tanis and their neighbours: A primitive civilization of the eastern Himalayas (London: Routledge & Kegan Paul, 1962)

The Konyak Nagas: An Indian frontier tribe (New York: Holt, 1969)

Return to the naked Nagas: An anthropologist's view of Nagaland, 1936–1970, new edn (London: J. Murray, 1976)

A Himalayan tribe: From cattle to cash (Berkeley: University of California Press, 1980)

Highlanders of Arunachal Pradesh: Anthropological research in north-east India (New Delhi: Vikas, 1982)

Gadgil, Madhav and Ramachandra Guha, *This fissured land: An ecological history of India* (Delhi; Oxford: OUP, 1993)

Galbraith, John S., 'The "turbulent frontier" as a factor in British expansion', *Comparative Studies in Society and History*, 2 (1960), 150–168

Ganguly, Sumit and Manjeet S. Pardesi, ed., *India's foreign policy: Retrospect and prospect* (New Delhi: OUP, 2010)

Garver, John W., 'Review: India and the China crisis', *China Quarterly*, 129 (1992), 232–233

Foreign relations of the People's Republic of China (Englewood Cliffs, NJ: Prentice Hall, 1993)

Protracted contest: Sino-Indian rivalry in the twentieth century (New Delhi: OUP, 2001)

'The security dilemma in Sino–Indian relations', *India Review*, 1 (2002), 1–38

'Review essay: India, China, the United States, Tibet, and the origins of the 1962 war', *India Review*, 3 (2004), 171–182

'China's decision for war with India in 1962', in *New directions in the study of China's foreign policy*, ed. by Alastair Iain Johnston and Robert S. Ross (Stanford, CA: Stanford University Press, 2006), pp. 86–130

Ge, Yikun and Wei Li, 'Links between Yunnan and India during the Second World War', in *India and China in the colonial world*, ed. by Madhavi Thampi (New Delhi: Social Science Press, 2005), pp. 193–198

Glassman, Jim, 'On the borders of Southeast Asia: Cold War geography and the construction of the other', *Political Geography*, 24 (2005), 784–807

Glover, Denise Marie, ed., *Explorers & scientists in China's borderlands, 1880–1950* (Seattle: University of Washington Press, 2011)

Goldstein, Melvyn C. and Gelek Rimpoche, *A history of modern Tibet, 1913–1951: The demise of the Lamaist state* (Berkeley: University of California Press, 1989)

The snow lion and the dragon: China, Tibet, and the Dalai Lama (Berkeley: University of California Press, 1997)

'The United States, Tibet, and the Cold War', *Journal of Cold War Studies*, 8 (2006), 145–164

A history of modern Tibet, Volume 2: The calm before the storm, 1951–1955 (Berkeley: University of California Press, 2007)

A history of modern Tibet, Volume 3: The storm clouds descend, 1955–1957 (Berkeley: University of California Press, 2013)

Gonon, Emmanuel, *Marches et frontières dans les Himalayas: Géopolitique des conflits de voisinage* (Québec: Presses de l'université du Québec, 2011)

Goodman, David S., *China's campaign to 'open up the West': National, provincial and local perspectives* (Cambridge: CUP, 2004)

Centre and province in the People's Republic of China (Cambridge: CUP, 2009)

Goswami, Manu, *Producing India: From colonial economy to national space* (Chicago: University of Chicago Press, 2004)

Graff, David Andrew and Robin Higham, eds., *A military history of China* (Boulder, CO: Westview, 2002)

Grothmann, Kerstin, 'Population, history and identity in the hidden land of Pemakö', *Journal of Bhutan Studies*, 26 (2012), 21–52

Grunfeld, Tom, *The making of modern Tibet* (Armonk, NY: ME Sharpe, 1996)

Guha, Amalendu, 'The McMahon Line in contemporary history', in *Studies in politics: National and international*, ed. by M.S. Rajan (New Delhi: Vikas, 1970), pp. 431–460

Guha, Ramachandra, *Savaging the civilized: Verrier Elwin, his tribals, and India* (New Delhi: OUP, 2001)

Guite, Jangkhomang, 'Colonialism and its unruly? The colonial state and Kuki raids in nineteenth century northeast India', *Modern Asian Studies*, 48 (2013), 1188–1232

Gupta, Karunakar, 'Distortions in the history of Sino-Indian frontiers', *Economic and Political Weekly*, 30 (1980), 1265–1270

Guyot-Réchard, Bérénice, 'Nation-building or state-making? India's north-east frontier and the ambiguities of Nehruvian developmentalism, 1950–1959', *Contemporary South Asia*, 21 (2013), 22–37

'Reordering a border space: Relief, rehabilitation, and nation-building in northeastern India after the 1950 Assam earthquake', *Modern Asian Studies*, 49 (2015), 931–962

Harrell, Steven, *Cultural encounters on China's ethnic frontiers* (Seattle, OR: University of Washington Press, 1995)

Harris, Cole, 'How did colonialism dispossess? Comments from an edge of empire', *Annals of the Association of American Geographers*, 94 (2004), 165–182

Harris, Tina, *Geographical diversions: Tibetan trade, global transactions* (Athens: University of Georgia Press, 2013)

Hellström, Jerker and Kaan Korkmaz, 'China and India: Great powers on a collision course', in *Strategic Outlook 2012*, ed. by Emma Skeppström, Stefan Olsson, and Åke Wiss (Stockholm: Swedish Defence Research Agency, June 2012), pp. 76–84

Henrikson, Alan K., 'Distance and foreign policy: A political geography approach', *International Political Science Review / Revue internationale de science politique*, 23 (2002), 437–466

Ho, David Dahpon, 'The men who would not be amban and the one who would: Four frontline officials and Qing Tibet policy, 1905–1911', *Modern China*, 34 (2008), 210–246

Hobsbawn, Eric and Terence Ranger, eds., *The invention of tradition* (Cambridge: CUP, 1983)

Hoffmann, Steven A., 'Anticipation, disaster, and victory: India 1962–71', *Asian Survey*, 12 (1972), 960–979

India and the China crisis (Berkeley: University of California Press, 1990)

'Rethinking the linkage between Tibet and the China–India border conflict: A Realist approach', *Journal of Cold War Studies*, 8 (2006), 165–194

Holslag, Jonathan, *China and India: Prospects for peace* (New York; Chichester: Columbia University Press, 2010)

Hopkins, Benjamin D., 'The Frontier Crimes Regulation and frontier governmentality', *Journal of Asian Studies*, 74 (2015), 369–389

Hostetler, Laura, *Qing colonial enterprise: Ethnography and cartography in early modern China* (Chicago: University of Chicago Press, 2001)

Huang, Jing, *Factionalism in Chinese Communist politics* (Cambridge: CUP, 2000)

Huber, Toni, *The cult of Pure Crystal Mountain: Popular pilgrimage and visionary landscape in southeast Tibet* (New York; Oxford: OUP, 1999)

The holy land reborn: Pilgrimage and the Tibetan Reinvention of Buddhist India (Chicago, IL: University Of Chicago Press, 2008)

'Pushing south: Tibetan economic and political activities in the far eastern Himalaya, ca. 1900–1950', in *Sikkim Studies: Proceedings of the Namgyal Institute Jubilee Conference, 2008*, ed. by Alex McKay and Anna Balikci (Gangtok: Namgyal Institute, 2011a), 259–276

'Blutrache: Hoch oben in den Bergen des östlichen Himalaya', in *Von der Lust am Unbekannten: Humboldts Erben auf Forschungsreisen*, ed. by Heike Zappe (Berlin: Panama Verlag, 2011b), pp. 87–93

Ispahani, Mahnaz Z., *Roads and rivals: The political uses of access in the borderlands of Asia* (Ithaca, NY; London: Cornell University Press, 1989)

Jacob, Jabin T., 'The Sino-Indian boundary dispute: Sub-national units as ice-breakers', *Eurasia Border Review*, 2:1 (2011), 35–45

Jacobs, Justin M., 'Nationalist China's "Great Game": Leveraging foreign explorers in Xinjiang, 1927–1935', *Journal of Asian Studies*, 73 (2014), 43–64

Jacobsen, John Kurt and Lloyd I. Rudolph, eds., *Experiencing the state* (New Delhi: OUP, 2006)

Jalal, Ayesha, *Democracy and authoritarianism in South Asia: A comparative and historical perspective* (Cambridge: CUP, 1995)

Kalia, S.L., 'Sanskritization and tribalization', *Bulletin of the Tribal Research Institute*, 2:4 (1959), 43–53

Kar, Boddhisattva, *What is in a name? Politics of spatial imagination in colonial Assam* (Guwahati: Omeo Kumar Das Institute of Social Change and Development, 2004)

'When was the postcolonial? A history of policing impossible lines', in *Beyond counter-insurgency: Breaking the impasse in northeast India*, ed. by Sanjib Baruah (New Delhi: OUP, 2009), pp. 49–77

'Historia Elastica: A note on the rubber hunt in the north-east frontier of British India', *Indian Historical Review*, 36 (2009), 131–150

Kasza, Gregory J., 'War and comparative politics', *Comparative Politics*, 28 (1996), 355–373

Kennedy, Andrew Bingham, *The international ambitions of Mao and Nehru: National efficacy beliefs and the making of foreign policy* (Cambridge: CUP, 2011)

Khan, Rasheeduddin, 'The total state: The concept and its manifestation in the Indian political system', in *The state, political processes, and identity: Reflections on modern India*, ed. by Zoya Hasan, Rasheeduddin Khan, and S.N. Jha (New Delhi: Sage, 1989), pp. 33–72

Khan, Sulmaan Wasif, 'Cold War co-operation: New Chinese evidence on Jawaharlal Nehru's 1954 visit to Beijing', *Cold War History*, 11 (2011), 197–222

Muslim, trader, nomad, spy: China's Cold War and the Tibetan borderlands (Duke, NC: UNC Press, 2015)

Kinzley, Judd, 'Crisis and the development of China's southwestern periphery: The transformation of Panzhihua, 1936–1969', *Modern China*, 38:5 (2012), 559–584

Kirby, William C., 'When did China become China? Thoughts on the twentieth century', in *The teleology of the modern nation-state: Japan and China*, ed. by Joshua A. Fogel (Philadelphia: University of Pennsylvania Press, 2005), pp. 105–114

Kit-ching, Chan Lau, 'Symbolism as diplomacy: The United States and Britain's China policy during the first year of the Pacific War', *Diplomacy and Statecraft*, 16:1 (2005), 73–92

Klieger, Christiaan, ed., *Tibetan borderlands* (Leiden: Brill, 2006)

Knaus, John Kenneth, *Orphans of the Cold War: America and the Tibetan struggle for survival* (New York: Public Affairs, 1999)

Kramer, Mark, 'Great-power rivalries, Tibetan guerrilla resistance, and the Cold War in South Asia: Introduction', *Journal of Cold War Studies*, 8 (2006), 5–14

Krasner, Stephen D., 'Rethinking the sovereign state model', *Review of International Studies*, 27 (2001), 17–42

Kratoska, Paul H., R. Raben and Henk Schulte Nordholt, *Locating Southeast Asia: Geographies of knowledge and politics of space* (Singapore: Singapore University Press; Athens: Ohio University Press, 2005)

Krishna, Sankaran, 'Cartographic anxiety: Mapping the body politic in India', *Alternatives: Global, Local, Political*, 19 (1994), 507–521

Kuhn, Philip A., *Origins of the modern Chinese State*, English edn (Stanford, CA: Stanford University Press, 2002)

Lamb, Alastair, *The China–India border: The origins of the disputed boundaries* (London: OUP, 1964)

The McMahon line: A study in the relations between India, China and Tibet, 1904–1914 (London: Routledge & Kegan Paul, 1966)

Tibet, China & India, 1914–1950: A history of imperial diplomacy (Hertingfordbury: Roxford Books, 1989)

Larsen, Kirk W., 'The Qing Empire (China), imperialism, and the modern world', *History Compass*, 9 (2011), 498–508

Lary, Diana, ed., *The Chinese state at the borders* (Vancouver: University of British Columbia Press, 2007)

Lattimore, Owen, *Inner Asian frontiers of China* (Hong Kong; Oxford: OUP, 1988)

Lawson, Joseph D., 'Warlord colonialism: State fragmentation and Chinese rule in Kham, 1911–1949', *Journal of Asian Studies*, 72 (2013), 299–318

'Unsettled lands: Labour and land cultivation in western China during the War of Resistance (1937–1945)', *Modern Asian Studies*, 49 (2015), 1442–1484

Lazcano, Santiago, 'La cuestión de la servidumbre en el sudeste de Tíbet y regiones colindantes del Himalaya oriental hasta la ocupación china de 1950', *Boletín de la Asociación Española de Orientalistas*, 35 (1999), 229–244

'Ethno-historic notes on the ancient Tibetan kingdom of sPo Bo and its influence on the eastern Himalayas (translated by Rita Granda)', *Revue d'Etudes Tibétaines*, 7 (2005), 41–63

Leach, Edmund Ronald, *Political systems of Highland Burma: A study of Kachin social structure*, 3rd edn (London: Athlone Press, 1970)

Lee, James Z., *The political economy of a frontier: Southwest China, 1250–1850* (Cambridge, MA: HUP, 2000)

Leibold, James, *Reconfiguring Chinese nationalism: How the Qing frontier and its indigenes became Chinese*, 1st edn (New York: Palgrave Macmillan, 2007)

Lieberman, Victor B., 'A zone of refuge in Southeast Asia? Reconceptualizing interior spaces', *Journal of Global History*, 5 (2010), 333–346

Lieberthal, Kenneth, *Governing China: From revolution through reform* (New York; London: W.W. Norton, 1995)

Lin, Hsiao-Ting, 'Boundary, sovereignty, and imagination: Reconsidering the frontier disputes between British India and Republican China, 1914–47', *Journal of Imperial and Commonwealth History*, 32 (2004), 25–47

Tibet and Nationalist China's Frontier: Intrigues and Ethnopolitics, 1928–49 (Vancouver: University of British Columbia Press, 2006a)

'War or stratagem? Reassessing China's military advance towards Tibet, 1942–1943', *China Quarterly*, 186 (2006b), 446–462

Modern China's ethnic frontiers: A journey to the west (London: Routledge, 2011)

Lintner, Bertil, 'Missions to China by insurgents from India's northeast', in *Indian and Chinese foreign policy in comparative perspective*, ed. by Surjit Mansingh (New Delhi: Radiant, 1998), 433–438

Great Game east: India, China, and the struggle for Asia's most volatile frontier (New Haven, CT: Yale University Press, 2015)

Liu, Xiaoyuan, *Frontier passages: Ethnopolitics and the rise of Chinese communism, 1921–1945* (Stanford: Stanford University Press, 2004)

'Entering the Cold War and other "wars": The Tibetan experience', *Chinese Historical Review*, 19:1 (2012), 47–64

Liu, Xuecheng, *The Sino-Indian border dispute and Sino-Indian relations* (Lanham, MD: University Press of America, 1994)

Low, Donald A., *Eclipse of empire* (Cambridge: CUP, 1991)

Ludden, David, 'Where is Assam?', Himal South Asian, (2005), http://himalmag .com/component/content/article/1676-Where-is-Assam?.html

'The process of empire: Frontiers and borderlands', in *Tributary empires in global history*, ed. by C.A. Bayly and Peter Fibiger Bang (New Delhi: Palgrave Macmillan, 2011), pp. 132–150

'Spatial inequity and national territory: Remapping 1905 in Bengal and Assam', *Modern Asian Studies*, 46 (2012), 1–43

Lunstrum, Elizabeth, 'Articulated sovereignty: Extending Mozambican state power through the Great Limpopo Transfrontier Park', *Political Geography*, 36 (2013), 1–11

Lustick, Ian, *Unsettled states, disputed lands: Britain and Ireland, France and Algeria, Israel and the West Bank-Gaza* (Ithaca, NY: Cornell University Press, 1993)

Brendan O'Leary and Tom Callaghy, eds., *Right-Sizing the State: The politics of moving borders* (Oxford: OUP, 2001)

Luthra, P.N., 'North-East Frontier Agency tribes: Impact of Ahom and British policy', *Economic and Political Weekly*, 6 (1971), 1143–1145; 1147–1149

MacFarquhar, Roderick and John K. Fairbank, eds., *The Cambridge history of China* (Cambridge: CUP, 1987), vol. XIV: The People's Republic

MacKenzie, Alexander, *The north-east frontier of India (History of the relations of the government with the hill tribes of the north-east frontier of Bengal)* (Delhi: Mittal, 1979 [1884])

Mackerras, Colin, *China's minority cultures: Identities and integration since 1912* (Melbourne: Longman; New York: St. Martin's Press, 1995)

ed., *Ethnic minorities in modern China*, 4 vols (London; New York: Routledge, 2011)

Mahmud Ali, S., *Cold War in the high Himalayas: The USA, China and South Asia in the 1950s* (New York: St. Martin's Press, 1999)

Malik, Mohan, *China and India: Great power rivals* (Boulder, CO: FirstForumPress, 2011)

Malkki, Liisa, 'National geographic: The rooting of peoples and the territorialisation and national identity among scholars and refugees', *Cultural Anthropology*, 7 (1992), 24–44

Malone, David M. and Rohan Mukherjee, 'India and China: Conflict and cooperation', *Survival*, 52 (2010), 137–158

Mankekar, D.R., *The guilty men of 1962* (Bombay: Tulsi Shah, 1968)

Marsden, Magnus and A.G. Hopkins, *Fragments of the Afghan frontier* (London: Hurst, 2011)

Marshall, Julie G., *Britain and Tibet 1765–1947: The background to the India–China border dispute; a select annotated bibliography of printed material in European languages* (Bundoora: La Trobe University Library, 1977)

Maxwell, Neville, *India's China war* (London: Cape, 1970)

Mbembé, Achille, 'At the edge of the world: Boundaries, territoriality, and sovereignty in Africa', *Public Culture*, 12 (2000), 259–284

McConnell, Fiona, 'De facto, displaced, tacit: The sovereign articulations of the Tibetan Government-in-Exile', *Political Geography*, 28 (2009), 343–352

Rehearsing the state: The governance practices of the exile Tibetan government (Oxford: John Wiley, 2016)

McGarr, Paul M., *The Cold War in South Asia: Britain, the United States and the Indian subcontinent, 1945–1965* (Cambridge: CUP, 2013)

McGranahan, Carole, 'Empire out of bounds: Tibet in the era of decolonisation', in *Imperial formations*, ed. by Ann Laura Stoler, Carole McGranahan, and Peter C. Perdue (Oxford: James Currey, 2007), pp. 173–210

Arrested histories: Tibet, the CIA, and memories of a forgotten war (Durham, NC: Duke University Press, 2010)

McKay, Alex, *Tibet and the British Raj: The frontier cadre 1904–47* (London: Curzon, 1997)

'The British invasion of Tibet, 1903–04', *Inner Asia*, 14 (2012), 5–25

McMahon, Robert J., *The Cold War on the periphery: The United States, India, and Pakistan* (New York; Chichester: Columbia University Press, 1994)

'U.S. policy toward South Asia and Tibet during the early Cold War', *Journal of Cold War Studies*, 8 (2006), 131–144

Mehra, Parshotam, *The northeastern frontier: A documentary study of the internecine rivalry between India, Tibet and China vol 2, 1914–54* (New Delhi: OUP, 1980)

'India-China border: A review and critique', *Economic and Political Weekly*, 17 (1982), 834–838

Mibang, Tamo, *Social change in Arunachal Pradesh (the Minyongs) 1947–1981* (Delhi: Omsons, 1994)

'Bogum-Bokang-Kebang', *Yaaro Moobang: A Land of Peace, Prosperity and Happiness (Bilingual Magazine of the Adi Baane Kebang Youth Front, HQ Pasighat, East Siang)*, 1 (2001), 26–29

Migdal, Joel S., *Strong societies and weak states: State–society relations and state capabilities in the Third World* (Princeton: Princeton University Press, 1988)

State in society: Studying how states and societies transform and constitute one another (Cambridge: CUP, 2001)

Boundaries and belonging: States and societies in the struggle to shape identities and local practices (Cambridge; New York: CUP, 2004)

Millward, James A., *Qing colonial enterprise: Ethnography and cartography in early modern China* (Chicago: University of Chicago Press, 2001)

Mimi, Raju, '"Power" house or powerless: A debate on dams in Arunachal Pradesh', *India Water Portal* (19 March 2014), www.indiawaterportal.org/a rticles/powerhouse-or-powerless-debate-dams-arunachal-pradesh

Misra, Sanghamitra, 'The nature of colonial intervention in the Naga Hills, 1840–80', *Economic and Political Weekly*, 33 (1998), 3273–3279

'Law, migration and new subjectivities: Reconstructing the colonial project in an eastern borderland', *Indian Economic and Social History Review*, 44 (2007), 425–461

Becoming a borderland: The politics of space and identity in colonial northeastern India (New Delhi: Routledge, 2011)

Mizuno, Kazuharu and Lobsang Tenpa, *Himalayan nature and Tibetan Buddhist culture in Arunachal Pradesh, India: A study of Monpa* (Berlin: Springer, 2015)

Mosca, Matthew M., *From frontier policy to foreign policy: The question of India and the transformation of geopolitics in Qing China* (Stanford, CA: Stanford University Press, 2013)

Mukherjee, Mithi, '"A world of illusion": The legacy of empire in India's foreign relations, 1947–62', *International History Review*, 32 (2010), 253–271

Mullaney, Thomas S., *Coming to terms with the nation: Ethnic classification in modern China* (Berkeley, CA; London: University of California Press, 2012)

Nag, Sajal, *Contesting marginality: Ethnicity, insurgency and subnationalism in north-east India* (New Delhi: Manohar, 2002)

Pied pipers in the hills: Bamboo flowers, rat famine and colonial philanthropy in north east India, 1881–1931 (Cambridge: University of Cambridge, Centre of South Asian Studies, 2008)

Nath, Jogendra, 'Anglo-Abor treaty 1862 and its significance in relation to the Inner Line Regulation, 1873', in *Proceedings of the North-East India History Association, Tenth Session* (Shillong: Singhania, 1989), pp. 409–419

'The Kebang: Aboriginal self-government of the Adis of Arunachal Pradesh', in *Proceedings of the North-East India History Association, Eleventh Session* (Shillong: Singhania, 1990), pp. 109–116

Nathan, Andrew J. and Robert S. Ross, *The great wall and the empty fortress: China's search for security* (New York; London: W.W. Norton, 1997)

Norbu, Dawa, 'Tibet in Sino-Indian relations: The centrality of marginality', *Asian Survey*, 37 (1997), 1078–1095

Nugent, Paul, *Smugglers, secessionists and loyal citizens on the Ghana–Togo frontier: The lie of the borderlands since 1914* (Oxford: James Currey, 2002)

Palit, D.K., *Sentinels of the north-east: The Assam Rifles* (New Delhi: Palit & Palit, 1984)

Pant, Harsh V., ed., *The rise of China: Implications for India* (Cambridge: CUP, 2012)

'Rising China in India's vicinity: a rivalry takes shape in Asia', Cambridge Review of International Affairs (2013), 1–18

Patterson Giersch, Charles, *Asian borderlands: The transformation of Qing China's Yunnan frontier* (Cambridge, MA; London: HUP, 2006)

'Across Zomia with merchants, monks, and musk: Process geographies, trade networks, and the Inner-East–Southeast Asian borderlands', *Journal of Global History*, 5 (2010), 215–239

'Commerce and empire in the borderlands: How do merchants and trade fit into Qing frontier history?', *Frontiers of History in China*, 9:3 (2014), 361–383

Perdue, Peter C., *China marches west: The Qing conquest of Central Eurasia* (London: Belknap, 2005)

'Erasing empire, re-racing the nation: Racialism and culturalism in imperial China', in *Imperial Formations*, ed. by Ann Laura Stoler, Carole McGranahan, and Peter C. Perdue (Santa Fe, NY: School for Advanced Research Press, 2007), pp. 141–169

'China and other colonial empires', *Journal of American—East Asian Relations*, 16 (2009), 85–103

Pfaff-Czarnecka, Joanna and Gérard Toffin, eds., *The politics of belonging in the Himalayas: Local attachments and boundary dynamics* (Delhi: Sage, 2011)

Facing globalization in the Himalayas: Belonging and the politics of the self (Delhi: Sage, 2014)

Pinney, Christopher, *Photos of the gods: The printed image and political struggle in India* (London: Reaktion, 2004)

Pirie, Fernanda and Toni Huber, eds., *Conflict and social order in Tibet and inner Asia* (Leiden: Brill, 2008)

'The limits of the state: Coercion and consent in Chinese Tibet', *Journal of Asian Studies*, 72 (2013), 69–89

Plating, John D., *The Hump: America's strategy for keeping China in World War II* (College Station: Texas A&M University Press, 2011)

Pomeranz, Kenneth, 'The great Himalayan watershed: Agrarian crisis, mega-dams and the environment', *New Left Review*, 58 (2009), 5–39

Pommaret, Françoise, 'The Mon-Pa revisited: In search of Mon', in *Sacred spaces and powerful places in Tibetan culture: A collection of essays*, ed. by Toni Huber (Dharamsala: Library of Tibetan Works and Archives, 1999), pp. 52–73

Prozumenschikov, M.Y. and others, 'The Sino–Indian conflict, the Cuban Missile Crisis, and the Sino–Soviet split, October 1962: New evidence from the Russian archives', *Cold War International History Project Bulletin* 8–9 (1996), 251–257

Raghavan, Srinath, 'Sino-Indian boundary dispute, 1948–60: A reappraisal', *Economic and Political Weekly*, 41 (2006), 3882–3892

'A bad knock: The war with China, 1962', in *A military history of India and South Asia: From the East India Company to the nuclear era*, ed. by Daniel P. Marston and Chandar S. Sundaram (Westport, CT: Prager Security International, 2007), pp. 157–174

'Civil–military relations in India: The China crisis and after', *Journal of Strategic Studies*, 32 (2009), 149–175

War and peace in modern India (Basingstoke: Palgrave Macmillan, 2010)

Ramirez, Philippe, 'Belonging to the borders: Uncertain identities in north-east India', in *The politics of belonging in the Himalayas: Local attachments and boundary dynamics*, ed. by Joanna Pfaff-Czarnecka and Gérard Toffin (New Delhi: Sage, 2011), pp. 77–97

Relyea, Scott, 'Yokes of gold and threads of silk: Sino–Tibetan competition for authority in early twentieth century Kham', *Modern Asian Studies*, 49 (2015), 963–1009

Richardson, Hugh, *Tibet and her neighbours: A presentation of the historic facts of Tibet's relations with neighbouring states* (London: Tibet Society, 1960)

Tibet and its history, 2nd edn (Boulder: Shambhala, 1984)

High peaks, pure earth: Collected writings on Tibetan history and culture, ed. by Michael Aris (London: Serindia, 1998)

Robb, Peter, 'The colonial state and constructions of Indian identity: An example on the northeast frontier in the 1880s', *Modern Asian Studies*, 31 (1997), 245–283

Rodriguez, Andres, 'Building the nation, serving the frontier: Mobilizing and reconstructing China's borderlands during the War of Resistance (1937–1945)', *Modern Asian Studies*, 45 (2011), 345–376

'"Decolonizing" the borderlands: Yunnan–Burmese borderlands and the dilemmas of the early postwar period (1945–1948)' (paper presented at the 4th Asian Borderlands Research Network Conference, Hong Kong, December 2014)

Roy, Srirupa, *Beyond belief: India and the politics of postcolonial nationalism* (Durham, NC; London: Duke University Press, 2007)

Roy, Tirthankar, 'State, society and market in the aftermath of natural disasters in colonial India: A preliminary exploration', *Indian Economic Social History Review*, 45 (2009), 261–294

Sahlins, Peter, *Boundaries: The making of France and Spain in the Pyrenees* (Berkeley; Oxford: University of California Press, 1989)

Saikia, Yasmin, *Fragmented memories: Struggling to be Tai-Ahom in India* (Durham: Duke University Press, 2004)

Sali, M.L., *India–China border dispute: A case study of the eastern sector* (New Delhi: APH Publishing Company, 1998)

Samuel, Geoffrey, *Civilized shamans: Buddhism in Tibetan societies* (Washington; London: Smithsonian Institution Press, 1993)

Sarkar, Ratna and Indrajit Ray, 'Trend of Bhutan's trade during 1907–26: Export', *Journal of Bhutan Studies*, 26 (2012), 100–122

Sarkar, Sumit, 'Nationalism and poverty: Discourses of development and culture in 20th century India', *Third World Quarterly*, 29 (2008), 429–445

Scott, David, 'The great power "Great Game" between India and China: "The logic of geography"', *Geopolitics*, 13 (2008), 1–26

Scott, James C., *The moral economy of the peasant: Rebellion and subsistence in Southeast Asia* (New Haven, CO: Yale University Press, 1976)

Seeing like a state: How certain schemes to improve the human condition have failed (New Haven, CO; London: Yale University Press, 1998)

The art of not being governed: An anarchist history of upland Southeast Asia (New Haven, CO; London: Yale University Press, 2009)

Shakya, Tsering W., *The dragon in the land of snows: A history of modern Tibet since 1947* (London: Pimlico, 1999)

Shambaugh, David L., ed., *The modern Chinese state* (Cambridge: CUP, 2000)

Shang, Quanyu, 'Sino-Indian friendship in the Nehru era: A Chinese perspective', *China Report*, 41 (2005), 237–252

Sharma, Jayeeta, *Empire's garden: Assam and the making of India* (Ranikhet: Permanent Black, 2011)

Shen, Simon, 'Exploring the neglected constraints on Chindia: Analysing the online Chinese perception of India and its interaction with China's Indian policy', *China Quarterly*, 207 (2011), 541–560

Sheng, Michael M., 'Mao, Tibet, and the Korean War', *Journal of Cold War Studies*, 8 (2006), 15–33

Shirk, Susan L., *China: Fragile superpower* (Oxford: OUP, 2008)

Shneiderman, Sara, 'Barbarians at the border and civilizing projects: Analyzing ethnic and national identities in the Tibetan context', in *Tibetan borderlands*, ed. by Christiaan Klieger (Leiden: Brill, 2006), pp. 9–34

'Are the Central Himalayas in Zomia? Some scholarly and political considerations across time and space', *Journal of Global History*, 5(2010), 289–312

Shue, Vivienne, *The reach of the state: Sketches of the Chinese body politic* (Stanford, CA: Stanford University Press, 1988)

Sidaway, James, 'Sovereign excesses? Portraying postcolonial sovereigntyscapes', *Political Geography*, 22 (2003), 157–178

Carl Grundy-Warr, and Bae-Gyoon Park, 'Asian sovereigntyscapes', *Political Geography*, 24 (2005), 779–783

Sidhu, Waheguru Pal Singh and Jing-Dong Yuan, *China and India: Cooperation or conflict?* (New Delhi: India Research Press, 2003)

Sikdar, Sudatta, 'Tribalism vs. colonialism: British capitalistic intervention and transformation of primitive economy of Arunachal Pradesh in the nineteenth century', *Social Scientist*, 10 (1982), 15–31

Simpson, Thomas, 'Bordering and frontier-making in nineteenth-century British India', *Historical Journal*, 58 (2015), 513–542

Singh, Chandrika, *Emergence of Arunachal Pradesh as a state* (New Delhi: Mittal, 1989)

Singh, Nitya, 'How to tame your dragon: An evaluation of India's foreign policy toward China', *India Review*, 11 (2012), 139–160

Singha, Radhika, 'Front lines and status lines: Sepoy and "menial" in the Great War, 1916–1920', in *The world in world wars: Experiences, perceptions and perspectives from the South*, ed. by Heike Liebau and others (Leiden: Brill, 2010), 55–106

Sinha, A.C., 'In search of the tribes of north-east India', *NEHU Journal*, 3 (2005), 17–30

Sinha, Aseema, 'Rethinking the developmental state model: Divided leviathan and subnational comparisons in India', *Comparative Politics*, 35 (2003), 459–476

Skocpol, Theda and Meyer Kestnbaum, 'War and the development of modern national states', *Sociological Forum*, 8 (1993), 661–674

Slater, Dan and Diana Kim, 'Standoffish states: Nonliterate leviathans in Southeast Asia', *TRaNS: Trans-Regional and National Studies of Southeast Asia*, 3 (2015), 25–44

Sonwalkar, Prasun, 'Mediating otherness: India's English-language press and the northeast', *Contemporary South Asia*, 13 (2004), 389–402

Spence, Jonathan, *The search for modern China*, 2nd edn (New York; London: W.W. Norton, 1999)

Sperling, Elliot, 'The Chinese venture in Kham 1904–11, and the role of Chao Er-feng', *Tibet Journal*, 1 (1976), 10–35

'The politics of history and the Indo-Tibetan border (1987–88)', *India Review*, 7 (2008), 223–239

'Tibet and China: The interpretation of history since 1950', *China Perspectives*, 3 (2009), 25–37

Stepan, Alfred C., Juan J. Linz, and Yogendra Yadav, eds., *Crafting state-nations: India and other multinational democracies* (Baltimore: Johns Hopkins University Press, 2011)

Subba, Tanka Bahadur, Sujit Som, and K.C. Baral, *Between ethnography and fiction: Verrier Elwin and the tribal question in India* (New Delhi: Orient Longman, 2005)

Sundar, Nandini, *Subalterns and sovereigns: An anthropological history of Bastar, 1854–1996*, 1st edn (Delhi: OUP, 1997)

Swaine, Michael D. and Ashley J. Tellis, *Interpreting China's grand strategy: Past, present, and future* (Santa Monica, CA: Rand, 2000)

Syiemlieh, D.R., 'The Crown Colony scheme for north east India 1928–47: An analysis of official views', in *Proceedings of the North-East India History Association, Second Session* (Shillong: Singhania, 1981), pp. 172–178

'Response of the north-eastern hill tribes of India towards Partition and independence', *Indo-British Review: A Journal of History*, 17 (1989), 27–35

Tagliacozzo, Eric, 'Ambiguous commodities, unstable frontiers: The case of Burma, Siam, and imperial Britain, 1800–1900', *Society for Comparative Study of Society and History*, 46 (2004), 354–377

Tarlo, Emma, *Clothing matters: Dress and identity in India* (London: Hurst, 1996)

Taylor Fravel, M., *Strong borders, secure nation: Cooperation and conflict in China's territorial disputes* (Princeton, NJ; Oxford: Princeton University Press, 2008)

Thakur, Amrendra Kumar, *Slavery in Arunachal Pradesh* (New Delhi: Mittal, 2003a)

'Process and agency of precolonial in Arunachal Pradesh', *NEHU Journal*, 1 (2003b), http://hdl.handle.net/123456789/2088

Thampi, Madhavi, *India and China in the colonial world* (New Delhi: Social Science Press, 2005)

Thant Myint, U., *The making of modern Burma* (Cambridge: CUP, 2001)

Tilly, Charles, *Coercion, capital, and European states, AD 990–1990* (Cambridge, MA: B. Blackwell, 1990)

Tinker, Hugh, 'A forgotten long march: The Indian exodus from Burma, 1942', *Journal of Southeast Asian Studies*, 6 (1975), 1–15

Tripodi, Christian, 'Negotiating with the enemy: "Politicals" and tribes 1901–47', *Journal of Imperial and Commonwealth History*, 39 (2011), 589–606

Tsomu, Yudru, 'Taming the Khampas: The Republican construction of eastern Tibet', *Modern China*, 39 (2013), 319–344

Tsui, Brian, 'The plea for Asia – Tan Yunshan, Pan-Asianism and Sino-Indian relations', *China Report*, 46:4 (2010), 353–370

Tuttle, Gray, *Tibetan Buddhists in the making of modern China* (New York; Chichester: Columbia University Press, 2005)

Van de Ven, Hans J., *War and nationalism in China, 1925–1945* (London; New York: RoutledgeCurzon, 2003a)

'Stilwell in the stocks: The Chinese Nationalists and the Allied powers in the Second World War', *Asian Affairs*, 34:3 (2003b), 243–259

Vang, Pobzeb, *Five principles of Chinese foreign policies* (Bloomington, IN: AuthorHouse, 2008)

Van Schendel, Willem, 'Geographies of knowing, geographies of ignorance: Jumping scale in Southeast Asia', *Environment and Planning D: Society and Space*, 20 (2002), 647–668

The Bengal borderland: Beyond state and nation in South Asia (London: Anthem, 2005)

'The dangers of belonging: Tribes, indigenous peoples and homelands in South Asia', in *The politics of belonging in India: Becoming Adivasi*, ed. by Daniel Rycroft and Sangeeta Dasgupta (London: Routledge, 2011), pp. 19–43

Van Spengen, Wim, *Tibetan borderworlds: A geohistorical analysis of trade and traders* (London: Kegan Paul, 2000)

'Frontier history of southern Kham: Banditry and war in the multi-ethnic fringe lands of Chatri, Mili, and Gyethang 1890–1940', in *Khams Pa histories: Visions of people, place and authority*, ed. by Lawrence Epstein (Leiden: Brill, 2002), pp. 7–29

'Beyond Annapurna or how to interpret success in Himalayan trade', *Himalaya: The Journal of the Association for Nepal and Himalayan Studies*, 33 (2014), 107–111

Venkata Rao, V., *A century of tribal politics in North East India, 1874–1974* (New Delhi: S. Chand, 1978)

Vertzberger, Yaacov, *Misperceptions in foreign policymaking: The Sino-Indian conflict, 1959–1962* (Boulder, CO: Westview, 1984a)

'Bureaucratic organisational politics and information processing in a developing state', *International Studies Quarterly*, 28 (1984b), 69–95

China's southwestern strategy: Encirclement and counter-encirclement (New York: Praeger, 1985)

Vumlallian Zou, David and M. Satish Kumar, 'Mapping a colonial borderland: Objectifying the geo-body of India's northeast', *Journal of Asian Studies*, 70 (2011), 141–170

Wang, Xiuyu, *China's last imperial frontier: Late Qing expansion in Sichuan's Tibetan borderlands* (Lanham, MD: Lexington Books, 2011)

Warner, Catherine, 'Flighty subjects: Sovereignty, shifting cultivators, and the state in Darjeeling, 1830–1856', *Himalaya, the Journal of the Association for Nepal and Himalayan Studies*, 34 (2014), 23–35

Wei, William, '"Political power grows out of the barrel of a gun": Mao and the Red Army', in *A military history of China*, ed. by David Andrew Graff and Robin Higham (Cambridge, MA: Westview, 2002), pp. 229–248

Wenbin, Peng, 'Frontier processes, provincial politics and movements for Khampa autonomy during the Republican period', in *Khams Pa histories: Visions of people, place and authority*, ed. by Lawrence Epstein (Leiden: Brill, 2002), pp. 57–84

Westad, Odd Arne, ed., *Brothers in arms: The rise and fall of the Sino-Soviet alliance, 1945–1963* (Washington, DC: Woodrow Wilson Center Press, 1998)

    Decisive encounters: The Chinese Civil War, 1946–1950 (Stanford, CA: Stanford University Press; London: Eurospan, 2003)

Whiting, Allen, *The Chinese calculus of deterrence: India and Indochina* (Ann Arbor, MI: University of Michigan Press, 1975)

Whitson, William W., 'Organisational perspectives and decision-making in the Chinese Communist high command', in *Elites in the People's Republic of China*, ed. by Robert A. Scalapino (Seattle: University of Washington Press, 1972), pp. 381–415

Wiener, Martin J., 'The idea of "colonial legacy" and the historiography of empire', *Journal of the Historical Society*, 13 (2013), 1–32

Williams, J.E., 'Chiang Kai-shek's intervention in Indian politics: An episode in Sino-British relations, February–September 1942', *International Relations*, 5:5 (1977), 49–70

Wouters, Jelle J.P. and Tanka B. Subba, 'The "Indian face", India's northeast, and "the idea of India"', *Asian Anthropology*, 12 (2013), 126–140

Wyatt, Don J., Nicola Di Cosmo, and Benjamin I. Schwartz, *Political frontiers, ethnic boundaries, and human geographies in Chinese history* (London: RoutledgeCurzon, 2003)

Xaxa, Virginius, 'Transformation of tribes in India: Terms of discourse', *Economic and Political Weekly*, 34 (1999), 1519–1524

Yang, Huei Pang, 'Helpful allies, interfering neighbours: World opinion and China in the 1950s', *Modern Asian Studies*, 49:1 (2015), 204–240

Yeh, Emily T., *Taming Tibet: Landscape transformation and the gift of Chinese development* (Ithaca, NY: Cornell University Press, 2013)

Yunuo, Asoso, *The rising Nagas: A historical and political study* (Delhi: Vivek, 1974)

Zachariah, Benjamin, *Developing India: An intellectual and social history, c. 1930–50* (New Delhi; Oxford: OUP, 2005)

Zamindar, Vazira Fazila-Yacoobali, *The long Partition and the making of modern South Asia: Refugees, boundaries, histories* (New York: Columbia University Press, 2007)

Zartman, William I., ed., *Understanding life in the borderlands: Boundaries in depth and in motion* (Athens; London: University of Georgia Press, 2010)

Zhai, Qiang, 'Tibet and Chinese–British–American relations in the early 1950s', *Journal of Cold War Studies*, 8 (2006), 34–53

Zhang, Yongjin and Greg Austin, *Power and responsibility in Chinese foreign policy* (Canberra: Asia Pacific Press, 2001)

Zhao, Suisheng, *A nation-state by construction: Dynamics of modern Chinese nationalism* (Stanford: Stanford University Press, 2004)

Chinese foreign policy: Pragmatism and strategic behavior (London: M.E. Sharpe, 2004)

Unpublished Secondary Sources

Aisher, Alexander, 'Through "spirits": Nyishi tribal cosmology and landscape ecology in Arunachal Pradesh, northeast India' (unpublished doctoral thesis, University College London, 2005)

Aziz, Barbara Nimri, 'The people of Dingri: A socio-historical portrait of a district in south west Tibet' (unpublished doctoral thesis, University of London, 1974)

Coleman IV, William M., 'Making the state on the Sino-Tibetan frontier: Chinese expansion and local power in Batang, 1842–1939' (unpublished doctoral thesis, Columbia University, 2014)

Goswami, Sandhya, 'Assam's language question: A political analysis for the period 1947 through 1961' (unpublished doctoral thesis, Gauhati University, 1990)

Grothmann, Kerstin, 'From a dominant power to a "backward tribe": The effects of Indian territoriality on Memba society of Mechukha''', in 4th Conference of the Asian Borderlands Research Network (Hong Kong, December 2014)

Jacobs, Justin M., 'Empire besieged: The preservation of Chinese rule in Xinjiang, 1884–1971' (unpublished doctoral thesis, University of California, San Diego, 2011)

Relyea, Scott, 'Gazing at the Tibetan plateau: Sovereignty and Chinese state expansion in the early twentieth century' (unpublished doctoral thesis, University of Chicago, 2012)

Rodriguez, Andres, 'China's frontier enterprise: Frontier studies and nation-building during the Republican period (1912–1949)' (unpublished doctoral thesis, Oxford University, 2009)

Sen, Uditi, 'Refugees and the politics of nation-building in India, 1947–1971' (unpublished doctoral thesis, Cambridge University, 2009)

Sikdar, Sudatta, 'The Eastern Himalayan trade of Assam in the 19th century: A study of British policy' (unpublished doctoral thesis, NEHU, 1984)

Weiner, Benno Ryan, 'The Chinese Revolution on the Tibetan frontier: State building, national integration and socialist transformation, Zeku (Tsékhok) County, 1953–1958' (unpublished doctoral thesis, Columbia University, 2012)

Index